Royal Air Force
BOMBER COMI
LOSSES
of the Second World war

Volume 2
Aircraft and Crew Losses
1941

Royal Air Force
BOMBER COMMAND LOSSES
of the Second World War

Volume 2
Aircraft and Crew Losses
1941

W R CHORLEY

Copyright © 1993 W R Chorley and
Midland Counties Publications.

First published in 1993 by
Midland Counties Publications,
24 The Hollow, Earl Shilton, Leicester,
LE9 7NA, England.

ISBN 0 904597 87 3

Printed in England by
Redwood Books
Trowbridge, Wiltshire.

The Royal Air Force Bomber Command
badge featured on the front cover
and title page is acknowledged as a
Crown copyright / RAF photograph.

Contents

Acknowledgements

In preparing this second volume of bomber losses, I acknowledge the kind assistance given by the Ministry of Defence (Air Historical Branch), the Public Record Office and the Commonwealth War Graves Commission. Also, I express my appreciation to the staff of the local studies department at Salisbury Library, where I have been able to use their facilities for examination of microfiche and microfilm, often at very short notice.

I am also indebted to the host of private individuals who have sent me material from their own files for use in this, and future volumes. With much pleasure, I warmly thank Brian Walker and Wilf Baguley for providing copies of the Group Rolls of Honour and for their help concerning Polish burials at Newark. Similarly, Geoffrey Negus has made a valuable contribution in this area, as has Mike Ingham with his notes on 300 Squadron.

Bob Collis, Historian for the Norfolk and Suffolk Aviation Museum, has sent details of crash sites in the East Anglia region, likewise Graham Sharpe has been most helpful in respect of 4 Group crashes in Yorkshire.

Manchester bomber losses have been covered by Dr. Robert Kirby, while Frank Haslam and Raymond Glynne-Owen have assisted in matters concerning 207 Squadron. Similarly, Frank Harper, Chris Goss, Peter Wilson and John Whitehouse have kindly checked my notes for 83, 102, 149 and 214 Squadrons, while Bryce Gomersall has cast his experienced eye over the Stirling losses for 1941. Bob Pearce, who flew as a wireless operator/air gunner with 142 Squadron and Don Bruce, an observer on 115 Squadron, have also been extremely helpful and I am particularly grateful to Don for allowing me to draw on his private material for use in many of the 115 Squadron summaries. I am also grateful to Keith Ford for his help in supplying individual letters carried by 51 Squadron aircraft.

Philip Baldock and Frank Wilson have sent notes on crashes in south-east England, and Peter Sharpe has generously checked numerous squadron lists, adding many useful notes especially in respect of those losses where night-fighters were involved.

Both Norman Ling and Ray Sturtivant have come to my aid, at the eleventh hour, with answers to questions concerning aircraft accidents in the United Kingdom and various matters in respect of the bomber OTUs.

My grateful thanks is also extended to Jacques De Vos of Gent for help with Belgian crashes, while Hans de Haan of Wijchen has been a mine of information, not only where crash sites in Holland are concerned, but in his general coverage of bomber casualties sustained during the period covered by this volume.

Drs. Theo Boiten has assisted with his knowledge of losses in northern Holland and off the Frisian Islands.

From Germany, help in trying to identify some of the obscure crash locations has been forthcoming from Hans-Günther Ploes and Franz Zimmermann.

I also freely acknowledge the help given by Jean-Louis Roba, Leo Zwaaf, Martin va Sleeuwen, Willi Offermann, Jim Habberfield, Brandon White, Gerrie Zwanenburg MBE, Douw Drijver and Dave Morris.

My appreciation is also extended to Martin Middlebrook and Chris Everitt for permitting me to draw from their acclaimed work, The Bomber Command War Diaries. Also, to Michael J F Bowyer, Norman Franks, James J Halley and Harry Moyle for allowing me to use material from their published works.

Finally, I wish to thank Chris Salter and the staff at Midland Counties Publications for their help and encouragement throughout the preparation of this volume.

Bill Chorley
Farthings Oak
10 Sycamore Close
Sixpenny Handley
Salisbury
Wiltshire
SP5 5QQ

July 1993

Introduction

This second volume of Royal Air Force bomber losses follows much the same pattern set by the first. The intention continues as before, that is to present a record of the tremendous sacrifice made in human lives by the airmen of Bomber Command in carrying through the bombing campaign, while at the same time producing a broad picture of the events that shaped the course of the Command's history.

The sequence of reporting is in chronological order of date, followed by the lowest Squadron Number within a sequence of losses. Squadron details are followed by aircraft type and Mark, serial, squadron code combination and, where known, the aircraft's individual letter and the target identity. Where a non-operational loss occurs, an appropriate term is used to describe the duty under which the crew were flying at the time of the accident. The summary that follows shows, where reported, all available crew details, the time and place of departure for an operational sortie and, if established, a brief description of what subsequently happened to the aircraft and its crew. Where deaths occurred, burial or memorial details have been included in many of the summaries. The abbreviated annotations following the crew names should be self evident; pow being the common abbreviation for prisoner of war. Other symbols used are explained in the Glossary of Terms.

Reported casualties are confined to airmen whose aircraft were destroyed, or damaged beyond all reasonable repair and thus deaths that occurred in aircraft that made a safe return and continued in service are not recorded. I have, however, shown where possible the names of airmen who were killed, or injured, in incidents involving the loss of a bomber through ground explosions, or became casualties after being hit by aircraft crashing in their vicinity.

Where information is available, an attempt has been made towards identifying the losses incurred by the Special Duty units which were responsible for dropping agents and supplies into occupied Europe. Nominal control of these units was exercised by 3 Group, hence their inclusion in this series of volumes. During 1941, 2 Group frequently detached its squadrons for Coastal Command duties and, in the summer, for operations in the Mediterranean theatre. Records for the latter are sparse and, therefore, casualties suffered during these periods of detachment to Coastal Command and away from the United Kingdom are excluded.

In preparing this work five major sources of information have been examined; the squadron Operational Record Books (ORBs) retained by the Public Record Office, Kew, the Bomber Command loss cards and the aircraft accident cards which are lodged with the Ministry of Defence (Air Historical Branch). Included in the primary source material are the cemetery and memorial registers published by the Commonwealth War Graves Commission (CWGC) and the official air forces prisoner of war file (AIR20/2336) which is amongst the many AIR Class documents at Kew. Reference has also been made to the WO208 Class files which contain the escape and evasion reports of servicemen who broke from their bonds of captivity, or evaded capture after finding themselves in enemy territory.

It will be helpful to explain how the principal sources have been used. The squadron ORBs (AIR27 Class) are compiled in two sections; the Form 540 which sets out the day to day events of the squadron and which often contain brief, or at times quite detailed, references to operational matters, and the Form 541 which records details of operational flying including the names of participating crews. These details take either the form of condensed individual crew reports, or a general compilation of the statements made by the crews at their de-briefing. The quality of reporting varies greatly between squadrons. Some ORBs have been meticulously maintained while others are far less revealing, with quite serious omissions regarding losses of aircraft and crews. Variances between what is reported in the Form 540 and that shown in the Form 541 are not uncommon. Of equal importance has been a study of the surviving loss cards and accidents cards. The former supplements the information published in the squadron ORBs while the latter are usually more accurate than the ORBs in respect of crash locations and cause. Most squadrons were at fault in the reporting of non-operational accidents where no loss of life occurred and few ORBs identify such incidents.

Two cautionary notes. Occasionally, the dates shown on the loss cards differ from those recorded in the ORBs. During research into the 1941 casualties, differences of 24-hours were noted on several cards.

Secondly, some cards are at variance with the ORBs in respect of target information. After a span of fifty years, and bearing in mind that all documents are subject to human errors of one sort or the other, it is extremely difficult to decide which source of information is the most accurate. Sometimes, evidence in headquarters records can resolve the matter and, occasionally, the CWGC registers give a useful pointer in the right direction.

The remaining prime source avenues, the CWGC registers and the prisoner of war file, have been invaluable in all matters pertaining to names and initials of airmen posted missing from air operations, or becoming victims in the all too frequent crashes that affected bomber units. These documents have enabled me to establish the accuracy of over ninety per cent of the names and initials reported in this second volume.

Establishing the function of each member of the crew has not been easy. In 1941, ORBs rarely identified individual crew positions but, by comparing the information published in the CWGC registers against entries made in the ORBs, or on the loss cards, a reasonably accurate order can be established. Thus a Blenheim crew is reported in the assumed order of pilot, observer and wireless operator/air gunner, while a typical Hampden pattern follows the sequence of pilot, observer and two wireless operator/air gunners. Wellingtons and Whitleys operated throughout 1941, usually with two pilots. Both types tended to employ an observer and two wireless operator/air gunners but the sixth and last named in a Wellington crew may be regarded as an air gunner.

Generally, this pattern was retained when the Manchester entered service early in the year, but with the introduction of the more complex four-engined bombers, the post of flight engineer was established and his name appears after that of the pilot. The practice of carrying two pilots was not rigidly enforced in the four-engined bombers but where eight names are shown it may be assumed that the first two named are pilots, followed by the flight engineer.

The task of bomb aiming in 1941 continued, mainly, as the duty of the observers, though some of the squadrons equipped with the new Halifaxes and Stirlings employed wireless operators for this function.

Absolute accuracy cannot be assured for all the crew patterns reported, this being especially so when aircraft were lost without trace and where the names of the deceased crew appear on the Runnymede Memorial. When publishing the Memorial registers, CWGC omitted all reference to crew function and without a positive guide in the ORBs proof of the correct order is impossible to ascertain. Furthermore, the cemetery registers do not identify crew function in respect of RAAF and Czechoslovak airmen, while Polish casualties are excluded.

The times quoted in the summaries follow the 24-hour clock system. Cardinal points of the compass are abbreviated and while distances within the United Kingdom are expressed in miles, for the Continent I have used kilometres. United Kingdom county titles are appropriate for the period and are given in all instances apart from those reports which identify county towns.

Locations in the occupied countries are usually followed by the province, shown in parenthesis. Likewise, spellings of towns and villages will be appropriate to the country being reported. Country identity will be included in most reports, except where the capital and well known towns and cities are identified.

As the intensity of night-bombing grew in scale and losses directly attributable to night-fighters rose accordingly, it has been possible to include some details of the Luftwaffe unit responsible. However, where such entries appear readers are advised that the information reported is based on the evidence available and as such can be open to challenge.

Identity of enemy aircraft is standard throughout with Me being used as an abbreviation for all Messerschmitt aircraft (as opposed to the more technically accurate Bf) followed by their type number.

In compiling this volume I have tried to convey as much information as possible, while at the same time maintaining a balance to the summaries. Where appropriate, notes have been appended.

Sources & Bibliography

Air Historical Branch:
Aircraft Accident Cards
Aircraft Movement Cards
Bomber Command Loss Cards

Commonwealth War Graves Commission:
Cemetery & Memorial Registers

Public Record Office, Kew:
Squadron Operational Record Books
Escape & Evasion Reports

Air-Britain (Historians) Ltd:
Battle Axe, A History of 105 Squadron Royal Air Force, Derek Ransom
Royal Air Force Aircraft K1000 to K9999, James J Halley
Royal Air Force Aircraft L1000 to L9999, James J Halley
Royal Air Force Aircraft N1000 to N9999, James J Halley
Royal Air Force Aircraft P1000 to P9999, James J Halley
Royal Air Force Aircraft R1000 to R9999, James J Halley
Royal Air Force Aircraft T1000 to T9999, James J Halley
Royal Air Force Aircraft V1000 to W9999, James J Halley
Royal Air Force Aircraft X1000 to Z9999, James J Halley
The Halifax File, R N Roberts
The Hampden File, Harry Moyle
The Squadrons of the Royal Air Force, James J Halley
The Stirling File, Bryce B Gomersall
The Whitley File, R N Roberts
110 Squadron History, Elwyn D Bell

Battle over the Reich, Alfred Price, Ian Allan, 1973
Boldness be my Friend, Richard Pape, Elek Books Ltd, 1953
Bomber Command, Max Hastings, Michael Joseph, 1979
Bomber Squadrons of the RAF and their Aircraft, Philip Moyes, Macdonald, 1964
Despite the Elements, The History of 115 Squadron 1917-1982, Nettlebed Press, 1983
Exemplary Justice, Allen Andrews, Harrap, 1976
Flyer's Tale, William W Hall, Merlin Books, 1989
Forever Strong: Story of 75 Squadron RNZAF 1916-1990, Norman Franks, Random Century, 1991
For Valour, The Air VCs, Chaz Bowyer, William Kimber, 1978
From Hull, Hell and Halifax, Chris Blanchett, Midland Counties Publications, 1992
Hampden & Hereford Crash Log, Nicholas Roberts, Midland Counties Publications, 1980
Lincolnshire Air Warfare 1939-1945, S Finn, Aero Litho Company, 1973
Messerschmitt Bf110 at War, Armand van Ishoven, Ian Allan, 1985
No Landing Place, Edward Doylerush, Midland Counties Publications, 1985
Somerset at War 1939-1945, Mac Hawkins, Dovecote Press, 1988
The Airmen of St. John's - Beck Row, P & M Wilson, Private, 1987
The Bomber Command War Diaries, Martin Middlebrook & Chris Everitt, Viking, 1985
The Distinguished Flying Medal, I T Tavender, Hayward, 1990
The Polish Air Force in Lincolnshire, M J Ingham, Beckside Design, 1988
The Right of the Line, John Terraine, Hodder & Stoughton, 1985
The Stirling Bomber, Michael J F Bowyer, Faber, 1980
The Wellington Bomber, Chaz Bowyer, William Kimber, 1986
They Shall Not Grow Old, A Book of Remembrance, Allison & Hayward, CATP Museum, 1992
To See The Dawn Breaking, William R Chorley, Chorley, 1981
Vickers Wellington Crash Log, Volume 1 1937-1942, David J Smith, Smith
White Rose Base, Brian J Rapier, Aero Litho Company, 1972
2 Group RAF A Complete History 1936-1945, Michael J F Bowyer, Faber, 1974
44(Rhodesia) Squadron RAF, A N White, White, 1977
83 Squadron 1917-1969, Ronald G Low & Frank Harper, Low, 1992

Glossary of Terms

AA	Anti-aircraft (fire)
AACU	Anti-aircraft Co-operation Unit
AASF	Advanced Air Striking Force
ACM	Air Chief Marshal
AC1	Aircraftman First Class
AC2	Aircraftman Second Class
AFC	Air Force Cross
AFM	Air Force Medal
ASI	Air speed indicator
asl	Above sea level
ASR	Air Sea Rescue (launch)
ATC	Air Training Corps
AVM	Air Vice-Marshal
BEF	British Expeditionary Force
BEM	British Empire Medal
CB	Companion of the Order of the Bath
CBE	Commander of the Order of the British Empire
Ch B	Bachelor of Surgery
Cmdr	Commander
CMG	Companion of (the Order of) St. Michael and St. George
CO	Commanding Officer
Cpl	Corporal
CWGC	Commonwealth War Graves Commission
D/F	Direction Finding (station)
DCM	Distinguished Conduct Medal
DFC	Distinguished Flying Cross
DFM	Distinguished Flying Medal
DSO	Distinguished Service Order
EGM	Empire Gallantry Medal
Evd	Evaded (capture)
F/L	Flight Lieutenant
F/O	Flying Officer
F/S	Flight Sergeant
Fw	Feldwebel
GC	George Cross
G/C	Group Captain
GCB	Grand Cross of the Bath
GM	George Medal
HCU	Heavy Conversion Unit
HMS	His Majesty's Ship
Hptm	Hauptmann
HSL	High Speed Launch
H/T	High tension (cable)
IFF	Identification Friend or Foe
Inj	Injured
Int	Interned
JG	Jagdgeschwader
JP	Justice of the Peace

KCMG	Knight Commander of the Order of St. Michael and St. George
LAC	Leading Aircraftman
Lt	Leutnant/Lieutenant
MB	Bachelor of Medicine
MBE	Member of the Order of the British Empire
MC	Military Cross
MiD	Mentioned in Despatches
MM	Military Medal
MTB	Motor Torpedo Boat
MU	Maintenance Unit
MVO	Member of the Royal Victorian Order
NCO	Non-commissioned Officer
Oblt	Oberleutnant
Ofw	Oberfeldwebel
Op:	Operation
ORB	Operational Record Book
OTU	Operational Training Unit
P/O	Pilot Officer
POW	Prisoner of War
RAAF	Royal Australian Air Force
RAE	Royal Aircraft Establishment
RAF	Royal Air Force
RCAF	Royal Canadian Air Force
RIAF	Royal Indian Air Force
RN	Royal Navy
RNethAF	Royal Netherlands Air Force
RNZAF	Royal New Zealand Air Force
Sgt	Sergeant
SHQ	Station Headquarters
S/L	Squadron Leader
S/L(A)	Sub Lieutenant (Air)
SMO	Senior Medical Officer
SOS	Save our Souls (distress message)
Sqn	Squadron
SS	Schutzstaffel/Steamship
T/o	Took off
Uffz	Unteroffizier
USAAC	United States Army Air Force
VC	Victoria Cross
W/C	Wing Commander
W/O	Warrant Officer
W/T	Wireless Telegraphy
ZG	Zerstörergeschwader
+	Fatal Casualty

Chapter 1

A Confident Start

1 January to 10 February 1941

Bomber operations in the New Year commenced with a daylight raid by Blenheims on targets in north-west Germany. Nine aircraft set out but cloud cover was insufficient and all returned without making any attacks.

As dusk fell, over 100 bombers headed for the inland port of Bremen. The night was bitterly cold, but visibility was good and fires started by the early arrivals acted as a beacon for those following. Much damage was inflicted on this attack, and in the two raids that followed. Many industrial buildings suffered, including the Focke-Wulf aircraft factory and damage was also reported from commercial and residential areas in the centre of Bremen. On the debit side, enemy intruder aircraft shot down two Wellingtons from 301 Squadron, killing eleven airmen, and three other bombers crashed, resulting in the death of a pilot from 78 Squadron.

Following on from these attacks, the Command made an unsuccessful attempt to bomb enemy shipping in the occupied port of Brest but scored a good success when thirty-two crews attacked Wilhelmshaven on 8-9 January. Bombs exploded in close proximity to the battleship Tirpitz and quite serious damage was caused to dockyard buildings and naval installations.

The first major incursion towards the Ruhr came on 9-10 January when synthetic oil plants at Gelsenkirchen were attacked. The results were disappointing. Well under half of the 135 bombers employed claimed to have reached the target area. Two Whitleys were lost; one fell to a night-fighter while crossing Holland and the other crashed on return to base.

Blenheim activity had been a mixture of day and night raiding and for the squadrons of 2 Group this pattern was to become a way of life for the next few months. Initially, their losses were light but as the demands for increased daylight operations were made, so their casualties rose to a level that had last been experienced during the fighting that marked the withdrawal of the BEF from France in the summer of 1940. And, it was to France that the Group focused attention on 10 January, with 114 Squadron providing six crews for a raid on an ammunition dump in the Forêt de Guines, south of Calais.

Heavily escorted by Fighter Command, the Blenheims carried out a successful attack and all returned safely. The first Circus operation, as these raids were titled, had been successfully completed. In due course other bomber types would take part in these operations to targets in the occupied areas

of Northern France. Their primary purpose was to entice the Luftwaffe to join battle with the escorting fighters and thus it can only be deduced that the handful of bombers sent on these operations were the inducement necessary to achieve this objective.

Inclement weather had been a factor in the failure of the recent Gelsenkirchen raid and for the remainder of the month and well into February, operations were severely hampered due to the severe winter weather conditions. But, despite the elements, port facilities in the occupied countries were attacked, as were industrial targets in Northern Italy.

In the middle of January, a particularly good raid was carried out on port facilities at Wilhelmshaven. Visibility was excellent and, once again, the leading crews started a series of fires which were effectively bombed for the remainder of the night.

On the ground the defenders, many from brigades called in from neighbouring towns, fought throughout the night in sub-zero temperatures to bring the dozens of fires under control. Vast sheets of ice formed around them as they laboured. None had experienced a raid of this magnitude before.

Bomber losses were confined to a Whitley from 58 Squadron which was shot down south of the Dutch town of Den Helder by a radar guided night-fighter.

Within twenty-four hours the bombers were back over Wilhelmshaven, but this time only minor damage resulted and casualties amongst the attackers rose to five. Four disappeared without trace, but from the fifth aircraft, a Whitley, all survived to become prisoners of war.

Towards the end of January, 2 Group were ordered to standby for further Circus style operations and during the first ten days of February three such operations were mounted. The first was an attack by four Blenheims on the docks at Boulogne, followed by a strike at the snow covered airfield at St-Omer. Then, on 10 February, half-a-dozen aircraft from 139 Squadron headed out from their base at Horsham St. Faith and executed a quite brilliant raid on the docks at Dunkerque. Approaching from the east all six Blenheims bombed and were far out to sea before the guns opened up.

No bombers were lost from these operations and their purpose in persuading the enemy to rise to the challenge had also been achieved.

In the wake of the attacks on targets in north-west Germany, night raiding was much reduced, but on 4-5 February the Command was able to field 142 bombers for operations against Germany and the occupied countries.

For the first time since the beginning of night raiding, each Group was allocated its own target. Thirty Hampdens from 5 Group were ordered to bomb Düsseldorf, while the remaining Groups despatched small forces of bombers to locations along the French and Belgian coasts.

Generally, the results were encouraging. A Wellington crew claimed a direct hit on a cruiser at Brest and good bombing was also reported at Bordeaux. Losses were minimal. The crew from a 49 Squadron Hampden were reported prisoner after failing to return from Düsseldorf and 106 Squadron lost a similar machine in a fatal crash at Nantes.

Since the start of the year, a total of forty-six bombers had been lost. Roughly, a third had been destroyed in non-operational flying accidents and one of the most tragic of these occurred during the morning of 13th January. Setting out from Linton-on-Ouse, the crew of the 35 Squadron Halifax had been briefed to carry out a measured climb to 12000 feet and monitor fuel consumption. Shortly before midday, the Halifax was seen flying at approximately 8000 feet in the vicinity of Baldersby St. James with smoke and flame trailing in its wake. Then, a steep dive developed and the bomber cartwheeled before plunging into the ground.

Introducing the new breed of heavy bombers into service was not proving to be an easy task but by 10th February, their operational debut was imminent.

1-2 Jan 1941	50 Sqn	Hampden I		X3143 VN-	Op: Bremen
	P/O T N C Burrough			T/o 1659 Lindholme. Crashed 0027 while trying to land at base in marginal weather conditions. No injuries reported.	
	P/O P B Hodgson				
	Sgt Hobson				
	Sgt A B Brooks				

	78 Sqn	Whitley V		T4204 EY-	Op: Bremen
	Sgt H A Davis			T/o 1630 Dishforth. Unable to locate target and bombs jettisoned due to severe icing. Abandoned 2200 though the body of P/O Bates was found in the wreckage near Lindholme airfield, Yorkshire.	
	P/O W A Bates		+		
	Sgt F Waldron				
	Sgt E O T Balcomb				
	Sgt E A Grunsell				

	301 Sqn	Wellington IC		T2517 GR-	Op: Bremen
	S/L S Floryanowicz		+	T/o 1558 Swinderby. Believed shot down by an intruder (Lt Rudolf Stradner, I./NJG2) and crashed 2225 near Digby airfield, Lincolnshire. All are buried in Newark Cemetery. Lt Stradner was killed on 9 July 1941, without, it is believed, adding any further victories.	
	P/O M Olszyna		+		
	F/O H Kulbacki		+		
	Sgt J Hejnowski		+		
	Sgt A Guzowski		+		
	Sgt L Gackowski		+		

	301 Sqn	Wellington IC		T2518 GR-	Op: Bremen
	P/O B R Murawski		+	T/o 1616 Swinderby. Believed shot down by an intruder (Uffz Arnold, I./NJG2) and crashed 0135 at Wellingore, 9 miles S of Lincoln. Mishandling of the wing flaps is also quoted as being a possible cause. Those who died are buried in Newark Cemetery.	
	P/O T Dzuibinski		+		
	F/O B Sadowski		+		
	Sgt K Sawick		+		
	Sgt G Kasianowski		+		
	Sgt Wancisiewicz		inj		

Note. Names and initials have been checked against the original burial register.

2-3 Jan 1941	61 Sqn	Hampden I		X3126 QR-	Op: Bremen
	F/L Powdrell		inj	T/o 0312 Hemswell. Turned back while 70 miles short of the target with an over heating port engine. Crashed 0736 some 500 yards from the Officers' Mess at Hemswell, when both engines cut through lack of fuel.	
	Sgt Horn		inj		
	Sgt R R B Durtnall				
	Sgt Clelland				

	102 Sqn	Whitley V		T4227 DY-R	Op: Bremen
	F/O D C F Coutts		+	T/o 1641 Topcliffe. Believed shot down by an intruder (Fw Hans Hahn, 3./NJG2) and crashed 1900 some 30 miles E of Withernsea, Yorkshire. All are commemorated on the Runnymede Memorial.	
	Sgt K H Smith		+		
	Sgt N Stephenson		+		
	Sgt J Kennedy		+		
	Sgt T F Behan		+		

3 Jan 1941	106 Sqn	Hampden I		P4314 ZN-	Training
	Sgt I P Mapp			Forced-landed 2055 approximately 1 mile S of Finningley airfield, Yorkshire. No injuries reported. Sgt Mapp was on attachment from 61 Squadron.	

3-4 Jan 1941	51 Sqn	Whitley V	P5060 MH-	Op: Bremen

Sgt A D Wright   +
P/O R W Trehern   +
Sgt J D L Kelly   +
Sgt C G Sinclair   +
Sgt C T Swaffield   +

T/o 1705 Dishforth. Lost without trace. All are commemorated on the Runnymede Memorial.

---

78 Sqn   **Whitley V**   **P4937 EY-**   **Op: Bremen**

P/O P S James
Sgt L R Blackwell
Sgt R J Garlish
Sgt C E Simpson
Sgt M W Chadwick

T/o 1700 Dishforth. Abandoned, due to w/t failure, 0340 in the vicinity of South Molton, Devon. Sgt Blackwell was later commissioned and lost his life in a flying accident on 21 July 1941, while serving with 76 Squadron.

---

4 Jan 1941   **99 Sqn**   **Wellington IA**   **L7783 LN-D**   **Training**

F/O J P A Davidson   inj
Sgt J M Keddie   inj
P/O Bellerby   inj
Sgt Truscott   inj

Crashed 1255 on Newmarket race course after two unsuccessful attempts to land. All four airmen were admitted to White Lodge Hospital where F/O Davidson and Sgt Keddie died from their injuries.

5-6 Jan 1941   **49 Sqn**   **Hampden I**   **P4322 EA-N**   **Op: Gardening**

P/O G E Price DFM   +
Sgt W B C Winning   +
Sgt C A Small   +
Sgt T H Chamberlain   +

T/o 1705 Scampton for a mining operation in French waters. Believed to have crashed in the sea 10 miles S of Sidmouth, Devon. All are commemorated on the Runnymede Memorial.

---

6 Jan 1941   **82 Sqn**   **Blenheim IV**   **V5375 UX-**   **Op: Rotterdam**

Sgt Jackman   inj
Sgt T H Cooke   inj
Sgt Perry

T/o 1506 Bodney. Crashed 1825 into a field at Strumpshaw, 8 miles E of Norwich. The pilot was trapped in the burning wreckage and was saved from death by the prompt action of local villagers. Prior to the crash, Sgt Jackman had ordered his crew to bale out.

---

8 Jan 1941   **214 Sqn**   **Wellington IC**   **T2956 BU-**   **Air Test**

P/O T E Timmins   +
P/O C N Walker   +
Sgt P R Peart   +
Sgt A S Roberts   +
Sgt R Cain   +
Sgt W E Griswold   +

Believed to have iced up while flying in cloud and crashed 1240 at Great Wratting, 2 miles NNE of Haverhill, Suffolk. P/O Walker was on the strength of 38 Squadron, a unit that had moved recently to the Middle East.

9-10 Jan 1941   **51 Sqn**   **Whitley V**   **T4270 MH-M**   **Op: Gelsenkirchen**

P/O G F Shaw   +
Sgt H G Soffe   +
Sgt W M Hyslop   +
Sgt Hart   inj
Sgt K L Minassian   inj

T/o 1730 Dishforth. Crashed 0043 on return to base and burst into flames. Rescue attempts were severely hampered by exploding ammunition and of the two survivors, Sgt Minassian died in Harrogate Hospital on 12 January.

---

78 Sqn   **Whitley V**   **T4203 EY-**   **Op: Gelsenkirchen**

Sgt C A Smith   +
Sgt S H Burley   +
Sgt L D Norman   +
Sgt A W Astle   +
Sgt V Tarrant   +

T/o 1757 Dishforth. Shot down by a night-fighter (Oblt Reinhold Eckardt, II./NJG1) and crashed 2318 through ice encrusted flood-water between Millingen and Kekerdom (Gelderland), Holland. All are buried in Mook War Cemetery.

---

10 Jan 1941   **75 Sqn**   **Wellington IC**   **T2550 AA-L**   **Air Test**

P/O B P McNamara RNZAF   +
P/O A J Ryan RNZAF   +
Sgt R B Elliott   +
Sgt J Olive   +
Sgt M R Ritchie   +
Sgt R E Ashby-Peckham   inj

T/o 1130 Feltwell. Crashed at Heath Farm near Stapleford, 4 miles SE of Cambridge, while heading for Bassingbourn. P/O Ryan RNZAF was due to remain here, his place being taken by another pilot. Sgt Ashby-Peckham was admitted to Addenbrooke Hospital very seriously injured.

---

11 Jan 1941   **82 Sqn**   **Blenheim IV**   **T2163 UX-**   **Op: Amsterdam**

P/O A H Poulsen   +
Sgt J Burton   +
Sgt H Summers   +

T/o 1450 Bodney. Lost without trace. All are commemorated on the Runnymede Memorial.

11-12 Jan 1941	**9 Sqn**	**Wellington IC**		**R1244 WS-**	**Op: Torino**

Sgt S M P Parkes — int
Sgt L R Willis — int
Sgt L D Goldingay — int
Sgt H W Bratley — int
Sgt R Vivian — int
Sgt R W Blaydon — int

T/o 1739 Honington. Forced-landed near Misérieux in Vichy France and the crew were interned by the authorities. However, apart from Sgt Willis, all returned safely and resumed operational flying by June 1941. Sgt Willis eventually made his way to freedom and was awarded the MM, details appearing in the London Gazette on 18 August 1942. Almost two years later Sgt Blaydon was killed on operations with 582 Squadron.

---

49 Sqn   **Hampden I**   **L4045 EA-Q**   **Op: Wilhelmshaven**

P/O H Newhouse +
Sgt H Irving +
Sgt L Jackson +
Sgt P C Prosser +

T/o 0135 Scampton. Crashed 0745 at Northorpe, Lincolnshire. Witnesses to this accident say the pilot pulled up sharply to avoid flying into some houses and by doing so he lost control.

---

12 Jan 1941   **142 Sqn**   **Wellington II**   **W5373 QT-**   **Training**

P/O Bilton inj
Sgt Rogers inj
Sgt Phillips inj
P/O M Jacoby
Sgt Rowe
Sgt T H Harrower
Sgt Durham

T/o Binbrook and crashed almost immediately due to failure of the port engine. Two of the crew were treated in Louth Hospital.

12-13 Jan 1941   **149 Sqn**   **Wellington IC**   **T2807 OJ-**   **Op: Italy**

Sgt R A Hodgson pow
P/O L K S Wilson pow
Sgt L W Hatherly pow
Sgt E E Harding pow
Sgt J McAnnally pow
Sgt C F Plummery pow

T/o 2130 Mildenhall.

---

13 Jan 1941   **35 Sqn**   **Halifax I**   **L9487 TL-**   **Air Test**

F/O M T G Henry DFC +
P/O L J McDonald +
Sgt J N Hall +
Sgt A C H R Russell +
Sgt W C B Jesse DFM +
Sgt F L Plowman +

T/o 1120 Linton-on-Ouse for a fuel consumption test and a measured climb to 12000 feet. Shortly before noon eye witnesses reported seeing the bomber flying at 8000 feet with its undercarriage down and trailing smoke and flame. It then cart-wheeled and crashed at Howefield House, just SW of Baldersby St. James, 4 miles N of Dishforth, Yorkshire.

---

13 Jan 1941   **114 Sqn**   **Blenheim IV**   **T1858 RT-**   **Op: Reconnaissance**

P/O D Lowther-Clarke +
Sgt A R Grindley +
Sgt N O Allen +

T/o 0855 Oulton. Believed shot down by fighters at 1055 and crashed into the sea NW of Bergen, Holland. All are commemorated on the Runnymede Memorial.

---

15 Jan 1941   **218 Sqn**   **Wellington IA**   **P9207 HA-**   **Training**

F/O P F MacLaren +

Crashed 1155 between Wormegay and Pentney, some 6 miles SE of King's Lynn, Norfolk. F/O MacLaren was making his first solo flight in a Wellington bomber.

15-16 Jan 1941   **58 Sqn**   **Whitley V**   **N1521 GE-J**   **Op: Wilhelmshaven**

P/O W E Peers +
Sgt H P Shipley +
P/O M P Griffiths +
Sgt R J Couser DFM +
Sgt R F J Duncan +

T/o 1755 Linton-on-Ouse. Heard on w/t at 2145, but shot down by a night-fighter (Oblt Egmont Prinz zur Lippe Weissenfeld, 4./NJG1) and crashed 2246 between the Zwanenwater lake and Callantsoog (Noord Holland), below Den Helder, Holland. It is further reported that the night-fighter was being radar controlled by Lt Jauk at Station Salzhering, not far from Den Helder.

16-17 Jan 1941   **10 Sqn**   **Whitley V**   **T4220 ZA-S**   **Op: Wilhelmshaven**

F/O H B Skyrme +
Sgt J E Rowlett +
Sgt G C Sandland +
Sgt E D Polkinghorne +
Sgt L P Brookman +

T/o 1832 Leeming. Last heard on w/t at 2115. All are commemorated on the Runnymede Memorial.

| 16-17 Jan 1941 | 40 Sqn | Wellington IC | T2912 BL-S | Op: Wilhelmshaven |

16-17 Jan
1941

40 Sqn　　　　　**Wellington IC**
Sgt A E Jones　　　　+
Sgt E G Robertson　　+
Sgt J H Lee　　　　　+
Sgt H F Lander　　　+
Sgt D R C Cannell　+
Sgt E F Todd　　　　+

T2912 BL-S　　　　　**Op: Wilhelmshaven**
T/o 1756 Wyton. Signal received indicating task completed, after which the Wellington vanished without trace. All are commemorated on the Runnymede Memorial

58 Sqn　　　　　**Whitley V**
Sgt A E Barlow　　　pow
F/O J H Frampton　　pow
Sgt R P London　　　pow
Sgt C H Steven　　　pow
Sgt R M Wade　　　　pow

Z6462 GE-D　　　　　**Op: Wilhelmshaven**
T/o 1745 Linton-on-Ouse. Last heard on w/t at 2030 by a monitoring station at Lympne in Kent. Shot down by marine flak and crashed 2115 at Anna Paulowna (Noord Holland), 12 km SE of Den Helder.

83 Sqn　　　　　**Hampden I**
P/O P J Strong　　　+
Sgt D Brand　　　　　+
Sgt A G S White　　+
Sgt D V House　　　+

AD731 OL-M　　　　　**Op: Wilhelmshaven**
T/o 0250 Scampton. Crashed in the sea 80 miles ENE of Great Yarmouth, Norfolk. The Runnymede Memorial commemorates the names of this crew.

311 Sqn　　　　　**Wellington IC**
P/O A Kubiznak　　　+
Sgt B Baumruk　　　　+
P/O J Hudec　　　　　+
P/O J Leskauer　　　+
Sgt R Bolfik　　　　+
P/O J O Kral　　　　+

T2519 KX-Y　　　　　**Op: Wilhelmshaven**
T/o 1750 East Wretham. Encountered technical problems and was last heard on w/t at 2221. All are commemorated on the Runnymede Memorial.

22 Jan
1941

139 Sqn　　　　　**Blenheim IV**
F/L G J Menzies DFC　+
Sgt E J Bonney　　　+
Sgt R Tribick　　　+

T2435 XD-　　　　　**Op: NW Germany**
T/o 1020 Horsham St. Faith. On return, and while crossing the East Anglia coast at 1220, the crew failed to give any recognition signals and the Blenheim was promptly engaged by AA fire from naval ships. Shortly afterwards the tail assembly broke away and the bomber dived into a field 250 yards from the police house at Oulton, 2 miles WNW of Lowestoft, Suffolk.

22-23 Jan
1941

82 Sqn　　　　　**Blenheim IV**
P/O P H Moller　　　+
Sgt A J Norman　　　inj
Sgt F H H Taylor　　+

N3553 UX-　　　　　**Op: Düsseldorf**
T/o 1939 Bodney and crashed almost immediately at Merton Park, SW of the airfield. The Blenheim came down amongst trees and then hit a brick wall. Sgt Norman was thrown clear, but died soon afterwards from his injuries.

29-30 Jan
1941

214 Sqn　　　　　**Wellington IC**
Sgt J Smiles
Sgt J R Turner
Sgt Turner
Sgt Foster
Sgt Rothorn
Sgt M Elelman

T2841 BU-K　　　　　**Op: Wilhelmshaven**
T/o 0302 Stradishall but as the bomber left the ground the port engine failed and the Wellington sank back onto the runway and burst into flames. Padre Harrison was one of the first to reach the scene and despite the risk of explosion, he was instrumental in saving the lives of the crew. For this act of great heroism, Padre Harrison was awarded the George Medal.

31 Jan
1941

99 Sqn　　　　　**Wellington IC**
Sgt Fennell

T2541 LN-O　　　　　**Training**
Forced-landed at Looms Lane, Burgh, 3 miles NW of Woodbridge, Suffolk and ran into a shallow ditch. The engines were closed down, but at 1645 the pilot decided he would restart. On doing so the port motor burst into flames and the bomber was destroyed by fire.

1 Feb
1941

61 Sqn　　　　　**Hampden I**
Sgt N M Lloyd　　　inj
Sgt R Guest　　　　+

AD725 QR-　　　　　**Training**
Crashed 2000 onto a snow covered dispersal at Hemswell airfield, Lincolnshire.

144 Sqn　　　　　**Hampden I**
Sgt J K Thurlbeck　+
Sgt J T Hawthorne　+

P1328 PL-　　　　　**Training**
Crashed 2015 at Willingham, 11 miles NNW of Lincoln, after flying into a snow storm.

2 Feb 1941	101 Sqn	Blenheim IV	N3570 SR-	Training
	Sgt Langrish	inj	Crashed on the beach near Freiston, 3 miles SSE	
	Sgt H F Rampley	inj	of Boston, Lincolnshire. Sgt Rampley died from	
	Sgt E W De´ath	+	his injuries the next day.	
	LAC Plunkett	inj		

4-5 Feb 1941	49 Sqn	Hampden I	P4299 EA-	Op: Düsseldorf
	Sgt W J Baird	pow	T/o 1800 Scampton.	
	Sgt R I Eastwood	pow		
	Sgt T R H Hawkes	pow		
	Sgt L W Homard	pow		

	106 Sqn	Hampden I	AD750 ZN-	Op: Gardening
	F/O W K B Thomas	+	T/o 1730 Finningley for a mining operation off	
	P/O G H F Inniss	+	St-Nazaire. Crashed near Nantes (Loire-	
	Sgt J L Franco	+	Atlantique), where all are buried in the	
	Sgt F A Colson	+	Pont-du-Cens Communal Cemetery.	

6 Feb 1941	107 Sqn	Blenheim IV	L8777 OM-	Training
	Sgt E G Clarke		Crashed while trying to make an emergency landing 2 miles SW of Wattisham, Suffolk.	

	304 Sqn	Wellington IC	R1014 NZ-	Training
	Sgt S Tofin	+	T/o Syerston but crashed almost immediately	
	Sgt W Lichota	+	at Bleasby, 11 miles NE of Nottingham. All	
	Sgt C A Cymborski	+	are buried in the Polish Plot at Newark	
	Sgt J Jonczyk	+	Cemetery.	

6-7 Feb 1941	214 Sqn	Wellington IC	N2776 BU-	Op: Boulogne
	P/O W Spooner		T/o 1803 Stradishall. Crash-landed 2025 on	
	P/O Gilson		return to base. The accident was attributed	
	Sgt Murphy		to hydraulic failure, which caused the bomber	
	Sgt Horobin		to overshoot the runway.	
	Sgt Ludkin			
	Sgt Trevillian			

	311 Sqn	Wellington IC	L7842 KX-T	Op: Boulogne
	P/O F Cigos	pow	T/o 1806 East Wretham. Forced-landed, intact,	
	Sgt P Uraba	pow	and later test flown by the Luftwaffe at its	
	P/O E Busina	pow	Experimental and Test facility at Rechlin. P/O	
	P/O A Valenta	pow	Valenta was murdered by the Gestapo in late	
	Sgt G Kopal	pow	March 1944, following the mass escape from	
	P/O K Krizek	pow	Sagan. He is buried in the Old Garrison	
			Cemetery at Poznan, Poland.	

Note. It is reported that P/O Valenta was amongst the early pairs of escapers from the tunnel on 24 March. He was recaptured in the Görlitz area and was last seen alive on 31 March amongst a group of ten officers in the charge of Oberreigierungsrat Scharpwinkel.

8 Feb 1941	12 Sqn	Wellington II	W5365 PH-	Training
	S/L P C Lawrence	+	Stalled and crashed while trying to land at	
	P/O R Atkinson	+	Tollerton. The Wellington came down near	
	Sgt J J C Batty	+	Cotgrave, 5 miles SE of Nottingham. Sgt Boyle	
	Sgt R T Tomlinson DFM	+	was a New Zealander whose father, Sgt J McK	
	Sgt A Crooks	+	Boyle MM, had been killed in action with the	
	Sgt E F Carter	+	Otago Regiment on 12 October 1917.	
	Sgt N C Boyle	+		

Note. On this day AC1 J D Boxall of 12 Squadron lost his life. He may have been flying as a passenger in the Wellington described above.

8-9 Feb 1941	144 Sqn	Hampden I	P4359 PL-	Op: Mannheim
	Sgt R H Pearman		T/o 0107 Hemswell. Abandoned 0615 and the	
	Sgt H Masters		Hampden crashed and burst into flames between	
	Sgt H E Turner		two army Nissen huts at Taverham Park, Taverham,	
	Sgt A R Simmons		7 miles NW of Norwich. At the time of the crash	
			the crew were lost and due to an unserviceable	

wireless were unable to ascertain their position.

9-10 Feb	61 Sqn	Hampden I	P4405 QR-	Op: **Wilhelmshaven**
1941	F/L W E Frutiger	+	T/o 0220 Hemswell. Crashed 0650, after calling
	Sgt R A Chanin	+	for assistance, into Bluestone Plantation between
	Sgt J E Hill	+	Heydon and Cawston, Norfolk.
	F/S R A Gapp	+	

Chapter 2

Arrival of the Heavyweights

10-11 February to 10-11 March 1941

The first Stirling arrived with the reformed 7 Squadron at Leeming on 12 August 1940. At the time, the outcome of the Battle of Britain was still to be decided.

Three months later, at Boscombe Down, 35 Squadron took charge of its first Halifax. In the same month, November 1940, the first production twin-engined Manchesters landed at Waddington where 207 Squadron had been re-established on the 1st.

The three types represented a considerable advance over the bombers currently in service, and squadron commanders found themselves under immense pressure to achieve operational readiness in the shortest time possible.

Prevailing conditions were not conducive to a measured introduction. Atrocious weather turned the airfields into quagmires, making life a misery for air and ground staff alike, while technical problems were soon forthcoming. The Rolls-Royce Vulture engines which powered the Manchester were relatively untested power plants and engine faults were destined to bedevil this bomber throughout its eighteen months of front line service.

Frequent grounding orders reduced flying practice to a minimum, resulting in only a handful of crews that could be considered familiar with their new aircraft, and this unfortunate situation was not confined just to the Manchester. The early production Stirlings provided the ground staff with a myriad of technical problems; its undercarriage units being particularly prone to fault.

Flying characteristics of the early model Halifaxes left much to be desired and neither type, in their present form, could be described as satisfactory.

As history now shows us, the Manchester's long run of problems was eventually solved by replacing the two Vultures with four Merlins. With changes to the mainplanes and tail assembly, the new bomber fully met its design potential and thus was conceived the Lancaster.

Gradually, the reliability of the Stirling and the Halifax improved and though the former was to be stood down from front line bomber service in 1944, the type soldiered on in active service to the end of the war, and beyond - as did the Halifax.

But, at the beginning of February 1941, production of all three types was proving to be painfully slow and, as recounted, the constant interruptions affecting the flying programme was seriously delaying their introduction to active service. Indeed, so concerned was the Commanding Officer of one of the new squadrons that in an interview with Air Chief Marshal Sir Charles Portal he voiced his serious concern that if his crews were ordered to attack Berlin, he doubted if any would return. Fortunately, despite the undisguised desires of politicians and Bomber Command headquarters for such an audacious action, common sense prevailed and when 7 Squadron did become operational on 10-11 February, their target was oil storage facilities at Rotterdam.

From Oakington, where the squadron had arrived the previous October, it took over an hour to get the three Stirlings away, but once airborne all three crews enjoyed a relatively trouble free raid and all made a safe return.

The first bombs landed in the Rotterdam area shortly after 2030 and explosions continued, at intervals, over the next two hours. At this stage of the war, little emphasis was placed on concentrated bombing, and the raid by over 200 aircraft on the primary objective of Hannover was an even more protracted affair.

Nonetheless, despite this piecemeal approach, the overall results were described by the crews as satisfactory. Fires were started at both locations and the general feeling of satisfaction at headquarters in the aftermath of the raids on Wilhelmshaven and Bremen was maintained. Furthermore, not only had the Stirling made its debut, but 3 Group had also fielded over 100 Wellingtons. This feat alone was, at this stage of the war, a magnificent achievement and marked the first time that a single bomber group had been able to muster such a number.

Not surprisingly, from the eight aircraft written off, four were Wellingtons, while the remaining casualties comprised of two Blenheims and two Hampdens. Of the eight crews involved, only three were down over enemy territory, the rest having crashed during the final stages of their return flight. Three, a Wellington from 115 Squadron, a 21 Squadron Blenheim and a 49 Squadron Hampden crew, had been successfully intercepted and shot down by enemy intruders operating over Lincolnshire and East Anglia, while a Wellington from 103 Squadron was obliged to ditch in the North Sea.

The remaining casualty, a bomber from 9 Squadron, had been shot down by AA fire from an Allied convoy, fortunately without fatal consequences.

The following night seventy-nine bombers

set out for Bremen, only to encounter very poor weather conditions which prevented the majority of crews from bombing. There was scant respite in the weather as tired crews headed for home, and to add to their growing concern, fog shrouded the greater part of eastern England. Unable to pinpoint their positions and with fuel reserves critically low, some crews abandoned their aircraft, while others decided to take their chances at getting down through the mist.

In the event, eighteen aircraft crashed, though fatal casualties were remarkably light. Tragically, a Wellington fell onto a house in Cambridge, killing three elderly lady occupants. The perils associated with bomber operations were not confined to those in the air.

Over the next two weeks night raiding was possible on only seven occasions, during which the Manchester received its baptism of fire. Six aircraft were despatched with orders to bomb naval installations at Brest. With the steady increase in U-boat activity in the Western Atlantic, Allied convoy losses were reaching alarming proportions. Supplies, critical to British needs, were being sent to the bottom on a scale that if allowed to continue unchecked would, in the long run, signal defeat.

The Battle of the Atlantic, as it came to be known, was contested throughout the war, though from 1943 onwards the scales had tilted in Britain's favour.

It was a battle fought principally between seamen, though hundreds of airmen were also involved in long-range air patrols.

Casualties amongst the escorting naval ships and aircraft, sent out to aid in the hunt for the U-boats, were significant. And let it not be forgotten that thousands of German sailors perished beneath the waves in depth charge attacks on their submarines.

Thus, it was the gravity of the situation early in March 1941 that prompted the Prime Minister, Winston Churchill, to issue a directive ordering Bomber Command to devote its energy towards countering the growing threat posed by the U-boats. A copy of his order reached High Wycombe from the Air Ministry on the 9th and for the next four months, the principal effort was focused on

the submarine construction yards in Germany and their operational bases along the Brittany coast.

For 2 Group, this new order signalled the start of a campaign that was to prove to be every bit as brutal and demanding as that fought in the skies over France and Belgium in the summer of 1940. The recently started Circus operations were suspended as the Group planners drew up orders that in the weeks ahead sent the Blenheims into action against shipping over an area stretching from the Bay of Biscay to the waters off southern Norway.

But this chapter ends, as it began, with the introduction of one of the new bomber types to the night bombing campaign.

At Linton-on-Ouse a cable from the Air Officer Commanding, Air Marshal Sir Richard Peirse, arrived during the morning of 10th March, addressed to the Commanding Officer of 35 Squadron. His message read, "Good wishes to 35 Squadron and the heavyweights on the opening of their Halifax operations tonight. I hope the full weight of the Squadron's blows will soon be felt further afield."

Throughout the day, groundcrews worked on preparing seven aircraft for despatch to the port of Le Havre. At 1900 the first Halifax departed, followed during the next twenty minutes by five others. There should have been a seventh, but this bomber remained firmly grounded with hydraulic problems.

Four of the six Halifaxes located and attacked the primary target, while a fifth bombed Dieppe. The sixth crew aborted their sortie after encountering dense cloud over the primary target and then running short of petrol while heading for the secondary objective, Boulogne.

From the four successful crews, one was making for home with a wounded navigator and an engine stopped after being hit by flak, while another was intercepted by an Allied night-fighter over the southern counties and sent crashing down near Aldershot. In the last moments before it hit the ground, the pilot and his flight engineer managed to parachute to safety.

Introducing the heavy bombers was turning out to be a difficult task.

10-11 Feb	9 Sqn	Wellington IC	R1096 WS-	Op: Hannover
1941	Sgt A G D McKay			T/o 1919 Honington. On return, and while some 30
	Sgt Millington			miles off the East Anglia coast, the bomber was
	Sgt McRiner			hit by AA fire from an Allied convoy. The pilot
	Sgt House			headed for Martlesham Heath, but overshot the
	Sgt Bevan			runway and crashed 0210 at Mill Field, Bredfield,
	Sgt Ainsbury			2 miles N of Woodbridge, Suffolk.

	15 Sqn	Wellington IC	T2702 LS-H	Op: Hannover
	Sgt W R Garrioch	pow		T/o Wyton. Last heard on w/t at 2135 indicating
	Sgt R F Beisley	pow		task completed. Shot down by a night-fighter
	Sgt J Hall	pow		(Hptm Walter Ehle, II./NJG1) and crashed 2335
	Sgt H G Hedge RNZAF	pow		some 15 km W of Kampen (Overijssel), Holland. The
	Sgt G Reardon	+		remains of Sgt Reardon were recovered in 1967 by
	Sgt W H Jordan	pow		RNethAF and taken for burial at Nijmegen.

10-11 Feb	21 Sqn	Blenheim IV	T2282 YH-	Op: Hannover

1941	F/L R J McConnell	pow	T/o 2205 Watton.
	Sgt E W Green	pow	
	Sgt D E Bristow	pow	

	21 Sqn	Blenheim IV	Z5877 YH-	Op: Hannover
	Sgt A Chatteway	+	T/o 2210 Watton. Shot down 0310 in the airfield
	P/O G E Sharvell	inj	circuit by a Ju 88C flown by Oblt Paul Semrau,
	Sgt Birch	inj	3./NJG2. P/O Sharvell died from his injuries.

Note. Believed to have been the first of forty-six combat victories claimed by Oblt Semrau who was himself shot down by Spitfires and died on 8 February 1945.

	49 Sqn	Hampden I	X3001 EA-H	Op: Hannover
	P/O J H Green	pow	T/o 2248 Scampton. Shot down by a night-fighter
	Sgt D A Cruickshank	+	(Lt Leopold Fellerer, 5./NJG1) and crashed 0350
	Sgt A L Bryceson	pow	some 10 km N of Alkmaar (Noord Holland), where
	Sgt H E Fisher	pow	Sgt Cruickshank is buried.

	49 Sqn	Hampden I	AD719 EA-	Op: Hannover
	Sgt G M Bates	inj	T/o 2240 Scampton. Shot down by an intruder
	Sgt J Butterworth	+	(Oblt Kurt Herrmann, I./NJG2) and crashed 0630
	Sgt Blower	inj	some 200 yards N of Sudbrooke Lane near Grange
	Sgt D A Caldwell	+	Farm, Sudbrooke, 3 miles NE of Lincoln.

	103 Sqn	Wellington IC	T2610 PM-	Op: Hannover
	Sgt W R Crich DFM	inj	T/o 1847 Newton. Lost engine power and ditched
	Sgt G A Farley	inj	in the North Sea. The crew were rescued two days
	Sgt L F Waern DFM	inj	later by the SS Tovelil; Sgt Farley suffering
	Sgt R Layfield	inj	from a fractured collar bone and Sgt Cameron with
	Sgt N Cameron	inj	a broken wrist.
	Sgt G G Chadd	inj	

	115 Sqn	Wellington IC	R1084 KO-Q	Op: Hannover
	Sgt H H Rogers		T/o 2035 Marham. Damaged by a night-fighter
	Sgt Robson		(Hptm Rolf Jung, 4./NJG2) and crash-landed 0145
	Sgt R Benson		at Narborough, 5 miles NW of Swaffham, Norfolk.
	Sgt Baird		Sgt Rogers later gained a DFM, was commissioned
	Sgt Bennett		and died on operations flying with 76 Squadron
	Sgt Hill	inj	on 8 April 1943.

11-12 Feb	51 Sqn	Whitley V	P4974 MH-	Op: Bremen
1941	Sgt I H Fenton		T/o 1842 Dishforth. Ordered to divert to Drem
	Sgt Clarke		but misunderstood the instruction and remained
	P/O Carter		over eastern England. Ran out of petrol and
	Sgt J R Wanbon		successfully abandoned.
	Sgt Henderson		

	51 Sqn	Whitley V	P4981 MH-	Op: Bremen
	Sgt D L Boyer		T/o 1830 Dishforth. Ordered to divert to Drem
	P/O Flower	inj	but encountered poor weather and the Whitley was
	Sgt W F Hurst		abandoned in the vicinity of Grimethorpe, 9 miles
	Sgt Radford	inj	SE of Wakefield, Yorkshire.
	Sgt J N A James	inj	

	51 Sqn	Whitley V	P5013 MH-	Op: Bremen
	Sgt D C Beddow		T/o 1840 Dishforth. Unable to comply with the
	Sgt E S C Halsall	inj	diversion order and abandoned the aircraft over
	Sgt E Hughes		Hatfield Military Camp, 10 miles NE of Doncaster
	Sgt Garnett	inj	Yorkshire.
	Sgt G H Carter		

	51 Sqn	Whitley V	T4217 MH-	Op: Bremen
	P/O M E Sharp	inj	T/o 1843 Dishforth. Crew unable to pinpoint
	Sgt Mathewman		their position and abandoned the Whitley near
	Sgt S J Congdon	inj	Bircham Newton. Sgt Congdon died on 15 August
	Sgt Salt		1943 while serving with 138 Squadron, and Sgt
	Sgt L J Allum	inj	Allum was posted missing on 24 November 1943,
			while on operations with 7 Squadron.

11-12 Feb 1941

58 Sqn   **Whitley V**   **T4213 GE-K**   **Op: Bremen**
Sgt W A Fullerton
P/O R McC Carrapiett
Sgt P C Morgan
Sgt Bell
Sgt Keatley

T/o 1830 Linton-on-Ouse. Abandoned in the area of Bagthorpe, N of Heanor, Nottingham, after which the Whitley crashed 0330 and caught fire at Fulbeck, Lincolnshire.

58 Sqn   **Whitley V**   **T4322 GE-R**   **Op: Bremen**
Sgt H J Walters
Sgt T J Thurling
Sgt A Sayner
Sgt G B Boreham
Sgt Halliday

T/o 1835 Linton-on-Ouse. Abandoned and crashed 0445 at Wishaw, 15 miles SE of Glasgow. Sgt Sayner was reported missing in action on 15 October 1942 while serving with 156 Squadron.

78 Sqn   **Whitley V**   **N1490 EY-**   **Op: Bremen**
Sgt J W Quincey
Sgt P F G Alcock
Sgt R Clark
Sgt R Bradbury
Sgt J F Hollingworth

T/o 1850 Dishforth. Crash-landed at Hill House Farm, Newmilns, 7 miles E of Kilmarnock, Ayrshire.

83 Sqn   **Hampden I**   **AD722 OL-X**   **Op: Bremen**
F/L D W F Barker DFC   +
Sgt W H Lowson   +
Sgt G Targett   +
F/O F S Wilson   +

T/o 2010 Scampton. Crashed after flying into a building while trying to land at Finningley.

83 Sqn   **Hampden I**   **AD734 OL-K**   **Op: Bremen**
F/L R Anderson
F/O J Badcock
Sgt D V Weaving
Sgt T P Byrne

T/o 1820 Scampton. Abandoned 0200 after flying into a balloon cable over Birmingham. It is believed that the Hampden, which was set on auto pilot following the collision, eventually crashed in the Irish Sea.

99 Sqn   **Wellington IC**   **T2888 LN-R**   **Op: Bremen**
Sgt Robinson
Sgt D N Beal   +
Sgt A R Clough   +

T/o Newmarket. Abandoned and crashed at Stags Holt Elm, 5 miles S of Wisbech, Cambridgeshire. Sgt Clough fell into water and drowned.

115 Sqn   **Wellington IC**   **R1004 KO-U**   **Op: Bremen**
P/O Clarke
Sgt Douglas
Sgt Tilson
Sgt White
Sgt Hoy
Sgt Campbell

T/o 1823 Marham. Abandoned in the vicinity of Cambridge, after which the bomber fell across houses in Histon Road, Cambridge, killing three elderly ladies, Miss Catherine Allen, Mrs Ann Warland and Mrs Ada Sara Blackwell. Mrs Mary Hewitt was badly injured and taken to hospital.

115 Sqn   **Wellington IC**   **R1238 KO-A**   **Op: Bremen**
Sgt Whittaker
Sgt Thompson
P/O Searle
Sgt Kerr
Sgt Welch
Sgt Tough

T/o 1900 Marham. Diverted to Finningley, but hit an obstruction while approaching to land and crashed short of the runway.

115 Sqn   **Wellington IC**   **R3238 KO-H**   **Op: Bremen**
W/C A C Evans-Evans
Sgt Jones
F/O Gilliat
P/O S S Barnett
Sgt J S C Sherman
Sgt E Keetley

T/o 1814 Marham. Abandoned over Wicken Bonhunt, 4 miles SSW of Saffron Walden, Essex. W/C Evans-Evans was killed on 21-22 February 1945 while on operations with 83 Squadron.

11-12 Feb **1941**	**144 Sqn** Sgt E Dainty Sgt L A F Wilmot Sgt T Grosvenor Sgt G Bottomley	**Hampden I**		**X3007 PL-** **Op: Hannover**

11-12 Feb 1941 — **144 Sqn** — **Hampden I** — **X3007 PL-** — **Op: Hannover**
Sgt E Dainty
Sgt L A F Wilmot
Sgt T Grosvenor
Sgt G Bottomley
T/o 1730 Hemswell. Abandoned near Kirton Lindsey airfield, Lincolnshire, after which the bomber flew on for nearly 70 miles before crashing 0325 at Kenhill Wood, Snettisham, Norfolk. Sgt Dainty was killed while flying Lancasters with 100 Squadron on 13 June 1943. He is buried in the Reichswald Forest War Cemetery.

149 Sqn — **Wellington IC** — **L7811 OJ-C** — **Op: Bremen**
Sgt Turner
Sgt Campbell
Sgt McKnight
Sgt Pates   inj
Sgt Piper
Sgt Rae
T/o 1822 Mildenhall. Abandoned 0200 in the vicinity of Conksbury. Sgt Pates sprained his ankle on landing.

149 Sqn — **Wellington IC** — **P9247 OJ-M** — **Op: Hannover**
Sgt R Warren
Sgt F F Early   +
Sgt Archer
Sgt H Chapman
Sgt Cook
Sgt MacDonald
T/o 1820 Mildenhall. On return, and while flying above cloud, the crew observed Very lights which were being fired from Waddington. While attempting to get below the cloud base, the Wellington crashed 0130 near Digby airfield, Lincolnshire.

218 Sqn — **Wellington IC** — **R1210 HA-D** — **Op: Bremen**
F/O Anstey
Sgt Shaw
Sgt Jackson
Sgt Thomas
Sgt Robinson   inj
Sgt Stephens
T/o 1750 Marham. Abandoned 0215, out of fuel, over Tebay, 9 miles NNE of Kendal, Westmorland. Sgt Robinson required treatment for a sprained ankle. Earlier, the Wellington had come under AA fire from the London area.

218 Sqn — **Wellington IC** — **T2885 HA-D** — **Op: Bremen**
Sgt W S Adam
Sgt Madgwick
Sgt J H Collopy
Sgt Millatt
Sgt Reardon
Sgt Payne
T/o 1810 Marham. Unable to make w/t contact on return and eventually the crew sighted a search-light beam pointing along the ground, but as the Wellington broke through the cloud, the light was extinguished and a forced-landing was made at 0040 in the mud of the River Severn some 300 yards from its banks near Frampton on Severn, 9 miles SW of Gloucester. No injuries reported.

14-15 Feb 1941 — **50 Sqn** — **Hampden I** — **X2983 VN-** — **Op: Gardening**
P/O P G Tunstal   +
Sgt J B Barclay   +
Sgt F C Bailey   pow
Sgt B Dixon   pow
T/o St. Eval to lay mines in the Garonne Estuary. Believed shot down inland from Pointe de la Chambrette. Both pilots are buried in Verdon-sur-Mer Communal Cemetery, France.

15 Feb 1941 — **114 Sqn** — **Blenheim IV** — **T2125 RT-** — **Op: Reconnaissance**
Sgt T E Barnes AFM   +
Sgt H S Seward   +
Sgt L S Walsh   +
T/o 0835 Oulton. Shot down by a fighter from JG52 and crashed 1040 at Oostkapelle (Zeeland), Holland. All are buried at Vlissingen.

15-16 Feb 1941 — **15 Sqn** — **Wellington IC** — **T2847 LS-R** — **Op: Sterkrade**
P/O C B Dove   +
Sgt P M Smith   +
P/O J E Russell   pow
Sgt W Jessop DFM   pow
Sgt G Simpson   +
Sgt G F Hurworth   +
T/o Wyton. Shot down by a night-fighter (Fw Kalinowski, 6./NJG1) and crashed 2305 near Barchem (Gelderland), 12 km S of Laren, Holland. Those who died are buried in Barchem General Cemetery.

77 Sqn — **Whitley V** — **T4164 KN-T** — **Op: Sterkrade**
P/O C R Hubbard   pow
Sgt D H Gilbert   pow
Sgt A Bocking   pow
Sgt T F Keeley   pow
Sgt M F Hurlston   pow
T/o 1839 Topcliffe. Attacked by a night-fighter (Oblt Jüsgen, I./NJG3) and crashed 2319 at Malden (Gelderland), 5 km S of Nijmegen.

| 15-16 Feb
1941 | 144 Sqn
S/L Lerwill | Hampden I | X3048 PL-
T/o Hemswell. Crash-landed 2247 on return to
base when the pilot, inadvertently, failed to | Op: Homberg |

lower the undercarriage. Extreme fatigue was judged to have been a factor.

| 17 Feb
1941 | 114 Sqn
F/L M J C Marks DFC
Sgt H Teeton
Sgt I H Adkins | Blenheim IV
+
+
+ | Z5902 RT-
T/o 0935 Oulton to reconnoitre the Den Helder
area. Shot down by flak. All are commemorated
on the Runnymede Memorial. | Op: Reconnaissance |

| 17-18 Feb
1941 | 1419 Flt
F/O E N Baker
S/L F J B Keast
Sgt D H Bernard
Sgt A J Cameron
Sgt D W Davies
F/L K S McMurdie | Whitley V
pow
pow
pow
pow
pow
pow | T4264
T/o Stradishall. F/L McMurdie was included in
the crew, his name annotated for "flying duties". | Op: Special Duties |

Note. It is believed this aircraft was the first to be reported missing from a clandestine operation.

| 21-22 Feb
1941 | 75 Sqn
P/O A J Falconer RNZAF
S/L E U G Solbe
P/O A V Muir RNZAF
Sgt W D Morrison
Sgt H T Hellier
Sgt A M Brodie RNZAF | Wellington IC
+
+
+
+
+
+ | T2503 AA-
T/o Feltwell. Presumed lost over the sea. S/L
Solbe is buried in Kiel War Cemetery; Sgt Brodie
RNZAF rests in Sage War Cemetery, Oldenburg.
Their companions are commemorated on the
Runnymede Memorial. | Op: Wilhelmshaven |

| | 75 Sqn
P/O R Hewitt
Sgt Reid
Sgt Evison
Sgt Wilson
Sgt Chatterley
Sgt Tong | Wellington IC | T2547 AA-
T/o 1910 Feltwell. Crashed 0030 on return to
base, colliding with a fence near the airfield
perimeter. | Op: Wilhelmshaven |

| | 149 Sqn
F/O I S Henderson
Sgt W P Jinks
Sgt W H Macleod
Sgt F May
Sgt J P Redmond
Sgt J Stewart | Wellington IC
+
+
+
+
+
+ | R1045 OJ-M
T/o 1825 Mildenhall. Lost without trace. All
are commemorated on the Runnymede Memorial. | Op: Wilhelmshaven |

| 22-23 Feb
1941 | 115 Sqn
Sgt E J Milton
Sgt D W M Thomas
Sgt J H Eades
Sgt K Kennard
Sgt T H M Simmonds
Sgt R H Gray | Wellington IC
+
+
+
+
+
+ | R1221 KO-F
T/o 0251 Marham. Crashed 0830 and burst into
flames after flying into a tree at East Winch,
5 miles SE of King's Lynn, Norfolk. The crew
were in w/t contact with Marham until moments
before the crash. | Op: Brest |

| 23-24 Feb
1941 | 107 Sqn
S/L C S Kemp
P/O P Moody
Sgt A Lloyd | Blenheim IV
+
+
+ | T2138 OM-
T/o 1845 Wattisham. Crashed 2213 just to the
SE of Swanton Morley airfield, Norfolk, while
trying to land. | Op: Boulogne |

| | 115 Sqn
P/O K N Arthurs
Sgt M F Lloyd
Sgt C E Donehue RNZAF
Sgt A E Law
Sgt S Charlton
Sgt J H S Jacobs | Wellington IC
+
+
+
+
+
+ | L7810 KO-R
T/o 1943 Marham. Crashed in the vicinity of
Pihen-lès-Guines (Pas-de-Calais), 10 km SW of
Calais. All are buried in Pihen-lès-Guines
War Cemetery. | Op: Boulogne |

25 Feb 1941	105 Sqn P/O M I Dore	Blenheim IV	T1989 GB–	Training

Crashed 2225 while attempting to land at Swanton Morley.

	106 Sqn F/O C P D Pruce	Hampden I	AD790 ZN–	Training

T/o 1115 Coningsby but both engines lost power and the Hampden glided into a field bordering the aerodrome. No injuries reported.

	139 Sqn	Blenheim IV	T2320 XD–	Ground

Destroyed by fire at Horsham St. Faith.

25-26 Feb 1941	103 Sqn	Wellington IC	T2621 PM–	Op: Düsseldorf

P/O J K C Ralston   +
Sgt J R C Pratt   +
Sgt L C Butcher   +
Sgt A E Laing   +
Sgt W McIntosh   +
Sgt D G Watt   +

T/o 1815 Newton. Believed to have exploded in the air. Four of the crew have no known graves and their names are commemorated on the Runnymede Memorial. Sgt Laing and Sgt Watt are buried in the Reichswald Forest War Cemetery.

	214 Sqn	Wellington IC	L7859 BU–	Op: Düsseldorf

P/O H C S Hordern   inj
Sgt Russell   inj
P/O McKenzie   inj
Sgt Cross   inj
Sgt Platt   inj
Sgt Stuart   inj

T/o 1830 Stradishall. On return to base with failing engines, the crew requested immediate landing precedence. Due to another Wellington obstructing the runway, permission was denied and the bomber stalled and crashed from 150 feet while trying to make a second circuit.

	218 Sqn	Wellington IC	R1009 HA-L	Op: Düsseldorf

Sgt Hoos
Sgt Brummwell   inj
Sgt Groves
Sgt Caswell
Sgt Stanley   inj
Sgt Heywood   inj

T/o 1825 Marham. Badly shot about by a Ju 88C (Fw Ernst Ziebarth, 1./NJG2) and crash-landed 2320 in the corner of a field near Red Lodge, 2 miles S of Swaffham, Norfolk. Sgt Brummwell broke an arm, Sgt Stanley suffered burns and Sgt Heywood dislocated a shoulder bone.

26 Feb 1941	21 Sqn	Blenheim IV	N3618 YH–	Training

Damaged in a flying accident for which no accident card has been traced; neither are there any indications as to what happened in the Squadron records.

26-27 Feb 1941	51 Sqn	Whitley V	P4934 MH-A	Op: Köln

Sgt I H Fenton   +
Sgt Clarke
P/O Carter
Sgt J A Patterson DFM   +
Sgt J Bowes   +

T/o 1858 Dishforth. Returned with failing engines and an unserviceable radio. Encountered heavy snow and the pilot ordered the crew to bale out, but only two complied before the bomber crashed 0500 into the sea off the Durham coast.

	51 Sqn	Whitley V	T4148 MH-R	Op: Köln

Sgt T C Wall
Sgt Walker
Sgt Chappell
Sgt Jackson
Sgt Chapman

T/o 1901 Dishforth but suffered a generator failure. In poor light the crew attempted to turn back, but crashed into a hill at Sutton Bank on the Yorkshire Moors, 14 miles NE of Dishforth. Miraculously, the crew escaped serious injury.

	78 Sqn	Whitley V	P4996 EY–	Op: Köln

W/C G T Toland   +
Sgt G A Forsyth   +
P/O D H Gates   +
Sgt G R Armstrong   +
Sgt N L Lane   +

T/o 1845 Dishforth. Strayed from track on return and crashed 0445 into a mountain 3 miles E of Craig, Ross and Cromarty, Scotland.

	82 Sqn	Blenheim IV	T2031 UX–	Op: Boulogne

Sgt K Dalton   +
Sgt R H Thomas   +
Sgt W Lake   +

T/o Bodney. Lost without trace. All are commemorated on the Runnymede Memorial.

26-27 Feb 1941	83 Sqn	Hampden I	X3124 OL-H	Op: Köln
	W/C W W Stainthorpe AFC	+	T/o 2150 Scampton. Strayed from track and	
	P/O A McD Melville	+	crashed 0130 into high ground near Derrington	
	Sgt L Emmerson	+	Cross, 2 miles WSW of Stafford. Sgt Weaving	
	Sgt D V Weaving	+	had parachuted safely a fortnight previous.	

28 Feb 1941	139 Sqn	Blenheim IV	L9402 XD-	Op: Den Helder
	Sgt R Bennett	inj	T/o 1806 Horsham St. Faith. Crash-landed 2032	
	Sgt Mills	inj	on return to base, colliding with another air-	
	Sgt E W Laban		craft from the Squadron.	

	139 Sqn	Blenheim IV	T1799 XD-	Op: Vlissingen
	Sgt Vivian	inj	T/o 1758 Horsham St. Faith. Landed 2022 and	
	Sgt A R Severn	inj	struck ten minutes later by L9402. Sgt Severn	
	Sgt Handley	inj	died the next day from his injuries.	

28 Feb- 1 Mar 1941	105 Sqn	Blenheim IV	T1895 GB-	Op: Wilhelmshaven
	Sgt J S H Heape	pow	T/o 2325 Swanton Morley. Shot down by a night-	
	Sgt S Jones	+	fighter (Ofw Paul Gildner, 4./NJG1) and crashed	
	Sgt J Bimson	+	0258 at Oosterhogebrug (Groningen), 5 km E of	
			Groningen, Holland.	

1 Mar 1941	106 Sqn	Hampden I	AD763 ZN-	Ferry
	P/O W A Brown		T/o 1505 Ternhill. Crashed 1550 while landing at	
	Sgt Stevens		Coningsby on completion of the ferry from 24 MU.	

1-2 Mar 1941	9 Sqn	Wellington IC	R1288 WS-D	Op: Köln
	F/O H G L Lawson	+	T/o 2215 Honington. Last heard on w/t at 0157	
	Sgt J N Murray	+	asking for a bearing. Crashed into the sea off	
	Sgt J N Huddlestone	+	Spurn Head. The body of Sgt Heslop was washed	
	Sgt A E Waters	+	ashore and buried in Patrington (Welwick Road)	
	Sgt E Routledge	+	Cemetery. The rest of the crew are commemorated	
	Sgt D A T Heslop	+	on the Runnymede Memorial.	

	10 Sqn	Whitley V	T4265 ZA-J	Op: Köln
	Sgt A C Hoare	+	T/o 1930 Leeming. Last heard on w/t at 0048	
	Sgt P H Woodbridge	+	calling for help. It was estimated the bomber	
	P/O A A Florigny	+	was W of Haamstede (Zeeland), Holland and on	
	Sgt C J Woods	+	course for Orford Ness, Suffolk. All are	
	Sgt A Coates	+	commemorated on the Runnymede Memorial.	

	50 Sqn	Hampden I	X2984 VN-	Op: Köln
	P/O H C Pexton		T/o 2015 Lindholme. Crashed 0335 on high ground	
	Sgt L T Richards	+	at Wold Newton, 9 miles NW of Bridlington,	
	Sgt Wheeler		Yorkshire. Sgt Richards is buried in Hatfield	
	Sgt J H Tittley		(Woodhouse) Cemetery.	

	51 Sqn	Whitley V	N1481 MH-	Op: Köln
	Sgt D C Beddow	+	T/o 1914 Dishforth. Last heard on w/t at 0140	
	Sgt E S C Halsall	+	asking for a bearing. All are commemorated on	
	Sgt E Hughes	+	the Runnymede Memorial.	
	Sgt G H Carter	+		
	Sgt K J Cooper	+		

	51 Sqn	Whitley V	P5108 MH-Q	Op: Köln
	Sgt V W Bruce	pow	T/o 1932 Dishforth. Last heard on w/t at 0524	
	Sgt R Smith	+	and six minutes later the Whitley crash-landed	
	Sgt R V Huston	+	on a sandbank NW of Pilsum, Germany. From a	
	Sgt E F Matthews	+	report given by Sgt Bruce, it would appear that	
	Sgt A Mather	pow	all survived the crash, but three were killed	

when the floatplane, that had taken off part of the bomber's crew, crashed on landing at its Borkum base. Two of the dead are buried in Sage War Cemetery, Oldenburg, but Sgt Matthews rests in Holland at the Schiermonnikoog (Vredenhof) Cemetery.

1-2 Mar 1941	61 Sqn	Hampden I	P1253 QR-	Op: **Köln**
	P/O J T Noble	inj	T/o 2004 Hemswell. Diverted to Stradishall,	
	Sgt R MacKinnon	+	but ran out of fuel and crashed 0320 at Great	
	Sgt A Fletcher	inj	Wratting, 15 miles SW of Bury St. Edmunds,	
	Sgt F D Healing	inj	Suffolk. Sgt Healing died from his injuries.	

	61 Sqn	Hampden I	X3147 QR-	Op: **Köln**
	Sgt R W T Clarke	+	T/o 2014 Hemswell. Crashed 0414 at Syderstone,	
	Sgt A D Cox	+	6 miles WNW of Fakenham, Norfolk, and burst into	
	Sgt P Thomas	+	flames. Sgt Loates was a Canadian serving in	
	Sgt H G Loates	+	the RAF.	

	61 Sqn	Hampden I	AD723 QR-	Op: **Köln**
	Sgt K G Cooper	+	T/o 2001 Hemswell. Crashed 0500 near Caistor,	
	Sgt H Windle	+	11 miles SW of Grimsby, Lincolnshire.	
	Sgt M Gough	+		
	Sgt G Hall	+		

	77 Sqn	Whitley V	Z6463 KN-	Op: **Köln**
	P/O J G Rogers		T/o Topcliffe. Ordered to divert to Benson	
	Sgt D B Flanders	+	in Oxfordshire, but reported crashed, after	
			hitting telegraph poles in Dunstable Road,	

Catterick, Yorkshire, while trying to land at the nearby airfield. Details of this incident are omitted from the Squadron records.

	78 Sqn	Whitley V	N1525 EY-E	Op: **Köln**
	Sgt J W Quincey	+	T/o 1901 Dishforth. A w/t message was received	
	P/O M J David	+	indicating a successful attack, after which the	
	Sgt R Clark	+	bomber and its crew disappeared without trace.	
	Sgt R Bradbury	+	All are commemorated on the Runnymede Memorial.	
	Sgt J G Earley	+		

	102 Sqn	Whitley V	T4261 DY-S Ceylon	Op: **Köln**
	S/L C E E Florigny	+	T/o 1844 Topcliffe. Ditched 2307 off Cromer,	
	Sgt R F Martin		Norfolk. S/L Florigny, who was brother of P/O	
	Sgt W E Hool		Florigny flying in the 10 Squadron Whitley	
	Sgt A Bush		previously described, was last seen atop the	
	P/O R C Rivaz		fuselage and unable to reach the dinghy that	
			was being blown away from the bomber by the	

strong wind. The names of both brothers appear on the Runnymede Memorial.

	144 Sqn	Hampden I	P4394 PL-	Op: **Hannover**
	P/O D H Skinner	inj	T/o Hemswell. Crashed 2215 between Wainfleet	
	Sgt F E Darnell	+	Bank and Wainfleet All Saints, 6 miles SW of	
	Sgt J F Shutt	+	Skegness, Lincolnshire.	
	Sgt R J Jones	+		

	144 Sqn	Hampden I	AD737 PL-	Op: **Hannover**
	P/O W A McVie		T/o Hemswell. Undershot and crashed while	
	Sgt Dyke		trying to land at base with failing engines.	
	Sgt J K Scouller			
	Sgt C W Carter			

Note. This had been the worst night for the Command since mid-February when eighteen bombers were lost, mainly in crashes within the United Kingdom and, mercifully, casualties had been light. Now, thirteen aircraft had failed to return, or crashed and over forty airmen were either dead, or badly injured.

2-3 Mar 1941	21 Sqn	Blenheim IV	Z5901 YH-	Op: **Rotterdam**
	Sgt A Warcup	+	T/o 2040 Watton. Lost without trace. All are	
	Sgt A B Ferguson	+	commemorated on the Runnymede Memorial.	
	Sgt T S Courtman	+		

	58 Sqn	Whitley V	Z6465 GE-U	Op: **Brest**
	Sgt S V Bunn	+	T/o 1805 Linton-on-Ouse. Called on w/t at	
	Sgt T J Thurling	+	2350 indicating the sortie had been abandoned.	
	Sgt H Gordon	+	Crashed 0156 and burst into flames 3 miles NE	
	Sgt H F Jennings	+	of Ternhill, Shropshire.	
	Sgt K Wright	+		

2-3 Mar 1941	**115 Sqn** Sgt G R Pike Sgt G L Elliott Sgt R C Brockway Sgt H W Green Sgt A W White Sgt E Fenwick	**Wellington IC** + + + + + +	**R3279 KO-D** — **Op: Brest** T/o 1828 Marham. Crashed in the sea. Apart from Sgt Fenwick, buried in Felton Cemetery, Northumberland, the crew are commemorated on the Runnymede Memorial.

2-3 Mar 1941

115 Sqn   **Wellington IC**
- Sgt G R Pike   +
- Sgt G L Elliott   +
- Sgt R C Brockway   +
- Sgt H W Green   +
- Sgt A W White   +
- Sgt E Fenwick   +

R3279 KO-D   **Op: Brest**

T/o 1828 Marham. Crashed in the sea. Apart from Sgt Fenwick, buried in Felton Cemetery, Northumberland, the crew are commemorated on the Runnymede Memorial.

3-4 Mar 1941

7 Sqn   **Stirling I**
- S/L J M Griffith-Jones DFC   +
- P/O W I Dalgliesh   +
- Sgt R Hinton   +
- Sgt J N Holdsworth   +
- Sgt J S Legge   +
- Sgt W T Watkins DFM   +
- Sgt R L McCarthy   +
- Sgt W J Richards   +

N3653 MG-   **Op: Brest**

T/o 1843 Oakington. Crashed in the English Channel, thus becoming the first of the new four-engined types to be lost on an operational sortie. All are commemorated on the Runnymede Memorial. Sgt Hinton was a South African from Bellair, Natal.

106 Sqn   **Hampden I**
- Sgt K Good   +
- Sgt A J W Ward   +
- Sgt D A D Crouch   +
- Sgt V T Essex   +

X3002 ZN-   **Op: Köln**

T/o 2010 Coningsby. All are buried in Schoonselhof Cemetery, Antwerpen.

4 Mar 1941

82 Sqn   **Blenheim IV**
- Sgt J N Harrison

R3812 UX-   **Training**

Crashed while trying to land at base during night-flying practice.

10-11 Mar 1941

35 Sqn   **Halifax I**
- S/L P A Gilchrist DFC
- Sgt R Lucas   +
- Sgt R G Aedy   inj
- P/O E R Arnold   +
- Sgt S Broadhurst   +
- F/O A E Cooper   +

L9489 TL-F   **Op: le Havre**

T/o 1908 Linton-on-Ouse. Intercepted on the return flight by an Allied night-fighter and shot down 2240 at Normandy, a small village on the Hampshire/Surrey border between Aldershot and Guildford.

44 Sqn   **Hampden I**
- P/O H R Stockings DFC   pow
- Sgt E W Dunkling   pow
- P/O E G M Bond   pow
- Sgt R J N Hanslip   pow

X2918 KM-   **Op: Köln**

T/o 1900 Waddington. Shot down by a night-fighter (Hptm Werner Streib, I./NJG1) and crashed 2218 near Venlo (Limburg), Holland.

144 Sqn   **Hampden I**
- Sgt T D Leitch   +
- Sgt T W Little   +
- Sgt D Lane   +
- Sgt G F Asbrey   +

AD720 PL-   **Op: Köln**

T/o Hemswell but lost height and crashed at Bishop Norton, 14 miles N of Lincoln.

Chapter 3

Increased Effort

12 March to 1 May 1941

In the first ten weeks of 1941, 123 bombers had been written off as against forty-nine in the corresponding period for 1940. This alarming trend was set to continue.

Casualties in the aftermath of the Köln raid in early March had totalled eleven aircraft, with two more destroyed in crashes after attacking Hannover. Then, during a night of mixed operations on 12-13 March, when the Command visited targets as far apart as Boulogne and Berlin, seven crews failed to return and a 102 Squadron Whitley crashed while trying to land at Bircham Newton, killing both pilots and injuring the remainder.

The increased effort of the past few weeks was being countered by correspondingly high losses.

Crew fatigue, technical failures, all were contributory factors, but the steadily growing influence of the night-fighter could not be ignored. Flak, too, was highly respected and in barrage form was not only spectacular but extremely lethal to any aircraft caught in the corridor of bursting shells.

Morale on the squadrons was high and the increasing numbers of recently trained aircrews were only too eager to get to grips with the demands imposed by the rigours of operational flying.

On 13-14 March, a particularly heavy blow fell on Hamburg. Fires were started over a wide area of the port, and for the second night in succession the key Blöhm & Voss ship building yards were hit. Seven bombers were lost, including the first Manchester to be shot down on operations. Its demise came at the hands of an intruder which picked up the bomber as it accelerated along the Waddington runway. Those watching on the ground saw a stream of tracer hit the Manchester which managed to stagger into the air before falling back to earth. In the ensuing explosion, one of the air gunners was blown from the aircraft and despite losing a leg, he survived. The rest of the crew, five in all, perished.

Night-fighters · are believed to have shot down at least three of the remaining missing bombers. Two, a Blenheim and a Wellington, went down near Groningen in northern Holland with only one survivor, while a 57 Squadron Wellington crew, the first to be lost from the Squadron following its recent conversion from Blenheims, were taken prisoner after a brief engagement which left the tail gunner with serious eye injuries.

Twenty-four hours later, a medium sized raid succeeded in halting oil production at the Hydriewerke Scholven synthetic oil plant at Gelsenkirchen. Good bombing was also reported in the wake of attacks on Bremen, Wilhelmshaven and Kiel, these operations taking place in the second half of a busy month. At Kiel, bombs fell on the U-boat yards of Deutsche Werke, which was welcome news for those responsible for co-ordinating anti-shipping operations.

Raids on the channel ports proved less successful, though some damage was caused to harbour installations at Brest when over 100 aircraft tried to hit the cruisers Gneisenau and Scharnhorst. Officially, there were no bomber losses from this attack, but in reality a Blenheim crashed heavily while trying to land at St. Eval in Cornwall and the CO of 103 Squadron was killed when his Wellington clipped a tree and crashed near Yeovil.

Running parallel with night raiding was an increasing tempo of anti-shipping operations by 2 Group. From a modest beginning by six aircraft on the 12th, daily sortie rates increased, culminating on the 31st when twenty Blenheims were sent out to hunt for shipping and targets of opportunity over the North Sea and along the channel coasts.

Shipping strikes called for a high degree of skill and courage. The enemy was quick to react to attacks on their coastal convoys and important shipping, such as tankers, was protected by means of both day fighter cover and flak ships.

Both forms of defence was highly effective and difficult for the Blenheims to counter. Crews were obliged to go in at extremely low level where they were immediately subjected to a barrage of anti-aircraft fire, while often waiting for them on the fringes were the fighters.

Crews also faced the attendant risk of being caught in the blast from their own bombs, thus further emphasising the dangers of anti-shipping operations.

At the beginning of the campaign losses were remarkably few. First to fall was an 82 Squadron crew, shot down off the Dutch coast on the 20th by an armed mine sweeper. Four days later the Squadron lost another Blenheim, this time to flak from a destroyer near Texel. Then, on the last day of the month, 21 Squadron reported two aircraft missing. Of the twelve airmen involved, not one had survived. An ominous pointer of what lay in store for the Group.

April began with attacks both by day and night against Brest. Ten aircraft were lost as a result, the majority being destroyed in crashes in the United Kingdom. One bomber, a Whitley from 51 Squadron, was shot down by a Hurricane night-fighter over Dorset during the raid on 3-4 April and a 115 Squadron Wellington crew were caught by a Ju 88C intruder while preparing to land at Marham.

Damage at Brest was difficult to judge but the following night bombs landed close to where the Gneisenau was lying, prompting her captain to move his vessel to a buoy in the harbour. This move resulted in a daring raid by Coastal Command Beauforts, during which the cruiser was seriously damaged and one of the attacking torpedo bomber pilots, F/O K Campbell of 22 Squadron, was awarded a posthumous VC for his outstanding courage.

The attention being given to the shipping campaign was having effect and following on from the Brest raids, the Command launched two very successful attacks on Kiel. The first, sent on 7-8 April, involved 229 aircraft, the largest number of bombers sent to a single target so far in the war. A bright moon shone throughout the raid and in five hours of bombing considerable damage was inflicted. Fires, small to start with, soon grew in intensity and by daybreak it was apparent that very serious damage had been caused to the U-boat building yards. Within twenty-four hours the bombers were back, slightly less in number but still operating to good effect. Closely grouped fires were reported and though the docks area escaped the worst of the attack, many commercial and residential properties were hit bringing misery to thousands who lost their homes and possessions in two nights of sustained bombing. Nine of the attackers were lost, all as a direct result of enemy action. Amongst them was a 207 Squadron Manchester that had been hit by flak on the second attack and was later abandoned north of Hamburg. Captained by the CO of the Squadron, all six airmen survived, but generally fatalities were high with not a single survivor from six of the nine crews that failed to return.

A departure from the customary shipping targets took place on 9-10 April when eighty aircraft raided Berlin. Five bombers were lost, including the first four-engined type, a Stirling, to be shot down while attacking Germany's capital city. Intercepted by a night-fighter the bomber fell near Lingen, killing six of the seven airmen aboard.

Anti-shipping operations were not ignored entirely. Small numbers of bombers operated against ship building facilities at Vegesack on the Weser, north-west of Bremen, while port installations at Emden were bombed by seven Wellingtons drawn from 1 Group.

Amongst them was a small contingent drawn from 12 Squadron at Binbrook, where, for the past four months the Squadron had been busy with a very demanding conversion programme.

Sadly, the occasion of their return to operations was marred by the loss of their Commanding Officer whose Wellington crashed into the sea off the Dutch coast with total loss of life. With two more Wellingtons failing to return from the Vegesack raid, the night had been relatively costly.

Night raiding for the remainder of April tended, in the main, to be centred on the French port of Brest, where repairs to the Gneisnau were in hand. These repairs were further hampered when the cruiser was hit by at least four bombs during the attack on 10-11 April, and later in the month further unsubstantiated reports for damage to this vessel and the Scharnhorst were claimed.

2 Group had an extremely busy April. Anti-shipping operations dominated, though night raiding featured on two occasions early in the month when Brest was the focal point of attention. From the first attack, the CO of 101 Squadron disappeared without trace and a second Blenheim, also from 101 Squadron, was destroyed in a fatal crash near Dorchester as the crew tried to locate Boscombe Down.

But, as to be expected, it was the hotly contested strikes on enemy shipping that brought about the majority of casualties. As already recounted, four bombers had been shot down in just over two weeks from the start of the campaign in March, and losses rose alarmingly as April progressed.

82 Squadron lost four crews before the middle of the month and 139 Squadron took a beating on the 7th when three of their aircraft were written off following an attack on a coastal target at IJmuiden, north-west of Amsterdam. One Blenheim, shot about by flak, was quickly finished off by a waiting fighter and two others sustained battle damage of such severity that both had to be reduced to scrap.

Losses were particularly heavy between the 15th and the 23rd. The CO of 18 Squadron was last seen flying towards the French coast following an attack on an armed trawler and it was during this period of intense activity that both 107 Squadron and 114 Squadron lost their Commanding Officers while on detachment to Coastal Command.

Then, in a further busy spell at the end of April, 82 Squadron lost a couple of crews on the 29th, the two Blenheims going into the sea off Norway while operating from a forward base at Lossiemouth.

In total, 2 Group had lost twenty-eight Blenheims from bomber operations and a further seven from the two squadrons attached to Coastal Command. Training accidents accounted for two more aircraft from which all six airmen died.

Despite these very serious casualties, the general consensus of opinion was that the campaign was achieving results. Few were the days when crews returned from a sweep without reporting any sightings and the Luftwaffe had been forced into the time consuming pastime of providing standing fighter cover over their coastal shipping.

For the present, 2 Group could not expect any slackening of effort, while for the rest of the Command the improving weather meant little change was likely over the coming months.

12-13 Mar 1941	9 Sqn	Wellington IC		N2744 WS-U	Op: Bremen

12-13 Mar 1941

9 Sqn   **Wellington IC**   **N2744 WS-U**   **Op: Bremen**

Sgt B P Hall	+
Sgt J R Brown	pow
Sgt W J Manger	+
Sgt W L Smith	+
Sgt J W Hammond	+
Sgt E Collins	pow

T/o 1936 Honington. Last heard on w/t at 2329. Crashed at Versen, 5 km NW of Meppen, Germany. Those who died are buried in the Reichswald Forest War Cemetery.

40 Sqn   **Wellington IC**   **R1013 BL-B**   **Op: Berlin**

S/L E H Lynch-Blosse	pow
P/O H Heaton	pow
F/O S H Palmer	pow
Sgt D R Clay	pow
Sgt A Hammond	pow
Sgt H Caldicott	pow

T/o 1955 Alconbury. Signalled task completed after which nothing further was heard.

40 Sqn   **Wellington IC**   **T2515 BL-U**   **Op: Boulogne**

Sgt D W Gough RNZAF	+
Sgt T G Webb RNZAF	+
Sgt T H Rose RCAF	+
Sgt H Jones	+
Sgt F Stones	+
Sgt W J Morgan	+

T/o 1950 Alconbury. Crashed near Wimille (Pas-de-Calais), 5 km N of Boulogne. This was an extremely young crew; the two pilots and their Canadian observer, were just 19 years of age, while the eldest, Sgt Morgan and Sgt Stones were both 21. All were on their first operational sortie.

50 Sqn   **Hampden I**   **AD721 VN-**   **Op: Berlin**

F/L D T Johnston	+
P/O L E Stannard	+
Sgt H Howell	+
Sgt W G Williams	+

T/o 2233 Lindholme. All are buried in Berlin at the 1939-1945 War Cemetery.

82 Sqn   **Blenheim IV**   **V5397 UX-**   **Op: Bremen**

Sgt L Stewart	+
Sgt E Richardson	+
Sgt P A Savage	+

T/o 2025 Bodney. All are buried in Becklingen War Cemetery, Soltau.

102 Sqn   **Whitley V**   **T4140 DY-H**   **Op: Berlin**

P/O F G Malin	+
F/O E G Cubitt	+
Sgt G E A Madgett	inj
Sgt N W Davies	inj
Sgt R D Davidson	inj

T/o 1945 Topcliffe. Returned from the Dutch coast on one engine and while trying to land at Bircham Newton the Whitley overshot the airfield and crashed 0100 into woods at Courtyard Farm, Ringstead, 3 miles NW of Docking, Norfolk.

102 Sqn   **Whitley V**   **T4326 DY-K**   **Op: Berlin**

F/L F H Long DFC	+
S/L A M Watts-Read	+
Sgt W E Van Klaveren	pow
Sgt V Hallas	+
Sgt E H Goodall	+

T/o 1940 Topcliffe. Shot down by flak and crashed 0005 at Noord-Deuringen (Overijssel), 3 km N of Denekamp, Holland. Four are buried at Denekamp, while Sgt Van Klaveren died from diptheria on 4 May 1941 and he rests in the 1939-1945 War Cemetery at Berlin.

Note. F/L Long, a New Zealander serving in the RAF, won his DFC in the winter of 1939 while flying as second pilot to the late F/O K N Gray. After forming his own crew he guided Leonard Cheshire VC, then a young and inexperienced P/O through his initial bomber operations.

218 Sqn   **Wellington IC**   **R1326 HA-G**   **Op: Bremen**

F/O W P Crosse	+
Sgt A E Binnie	pow
Sgt J H Collopy	+
Sgt W J Chamberlain	+
Sgt A Parfitt	pow
Sgt E J Coult	+

T/o 1911 Marham. Shot down by Me 110 G9+BM flown by Ofw Hans Rasper of 4./NJG1. The bomber fell into the Gouwe Sloot near Opperdoes (Noord-Holland), 3 km SW of Medemblik. Those who died are buried in Bergen General Cemetery.

13-14 Mar 1941

50 Sqn   **Hampden I**   **X3146 VN-**   **Op: Hamburg**

Sgt R L Grainger	+
Sgt R E F Wunderlich	+
Sgt J Cameron	+
Sgt R D Watson	+

T/o 1904 Lindholme. Lost without trace. All are commemorated on the Runnymede Memorial. At least three members of the crew were of Scottish parentage.

13-14 Mar	57 Sqn	Wellington IC	T2970 DX-	Op: Hamburg

1941

57 Sqn	Wellington IC	T2970 DX-		Op: Hamburg
Sgt J R Harvey	pow			T/o 1940 Feltwell. Shot down by a night-fighter.
Sgt A R Ward	pow			Both pilots sustained severe ankle wounds and Sgt
Sgt G G Patterson	pow			Gibberd received an eye injury which resulted in
Sgt L Pattinson	pow			his repatriation in October 1943.
Sgt S T Starkins	pow			
Sgt Gibberd	pow			

77 Sqn	Whitley V	N1493 KN-		Op: Hamburg
SGT D W Arkwright	+			T/o 1937 Topcliffe. Last heard on w/t calling
Sgt S W Snoddon	+			for assistance at 2353, after which the Whitley
Sgt N F Johnson	+			and its crew disappeared without trace. All
Sgt D A Smithies	+			are commemorated on the Runnymede Memorial.
Sgt D P Williams	+			

102 Sqn	Whitley V	T4273 DY-S		Op: Hamburg
Sgt A L R Cook	+			T/o 1920 Topcliffe. Shot down by flak and
Sgt A C Elliott	+			crashed at Kampstrasse 80-84, Hamburg-Lokstedt.
Sgt J M Oxley	+			All are buried in Hamburg Cemetery, Ohlsdorf.
Sgt N R Skinner	+			
Sgt S H A Jess	+			

110 Sqn	Blenheim IV	T2278 VE-		Op: Hamburg
F/L J Dickinson DFC	+			T/o 2027 Wattisham. Shot down by a night-fighter
Sgt C W Fry	+			(Ofw Paul Gildner, 4./NJG1) and crashed at Tolbert
Sgt R Mower	+			(Groningen), 14 km SW of Groningen, Holland. All
				are buried in the General Cemetery at Esserveld
				in the SE suburbs of Groningen.

207 Sqn	Manchester I	L7313 EM-C		Op: Hamburg
F/O H V Matthews DFC	+			T/o Waddington but as the Manchester accelerated
Sgt J Marsden	+			it was attacked by a Ju 88C intruder flown by Fw
Sgt H C Redgrave	+			Hans Hahn of 3./NJG2, probably operating from
Sgt R D Welch	+			Gilze Rijen in Holland. Somehow, F/O Matthews
Sgt W A W Cox	inj			got the bomber into the air but moments later
Sgt H W Hemingway	+			crashed and exploded at Whisby, Lincolnshire.
				Sgt Cox was thrown clear and survived, despite

losing one of his legs. This was the first Manchester loss, and in his report,
Fw Hahn timed his combat at 2200, claiming it to be a "Hudson".

214 Sqn	Wellington IC	N2746 BU-		Op: Hamburg
Sgt A G Elder	+			T/o 2000 Stradishall. Shot down by a night-
Sgt V L Bagley	+			fighter and crashed in the vicinity of Groningen,
Sgt S Glazer RNZAF	+			Holland, where those who died are buried in the
Sgt J la B Tomkinson	+			General Cemetery at Esserveld.
Sgt D W Waters	pow			
Sgt G C Daniel	+			

14 Mar	110 Sqn	Blenheim IV	R3832 VE-	Training

1941

110 Sqn	Blenheim IV	R3832 VE-		Training
Sgt Leadbeater				Crashed 1156 some 300 yards SW of Costessey Hall,
Sgt Cameron				Costessey, 4 miles WNW of Norwich. Sgt Stacey was
Sgt Stacey	inj			pulled from the burning wreckage by the pilot and
				his observer. Shortly afterwards, the bomb-load
				exploded, completely wrecking the Blenheim.

14-15 Mar	149 Sqn	Wellington IC	L7858 OJ-A	Op: Gelsenkirchen

1941

149 Sqn	Wellington IC	L7858 OJ-A		Op: Gelsenkirchen
Sgt L R Hawley	+			T/o 1940 Mildenhall. Shot down by a night-fighter
Sgt C B Rogers	+			(Hptm Werner Streib, I./NJG1) and crashed 2234 at
Sgt E G Prettyman	+			Sevenum (Limburg), 12 km NW of Venlo, Holland.
Sgt W G Marett	+			All were buried at Venlo, but since 1945 their
Sgt E White	+			remains have been reinterned at Nijmegen in the
Sgt C G H Ward	+			Jonkerbos War Cemetery.

17-18 Mar	21 Sqn	Blenheim IV	R3636 YH-	Op: Wilhelmshaven

1941

21 Sqn	Blenheim IV	R3636 YH-		Op: Wilhelmshaven
S/L A H Allen	+			T/o 0240 Watton but crashed 0305 and exploded
Sgt H F Linley	+			1 mile W of Garboldisham, 6 miles E of Thetford
Sgt A Parsons	+			Norfolk.

17-18 Mar 1941	149 Sqn	Wellington IC	R1474 OJ-M	Op: Bremen

149 Sqn   Wellington IC   R1474 OJ-M   Op: Bremen

17-18 Mar
1941

Sgt R Warren +
Sgt E R Cooke +
Sgt E A Lown +
Sgt H Chapman +
Sgt W J Greaves +
Sgt D J Capel +

T/o 0122 Mildenhall. While preparing to land, shot down by a Ju 88C intruder flown by Lt Rudolf Pfeiffer, I./NJG2 and crashed 0610 onto a bungalow at Beck Row, Mildenhall, Suffolk. The occupants, Mr and Mrs Titmarsh, are reported to have escaped injury.

18 Mar
1941

311 Sqn   Wellington IC   R1378 KX-K   Op: Bremen

Sgt Anderle
F/O Sejbl
P/O Konstacky
Sgt Plzak
P/O Horak
Sgt Valach

T/o 0030 East Wretham. Crashed 0530 while trying to land at base. The Wellington was consigned to Vickers for repairs, but these were not proceeded with and the bomber was struck off charge on 17 April 1941.

18-19 Mar
1941

10 Sqn   Whitley V   T4202 ZA-N   Op: Kiel

Sgt N Watson +
P/O W McN Spiers
Sgt Mole
Sgt Owen
Sgt Bok

T/o 2021 Leeming. At 0455 while returning to base and flying at 6000 feet, the port engine seized and caught fire. The flames spread to the fuselage and the crew were ordered to bale out. Four did so, but Sgt Watson was overcome by smoke and his body was found in the wreckage at Sutton Penn Farm, 2 miles NW of Masham, Yorkshire.

75 Sqn   Wellington IC   T2736 AA-   Op: Kiel

F/O Collins
Sgt A C Mee RNZAF
P/O Evans
Sgt D Gilmore +
Sgt Cole
Sgt Peters

T/o 1950 Feltwell. Crashed 0350 near Ryhill, 14 miles SSE of Leeds, Yorkshire. Earlier, the crew had requested Hull to provide searchlight assistance, but this was denied due to enemy air activity in the area. Sgt Gilmore was killed after his parachute failed to deploy.

101 Sqn   Blenheim IV   R3846 SR-   Op: Wilhelmshaven

P/O C R Brown DFC +
P/O G Collis DFM +
Sgt G Loughlin DFM +

T/o 1935 West Raynham. Presumed lost over the sea. P/O Brown is buried in Sage War Cemetery, Oldenburg; his crew have no known graves.

149 Sqn   Wellington IC   R1159 OJ-N   Op: Köln

Sgt W Hall
Sgt German
P/O K E Platt
Sgt Anderson
Sgt Baton
Sgt Seymour

T/o 1930 Mildenhall. Collided with trees after descending through dense haze and crash-landed 0300 in a field near Peasenhall, 4 miles NNW of Saxmundham, Suffolk.

20 Mar
1941

82 Sqn   Blenheim IV   R3604 UX-   Op: Anti-shipping

Sgt J H Kelly +
Sgt G R Wilson RNZAF +
Sgt S W Adair +

T/o 1109 Bodney. Shot down by Minenraumboot 64 and crashed into the sea off the Dutch coast. Sgt Adair has no known grave; his colleagues are buried in Bergen op Zoom War Cemetery.

20-21 Mar
1941

50 Sqn   Hampden I   AD742 VN-   Op: Gardening

P/O T N C Burrough
P/O P B Hodgson
Sgt Russell
Sgt A B Brooks   inj

T/o 1820 Lindholme to lay mines off Lorient. Crashed 0032 at Armthorpe, 4 miles SW of the airfield while trying to land in poor visibility.

83 Sqn   Hampden I   X3132 OL-L   Op: Gardening

Sgt C B James   pow
Sgt W E Miller +
Sgt D MacCallum   evd
Sgt N S Weir +

T/o 0300 Scampton to lay mines off Brest. Shot down at Morlaix (Finistère), France. Sgt James received serious arm injuries and while receiving treatment, the German authorities insisted his left arm be amputated. Despite this very severe disability, he succeeded in escaping and arrived in England on 4 March 1942. For his courage and tenacity, Sgt James received the MM. In due course he returned to operational flying, only to lose his life during operations on night-fighters. Sgt MacCallum is believed to have survived the war.

0-21 Mar 1941	144 Sqn	Hampden I	AD745 PL-	Op: **Gardening**

144 Sqn   Hampden I   AD745 PL-   Op: **Gardening**
P/O R N Harrison   T/o Hemswell to lay mines off Brest. On return,
Sgt E W Smith   collided with a barrage balloon cable and was
Sgt H E Turner   abandoned 0230 near Chelveston, Northamptonshire.
Sgt A R Simmons

207 Sqn   Manchester I   L7278 **EM-A**   Op: **Lorient**
Sgt F B Harwood DFM   +   T/o 0200 Waddington. Crashed 0225 while trying
Sgt N Birch   +   to make an emergency landing E of Wymondham,
Sgt Holland   inj   6 miles E of Melton Mowbray, Leicestershire.
Sgt W C Aitken   +   The crash was attributed to a silver bearing
Sgt B Hogg   +   failure in the port Vulture engine.
Sgt Hallam   inj

21 Mar 1941   301 Sqn   Wellington IC   L7874 GR-   Training
Sgt B Chrzanowski   +   Overshot and crashed near Swinderby airfield,
P/O J Korzcinski   +   Lincolnshire. All are buried in Newark Cemetery.
Sgt K Lenczowski   +

Note. Names and initials checked against the original burial register.

21-22 Mar 1941   18 Sqn   Blenheim IV   T2038 **WV-M**   Op: **Lorient**
P/O G H Cowings   +   T/o 2339 Boscombe Down. Crashed on return at
P/O R Daniel   +   Barkston, 4 miles NNE of Grantham, Lincolnshire.
Sgt E A Lee   +

49 Sqn   Hampden I   X3054 **EA-**   Op: **Lorient**
P/O R D Wilson   +   T/o 1820 Scampton. Crashed into high ground on
Sgt R Ellis   +   Hamel Down Tor, 1737 feet asl, Dartmoor, 5 miles
Sgt R Brames   +   SW of Moretonhampstead, Devon.
Sgt C J Lyon   +

57 Sqn   Wellington IC   X3162 **DX-**   Op: **Oostende**
F/L A L H Barber   +   T/o Feltwell. Crashed in the sea off Oostende.
P/O W W McMaster   +   F/L Barber is buried locally; his crew have no
P/O N C MacIver   +   known graves and their names are perpetuated by
Sgt J L Montague   +   the Runnymede Memorial.
Sgt W C Stone   +
Sgt S A Wilkins   +

105 Sqn   Blenheim IV   T1892 **GB-**   Op: **Lorient**
P/O I M Shirlaw   +   T/o 2034 Swanton Morley. Collided with a
P/O C P Dugdale   +   barrage balloon cable and crashed SW of
F/O J O Mair   +   Birmingham.

150 Sqn   Wellington IC   R3288 **JN-B**   Op: **Lorient**
F/O C H Elliot   +   T/o 1810 Newton. Crashed 2308 into Moel
P/O R C Parkhurst   +   Farlwyd on Snowdonia. The crash occurred
Sgt H Beddall   +   within seconds of the Wellington breaking
Sgt J Killen   +   through the cloud cover. Sgt Martlew was
Sgt L J Kirk   +   found still in the rear turret, which had
Sgt P Martlew   inj   broken off on impact, with a broken leg.

23 Mar 1941   105 Sqn   Blenheim IV   R3682 **GB-G**   Training
Sgt R Wood   Crashed while trying to land at Swanton
     Morley airfield.

23-24 Mar 1941   7 Sqn   Stirling I   N3643 **MG-G**   Op: **Calais**
S/L S A F Robertson   +   T/o Newmarket. Caught fire in flight and
Sgt A J Roberts   +   while trying to force-land collided with
Sgt G M Short   +   h/t cables and struck the roof of a house
Sgt E V Seymour   +   before crashing 0152 on Hazelwood Common
Sgt F B White   inj   near Leiston, Suffolk. Sgt White died
Sgt P Green   +   from his injuries on 30 March.
Sgt J B Clarke   +

23-24 Mar **1941**	**21 Sqn** Sgt S E Sproson Sgt W R Clinton Sgt E J Chinn	**Blenheim IV** inj inj +	**R3673 YH-**	**Op: Hannover** T/o 1955 Watton. Crashed 0040 on return to base and burst into flames. Sgt Clinton died a few hours later, followed on 25 March by Sgt Sproson

40 Sqn   **Wellington IC**   **R1166 BL-M**   **Op: Berlin**
P/O Billyeald   T/o 1940 Alconbury. Hit by flak which damaged
Sgt Youldon   the hydraulics. Crashed 0330 while making a
P/O Gill   second attempt to land. The bomber overshot
Sgt Williams   the runway and collided with a wooden hut and
Sgt A E Varnsverry   a nearby office trailer. Three crew members
Sgt Crook   required hospital treatment for their injuries.

61 Sqn   **Hampden I**   **X3005 QR-**   **Op: Kiel**
P/O P H H Pritchard   T/o 1841 Hemswell. Hit by flak and later in
P/O F A Caunter-Jackson   the flight, the port engine seized. Unable to
Sgt P J Breene   maintain height, the Hampdon was abandoned and
Sgt O W J Pearce   left to crash 0130 near Driffield, Yorkshire.

105 Sqn   **Blenheim IV**   **Z5903 GB-**   **Op: Hannover**
Sgt C H King   +   T/o 1951 Swanton Morley. Presumed lost over the
Sgt R F Murphy   +   sea. Sgt Gibbs is buried in Sage War Cemetery,
Sgt F Gibbs   +   Oldenburg; the remainder have no known graves.

300 Sqn   **Wellington IC**   **R1273 BH-**   **Op: Berlin**
S/L Cwynar   T/o Langham but crashed almost immediately when
the pilot was unable to prevent the Wellington
from swinging to starboard. Out of control, the bomber ran through the hedge
bordering the airfield and finished up in a field damaged beyond repair.

300 Sqn   **Wellington IC**   **T2719 BH-**   **Op: Berlin**
Sgt Hazierczak   T/o 2225 Langham but swung through 45 degrees
and smashed through the boundary fence before
coming to a stop in a field very severely damaged.

24 Mar
1941   **82 Sqn**   **Blenheim IV**   **L9389 UX-**   **Op: Anti-shipping**
F/L H J W Black DFC   +   T/o 1410 Bodney. Shot down while attacking a
Sgt T H Cooke   +   destroyer off the Dutch coast. F/L Black is
Sgt F Archer DFM   +   buried in Bergen op Zoom War Cemetery; his crew
are commemorated on the Runnymede Memorial.

27-28 Mar
1941   **9 Sqn**   **Wellington IC**   **R1335 WS-K**   **Op: Köln**
F/L J T L Shore   pow   T/o 1943 Honington. At 2248 Hull intercepted an
P/O J L R Long   pow   SOS from this aircraft, followed by "I am forced
Sgt H J Tomkins   pow   to land GN". Shot down by a night-fighter (Oblt
Sgt R D Bews   pow   Walter Fenske, III./NJG1) and crashed at Heusden
Sgt N D R Griffiths   pow   (Limburg), 12 km NNW of Hasselt, Belgium. F/L
Sgt R Parkin   pow   Shore escaped from captivity in the autumn of
1941 and arrived home via Sweden. Awarded the
MC, F/L Shore rose to the rank of W/C and was killed after the war while flying
in a Lincoln. P/O Long was amongst the officers that escaped from Sagan in
March 1944. He was captured, handed over to the SS and executed at Breslau
on 13 April 1944. His grave is now in Poznan Old Garrison Cemetery, Poland.

10 Sqn   **Whitley V**   **Z6477 ZA-**   **Op: Düsseldorf**
S/L H A R Holford   T/o 1951 Leeming. Abandoned 0215 N of Pickworth
Sgt Taylor   inj   8 miles ESE of Grantham, Lincolnshire, after
Sgt J F Bassett   which the bomber flew on to crash near Cottesmor
Sgt R R Hanson   airfield, Rutland.
Sgt A J Jones

57 Sqn   **Wellington IC**   **R1441 DX-**   **Op: Köln**
Sgt Emmerson   T/o 2005 Feltwell. Crashed 0020 while trying to
P/O Allan   land in poor visibility at East Wretham, Norfolk
P/O Gardner
Sgt Culver
Sgt Hagen
Sgt Dwyer

-28 Mar	**78 Sqn**	**Whitley V**	**Z6470 EY-G**	**Op: Düsseldorf**
41	P/O K F Seager	+		
	Sgt A K Mills	+		
	S/L(A) P J Hoad RN	+		
	Sgt E A F Grunsell MiD	+		
	Sgt J Mitchell	+		

T/o 1929 Dishforth. Last heard on w/t at 2137 and reported shot down by a night-fighter (Ofw Herzog, 3./NJG1) and crashed 2305 at Helenaveen (Noord Brabant), 16 km WNW of Venlo, Holland. All are buried in Jonkerbos War Cemetery.

	110 Sqn	**Blenheim IV**	**L8787 VE-**	**Op: Brest**
	F/L G P Yarrow	inj		
	P/O R Y Ashley	inj		
	Sgt J Grant	inj		

T/o 0111 St. Eval. Crashed 0320 at Carnewas Farm, 2 miles N of St. Mawgan airfield, Cornwall. F/L Yarrow died from his injuries on 30 March.

	207 Sqn	**Manchester I**	**L7307 EM-P**	**Op: Düsseldorf**
	F/L J A Siebert DFC	+		
	Sgt P C Robson	pow		
	Sgt G T J Fomison	pow		
	Sgt W J J McDougall	pow		
	Sgt J A Taylor	pow		
	Sgt P Gurnell	pow		

T/o Waddington. Abandoned and crashed between Roessel and Bakel (Noord Brabant), 6 km NE of Helmond, Holland. F/L Siebert was the last to leave the bomber and he hit the ground before his parachute had fully deployed. Moments later, the Manchester was attacked by a night-fighter (Ofw Herzog, 3./NJG1) operating from Eindhoven.

9-30 Mar	**83 Sqn**	**Hampden I**	**AD800 OL-X**	**Op: Gardening**
41	P/O E W Reynolds	+		
	Sgt C B Harrison	+		
	Sgt H R Northwood	+		
	Sgt J T Owen	+		

T/o 0130 Scampton to lay mines off Brest. Crashed in the sea 36 miles SSE of Start Point, Devon. All are commemorated on the Runnymede Memorial.

0-31 Mar	**101 Sqn**	**Blenheim IV**	**T2281 SR-**	**Op: Brest**
41	Sgt L E Kiddle	+		
	Sgt P E G Cammaerts	+		
	Sgt Kniveton	inj		

T/o 2048 St.Eval. Overshot and crashed into a field just beyond St. Eval airfield, Cornwall. Sgt Kniveton was admitted to Truro Hospital.

	103 Sqn	**Wellington IC**	**R1043 PM-**	**Op: Brest**
	W/C C E Littler	+		
	P/O Auliff	inj		
	Sgt Allen	inj		
	Sgt Summers	inj		
	Sgt Garbutt	inj		
	P/O Davies	inj		

T/o 1900 Newton. While making an emergency landing and banking steeply in order to avoid colliding with a house, the Wellington hit a tree and crashed at Manor Farm, Mudford, 2 miles NE of Yeovil, Somerset, bursting into flames. The injured were taken to Yeovil Hospital.

	103 Sqn	**Wellington IC**	**W5612 PM-**	**Op: Brest**
	S/L Mellor	inj		
	Sgt Elliott			
	F/O Roberts			
	F/S McCudden			
	Sgt Davies			
	Sgt S E Hamblin			

T/o 1900 Newton. Attacked by an intruder as the crew prepared to land and the Wellington forced-landed 0025 in a field 1 mile from the airfield.

Mar	**21 Sqn**	**Blenheim IV**	**R3884 YH-**	**Op: Anti-shipping**
41	Sgt P A Adams	+		
	Sgt T R Alston	+		
	Sgt R E Nichols	+		

T/o 1115 Watton. Shot down by a Kriegsmarine Vorpostenboot off the Dutch island of Texel. All are commemorated on the Runnymede Memorial.

	21 Sqn	**Blenheim IV**	**R3900 YH-**	**Op: Anti-shipping**
	P/O D A Rogers	+		
	P/O W L Gourlay	+		
	Sgt G H Howard	+		

T/o 1120 Watton. Lost in circumstances similar to those described above. All are commemorated on the Runnymede Memorial.

Mar-	**15 Sqn**	**Wellington IC**	**T2703 LS-A**	**Op: Bremen**
Apr 1941	Sgt B C Kelly	pow		
	Sgt E F Duncombe	pow		
	P/O H McCosh	inj		
	Sgt R Mount	pow		
	Sgt B J Moore	pow		
	Sgt T R McWalter	+		

T/o Wyton. Shot down by a night-fighter (Fw Karl-Heinz Scherfling, III./NJG1) and crashed near the railway station at Haren-Ems, Germany. P/O McCosh was found near Osterfeld suffering from bullet wounds and he died on 6 April while being treated in Lingen Hospital.

31 Mar 1 Apr 1941	149 Sqn Sgt G J P Morhen Sgt Sunderland Sgt Jones Sgt Barnes Sgt P E Butler Sgt L R Guymer	Wellington IC	R1229 OJ-H	Op: Emden

Sgt P E Butler — inj

T/o 1949 Mildenhall. Landed heavily on return to base, bounced and then climbed steeply before stalling at approximately 70 feet. A fire broke out when the bomber crashed at 0350. Sgt Butler died from his injuries.

| 1 Apr
1941 | 50 Sqn
Sgt J Ratcliffe | Hampden I | P4409 VN- | Training |

T/o Lindholme but swung and crashed following the collapse of the undercarriage.

| | 144 Sqn
P/O W C Hartop — pow
Sgt F H Sykes — +
F/S R G L Lambourne — +
Sgt J Riley — + | Hampden I | X3129 PL- | Op: Brest |

T/o Hemswell. Shot down at Lannilis (Finistère), 20 km N of Brest. Those who died are buried in Lannilis Communal Cemetery.

| | 311 Sqn
F/O J Stransky | Anson I | K6296 KX- | Training |

Crash-landed at Honington following the loss of the starboard aileron.

| 2 Apr
1941 | 82 Sqn
Sgt W C Haynes — +
P/O A A Ford — +
Sgt A Lee — + | Blenheim IV | Z5818 UX-P | Op: Anti-shipping |

T/o 1420 Bodney to patrol Beats E and A. Lost without trace. All are commemorated on the Runnymede Memorial.

| 3-4 Apr
1941 | 49 Sqn
Sgt Ball
Sgt Batchelor
Sgt J H Bentley
Sgt Calvert | Hampden I | P4403 EA-M | Op: Gardening |

T/o 1905 Scampton to lay mines off Lorient. Overshot and crashed 0155 into a hedge while trying to land at St. Eval. No injuries reported.

| | 51 Sqn
P/O M E Sharpe
Sgt Gibson
P/O R C Alabaster
Sgt L J Allum
Sgt W N Brindley — + | Whitley V | T4299 MH-B | Op: Brest |

T/o 1900 Dishforth. Shot down 2120 by Hurricane V6960 of 87 Squadron and crashed astride a hedge at Connegar Farm, a few hundred yards E of Manston village church, 2 miles NE of Sturminster Newton, Dorset.

| | 51 Sqn
F/L J Harrington — +
Sgt J K Purdon — +
Sgt T H Knighton — +
Sgt D G Farmer — +
Sgt C Calvert — + | Whitley V | Z6556 MH-Q | Op: Brest |

T/o 1856 Dishforth. Obtained a bearing while over the channel, but subsequently crashed at Trébeurden (Côtes-du-Nord), 8 km NW of Lannion, France. All are buried in Trébeurden Communal Cemetery.

| | 77 Sqn
Sgt K G W Kyle — +
Sgt W E Godfrey — +
Sgt P C L Wicks — +
F/S A L Kennedy — +
Sgt Engel — inj | Whitley V | P4947 KN- | Op: Brest |

T/o 1904 Topcliffe. Iced up and crashed 2240 while making a second circuit of Waddington. The Whitley is reported to have stalled at 300 feet before diving into the ground and bursting into flames.

Note. F/S Kennedy had already survived a number of serious crashes during 1940, badly injuring his back on 10 June 1940 when the Whitley in which he was flying crashed at Abingdon.

| | 77 Sqn
Sgt H J Dowling — +
P/O G A Bussy — +
Sgt W G Rawkins — +
Sgt Pryor — inj
Sgt J C Kesson — inj | Whitley V | Z6583 KN- | Op: Brest |

T/o 1901 Topcliffe. Ordered to divert to an airfield in southern England, the Whitley crashed 0049 at Eartham Wood, 6 miles NE of Chichester, Sussex, while circling Tangmere. It is believed the pilot became disorientated when the airfield lights were suddenly extinguished.

-4 Apr 1941	**83 Sqn**	**Hampden I**	**AD748 OL-M**	**Op: Gardening**

-4 Apr
1941

83 Sqn   **Hampden I**

F/L E D Thompson	+
P/O L R Evans	+
Sgt L R Eden	+
Sgt A M Murray	+

AD748 OL-M   **Op: Gardening**

T/o 1845 Scampton to lay mines off la Rochelle.
On return, crashed 0200 into high ground at
Hangingstone Hill on Dartmoor.

101 Sqn   **Blenheim IV**

W/C D Addenbrooke	+
P/O W J Fenton	+
Sgt E E Blomeley	+

N3552 SR-   **Op: Brest**

T/o 1940 West Raynham. Lost without trace.
All are commemorated on the Runnymede Memorial.

101 Sqn   **Blenheim IV**

Sgt P I Burrows	+
Sgt G B H Birdsell	+
Sgt H R Perry	+

T2439 SR-   **Op: Brest**

T/o 1915 West Raynham. Crashed and exploded
5 miles NW of Dorchester, while trying to locate
Boscombe Down.

115 Sqn   **Wellington IC**

Sgt C M Thompson	+
Sgt H Y Chard	+
P/O S S Barnett	+
Sgt J S C Sherman	+
Sgt E Keetley	+
Sgt Russell	

R1470 KO-H   **Op:Brest**

T/o 1847 Marham. Shot down by a Ju 88C intruder
(Lt Heinz Völker, I./NJG2) and crashed 0120 on
marshland at Ongar Hill, Terrington St. Clement,
5 miles W of King's Lynn, Norfolk.

Apr
1941

82 Sqn   **Blenheim IV**

Sgt A V M Farns	+
Sgt W W Fox	+
Sgt N A Geer	+

L9270 UX-X   **Op: Anti-shipping**

T/o 1250 Bodney to patrol Beat F off the Dutch
coast. Lost without trace. All are commemorated
on panel 43 of the Runnymede Memorial.

-5 Apr
1941

106 Sqn   **Hampden I**

W/C P J Polglase MiD	+
P/O W Brown	+
F/S G Allanson	+
Sgt E J Holman	+

AD738 ZN-   **Op: Brest**

T/o 1900 Coningsby. Shot down by flak at
St-Renan (Finistère), 11 km NW of Brest.
All are buried in St-Renan Churchyard.

Apr
1941

50 Sqn   **Hampden I**

P/O H M Macrossan	+
Sgt R F Cheesman	+
Sgt F R Worthington	+
Sgt J H Matthews	+

AD753 VN-   **Op: Brest**

T/o 1205 Lindholme. Dived vertically from 500
feet into the sea and exploded S of the Isles of
Scilly. The Hampden was flying No. 2 in the
leading formation. All are commemorated on the
Runnymede Memorial.

-7 Apr
1941

83 Sqn   **Hampden I**

P/O A E Jackson DFM	+
P/O A F Phillips	+
Sgt W A Foster	+
Sgt M A Hollingshead	+

X2899 OL-D   **Op: Gardening**

T/o 1950 Scampton to lay mines off Brest. Lost
without trace. All are commemorated on the
Runnymede Memorial. P/O Jackson won his DFM as
an NCO pilot in December 1940.

Apr
1941

139 Sqn   **Blenheim IV**

Sgt R Bennett	+
P/O E R Pierce	+
Sgt E W Laban	+

L9386 XD-   **Op: Hoogovens**

T/o 1543 Horsham St. Faith. Hit by flak and
finished off by a fighter (Uffz Krause, I./JG1)
off the Dutch coast. All are commemorated on
the Runnymede Memorial.

139 Sqn   **Blenheim IV**

Sgt Dennis	
Sgt S G Hill	inj
Sgt Waddington	

V5521 XD-E   **Op: Hoogovens**

T/o 1543 Horsham St. Faith. Crashed 1755 on
return to base. Sgt Hill died from his injuries
on 14 April.

139 Sqn   **Blenheim IV**

Sgt Jennings	
Sgt Scholefield	
Sgt Shrimpton	

V5826 XD-F   **Op: Hoogovens**

T/o 1543 Horsham St. Faith. Badly shot about by
Me 109s and on return to base at 1738 was deemed
to be beyond economical repair.

7-8 Apr	40 Sqn	Wellington IC	R1007 BL-L	Op: Kiel

7-8 Apr
1941

40 Sqn   **Wellington IC**   **R1007 BL-L**   **Op: Kiel**
Sgt T Gamble +
Sgt L E E Bundock +
Sgt J Sharkey +
Sgt N Benfield +
Sgt F Sherratt +
Sgt J S Crane +

T/o 1955 Alconbury. Crashed in the target area. All are buried in Kiel War Cemetery.

51 Sqn   **Whitley V**   **T4298 MH-K**   **Op: Kiel**
Sgt D L Bowyer pow
Sgt J J W Eames pow
Sgt W F Hurst pow
Sgt J N A James pow
Sgt C Snook pow

T/o 2044 Dishforth. Three members of this crew, including the pilot, had successfully abandoned their aircraft in poor weather while returning from Bremen in mid-February 1941.

58 Sqn   **Whitley V**   **T4145 GE-P**   **Op: Kiel**
P/O R McC Carrapiett +
Sgt A J White +
P/O C F Jones +
Sgt A R Mason pow
Sgt A C Wroath +

T/o 2055 Linton-on-Ouse. Shot down by a night-fighter (Ofw Paul Gildner, 4./NJG1) and crashed 0027 at Waterhuizen (Groningen), 7 km SW of Groningen, Holland. Those who died are buried in the Esserveld General Cemetery.

102 Sqn   **Whitley V**   **Z6468 DY-**   **Op: Kiel**
W/C F C Cole +
F/S W E Craven +
F/S J Derbyshire +
Sgt H R Martin +
Sgt R C Smith +

T/o 2027 Topcliffe. Last heard on w/t at 0152 and fixed approximately 5005N 0348E. All are commemorated on the Runnymede Memorial.

214 Sqn   **Wellington IC**   **R1380 BU-**   **Op: Kiel**
Sgt R A Williams +
Sgt K Manson RNZAF +
Sgt R A Chatfield +
Sgt R C Plummer +
Sgt H R Easton RCAF +
Sgt C H R Mercer +

T/o Stradishall. Lost without trace. All are commemorated on the Runnymede Memorial.

8-9 Apr
1941

44 Sqn   **Hampden I**   **AD899 KM-**   **Op: Gardening**
P/O J G Curley +
P/O E T Laverack +
Sgt F Ashurst +
Sgt K S Campbell +

T/o Waddington to lay mines off Calais. Crashed near Pihen-lès-Guines (Pas-de-Calais), 10 km SW of Calais. Both pilots are buried in the Communal Cemetery while their two companions rest in the nearby War Cemetery.

61 Sqn   **Hampden I**   **AD827 QR-**   **Op: Kiel**
F/O D G Glennie +
P/O G F Chipperfield +
Sgt J G Donnelly +
Sgt C P Thomas +

T/o 1950 Hemswell. Hit by flak and crashed in the target area. All are buried in Kiel War Cemetery. This was the first Hampden from the Squadron to be declared missing in 1941, the previous six losses having concerned aircraft that crashed in the United Kingdom and, therefore, could be accounted for.

149 Sqn   **Wellington IC**   **X3167 OJ-H**   **Op: Kiel**
Sgt J B C Jago +
Sgt F M Jarrett +
P/O J A Graham RNZAF +
Sgt A W Rose +
Sgt P E M Mertens +
Sgt A G Coster +

T/o Mildenhall. Presumed lost over the sea. Sgt Jarrett and Sgt Mertens are commemorated on the Runnymede Memorial; the remainder of the crew are buried in Kiel War Cemetery.

207 Sqn   **Manchester I**   **L7302 EM-R**   **Op: Kiel**
W/C N C Hyde pow
F/O H T Morgan pow
F/S J Wells DFM pow
Sgt W Buck pow
Sgt D A Budden pow
Sgt L W Hedges pow

T/o Waddington. Hit by flak in the starboard engine, which later caught fire. The bomber was successfully abandoned and left to crash near Hamburg. F/S Wells had previously served with 50 Squadron, his DFM being Gazetted on 13 September 1940.

8-9 Apr 1941	214 Sqn	Wellington IC	T2542 BU-	Op: Kiel

Sgt J P Cusworth	+
Sgt C M F Hitchcock	+
Sgt J C Cattell RNZAF	+
Sgt R Brown	+
Sgt A J McHardy	+
Sgt D C Rowland	+

T/o 2025 Stradishall. All are buried in Kiel War Cemetery.

9-10 Apr 1941	7 Sqn	Stirling I	N6011 MG-	Op: Berlin

F/L V F B Pike DFC	+
Sgt C Sumner	+
Sgt C MacDonald	pow
F/S G P C Smith	+
Sgt W E Osterfield	+
Sgt A J Whitby	+
F/S A C Jupp	+

T/o 2040 Newmarket. Shot down by a night-fighter (Fw Karl-Heinz Scherfling, 7./NJG1) and crashed near Lingen, Germany. Those who died are buried in the Reichswald Forest War Cemetery.

9 Sqn	Wellington IC	T2473 WS-M	Op: Berlin

P/O G G Sharp	+
P/O J N Fisher	+
P/O R C Rendle	+
Sgt J Anderson	+
Sgt C B Parris	+
P/O W P Strickland	+

T/o 2032 Honington. Crashed at Veldhausen, 12 km NW of Nordhorn, Germany. All are buried in the Reichswald Forest War Cemetery.

12 Sqn	Wellington II	W5375 PH-D	Op: Emden

W/C V Q Blackden	+
P/O J C A Bond	+
F/O J du V Broughton	+
F/S D McDougall	+
Sgt G H Bishop	+
F/O H Marshall	+

T/o 2230 Binbrook. Shot down by a night-fighter (Oblt Egmont Prinz zur Lippe Weissenfeld, 4./NJG1) and crashed 0059 in the IJsselmeer. All bodies were recovered and taken for burial in various Dutch cemeteries. W/C Blackden was the son of Brigadier-General L S Blackden CBE.

Note. The above loss marked the occasion of 12 Squadron's return to operations following conversion from the Fairey Battle, which began in November 1940.

57 Sqn	Wellington IC	R1437 DX-X	Op: Vegesack

Sgt D Day	+
Sgt D M Jameson	pow
Sgt A G Sutherland RNZAF	pow
Sgt S Terry	+
Sgt S Felman	+
Sgt J E Caddick	+

T/o 2035 Feltwell. Three of the crew are buried in Sage War Cemetery, Oldenburg, while Sgt Felman rests at Rheinberg War Cemetery. Sgt Jameson was seriously wounded and is believed to have been repatriated before the end of hostilities.

57 Sqn	Wellington IC	T2804 DX-	Op: Berlin

F/O G W S Ritchie	pow
Sgt C S Greager RNZAF	pow
Sgt D L Jones RNZAF	pow
Sgt R S Cairns	pow
Sgt L J Ferris	pow
Sgt J C F Everett	pow

T/o 2000 Feltwell. Sgt Ferris was badly wounded and may have been repatriated.

77 Sqn	Whitley V	Z6570 KN-	Op: Berlin

Sgt D N Lee	pow
P/O J S B Tyrie	pow
Sgt D G Young	pow
Sgt E W Budd	pow
Sgt T S Hull	pow

T/o 2041 Topcliffe. Last heard on w/t at 0125 indicating both engines were failing.

99 Sqn	Wellington IC	R1440 LN-	Op: Vegesack

P/O T Fairhurst	+
Sgt H V Wansbrough	+
Sgt W L Waldron RCAF	+
Sgt W R Moore	+
Sgt C W Hall	+
Sgt G W Brown	+

T/o 2020 Waterbeach. Sent NGZ signal on w/t at 2336, after which the bomber crashed in the IJsselmeer. Sgt Brown is buried in Harderwijk General Cemetery; his companions have no known graves.

9-10 Apr	**99 Sqn**	**Wellington IC**	**R3199 LN-**	**Op: Berlin**
1941	S/L D C Torrens	pow	T/o 2000 Waterbeach. Last heard on w/t at	
	Sgt E H Berry	pow	0130 calling for help.	
	P/O P A Goodwyn	pow		
	Sgt A A Jenner	pow		
	P/O J F Palmer	pow		
	F/S A J Smith	pow		

10 Apr	**50 Sqn**	**Hampden I**	**AD830 VN-**	**Training**
1941	Sgt J J Campbell	+	Crashed 1530 into houses at Evington on	
	F/S L A Carn	+	the eastern outskirts of Leicester. In	
		+	addition to the airmen killed, a civilian	
			also died in this tragedy.	

82 Sqn	**Blenheim IV**	**N3569 UX-T**	**Op: Anti-shipping**
F/S J M Irving	+	T/o 1256 Bodney. Lost without trace. All are	
P/O J W Gadsby	+	commemorated on the Runnymede Memorial.	
Sgt J G MacIlwraith	+		

82 Sqn	**Blenheim IV**	**V5596 UX-C**	**Op: Anti-shipping**
Sgt Crew		T/o 1257 Bodney. Ditched 1730 in the sea off	
Sgt Cartside		Birchington, 1 mile WSW of Margate, Kent.	
Sgt Drummond			

149 Sqn	**Wellington IC**	**R1181 OJ-W**	**Training**
P/O J H Fisher	inj	T/o Mildenhall but collided with trees and	
Sgt R J Uhrig RAAF	+	crashed, demolishing a cottage at Holmsey Green,	
Sgt J K Moseley	+	Mildenhall, Suffolk. The Wellington caught fire	
Sgt D C Smallbone	inj	and when the wreckage was searched the body of	
Sgt H J F Kerr	inj	Mrs Martha Brightwell was found in the rubble.	
Sgt C Ingleby	inj		
Sgt G H Goodwing	inj		
Sgt R L Clarke	inj		

10-11 Apr	**40 Sqn**	**Wellington IC**	**R1493 BL-P**	**Op: Mérignac**
1941	F/L F A Bowler	pow	T/o 2040 Alconbury. Ditched in the English	
	P/O A B Trench	pow	Channel. P/O Branson is commemorated on the	
	F/L L S Dunley RNZAF	pow	Runnymede Memorial.	
	Sgt E A Jewson	pow		
	Sgt E Spencer	pow		
	P/O J P L Branson	+		

50 Sqn	**Hampden I**	**AD789 VN-**	**Op: Düsseldorf**
P/O G J Cornish	pow	T/o Lindholme. Shot down by a night-fighter	
Sgt J Ratcliffe	+	(Lt Reese, I./NJG1) and crashed 2254 some 4 km	
F/S R A Royal	+	NNE of Roermond, Holland. Those who died are	
Sgt S R Cassey	+	buried at Nijmegen in Jonkerbos War Cemetery.	

50 Sqn	**Hampden I**	**AD828 VN-**	**Op: Düsseldorf**
P/O D E F Powell	+	T/o Lindholme. Shot down by a night-fighter	
Sgt J A Davis	pow	(Ofw Herzog, 3./NJG1) and crashed 2255 some	
Sgt R E Drake	pow	6 km N of Maastricht (Limburg), Holland.	
Sgt F C Snook	pow	P/O Powell is buried in Jonkerbos War Cemetery,	
		while Sgt Davis, who was very severely wounded,	

was eventually repatriated to the United Kingdom on 1 February 1945.

106 Sqn	**Hampden I**	**X3148 ZN-E**	**Op: Düsseldorf**
Sgt R J West	pow	T/o 2000 Coningsby. Shot down by a night-fighter	
Sgt J Spencer	+	(Hptm Werner Streib, I./NJG1) and crashed 2301 at	
Sgt J T Wright	+	Ittervoort (Limburg), 12 km SE of Weert, Holland.	
Sgt E J Butler	+	Those who died rest in Jonkerbos War Cemetery.	

106 Sqn	**Hampden I**	**X3153 ZN-**	**Op: Düsseldorf**
Sgt W F Osborne	pow	T/o 2000 Coningsby. Shot down by a night-fighter	
Sgt J F R Boyall	+	(Hptm Werner Streib, I./NJG1) and crashed 2249	
Sgt D Skene	+	between Kessel and Helden (Limburg), 12 km N of	
Sgt S A T Davies	pow	Roermond, Holland. The two airmen who died are	
		buried in Jonkerbos War Cemetery.	

10-11 Apr 1941	144 Sqn	Hampden I	X3066 PL-	Op: Düsseldorf

P/O N J Kerr +
P/O R J Hamilton +
Sgt J Howell DFM +
Sgt A R Wickens +

T/o Hemswell. Shot down by a night-fighter (Lt Hans-Dieter Frank, I./NJG1) and crashed 2332 some 2 km SW of Neeroeteren (Limburg), 6 km WSW of Maaseik, Belgium. All are buried in the Canadian War Cemetery at Adegem.

218 Sqn	Wellington IC	R1442 HA-D	Op: Brest

Sgt A G Plumb +
Sgt J D Brown +
SGT R E V Anderson RCAF +
Sgt D F Henderson +
Sgt G S Snoddon +
Sgt T W Dabinette RNZAF +

T/o 1930 Marham. Heard on w/t asking for help, after which the Wellington crashed into the sea off Brest. Sgt Anderson RCAF is buried in Kerfautras Cemetery; the rest of the crew have no known graves.

1419 Flt	Whitley V	T4165	Op: Special Duties

P/O J Molesworth inj
F/O Oettle inj
P/O Wilson inj
Sgt A J Cowan +
Sgt L G Morris +
Sgt Briscoe inj

T/o Tangmere with six Polish saboteurs, bound for a power station at Passac. While over the River Loire, the Whitley developed an electrical fault and turned back, only to stall and crash 0320 while trying to land at Tangmere.

11 Apr 1941	18 Sqn	Blenheim IV	T1829 WV-P	Op: Anti-shipping

P/O H P G Jones +
Sgt J F Horsham +
Sgt K C Walton +

T/o 1050 Oulton. Last seen flying towards Sylt from the direction of Amrum. P/O Jones is buried in Sondre Nissum Churchyard, Denmark; his crew are commemorated on the Runnymede Memorial.

12 Apr 1941	110 Sqn	Blenheim IV	R3905 VE-	Op: Anti-shipping

S/L D B Gericke pow
Sgt D S Staples +
F/S E W Rae +

T/o 1055 Wattisham. Hit by ship's flak during a low level attack and crashed into the sea 1 km W of Westkapelle (Zeeland), Holland. Those who died have no known graves.

12-13 Apr 1941	149 Sqn	Wellington IC	T2897 OJ-O	Op: Mérignac

Sgt R R Morison +
Sgt J L G Westley +
Sgt E J Holland DFM +
Sgt R Hutchinson +
Sgt K C H Rawlings pow
Sgt W H Wilkinson +

T/o 2150 Mildenhall. Crashed near St Sever-Calvados (Calvados), 14 km W of Vire, France. Those who died are buried in St-Sever-Calvados Communal Cemetery.

13 Apr 1941	18 Sqn	Blenheim IV	L9247 WV-L	Op: Anti-shipping

F/S J M Anderton +
F/O R F Tapp +
Sgt R G St James-Smith +

T/o 1051 Oulton. Last seen at 1230 off the Dutch coast. Believed shot down near Schiermonnikoog. Sgt St James-Smith has no known grave; the rest of the crew are buried in Sage War Cemetery.

14 Apr 1941	21 Sqn	Blenheim IV	R2784 YH-	Op: Leiden

Sgt E Newhouse +
Sgt V A Cobb +
Sgt J M C Bougin +

T/o 1514 Watton to attack a power station. Crashed 1645 at Oegstgeest (Zuid Holland), 2 km NW of Leiden. All are buried at Oegstgeest.

15 Apr 1941	18 Sqn	Blenheim IV	R3841 WV-	Op: Anti-shipping

W/C C G Hill DFC +
F/S C D McPhee +
F/S J Frodsham +

T/o 1345 Chivenor. Last seen 1537 in position 4815N 0441W, climbing to about 1000 feet and flying towards the French coast. All are commemorated on the Runnymede Memorial.

304 Sqn	Wellington IC	R1212 NZ-	Training

F/O R Chrystman +
Sgt W L Pietruszewski +
Sgt A Berger +
P/O Z Galczynski inj
Sgt A Aranowski inj
Sgt J Jarosz inj

Pilot lost control while trying to land in a strong cross-wind and crashed 1727 into Flintham Woods, just beyond Syerston airfield. Those who died are buried in Newark Cemetery.

Note. Names and initials of the dead have been checked in the burial register.

15-16 Apr 1941	35 Sqn	Halifax I	L9493 TL-G	Op: Kiel

Sgt Lashbrook
Sgt Robbins
Sgt Hewlett
Sgt Somerville
Sgt Muir
Sgt Broadbent
Sgt Stewart

T/o 2235 Linton-on-Ouse. Both port side engines damaged by flak over the target and on return to base the Halifax crash-landed, striking a tree in the process, at Tollerton, Yorkshire, a village on the NE side of the airfield. Two crew members were slightly hurt.

102 Sqn	Whitley V	T4260 DY-	Op: Boulogne

P/O B A Childs +
Sgt J A Norris +
P/O R J W Williams +
F/S A P Clifford-Reade +
Sgt R T Selley +

T/o 2135 Topcliffe. Hit by flak and crashed at Bourthes (Pas-de-Calais), 27 km SE of Boulogne. All are buried in Bourthes Churchyard.

149 Sqn	Wellington IC	R1439 OJ-U	Op: Kiel

Sgt P R B Meynell +
Sgt R C Payne +
Sgt H W Patten +
F/S T E Evans +
Sgt L G Gillam +
Sgt A G Humphries +

T/o 2110 Mildenhall. Last heard on w/t at 2146 when the crew made a routine frequency check with Manston. All are buried in Kiel War Cemetery.

16 Apr 1941	311 Sqn	Wellington IA	P9212 KX-	Training

P/O S Zeinert
Sgt M Svic

Crashed and caught fire 1 mile NW of Honington airfield, Suffolk, following engine failure.

Note. An air-to-ground photograph of the burning wreckage was taken from a 268 Squadron Lysander and a copy of this is lodged with the Norfolk and Suffolk Air Museum.

16-17 Apr 1941	10 Sqn	Whitley V	Z6557 ZA-	Op: Bremen

Sgt R V Salway +
Sgt V J Stickland +
Sgt N A Morant +
Sgt G Lynch +
Sgt N F Jackson +

T/o 2044 Leeming. Last heard on w/t at 2240 when the Whitley was plotted off the Dutch coast. All are buried in Sage War Cemetery, Oldenburg.

144 Sqn	Hampden I	AD761 PL-	Op: Gardening

Sgt H Kirby +
Sgt W A Tyler +
Sgt V G Elliott +
Sgt G Walsh inj

T/o Hemswell. Shot down four minutes later by an intruder (Fw Hans Hahn, 3./NJG2) and crashed 2 miles ENE of the airfield.

17 Apr 1941	105 Sqn	Blenheim IV	T2141 GB-	Op: Anti-shipping

Sgt I G Sarjeant +
Sgt L L Evered +
Sgt K G Gresty +

T/o 1310 St. Eval to patrol Beat 17. Shot down by Me 109s off the Brittany coast. All are commemorated on the Runnymede Memorial.

17-18 Apr 1941	9 Sqn	Wellington IC	N2745 WS-O	Op: Köln

Sgt G E Heaysman +
Sgt S F Whitlock pow
Sgt C J Mavor RCAF +
Sgt T Lancaster pow
Sgt B Hanlon pow
Sgt G C Balch pow

T/o 2023 Honington. Last heard on w/t at 2343 indicating the crew were preparing to bale out. Crashed at Neuwied, 12 km NW of Koblenz. The two airmen who died are buried in Rheinberg War Cemetery.

9 Sqn	Wellington IC	T2900 WS-L	Op: Berlin

Sgt R D C Stark +
Sgt F W Baker +
Sgt J W Nightingarl +
Sgt G Gibb +
Sgt J E Johnson +
Sgt H F Hurt +

T/o 2057 Honington. During the course of the next five hours a number of w/t signals were received, the last being at 0058 when SOS was heard. At this stage, the bomber was plotted 30 miles off Lowestoft, Suffolk, but despite an intensive investigation of the area by RN destroyers, no trace of this Wellington and its crew were found. All are commemorated on the Runnymede Memorial.

17-18 Apr **40 Sqn**   Wellington IC | R1331 BL-R   **Op: Berlin**
1941

40 Sqn   Wellington IC   R1331 BL-R   Op: Berlin
Sgt Jenner   T/o 2045 Alconbury. Crashed 0525 on a hillside
Sgt Bagnall   near Combe Martin, 4 miles E of Ilfracombe,
Sgt Noble   on the north Devon coast. Sgt Griffin baled
Sgt Jordan   out, but his parachute failed to deploy before
Sgt A Macaskill   he hit the ground. The rest of the crew stayed
Sgt J Griffin   +   in the aircraft and were not seriously hurt.

44 Sqn   Hampden I   X2999 KM-   Op: Berlin
F/S J N Sneeston   +   T/o 2015 Waddington. Presumed lost over the
Sgt E N Brundish   +   North Sea. The body of F/S Sneeston was washed
Sgt J M Taylor   +   ashore on 6 June 1941 at Sheerness, Kent, but
Sgt J W Mulford   +   his crew have never been found.

50 Sqn   Hampden I   AD730 VN-   Op: Berlin
P/O J K Hill   +   T/o 2030 Lindholme. Overflew the United Kingdom
Sgt J T Lamb   +   on return, crossed the Irish Sea and crashed on
Sgt S Wright   +   a hillside near Blessington, County Wicklow,
Sgt F H Erdwin   +   Eire.

58 Sqn   Whitley V   T4266 GE-O   Op: Berlin
P/O A A Law   T/o 2041 Linton-on-Ouse. Returning, hit by flak
Sgt A Whewell   over Hamburg, which wrecked the port engine. At
P/O McNeil   0350 the starboard motor seized and caught fire,
Sgt Rose   followed ten minutes later by a ditching in the
Sgt Steggall   North Sea. Late in the evening of 20 April, a
                                            Hudson sighted the crew in their dinghy and a
second Hudson later dropped Lindholme rescue gear in their vicinity. At 2230
that same evening one very exhausted bomber crew were rescued by an ASR launch,
some 64 hours after coming down in the sea.

77 Sqn   Whitley V   T4338 KN-   Op: Berlin
Sgt E I Pocock   +   T/o 2026 Topcliffe. All are buried in Berlin
Sgt P J Church   +   at the 1939-1945 War Cemetery.
Sgt J S Bools   +
Sgt A F Tweed   +
P/O W L Boon   +

77 Sqn   Whitley V   Z6582 KN-   Op: Berlin
Sgt Cradduck   T/o 2037 Topcliffe. Hit by flak and bombs were
Sgt Turner   jettisoned over Hamburg. Turned back and ditched
P/O Birch   60 miles off Blyth, Northumberland. No injuries
Sgt Morgan   reported.
Sgt J W Middleton

77 Sqn   Whitley V   Z6585 KN-   Op: Berlin
F/O L E Pearson   +   T/o 2027 Topcliffe. All are buried in Hamburg
F/L D Gibson   +   Cemetery, Ohlsdorf.
Sgt C E Gansler   +
Sgt H D Bowles   +
Sgt L W Flint   +

102 Sqn   Whitley V   T4334 DY-   Op: Berlin
F/O E G Libbey   pow   T/o 2032 Topcliffe. Hit by flak and crashed
Sgt J I Charlton   pow   in the vicinity of the German capital.
F/S L Barrows   pow
Sgt G A Hartley   pow
Sgt J J McCurdy   pow

149 Sqn   Wellington IC   P9248 OJ-G   Op: Köln
Sgt J Peel   +   T/o 0055 Mildenhall. Lost without trace.
Sgt T C C Clifton   +   All are commemorated on the Runnymede Memorial.
P/O K E Platt   +
Sgt E E Allnatt   +
Sgt H S Walters   +
Sgt J Wood   +

17-18 Apr 1941	311 Sqn	Wellington IC	R1599 KX-J	Op: **Berlin**

311 Sqn — Wellington IC — R1599 KX-J — Op: Berlin

Sgt F Kracmer +
F/O F Sixta +
P/O V Kubicek +
P/O V J J Kosulic +
Sgt V Stetka +
Sgt R Lifcic +

T/o 2055 East Wretham. Shot down by a night-fighter (Hptm Werner Streib, I./NJG1) and crashed 2339 at Kelpen (Limburg), 9 km ESE of Weert, Holland. The crew were first buried at Venlo, but since 1945 their remains have been taken to Jonkerbos War Cemetery.

18 Apr 1941 — 21 Sqn — Blenheim IV — T1814 YH- — Op: Anti-shipping

P/O H K Marshall +
Sgt L W Bacon +
Sgt A C Bonnett +

T/o 1028 Watton. Hit by flak and crashed into the sea off Heligoland. All are commemorated on the Runnymede Memorial.

21 Sqn — Blenheim IV — V5855 YH- — Op: Anti-shipping

Sgt J Dunning +
Sgt P Hope +
Sgt J H Bruce +

T/o 1028 Watton. Lost in circumstances similar to those described above. Sgt Dunning is buried in Sage War Cemetery; the bodies of his crew have not been identified and their names are commemorated on the panels of the Runnymede Memorial.

61 Sqn — Hampden I — AD732 QR- — Op: Cherbourg

F/L R S E Aldridge DFC +
P/O F W Holden +
Sgt K Downing pow
Sgt A Drury +

T/o 1520 Hemswell to attack an airfield near Cherbourg. Shot down by flak in the target area. Those who died are buried in Cherbourg Old Communal Cemetery.

61 Sqn — Hampden I — AD825 QR- — Op: Brest

Sgt L W Metcalfe inj
Sgt F A Armstrong
Sgt D Pearce
Sgt W Butler

T/o 1535 Hemswell. Damaged by flak, which wounded Sgt Metcalfe in his arms and legs, and on return the Hampden was abandoned 1 mile NW of Aldbourne and 6 miles NE of Swindon, Wiltshire.

110 Sqn — Blenheim IV — R2787 VE- — Op: Anti-shipping

Sgt H W Wright +
Sgt N E T Kendall +
F/S G S Cornwall +

T/o 0335 Wattisham but crashed almost immediately after colliding with a tree on the airfield boundary, bursting into flames on impact.

20 Apr 1941 — 77 Sqn — Whitley V — T4332 KN- — Training

Sgt P Singleton

Crashed 1230 following engine failure at Edwinstowe, 5 miles E of Warsop, Nottinghamshire. The Whitley caught fire, but no injuries are reported.

20-21 Apr 1941 — 7 Sqn — Stirling I — N6009 MG- — Op: Köln

F/L R A Cruikshank DFC
Sgt R S Havery
Sgt K F Wilson
Sgt G W Smith
Sgt J McIntyre
Sgt S A Hives
Sgt E Barratt

T/o 2150 Oakington. Crash-landed on a Q site at Stambourne, 8 miles NW of Halstead, Essex. The crew escaped unhurt, despite the efforts by an enemy aircraft to bomb the wrecked Stirling.

83 Sqn — Hampden I — X3119 OL-R — Op: Köln

F/S R B Hanmer +
Sgt F A Whitehead +
Sgt J R Ronnie +
Sgt E S Phillips +

T/o 0010 Scampton. Crashed at Houthulst (West-Vlaanderen), 9 km SE of Diksmuide, Belgium. All are buried in Houthulst Churchyard.

99 Sqn — Wellington IC — T2997 LN- — Op: Köln

P/O F H Cook +
P/O W E Bowden +
P/O R M Morrow RNZAF +
Sgt B M Evans +
Sgt F G Hindrup RNZAF +
Sgt M A J Savage +

T/o 2047 Waterbeach. Collided with a barrage balloon over Harwich harbour, burst into flames and crashed 0120 in the sea 3000 yards off the shore, bearing 125 degrees from Landguard, Felixstowe, Suffolk. The accident occurred close to where another 99 Squadron Wellington had crashed on 7 November 1940. Sgt Hindrup's father, Rifleman F J Hindrup of the 3rd NZ Rifle Brigade, was killed in France on 26 August 1918.

Date	Squadron	Aircraft	Serial / Code	Operation
20-21 Apr 1941	106 Sqn P/O R M A Lakin + P/O J Cutmore + Sgt W E Burrell + Sgt H E Preston DFM +	Hampden I	X2986 ZN-F	Op: Köln T/o 0015 Coningsby. Crashed near Köln. All are buried in Rheinberg War Cemetery. Sgt Preston had previously served with 44 Squadron, his award being Gazetted on 22 November 1940.
22 Apr 1941	18 Sqn P/O P T R Cook + Sgt G F Beever + LAC R S Prahl +	Blenheim IV	T2232 WV-	Training Crashed on Oulton airfield, Norfolk, following engine failure at low altitude.
	21 Sqn Sgt R Lloyd Sgt Fairey Sgt Wade	Blenheim IV	V6031 YH-	Op: Anti-shipping T/o Watton. Overshot the runway and crashed on return to base. No injuries reported.
	82 Sqn Sgt Miller Sgt Johnson Sgt Newbon	Blenheim IV	T2442 UX-F	Op: Anti-shipping T/o 1023 Lossiemouth. Believed crashed near Embleton while trying to reach Acklington airfield, Northumberland. No injuries reported.
22-23 Apr 1941	115 Sqn Sgt Palmer Sgt F E Shaw + Sgt Lewis Sgt Webb Sgt Bowes Sgt R W R Kerruish	Wellington IC	T2560 KO-E	Op: Brest T/o 2004 Marham. Crashed 2 miles E of Chiseldon, 4 miles SSE of Swindon, Wiltshire.
	218 Sqn Sgt W H Swain RNZAF + Sgt R E Finch + Sgt M B Crooks RNZAF + Sgt V M R Lloyd + Sgt G Molyneaux + Sgt J Clark RNZAF pow	Wellington IC	L7798 HA-S	Op: Brest T/o Marham. Crashed at Milizac (Finistère), 11 km NW of Brest. Those who died are buried in Milizac Churchyard.
	218 Sqn Sgt W S Adams Sgt Forster Sgt Jackson Sgt Dadd Sgt Pearse Sgt Payne	Wellington IC	R1368 HA-F	Op: Brest T/o 1945 Marham. Ran out of petrol while trying to reach Wyton, and was successfully abandoned. The Wellington crashed 0315 just to the N of Clenchwarton Station, 2 miles W of King's Lynn, Norfolk.
23 Apr 1941	105 Sqn Sgt A H Lister + Sgt W T Heaney + Sgt K W Porter +	Blenheim IV	V6318 GB-	Op: Anti-shipping T/o 1055 Swanton Morley. Hit by flak from the minesweeper M1404 and crashed into the sea off Domberg (Zeeland), Holland. Sgt Lister is buried at Vlissingen, Holland and Sgt Porter rests in Wenduine Communal Cemetery, Belgium. Sgt Heaney has no known grave.
24-25 Apr 1941	15 Sqn Sgt A W I Jones Sgt Brown Sgt Barrass Sgt Stewart Sgt Strang Sgt Galloway inj	Wellington IC	R1218 LS-H	Op: Kiel T/o Wyton. Abandoned, after failure to obtain a response from a call asking for landing instructions. The Wellington crashed at Sand Hutton, 7 miles NE of York.
	51 Sqn F/S J P Wilson + P/O G H Kidd + F/S K E Taylor + Sgt A H Norris + Sgt J M Gibson +	Whitley V	Z6482 MH-	Op: Kiel T/o 2135 Dishforth. Last heard on w/t at 0020 calling for help. Presumed lost over the sea. All are commemorated on the Runnymede Memorial.

24-25 Apr	218 Sqn	Wellington IC	T2958 HA-T	Op: **Kiel**
1941	Sgt E J Chidgey		T/o 0003 Marham. Crashed 0318 into trees just	
	Sgt H G Huckle		beyond the airfield while making a second attempt	
	Sgt R J Alexander		at landing. The Wellington came down in a field	
	Sgt T A E Bridewell		at Barton Bendish, 7 miles WSW of Swaffham,	
	Sgt Spilsbury		Norfolk.	
	Sgt E S Spong			

25 Apr	105 Sqn	Blenheim IV	V6370 GB-	Op: **Anti-shipping**
1941	P/O R Needham	+	T/o 0505 Swanton Morley. Shot down by fighters	
	P/O T Keightley-Smith	+	and came down in the North Sea, 5 km W of	
	Sgt F H Bridgman	+	Westkapelle (Zeeland), Holland. P/O Keightley-	
			Smith is buried in Westduin General Cemetery;	

the rest of the crew are commemorated on the Runnymede Memorial.

25-26 Apr	218 Sqn	Wellington IC	R1507 HA-V	Op: **Kiel**
1941	F/O G B S Agar	+	T/o 2054 Marham. Last heard on w/t at 2356	
	P/O G P L Redstone RNZAF	+	asking for assistance. A bearing, taken at	
	F/S C W Andrews	+	the time, placed the Wellington 80 miles off	
	Sgt V E Ashworth	+	the coast of Holland. All are commemorated	
	F/S W Thornhill	+	on the Runnymede Memorial.	
	P/O C E Blair	+		

26 Apr	21 Sqn	Blenheim IV	V5822 YH-	Op: **Anti-shipping**
1941	Sgt C F Spouge	+	T/o 0705 Watton. Shot down by ship's flak and	
	Sgt A Jordan	+	crashed in the sea off the Dutch Frisian Islands.	
	Sgt E P Acton	+	Sgt Acton is buried in Sage War Cemetery; his	
			two companions have no known graves.	

	21 Sqn	Blenheim IV	V6338 YH-	Op: **Anti-shipping**
	W/C G A Bartlett DFC	+	T/o 0705 Watton. Shot down by ship's flak and	
	F/O A F S Winder	+	crashed in the sea off Vlieland. All are	
	Sgt P K Eames DFM	+	commemorated on the Runnymede Memorial.	

	110 Sqn	Blenheim IV	V6063 VE-	Op: **Anti-shipping**
	F/L G O Lings DFC	+	T/o 0825 Wattisham to patrol Beat 9. Believed	
	F/S C I Martin	+	shot down by Lt Otto Vinzent, 3./JG54 and lost	
	Sgt S G Peplar	+	in the sea N of Texel. All are commemorated on	
			the Runnymede Memorial.	

Note. F/L Lings had been a long serving member of 110 Squadron and had fought
with distinction in the summer of 1940. His observer, F/S Martin, and his air
gunner, Sgt Peplar, had also served throughout this period.

	301 Sqn	Wellington IC	R1619 GR-	**Training**
	F/L S M Krzystiniak		Crashed 2155 and caught fire after landing	
			heavily on the starboard undercarriage leg	
			at Swinderby. No injuries reported.	

26-27 Apr	9 Sqn	Wellington IC	R1281 WS-	Op: **Emden**
1941	Sgt R G Damman RAAF	pow	T/o 2044 Honington. A fix on this aircraft made	
	Sgt R M Trundle	pow	at 0157 placed the Wellington W of Berlin and it	
	Sgt D B Reid	pow	is believed the crew had flown a reciprocal	
	Sgt R R Mc Graham	pow	course after acknowledging an earlier bearing.	
	Sgt B S Jacobs	pow	At 0223 the bomber was plotted S of Emden and	
	Sgt B W Channing	pow	shortly after this the crew force-landed at	
			Ommen (Overijssel), 24 km NW of Almelo, Holland.	

	44 Sqn	Hampden I	AD847 KM-	Op: **Hamburg**
	Sgt Lauderdale		T/o 2155 Waddington. Crash-landed 0530 near	
	Sgt Mallen		West Raynham airfield, Norfolk. No injuries	
	Sgt Hartley		reported.	
	Sgt R Oliver			

	83 Sqn	Hampden I	AD796 OL-D	Op: **Hamburg**
	P/O R H Crush	+	T/o 2110 Scampton. Crashed at Eddelak, 6 km NNW	
	Sgt G T Hall	+	of Brunsbüttel, Germany. All are buried in	
	Sgt E G Norman	+	Kiel War Cemetery.	
	Sgt W K Thompson	+		

Date	Squadron	Aircraft	Serial	Operation
28 Apr 1941	**101 Sqn** Sgt R Ridgman-Parsons + Sgt G W Hickman + Sgt H T H Downes +	**Blenheim IV**	**V5493 SR-G**	**Op: Anti-shipping** T/o 1054 Manston to attack trawlers reported in the Strait of Dover. Lost off Calais. All are commemorated on the Runnymede Memorial.
28-29 Apr 1941	**50 Sqn** S/L D C F Good DFC + P/O J G E Willis + Sgt A C Evans + Sgt H C Page +	**Hampden I**	**AD728 VN-**	**Op: Gardening** T/o Lindholme to lay mines off la Rochelle. Presumed lost in the target area. Three of the crew are buried at various locations along the French coast; S/L Good is commemorated on the Runnymede Memorial.
	50 Sqn F/O J A Whitecross evd Sgt J E Martin pow F/S D F Ross + Sgt J F O'Hare +	**Hampden I**	**AD834 VN-**	**Op: Gardening** T/o Lindholme. Last heard on w/t at 2359 indicating the mines had been planted, but the port engine was failing. Subsequently, the bomber crashed near Loudeac (Finistère), France, where the two airmen who died are buried.
29 Apr 1941	**82 Sqn** P/O D White + Sgt R G Hanson + Sgt W G Busby + Sgt H E Hollis +	**Blenheim IV**	**V6256 UX-W**	**Op: Anti-shipping** T/o 1402 Lossiemouth to search for shipping in Norwegian waters. Lost without trace. All are commemorated on the Runnymede Memorial.
	82 Sqn F/L R E Tallis DFC + Sgt D G Shayler + Sgt F E Davis +	**Blenheim IV**	**V6451 UX-**	**Op: Anti-shipping** T/o 1343 Lossiemouth. Presumed lost over the sea. F/L Tallis is buried in Sola Churchyard, Norway; his crew have no known graves.
29-30 Apr 1941	**99 Sqn** Sgt F Hewitson + Sgt N O Bennett + Sgt E C Stevens + Sgt S J Holt + Sgt W P James + Sgt R R Thomas RNZAF +	**Wellington IC**	**T2721 LN-**	**Op: Mannheim** T/o 2111 Waterbeach. Last heard on w/t at 0314 calling for help and it is believed the bomber was attacked at this time by a Ju 88C intruder flown by Ofw Hermann Sommer, I./NJG2 off the east coast. All are commemorated on the Runnymede Memorial.
30 Apr 1941	**18 Sqn** S/L H J N Lindsaye + Sgt A E Stone + F/O F Holmes +	**Blenheim IV**	**V6389 WV-**	**Training** Pilot lost control, while towing a target, and dived into the ground at Hillington, 7 miles NE of King's Lynn, Norfolk. An investigation into this accident, which occurred at 1052 found that the drogue had separated from its cable and had fouled the port elevator and trim tab.
	21 Sqn Sgt M S Dewing + Sgt W H R Smale + Sgt H Nathan +	**Blenheim IV**	**V5853 YH-**	**Op: Anti-shipping** T/o 0530 Watton. Hit by flak and crashed in the sea off the Dutch coast. All are buried in the General Cemetery at Hoek van Holland.
30 Apr- 1 May 1941	**7 Sqn** F/L N Williams DFC, RNZAF Sgt W T Williams LAC R C Watkins Sgt C T Webb Sgt R A Pickers Sgt W F Hodson Sgt L Smith	**Stirling I**	**N6014 MG-**	**Op: Berlin** T/o Oakington. Ran short of petrol and crash-landed 0430 in a wheatfield at Hinton Lodge, 3 miles SE of Halesworth, Suffolk. LAC Watkins had recently completed his flight engineer training, but his promotion to Sgt had still to be promulgated.
1 May 1941	**105 Sqn** F/L Goode inj P/O Hogan inj Sgt Roland inj	**Blenheim IV**	**V5823 GB-**	**Op: Anti-shipping** T/o 1215 Swanton Morley. Badly shot about by Me 109s and later a propeller fell off, causing the crew to make an emergency landing 1420 in a field at Buck's Farm, Cookley, 2 miles SW of Halesworth, Suffolk.

1 May	139 Sqn	Blenheim IV	V6177 XD–		Op: Anti-shipping
1941	W/C I W Braye DFC	+	T/o 1539 Horsham St. Faith. Believed shot down		
	F/S K C Peek	+	by flak off Den Helder, Holland. All are		
	Sgt J Hutchison	+	commemorated on the Runnymede Memorial.		

Chapter 4

A Week in May

2 May to 8-9 May 1941

During the night of 8-9 May, Bomber Command despatched a total of 364 aircraft, thus setting a new record and exceeding by nearly one hundred sorties the previous best which had been 265 bombers mustered on 10-11 February 1941. In the period between the end of April and 8-9 May, operations had been mounted on six consecutive nights and had involved a respectable total of 819 bombers. Then, to set a new record without first the benefit of a stand-down was an excellent achievement.

Day operations over the same period by 2 Group had witnessed the despatch of 131 Blenheims, continuing their hazardous anti-shipping strikes, while cloud cover raids to targets in north-west Germany and along the channel coasts had been attempted by a trio of Hampdens and two Stirlings. The latter incursions had been a failure, but 2 Group was able to report some positive results, albeit at a cost of seven Blenheims missing, and an eighth machine written off following a brave attempt to get in amongst a convoy making for La Pallice.

On 2 May, 101 Squadron came across a 2000 ton vessel off Oostende and in the briefest of engagements left the ship a sinking hulk. The following day the tables were turned and two Blenheims, both from 101 Squadron, were lost in the channel. Since 24 April, a detachment from the squadron had been flying out of Manston, engaged on what has become known as Channel Stop operations designed to prevent enemy shipping from passing through the Strait of Dover by day. At night the pressure was maintained on the enemy by fast motor torpedo boats of the Royal Navy.

Main force operations continued in much the same vein as before but with two notable exceptions. During 3-4 May, just over one hundred bombers were sent to Köln, while two nights later the key industrial centre of Mannheim, which straddles the Neckar where this river flows into the Rhine opposite Ludwigshafen, was attacked by a force of 141 aircraft.

Neither raid was considered a success. On both occasions weather conditions were poor, with crews reporting almost total cloud cover.

In contrast, twin attacks on Hamburg and Brest brought claims of good bombing and on each of the Brest operations, several sticks exploded in close proximity to the Gneisenau and the Scharnhorst. However, firm evidence of damage being inflicted on these capital ships could not be confirmed.

At Hamburg, meanwhile, fires were left burning in the wake of each raid, though the authorities say these were quite minor and damage was only slight. Then, throughout the night of 8-9 May, Hamburg and Bremen were heavily bombed by forces of 188 and 133 aircraft respectively. The worst destruction was felt at Hamburg where several loads of the relatively new 4000 pounders exploded, causing massive blast damage and havoc in the Barmbek district. This addition to the Command's growing arsenal of weapons was to prove a major problem to the enemy defences now being severely tested in the towns and cities of north-west Germany.

At Bremen, damage was not so extensive, but here, too, the clear weather conditions enabled the bombers to make good use of their resources and many fires were started.

In addition to the two main prongs of assault, a small force of Blenheims made an unsuccessful attempt to block the Kiel canal and minor operations were also conducted against targets at Rotterdam, Emden and Berlin.

Eleven bombers were lost; five from Hamburg and an equal number from Bremen, while Berlin claimed a single Wellington. Overall, however, the planners felt well pleased with the night's work.

2-3 May 1941	7 Sqn	Stirling I	N6012 MG-	Op: Hamburg
	F/L R A Cruikshank DFC & Bar	+	T/o 2107 Oakington. Crashed 0231 at Dry Drayton, 3 miles SW of Oakington, Cambridgeshire. It is	
	Sgt R S Havery	+	believed that the crew had fought an engagement	
	Sgt K F Wilkinson	+	with a night-fighter. Sgt Barratt died from his	
	Sgt G W Smith	+	injuries on 4 May. It will be recalled that F/L	
	Sgt S A Hives	+	Cruikshank had crash-landed on return from Köln	
	F/S J McIntyre	+	in April 1941, his crew escaping injury on that	
	Sgt E Barratt	inj	occasion.	

2-3 May 1941	44 Sqn	Hampden I	AD864 KM-	Op: **Hamburg**

P/O J E P Jeff   +
P/O H U A Tripp   +
Sgt R J Leaper   +
Sgt E Egar   +

T/o 2205 Waddington. P/O Jeff has no known grave, but the rest of the crew are buried in Hamburg Cemetery, Ohlsdorf.

77 Sqn	Whitley V	Z6461 KN-	Op: **Hamburg**

Sgt J F Hughes   +
Sgt D G Garn   +
P/O J A Basham   +
Sgt J B Seden   +
Sgt C Hutchinson   +

T/o 2129 Topcliffe. Crashed in the North Sea. On 7 August 1941, Patrol Boat 1207 recovered the body of Sgt Hutchinson from the sea off Weselbusen and he is buried, along with Sgt Garn, in Kiel War Cemetery. The rest of the crew are commemorated on the Runnymede Memorial.

207 Sqn	Manchester I	L7379 EM-T	Op: **Hamburg**

F/O D E Pinchbeck   pow
Sgt E A C Lee   pow
Sgt A S Duncan   pow
F/S S E Panton   pow
Sgt W M McGregor DFM   pow
Sgt C N Barron   pow

T/o Waddington. Hit by flak and set on fire over the target. The crew baled out, with the exception of F/O Pinchbeck who had mislaid his parachute. In pitch dark conditions he force-landed on farmland near Hamburg. Sgt McGregor had previously served with 144 Squadron.

305 Sqn	Wellington IC	R1214 SM-T	Op: **Emden**

F/O J Nogal   pow
Sgt T Kasprzyk   pow
P/O W J Malak   +
Sgt T Zuk   pow
F/O A Jastrzebski   pow
P/O M J Ryszkiewicz   +

T/o 2140 Syerston. Last heard on w/t at 0232 by Sealand. Shot down by a night-fighter (Lt Reinhold Knacke, I./NJG1) and crashed at Budel (Noord Brabant), 20 km SSE of Eindhoven, where those who died are buried in Woensel General Cemetery. This was the first Squadron crew to be posted missing since commencing operations on 25-26 April 1941, when three Wellingtons bombed Rotterdam.

3 May 1941	101 Sqn	Blenheim IV	T1825 SR-Y	Op: **Anti-shipping**

P/O C D Brown   +
P/O C H Farvis   +
Sgt A J Morgan   +

T/o 1929 Manston. Shot down by flak off Boulogne. All are commemorated on the Runnymede Memorial.

101 Sqn	Blenheim IV	T2234 SR-H	Op: **Anti-shipping**

Sgt C H Deane   +
Sgt G D Watkinson   +
Sgt J F Chell   +

T/o 1929 Manston. Hit by flak and ditched 19 miles off Dungeness, Kent. The pilot and his observer were seen getting out of the sinking Blenheim, but despite an extensive search, no survivors were found and all are commemorated on the Runnymede Memorial.

Note. These were the last two Blenheims lost by 101 Squadron prior to leaving 2 Group and converting to Wellingtons for operations with 3 Group. Twenty-four hours previous, P/O Brown had sunk a 2000 vessel off Oostende. Since the start of the year, the Squadron had lost eight Blenheims, seven on operations and one in a training accident, claiming the lives of twenty-two airmen.

3-4 May 1941	9 Sqn	Wellington IC	T2964 WS-N	Op: **Rotterdam**

Sgt Anderson
Sgt Williamson
Sgt Dove
Sgt Palmer
Sgt M Smith
Sgt Love

T/o 2100 Honington. Landed 2358 but believed to have been damaged. Following a technical inspection the Wellington was declared beyond economical repair and was struck off charge on 14 May 1941.

78 Sqn	Whitley V	Z6483 EY-	Op: **Köln**

Sgt L Hatcher
Sgt Chandos
Sgt H B Buttell
Sgt T K Moodie
Sgt T Hall

T/o 2045 Middleton St. George. Abandoned due to a combination of w/t failure and lack of fuel. The bomber crashed 0630 near Leominster, Herefordshire. No injuries reported.

Note. Sgt Hatcher was subsequently commissioned and rose to the rank of S/L, gaining a DFC and an AFM in the process. He lost his life on 22 December 1944 and is buried at Woolwich.

-4 May 941	115 Sqn	Wellington IC	R1280 KO-H	Op: Brest

Sgt Sayers
Sgt Tingley
Sgt Brittan
Sgt Taylor
Sgt Lambert
Sgt Walker

T/o 2119 Marham. Lost a propeller and crash-landed 0400 just to the N of Oakington railway station, 5 miles NW of Cambridge. No injuries reported.

-5 May 941	58 Sqn	Whitley V	T4336 GE-E	Op: Brest

F/L S P Daniels
P/O F J Joshua
Sgt Hardie
Sgt Kemp
Sgt Mole

T/o 2130 Linton-on-Ouse. Crashed 0040 while trying to land by the aid of Drem lights at Church Fenton. Later, Spitfire I X4609 of 485 Squadron swung taking off and collided with the Whitley, wrecking the fighter.

May 941	18 Sqn	Blenheim IV	V6377 WV-	Op: la Pallice

Sgt Burns
Sgt Kirkpatrick   inj
Sgt White

T/o 1154 Portreath. Clipped the mast of a ship while attacking a convoy at 4700N 0530W and crash-landed 1500 on return to Portreath.

	21 Sqn	Blenheim IV	L8758 YH-B	Training

Sgt D K Glass   +
Sgt H W C Norman-Arterton +
F/S G A Cole   +

Presumed lost while over the Irish Sea. F/S Cole is buried in Andreas (St. Andrew) Churchyard, Isle of Man; his companions are commemorated on the Runnymede Memorial.

	110 Sqn	Blenheim IV	V5620 VE-	Training

P/O D H Seale

Overshot while attempting to land and crashed near the fuel dump at Wattisham.

-6 May 941	99 Sqn	Wellington IC	T2477 LN-	Op: Mannheim

F/O Osborn

T/o Waterbeach and crashed almost immediately coming to rest near the airfield perimeter.

May 941	21 Sqn	Blenheim IV	Z5875 YH-W	Op: Anti-shipping

Sgt K B Fitzgerald   +
Sgt N Berry   +
Sgt A Barron   +

T/o 0600 Watton to patrol Beat 9. Last seen on fire in the target area. All are commemorated on the Runnymede Memorial.

	110 Sqn	Blenheim IV	R3600 VE-	Op: Anti-shipping

F/L E N Steel   +
F/S R A Freestone   +
Sgt J D Bramhall   +

T/o 1115 Wattisham to patrol Beat 7. Crashed in Sgt Bramhall is buried in Sage War Cemetery; his two companions have no known graves.

Note. F/L Steel was one of the dwindling band of native New Zealanders who crossed the world to join the pre-war regular Royal Air Force. His Blenheim was credited with at least forty-eight operational sorties, a remarkable record for this type.

	139 Sqn	Blenheim IV	V6196 XD-	Training

Sgt J Evans   inj
Sgt Tuppen   inj
Sgt Dumolo   inj

T/o 0015 Horsham St. Faith but collided with a tree. The pilot maintained control, but due to enemy air activity in the area, the crew were obliged to circle for ninety minutes before crash-landing in Back Street, Horsham St. Faith, 4 miles NNW of Norwich. Sgt Dumolo was seriously injured when a branch from an apple tree sliced into the Blenheim's gun turret.

-7 May 941	75 Sqn	Wellington IC	R3169 AA-	Op: Hamburg

Sgt D L Nola RNZAF   +
Sgt A C Mee RNZAF   +
P/O C F Page   +
Sgt J Hall   +
Sgt W Russell   +
Sgt Craven   inj

T/o Feltwell. Crossed the east coast on return and collided with barrage balloon cables. Out of control, the Wellington crashed in the River Humber near Trinity Sands. Sgt Mee RNZAF had successfully parachuted on 19 March 1941, while returning from Kiel.

| 6-7 May
1941 | 304 Sqn | Wellington IC | R1443 NZ- | Op: le Havre |

6-7 May	304 Sqn		Wellington IC	R1443 NZ-	Op: le Havre
1941	P/O A Sym	+		T/o 2201 Syerston. Crashed in the sea. The
	Sgt W Zolnowski	+		body of P/O Sobieralski was washed ashore on
	P/O F Sobieralski	+		14 September 1941, and he is buried in Holland
	Sgt J Hampel	+		at Noordwijk General Cemetery. This was the
	Sgt S Bialek	+		first loss suffered by the Squadron since
	P/O S Duchnicki	+		commencing operations on 25-26 April 1941.

7 May	18 Sqn		Blenheim IV	R3741 WV-X	Op: Anti-shipping
1941	S/L R B Barker	+		T/o 1025 Portreath to patrol Beat 15. Crashed
	Sgt N H Meanwell	+		1116, streaming flames, into the sea after
	Sgt V Hughes	+		attacking a cargo vessel. The Blenheim's

position was logged as 4834N 0321W and on
impact a plume of smoke was seen rising to over 100 feet. All are commemorated
on the Runnymede Memorial.

57 Sqn		Wellington IC	T2504 DX-	Ground
			Hit by incendiary bombs during a Luftwaffe	

raid on Feltwell and burnt out on its dispersal pan.

61 Sqn		Anson I	N5187 QR-	Training
			Crashed and burnt out. No accident card	
			raised.	

7-8 May	139 Sqn		Blenheim IV	P4860 XD-	Op: Anti-shipping
1941	Sgt J W Middleton	pow		T/o 2204 Horsham St. Faith. Ditched 0013 in the
	Sgt K R Coles	pow		Waddenzee off Wierum (Groningen), 9 km NNE of
	Sgt H R Hale	pow		Dokkum, Holland.

	150 Sqn		Wellington IC	R1374 JN-G	Op: St-Nazaire
	F/L F H Savage	+		T/o 2230 Newton. Crashed near Nantes (Loire
	Sgt J M Fulford	+		Atlantique). The crew are buried in Pont-du-
	Sgt W W Heywood RCAF	+		Cens Communal Cemetery.
	Sgt L F Harris	+		
	Sgt P V Read	+		
	Sgt J L Hart	+		

8 May	105 Sqn		Blenheim IV	V5828 GB-R	Op: Anti-shipping
1941	W/C A L Christian	+		T/o 0510 Lossiemouth. Last seen in the entrance
	Twice MiD			to Havs Fjord, Norway, with its port engine on
	F/S H F Hancock	+		fire. All are commemorated on the Runnymede
	Sgt G Wade	+		Memorial.

8-9 May	10 Sqn		Whitley V	P4946 ZA-P	Op: Bremen
1941	P/O G R Guest	pow		T/o 2215 Leeming. Signalled operation completed
	Sgt C A Stickland	pow		at 0159 but subsequently ditched off the Dutch
	Sgt M C Newlyn	pow		coast.
	Sgt W Gardner	pow		
	Sgt R R Hanson	pow		

	78 Sqn		Whitley V	T4147 EY-D	Op: Bremen
	Sgt L Thorpe	+		T/o 2225 Middleton St. George. Crashed at
	P/O R W Wallis-Stolzle	+		Heisfelde in the northern outskirts of Leer,
	Sgt P J Lewis	+		Germany. All are buried in Sage War Cemetery,
	Sgt H E Bailey	+		Oldenburg.
	Sgt P W R Emmett	+		

	83 Sqn		Hampden I	X3062 OL-Z	Op: Hamburg
	P/O F K Gill	+		T/o 2225 Scampton. Shot down by an intruder
	P/O G D G Hudson	+		and crashed in the sea off Mablethorpe,
	Sgt R C H Blatchford	+		Lincolnshire. All are commemorated on the
	Sgt H W Francis	+		Runnymede Memorial.

8-9 May 1941	99 Sqn	Wellington II	W5400 LN-	Op: Berlin

99 Sqn		Wellington II	W5400 LN-	Op: Berlin
S/L P H Jackson	+			
P/O I O M Smith	+			
P/O L H Mercer MiD	+			
Sgt G A Bennetts	+			
Sgt J Harding	+			
Sgt G J Talbot	+			

T/o 2159 Waterbeach. Last heard on w/t at 0520 calling for help. All are commemorated on the Runnymede Memorial.

144 Sqn	Hampden I	AD901 PL-M	Op: Hamburg
S/L Fleming			
Sgt Wathey			
Sgt G Crombie			
F/O Morgan			

T/o 2214 Hemswell. Force-landed 0500 in a field at White Hall Farm, Syderstone, 15 miles NE of King's Lynn, Norfolk. Sgt Crombie later gained the DFM, Gazetted 21 November 1941, and was killed while serving with 230 Squadron on 29 December 1943. He is buried in Nairobi (Forest Road) Cemetery, Kenya.

149 Sqn		Wellington IC	R1506 OJ-D	Op: Hamburg
F/S C R Burch	+			
Sgt G D K Jones	pow			
P/O D Martin	+			
Sgt W G H Dauncey	+			
Sgt J A Keates	+			
Sgt D Westmacott	pow			

T/o 2210 Mildenhall. Shot down by a night-fighter (Ofw Schönherr, II./NJG1) and crashed 0515 into the sea some 10 km N of Heligoland. It is believed the combat was concluded with both aircraft flying just 20 feet off the sea. Those who died are buried in Sage War Cemetery.

214 Sqn		Wellington IC	R1226 BU-L	Op: Hamburg
S/L F L H Eddison DFC	+			
P/O N M K Kirkcaldie RNZAF	+			
Sgt J Holt	+			
Sgt K Tait	+			
Sgt A F Wilson	+			
Sgt C Paton	+			

T/o 2210 Stradishall. Crashed at Anna Paulowna (Noord Holland), 12 km SE of Den Helder. All are buried in Bergen op Zoom War Cemetery. S/L Eddison was due to be posted to another squadron as a Flight Commander on completion of this sortie.

214 Sqn		Wellington IC	R3208 BU-	Op: Hamburg
F/S W H Browell	+			
Sgt A W Dean	+			
Sgt J L Smith	+			
Sgt R J Bennett	+			
Sgt W J S McGregor	+			
Sgt M G Robertson	+			

T/o 2222 Stradishall. Presumed crashed in the sea. F/S Browell is buried at Soltau in Becklingen War Cemetery. His crew are commemorated on the Runnymede Memorial.

301 Sqn		Wellington IC	R1227 GR-M	Op: Bremen
Sgt T Bojakowski	+			
P/O W F Brzozowski	+			
F/O S Rewkowski	+			
Sgt A Lipecki	+			
Sgt K Golebiowski	+			
F/O I Dudek	+			

T/o 2318 Swinderby. Last heard on w/t at 0155 when NGZ was received. Presumed lost over the sea. P/O Brzozowski is buried in Sage War Cemetery, Oldenburg, but the rest of the crew have no known graves.

304 Sqn		Wellington IC	R1473 NZ-	Op: Bremen
F/O G J Lynes DFC	+			
W/C W M Graham	+			
F/S T E Wady	pow			
F/S S R Gear DFM	+			
Sgt W C Hamilton	+			
F/O F S W Webb	+			

T/o 2308 Syerston. Hit by flak and crashed at Plantlünne, on the N bank of the Gr Aa, 12 km SSE of Lingen-Ems, Germany, where those who died were buried. Since 1945, their remains have been taken to the Reichswald Forest War Cemetery. F/S Gear had previously flown in Hampdens with 83 Squadron, details of his DFM being published in the London Gazette on 11 February 1941.

305 Sqn		Wellington IC	R1322 SM-F	Op: Bremen
Sgt J P Dorman	+			
Sgt Z Gwozdz	+			
P/O M Socharzki	+			
Sgt H F Sikorski	+			
Sgt S Pisarski	+			
Sgt L Karcz	+			

T/o 2256 Syerston. Shot down by a night-fighter (Ofw Hans Rasper, 4./NJG1) and crashed in the IJsselmeer, 12 km SW of Lemmer. Three bodies were later recovered and taken for burial in various Dutch cemeteries; P/O Socharzki, Sgt Sikorski and Sgt Pisarski have no known graves.

Chapter 5

Industrial Targets

9 May to 21-22 June 1941

The momentum of the recent night operations continued on 9-10 May, when a strong force of 146 aircraft attacked the twin cities of Ludwigshafen and Mannheim. Excellent bombing was achieved and, for this period of the war, damage was quite significant.

Within twenty-four hours, Bomber Command was active over north-west Germany, raiding the port of Hamburg as well as sending a small force further east to Berlin. Clear skies over Hamburg resulted in concentrated fires which by daybreak had burnt out much of the Stock Exchange as well as causing considerable damage to commercial buildings in the centre of the city.

Casualties for an attack on this well protected target were light and amounted to a Whitley and three Wellingtons. From the latter, one airman had a quite remarkable escape. Trouble for the crew started when their aircraft was held in searchlights over Tonning and it was not long before their plight was recognised by a night-fighter. In the attack that followed, the observer, Sergeant Legg, was knocked out but in the understandable confusion the crew thought their colleague had been killed.

Regaining consciousness, Sergeant Legg found himself alone in the bomber which was still flying on a reasonably even keel, having been set on automatic pilot by the captain prior to the survivors making their departure.

Still in a dazed state of mind, Legg found his parachute but as he made ready to make his exit, the parachute pack fell through the open escape hatch.

Undeterred by this setback, he climbed into the cockpit and after disengaging the automatic pilot, pulled off a miraculous crash-landing. By this time the Wellington was burning quite fiercely and in his weak state Sergeant Legg would have perished but for the bravery of two German soldiers who, having witnessed the sudden arrival of the burning bomber near their flak post, ran to the wreckage and pulled Sergeant Legg clear.

From this 115 Squadron crew, five had survived. Tragically, their skipper had fallen into the River Elbe and drowned.

While in captivity, the badly wounded Sergeant Legg underwent several operations at the hands of a fellow prisoner, Doctor Chatenay, but he never made a full recovery and in October 1943 he was amongst a group of prisoners repatriated to the United Kingdom.

By comparison, the Berlin raid was not a success. Only a dozen crews claim to have reached the capital and this long distance operation cost the Command a Manchester and two Stirlings. One of the Stirlings was captained by the CO of 15 Squadron, which had returned to operations at the beginning of May following a speedy conversion from Wellingtons. Picked up by a night-fighter, the Stirling fell, blazing, north-east of the Dutch town of Alkmaar. There were no survivors.

The following night, Hamburg underwent yet another sharp attack. Major fires sprang up in several parts of the city, while to the south Bremen, too, was experiencing a well aimed raid on the harbour area.

Much has been written about the ineffectiveness of early Bomber Command operations, but this series of raids on north-west Germany in the spring of 1941, was at the very least, an unmistakable signal to the German High Command of what the future held in store.

This pace of night operations could not, at this stage of the war, be maintained and following a disappointing raid on Mannheim the main force squadrons were stood down for forty-eight hours. When raiding recommenced the order was for an attack on Hannover by a medium force of just over one hundred aircraft. This was the first time since early February that Hannover had featured and the attack was a departure from the main thrust of operations which, until now, had been mainly associated with shipping related objectives.

The Hannover raid appears to have been mildly successful, but for the remainder of May and well into June, night raiding was at a much reduced level. This slackening of effort is reflected in fewer bomber losses, though a medium attack on Düsseldorf during the night of 2-3 June resulted in three crews failing to return and two more bombers were destroyed in crashes on return to base.

By day, however, a very different picture emerges. Anti-shipping operations were flown on most days and, as was now fully expected, losses were recorded amongst the hard-pressed Blenheim squadrons. On the 13th 82 Squadron lost two aircraft while bombing the docks at St-Nazaire and during a hectic spell between the 18th and the 25th, nine aircraft were lost. Of these, one was shot down during a rare Circus operation on the 21st and two others crashed during training exercises. The misery of 2 Group continued unabated.

As recounted, Düsseldorf was visited early in June and this excursion to the Ruhr was followed by a series of operations to the industrial heart of Germany in the middle of the month. Düsseldorf and Duisburg, both cities located on the east bank of the Rhine came under attack on 11-12 June, though the numbers sent to each target was relatively small and damage was slight. However, from down river at Köln, came reports of heavy bombing along the water front and around the central station.

In addition to the raids mentioned above, a force of twenty Hampdens carried out an important mining operation over Kiel Bay, 61 Squadron losing a crew to flak in the process.

Attention switched next to railway centres linking the Ruhr to central parts of Germany and for the first time a Canadian bomber unit, 405 Squadron, joined in the action with four crews ordered to attack the yards at Scwerte on 12-13 June.

Generally, the results were disappointing. A thick industrial haze shielded most of the Ruhr, totally obscuring ground detail. At Hamm, however, the Wellington force claim to have delivered a successful attack and good bombing was also reported at Osnabrück.

Casualties from the 339 sorties despatched came to eleven bombers missing, or destroyed in accidents. Amongst the latter category was a Wellington from 301 Squadron, wrecked on the ground at Swinderby when it was hit by a similar aircraft that had overshot its landing

Night operations of a similar nature were conducted over the next six nights, culminating in a medium sized raid on 20-21 June when 115 bombers tried to attack the Tirpitz

at Kiel. Since the epic chase and recent sinking of the Bismarck in the Atlantic by units of the Royal Navy, the importance of the Tirpitz had increased significantly.

An extremely hostile reception greeted the force with a fierce barrage of flak being maintained throughout the raid. A number of aircraft were hit and two Wellingtons, both from 218 Squadron, were lost without trace.

2 Group, meanwhile, continued the day offensive. On the 2nd, forty-four Blenheims carried out a particularly daring evening raid on the Kiel Canal. Braving the flak, which was murderous, the bombers came in low and in the late evening gloom left at least two ships sinking.

Two of the attackers failed to return, one from 18 Squadron, another from 139 Squadron. Flak may have claimed the latter, but it is believed that a patrolling fighter shot the 18 Squadron aircraft down west of Texel.

On the 4th, 139 Squadron lost two more crews during an evening strike on De Kooy aerodrome, while three days later more Blenheims were lost after attacking a convoy hugging the coast off IJmuiden. Further to the north, another convoy was intercepted off Terschelling and as the bombers beat a hasty retreat towards the comparative safety of the open sea, flames could be seen leaping high into the air from one of the stricken vessels.

Without question, the courage of those airmen who flew with the light-bomber squadrons in the spring and summer of 1941 cannot be over stated. Few, if any, had any illusions of the danger facing them, and yet they rose magnificently to the challenge.

9 May 1941	7 Sqn	Stirling I	N6019 MG-	Training
	S/L W T C Seale			

T/o Oakington but the starboard engine failed as the Stirling left the ground, followed at 100 feet by the port outer. This drastic reduction in power made a crash-landing inevitable and the bomber came down 1 mile NE of the airfield. The crew are reported to have escaped injury.

	18 Sqn	Blenheim IV	V6379 WV-	Op: Anti-shipping
	S/L R Langebear	+		
	P/O J R Stone	+		
	Sgt A K Newbery MiD	+		

T/o 1330 Portreath. Last seen 1525 heading NNW in position 4815N 0450W and flying at 200 feet, following an attack on a 1000 ton vessel. The Blenheim's port engine was on fire, but the aircraft was gaining height. All are commemorated on the Runnymede Memorial.

9-10 May 1941	51 Sqn	Whitley V	P5106 MH-0	Op: Ludwigshafen
	P/O P Myers	+		
	Sgt H G Browne	+		
	Sgt B Kipling	+		
	Sgt G A Selby	+		
	F/S A Jackson	+		

T/o 2159 Dishforth. Last heard on w/t at 0247 indicating a successful attack. Shot down by a night-fighter (Lt Reinhold Knacke, I./NJG1) and crashed 0305 at Boshoven (Limburg), 2 km W of Weert, Holland. All are buried at Eindhoven.

	77 Sqn	Whitley V	Z6559 KN-	Op: Ludwigshafen
	Sgt Mills			
	Sgt J R T Hazelton			
	P/O Heslop			
	Sgt Roberts			
	Sgt Holman			

T/o 2208 Topcliffe. Overshot the flare-path and crashed 0015 on return to base. Sgt Hazelton was killed on active service on 21 February 1943. At the time of his death he had been decorated with the DFM, Gazetted 23 December 1941.

| 9-10 May 1941 | 102 Sqn | Whitley V | T4146 DY- | Op: Ludwigshafen |

P/O J F W Elliott
Sgt E T Borsberry
Sgt C T F Baldwin
Sgt F V Braybrooke   inj
Sgt H Timlin   inj

T/o 2217 Topcliffe. Encountered very heavy rain, during which the port engine failed. Crash-landed 2340 after clipping trees at Winfarthing, 4 miles NNW of Diss, Norfolk.

| | 214 Sqn | Wellington IC | R1447 BU- | Op: Mannheim |

P/O I K Woodroffe   pow
Sgt H Barnes   pow
Sgt J R Fry RNZAF   pow
Sgt H Gillies   pow
Sgt B L Tillotson   pow
F/O M M Marsh   pow

T/o 2226 Stradishall. In peacetime, both before and after the war, F/O Marsh was a respected race horse trainer and amongst his many successes were two Derby winners. The first was Windsor Lad, which won the 1934 race and in 1952 he gained success with Tulyar.

| 10 May 1941 | 18 Sqn | Blenheim IV | V6376 WV- | Ground |

Destroyed at Portreath airfield, Cornwall, by enemy bombing.

| | 82 Sqn | Blenheim IV | T2330 UX- | Ground |

Destroyed at St. Eval airfield, Cornwall, by enemy bombing.

| | 82 Sqn | Blenheim IV | V6070 UX-N | Ground |

Lost in circumstances as described above.

| 10-11 May 1941 | 7 Sqn | Stirling I | N6010 MG- | Op: Berlin |

F/L N Williams DFC, RNZAF   +
Sgt E J Rapley   +
Sgt R C Watkins   +
F/O D Mackay   +
Sgt W F Hodson   +
Sgt R A Pickers   +
Sgt L Smith   +

T/o 2211 Oakington. Crashed near Cloppenburg, Germany. All are buried in Becklingen War Cemetery, Soltau.

| | 10 Sqn | Whitley V | P5048 ZA-H | Op: Hamburg |

P/O P B Gough   +
Sgt F G Stewart   +
Sgt L Manchip   +
Sgt R Richardson   +
Sgt D F F Watson   +

T/o 2225 Leeming. Last heard on w/t at 0223 indicating the target had been attacked. All are commemorated on the Runnymede Memorial.

| | 15 Sqn | Stirling I | N3654 LS-B | Op: Berlin |

W/C H R Dale   +
P/O P R S Bird   +
Sgt F A S Smith   +
P/O D McL Campbell RNZAF   +
Sgt E R Lucas RNZAF   +
Sgt N H Nuttall   +
Sgt S P Plumb   +

T/o Wyton. Shot down by a night-fighter (Oblt Egmont Prinz zur Lippe Weissenfeld, 4./NJG1) and crashed between Hoodwoud and Opmeer (Noord Holland), 16 km NE of Alkmaar. Apart from W/C Dale, who is buried in Bergen General Cemetery, the crew are commemorated on the Runnymede Memorial.

| | 97 Sqn | Manchester I | L7323 OF-A | Op: Berlin |

P/O R S Ayton   pow
F/S J Bryce DFM   pow
Sgt W J Chantler   pow
Sgt D J Harvey   pow
Sgt E W R Sykes DFM   pow
Sgt R Anderson   pow

T/o Coningsby. Ditched in the North Sea while returning to base. Sgt Bryce had previously served with 50 Squadron, his DFM being Gazetted on 22 October 1940. This was the first bomber lost by 97 Squadron since reforming on 25 February 1941.

| | 115 Sqn | Wellington IC | R1379 KO-B | Op: Hamburg |

Sgt J Anderson   +
Sgt A McB Kerr RAAF   pow
Sgt W J A Legg   pow
Sgt G W Hogg   pow
Sgt A B Morgan   pow
Sgt D W Fraser   pow

T/o 2217 Marham. Shot down by a night-fighter (Lt Eckart-Wilhelm von Bonin, II./NJG1) after being coned in searchlights over Tönning, Germany. Sgt Anderson is buried in Hamburg. This was von Bonin's first night victory. On 10 May 1991, at a special ceremony at Hohn Air Base, Germany, three of the survivors, including Sgt Legg, were introduced to Eckart-Wilhelm von Bonin, whose death was reported in January 1992.

10-11 May	149 Sqn	Wellington IC	R1512 OJ-H	Op: **Hamburg**

10-11 May 149 Sqn   Wellington IC   R1512 OJ-H   Op: Hamburg
1941
Sgt J G Keymer   +   T/o 2237 Mildenhall. Lost without trace. All
Sgt T C Pugh   +   are commemorated on the Runnymede Memorial. Sgt
P/O G R N Adams   +   Menage participated in the Battle of Britain
Sgt F C Ockenden   +   flying as an air gunner in Blenheims with 29
Sgt L G Sutherland   +   Squadron.
Sgt T N Menage   +

150 Sqn   Wellington IC   R1435 JN-H   Op: Hamburg
F/O V G D Spiller   +   T/o 2225 Newton. All are buried at Soltau
Sgt G W Rowe   +   in Becklingen War Cemetery.
F/S G Smith   +
F/S H K Trewhella   +
F/S A E Vickers   +
Sgt G B Paterson   +

11-12 May 40 Sqn   Wellington IC   R1330 BL-H   Op: Hamburg
1941
Sgt R W Finlayson RNZAF +   T/o 2225 Alconbury. Those who died are buried
Sgt J B Murray   +   in Kiel War Cemetery.
Sgt D Fletcher   +
F/S J Shaw   pow
F/S H C Tuckwell   +
F/S P H Beckett   +

40 Sqn   Wellington IC   R1461 BL-Z   Op: Hamburg
Sgt F T Luscombe   +   T/o 2230 Alconbury. Crashed in the sea. Three
Sgt D Chappell   +   bodies, those of Sgt Chappell, Sgt Mulligan and
Sgt E M Mulligan   +   Sgt Hodges, were washed ashore and they are
Sgt J A Harris   +   buried at Sage, Hambury and Becklingen cemeteries
Sgt J E Hodges   +   respectively. The remainder are commemorated on
Sgt J D C Long RNZAF   +   the Runnymede Memorial.

144 Sqn   Hampden I   AD900 PL-   Op: Bremen
S/L C G C Rawlins DFC pow   T/o Hemswell. Shot down by a night-fighter
P/O R F J Featherstone pow   (Oblt Helmut Woltersdorf, II./NJG1) and crashed
    RCAF   0257 at Hoogkarspel (Noord Holland), 6 km WSW of
P/O R H Vaughan   +   Enkhuisen. The two airmen who died are buried in
Sgt S A Taylor   +   Bergen General Cemetery.

214 Sqn   Wellington IC   R1462 BU-   Op: Hamburg
P/O J G Toplis   +   T/o Stradishall. All are buried in Hamburg
Sgt P R K Burley   +   Cemetery, Ohlsdorf.
Sgt A W Gibson   +
Sgt H W J Barr   +
Sgt A Livesey   +
Sgt T W James   +

12-13 May 44 Sqn   Hampden I   X2982 KM-   Op: Mannheim
1941
Sgt E D Tyler   T/o 2200 Waddington. Crashed 0652 in a field
Sgt Greig   bordering Catterick airfield, Yorkshire. No
Sgt Betts   injuries reported.
Sgt Campbell

13 May 82 Sqn   Blenheim IV   V5997 UX-   Op: St-Nazaire
1941
Sgt F H Miller   int   T/o 0811 Portreath.
Sgt N J Ingram   int
Sgt W E W Whiteman   int

82 Sqn   Blenheim IV   V6430 UX-   Op: St-Nazaire
S/L G S King   +   T/o 0807 Portreath. Presumed crashed in the
Sgt J E Austen-Johnson +   sea off the French coast. S/L King and his
Sgt D Owen   +   observer are buried in Escoublac-la-Baule War
                              Cemetery; Sgt Owen has no known grave.

15 May 21 Sqn   Blenheim IV   V6372 YH-H   Op: Anti-shipping
1941
P/O J F T Ogilvie   +   T/o 1102 Watton. Shot down into the sea by
Sgt R P Mayers   +   Me 109s off Heligoland. All are commemorated
Sgt W V Fillingham   +   on the Runnymede Memorial.

15-16 May	40 Sqn	Wellington IC	R1167 BL-N	Op: **Hannover**
1941	Sgt W E Moore	+	T/o 2210 Alconbury. Those who died are buried	
	P/O D F R Whyte	+	in the Reichswald Forest War Cemetery.	
	F/S L J Kennard	+		
	Sgt I J Adey	+		
	Sgt R Meech	+		
	Sgt P Addison	pow		

97 Sqn   Manchester I   L7324 OF-   Op: **Berlin**
F/L G O L Bird DFC   +   T/o 2200 Coningsby. Last heard on w/t at 2300
F/S K J Hutt   +   indicating the starboard engine had failed.
Sgt P N Nutt   +   Presumed lost over the sea. Two bodies were
P/O W A Brown   +   later washed ashore; F/S Hutt was found near
Sgt W P Hannigan   +   Blokhus and Sgt Hannigan was recovered from a
Sgt R G Pyatt   +   beach near Lokken, both places being on the
     shores of the Skagerrak. These two airmen
are buried in Denmark; their companions have no known graves.

103 Sqn   Wellington IC   R1494 PM-   Op: **Hannover**
P/O R G Eccles RNZAF   +   T/o Newton. Heard on w/t advising that the
P/O H J Sellers   pow   port engine had failed, after which it is
P/O A W Sulston   pow   believed the Wellington crashed at Oude Pekela
Sgt E C Easton   pow   (Groningen), 9 km E of Veendam, Holland. The
Sgt S E T Hamblin   pow   two airmen who died are buried in Esserveld
Sgt G Maclean   +   General Cemetery. It is also reported that
     the bomber had been hit by flak over Emden.

144 Sqn   Hampden I   AD841 PL-Q   Op: **Hannover**
P/O W A McVie   +   T/o 2300 Hemswell. Hit by flak and crashed
P/O S L Bailey   +   0235 in the Monnickenmeer polder near Ilpendam
Sgt J K Scouller   pow   (Noord Holland), 12 km NE of Amsterdam, where
Sgt C Carter   pow   those who died are buried in the New Eastern
     Cemetery.

16 May   105 Sqn   Blenheim IV   T2118 GB-   Op: **Anti-shipping**
1941   P/O R A Richards   +   T/o 1430 Lossiemouth. Last seen at the entrance
     Sgt A C North   +   to a Norwegian fjord. P/O Richards, along with
     Sgt E E J Snutch   +   Sgt North, is buried at Bergen (Mollendal)
     Church Cemetery; Sgt Snutch has no known grave.

16-17 May   9 Sqn   Wellington IC   R1267 WS-Y   Op: **Boulogne**
1941   Sgt L B Mitchell   +   T/o 2245 Honington. Crashed 0245 near the bomb
     Sgt T W Sutton   dump on return to base. G/C J A Gray, the
     Sgt D H Humphrey   Station Commander, and the Station Medical
     Sgt O J P Richards   inj   Officer, S/L J A McCarty, were quickly at the
     Sgt S D J Howorth   scene, entering the blazing bomber and pulling
     two of the crew, who were trapped, to safety.
In recognition of their heroism, both officers were awarded the George Medal.

78 Sqn   Whitley V   Z6493 EY-V   Op: **Köln**
P/O J A T Garrould   +   T/o 2243 Middleton St. George. Shot down by a
Sgt R S L Keymer   +   night-fighter (Uffz Pross, 3./NJG1) and crashed
F/S R J Garlish   +   0234 between Helenaveen (Noord Brabant) and
Sgt E Oakes   +   Maasbree (Limburg), Holland. All are buried
F/S A P Smith   +   in Jonkerbos War Cemetery, Nijmegen.

17 May   106 Sqn   Hampden I   P2099 ZN-K   **Training**
1941   P/O S J Harvey   +   Stalled and crashed 1545 while trying to make
     Sgt R R Adams   inj   an emergency landing at Uffington, 12 miles
     Sgt W A Campbell   +   ESE of Oakham, Rutland.
     AC2 T Kane   +

149 Sqn   Wellington IC   R1587 OJ-   **Training**
S/L A W J Clark   +   Crashed at Prickwillow, 4 miles NE of Ely,
P/O G H Cotton   +   Cambridgeshire, after colliding with Hurricane
Sgt C E Bushford   +   V7225 of 1401 Meteorology Flight. P/O Cotton,
Sgt A Pepper   +   who had trained before the war as an architect
Sgt R A Petter   +   at Sheffield University, died on his 21st
Sgt D G Gray   +   birthday.

17-18 May	**77 Sqn**	**Whitley V**	Z6578 **KN-**	**Op: Köln**
1941	Sgt K Gray	+	T/o 2230 Topcliffe. Crashed near Rotem	
	Sgt A Morris	pow	(Limburg), 6 km SSW of Maaseik, Belgium.	
	Sgt N B Pell	+	Those who died are buried in the Communal	
	Sgt T W A Crone	+	Cemetery at Rotem.	
	Sgt H Fraser	pow		

18 May	**139 Sqn**	**Blenheim IV**	L9413 **XD-D**	**Training**
1941	P/O A M Saunders RCAF	+	Crashed 1622 and burst into flames following	
	Sgt R L R Halbert	+	a low pass over an army gun battery at Acle,	
	Sgt P R Gordon	+	11 miles E of Norwich. The bomber collided with	
	Cpl G A Acton	+	a pear tree and then clipped the gable end of	
			Wingates House, causing severe structural damage	

to the building. Lt Packe was injured, along with another soldier at the camp.

	207 Sqn	**Manchester I**	L7393 **EM-V**	**Air Test**
	S/L J C Macintosh		T/o Waddington with a scratch crew to carry out	
			an engine test, following recent grounding of the	

Manchesters. An engine fire developed while over the Bristol Channel, but by skilful airmanship, S/L Macintosh succeeded in a crash-landing at Perranporth airfield, Cornwall. The airframe was later converted for instructional use.

	218 Sqn	**Wellington II**	W5448 **HA-Z**	**Training**
	P/O B E Lymbery	+	Crashed 1100 from a high speed dive, caused	
	Sgt K W Coates	+	by the dinghy breaking loose and fouling the	
	Sgt W F Webber RCAF	+	starboard elevator. The bomber came down at	
	Sgt L Crawshaw	+	Hilgay, 3 miles SSE of Downham Market, Norfolk.	
	Sgt G L M Bayley	+	Sgt Mew died two days later from his injuries.	
	Sgt R G Mew	inj		

21 May	**15 Sqn**	**Stirling I**	N3644 **LS-**	**Training**
1941	F/L E V Best		Undercarriage collapsed while taxying at Wyton.	

	83 Sqn	**Hampden I**	AD898 **OL-K**	**Transit**
	Sgt O N Stromberg	+	T/o 1735 Scampton but crashed ten minutes later	
	AC2 M F Cross	+	while preparing to land at the nearby airfield	
	AC2 J Metcalf	+	of Dunholme Lodge.	

	107 Sqn	**Blenheim IV**	L9272 **OM-**	**Op: Anti-shipping**
	Sgt R G Ratcliffe	pow	T/o 1400 Great Massingham. Ditched in the	
	F/S D J R Craig	+	vicinity of Heligoland. F/S Craig has no known	
	Sgt F J Smith	pow	grave. 107 Squadron had recently rejoined	
			Bomber Command from a long attachment with	

Coastal Command, during which time the Squadron lost at least three crews.

	110 Sqn	**Blenheim IV**	V6390 **VE-**	**Op: Circus 10**
	Sgt M G Jackson	+	T/o 1547 Wattisham to bomb a power station at	
	Sgt J A Donovan	+	Gosnay. Crashed near Allouagne (Pas-de-Calais),	
	Sgt T Beattie	+	32 km NNW of Arras, France. The crew are buried	
			in Allouagne Communal Cemetery.	

24 May	**105 Sqn**	**Blenheim IV**	T1826 **GB-**	**Training**
1941	W/C H I Edwards		Overshot and crashed while trying to land at	
	Sgt Ashplant		Hendon airfield, Middlesex. No injuries reported.	
	Sgt Quinn			

	110 Sqn	**Blenheim IV**	V5426 **VE-**	**Op: Anti-shipping**
	P/O M A Scott	+	T/o 1125 Wattisham. Believed shot down at 1430	
	P/O J Gill	+	N of Texel by Lt Runger, 2./JG52. All are	
	Sgt R A Hewlett	+	commemorated on the Runnymede Memorial.	

25 May	**18 Sqn**	**Blenheim IV**	L8864 **WV-W**	**Op: Anti-shipping**
1941	Sgt F Wood	+	T/o 0550 Oulton. Crashed 0810 in the vicinity of	
	Sgt E G Baker	+	Vrist (Ringkobing), Denmark, following an attack	
	Sgt C N Harris	pow	on 1500 ton cargo ship. Those who died are buried	
			in Lemvig Cemetery. This Blenheim is believed to	

have completed at least forty-two operational sorties.

25 May 1941	18 Sqn	Blenheim IV	V6248 WV-	Op: Norderney

F/S D G Keane +
Sgt G M Duffus +
Sgt I F Gow +

T/o 1407 Oulton. Became separated from the main formation and is believed to have been shot down by Oblt Leesman, I./JG52. All are commemorated on the Runnymede Memorial.

	105 Sqn	Blenheim IV	R3707 GB-U	Op: Anti-shipping

P/O G E J Rushbrooke +
Sgt G E Green +
Sgt S Parr +

T/o 1405 Swanton Morley. Last seen flying towards Ameland and is believed to have been shot down by Uffz Netter, I./JG52. All are commemorated on the Runnymede Memorial.

	139 Sqn	Blenheim IV	R2791 XD-	Op: Anti-shipping

Sgt G A Bye RCAF +
Sgt W G Thorneycroft +
Sgt S B Bransby +

T/o 0513 Horsham St. Faith to patrol Beat 9. Hit by flak, believed from the Spessbrecker Sylvia, and crashed in the sea off IJmuiden. All are commemorated on the Runnymede Memorial. It is reported that the Blenheim was engaged on its forty-eighth sortie.

	311 Sqn	Wellington IA	N3010 KX-L	Training

P/O S Zeinert inj
Sgt F Dusek +
Sgt M Stocek +
P/O M Svic inj
Sgt J Cermak inj
Sgt M Vild inj

T/o 1130 Langham for an air gunnery exercise but climbed erratically before stalling into trees bordering a field adjacent to the airfield. The Wellington burst into flames on impact. P/O Svic and P/O Zeinert died from their injuries. Along with the rest who died, they are buried in East Wretham (St. Ethelbert) Churchyard.

26-27 May 1941	106 Sqn	Hampden I	P2083 ZN-	Op: Gardening

Sgt L A Forty +
Sgt A Wood inj
Sgt N G Lines inj
Sgt R Thompson inj

T/o 2240 Coningsby for a mining operation off Brest. Ran short of fuel and crashed heavily while trying to land at Wellesbourne Mountford airfield, Warwickshire.

27-28 May 1941	49 Sqn	Hampden I	AD729 EA-N	Op: Gardening

S/L D A Smith +
Sgt J R Butler +
F/S J G Leslie +
Sgt G Hadaway +

T/o Scampton to lay mines off Brest. Lost without trace. All are commemorated on the Runnymede Memorial.

	150 Sqn	Wellington IC	R1044 JN-Y	Op: Boulogne

Sgt V D Huggett +
Sgt V E Pereira +
Sgt P Jarvis +
Sgt E B Wilcox +
Sgt M E Gardiner +
Sgt Edmunds inj

T/o 0145 Newton. Crashed 0445 on Colborough Hill, Halstead, 10 miles E of Leicester. Moments before the crash, the Wellington had emerged from the cloud in order for the crew to establish their position. On impact, the bomber broke into two sections.

	304 Sqn	Wellington IC	R1392 NZ-	Op: Boulogne

P/O J S Waroczewski +
F/O B Kuszczynski +
P/O C Wieczorek +
Sgt Nilski
Sgt Josefiak inj
Sgt J Drozdz +

T/o 2257 Syerston. Hit by flak in the port engine and later crashed at Darwell Hole, 1 mile S of Brightling, 11 miles NW of Hastings, Sussex. Sgt Drozdz baled out, either over the target or in the sea, while the two survivors parachuted over Kent, Sgt Josefiak being taken to a hospital at Tonbridge for treatment. Three of the four who died are buried in Newark Cemetery.

28 May 1941	82 Sqn	Blenheim IV	V6457 UX-T	Op: Heligoland

Sgt J H McGowan +
Sgt A L Walker +
Sgt D N Banks +

T/o 1258 Bodney. Presumed lost over the sea. Sgt McGowan is buried on Terschelling; his crew are commemorated on the Runnymede Memorial.

28-29 May 1941	78 Sqn	Whitley V	Z6484 EY-	Op: Kiel

Sgt A T Copley +
Sgt W B Smith RCAF +
Sgt A Cooke +
Sgt A Gregory +
Sgt D R Stickland +

T/o 2355 Middleton St. George. All are buried in Becklingen War Cemetery, Soltau.

30 May **1941**	**50 Sqn** P/O J C Cunningham Sgt W Hall	**Hampden I** + +	**AD867 VN-**	**Air Test**

Stalled while turning and crashed 1120 some 50 yards from Hale Hill Farm, between Hatfield and Hatfield Woodhouse, 2 miles NW of Lindholme.

2 Jun **1941**	**18 Sqn** F/L I A Mead Sgt C C G Ashcroft Sgt W F Richards	**Blenheim IV** + + +	**L9192 WV-Q**	**Op: Kiel Canal**

T/o 1902 Oulton. Believed to have been shot down some 160 km W of Texel by Ofw Karl Munz, 2./JG52. All are commemorated on the Runnymede Memorial. The Blenheim, it is reported, was engaged on its forty-third sortie when lost.

139 Sqn   **Blenheim IV**   **V6239 XD-**   **Op: Kiel Canal**
Sgt F Boroski RCAF   +
Sgt L A Slade   +
Sgt A Ball   +

T/o 1807 Horsham St. Faith. Lost without trace. All are commemorated on the Runnymede Memorial.

2-3 Jun **1941**	**7 Sqn** F/O J Mitchell Sgt P B E Smith Sgt D G Clark F/S A N Wynne Sgt J G Armstrong Sgt E Clarke Sgt W S Bellow	**Stirling I** + + + + + + pow	**W7430 MG-**	**Op: Berlin**

T/o 2250 Oakington. Last heard on w/t at 0018 and plotted W of Hamburg. Subsequently, shot down by a night-fighter from 2./NJG3 and crashed between Dobbrikow and Hennickendorf, 10 km NW of Luckenwalde, Germany. Those who died are buried in the 1939-1945 War Cemetery at Berlin.

40 Sqn   **Wellington IC**   **R1438 BL-U**   **Op: Düsseldorf**
Sgt P D Sargent   +
Sgt E A B Beadman   +
Sgt A Hicks RCAF   +
Sgt R W Body   +
Sgt L D Dougherty RCAF +
Sgt Hillebrandt   inj

T/o 0015 Alconbury. Stalled and crashed 0500 in the aerodrome circuit after returning to base.

50 Sqn   **Hampden I**   **AD797 VN-**   **Op: Düsseldorf**
P/O P B Hodgson   +
P/O P R D Brown   +
Sgt J T Donnelly   +
Sgt G T Cheetham   +

T/o Lindholme. All are buried in Leopoldsburg War Cemetery, Belgium. As a second pilot, P/O Hodgson had survived two crashes earlier in the year.

58 Sqn   **Whitley V**   **P4991 GE-N**   **Op: Düsseldorf**
Sgt D H Roberts   pow
Sgt J L S Flanagan   pow
P/O J K Lyon   pow
Sgt W S Donnelly   pow
Sgt C Bamford   pow

T/o 2314 Linton-on-Ouse.

61 Sqn   **Hampden I**   **P2144 QR-**   **Op: Düsseldorf**
Sgt P Sleight
Sgt Woods
Sgt Burrows
Sgt Lodington

T/o 2251 Hemswell. Force-landed 0445 at East Dereham, Norfolk, after running out of fuel while trying to reach Bircham Newton. No injuries reported.

61 Sqn   **Hampden I**   **X3120 QR-**   **Op: Düsseldorf**
Sgt W Asson   pow
Sgt N M Campbell   pow
Sgt H G Johnson   pow
Sgt C E Hawkes   pow

T/o 2258 Hemswell. Believed to have run short of petrol and ditched.

214 Sqn   **Wellington II**   **W5450 BU-**   **Op: Berlin**
W/C R B Jordan
P/O C McD Didsbury RNZAF
F/O K J Falconer DFC
Sgt Crofts
Sgt Jones
Sgt G A D Cotton

T/o 2220 Stradishall. Stalled and crashed 0600 at Mile End Farm, Hartest, 7 miles SSW of Bury St. Edmunds, Suffolk. The bomber collided with trees, but there was no fire and only one crew member was hurt. The crew returned to base riding in a farmer's cart!

3 Jun 1941	226 Sqn P/O D E S Hawkins	Blenheim IV +	Z7286 MQ- Collided, while taking-off from Wattisham with	Training

a Blenheim captained by the Squadron's CO and burst into flames. P/O Hawkins was flying solo at the time of the accident.

	226 Sqn W/C Harrison Sgt Woodward Sgt W R Mathias	Blenheim IV inj inj	Z7287 MQ- Lost in the circumstances described above. The injured airmen were admitted to Ipswich and East Suffolk Hospital.	Training

Note. Following the withdrawl of the AASF from France in mid-June 1940, 226 Squadron had been relegated to second-line duties in Northern Ireland and still equipped with Battles. Conversion to the Blenheim began in the early part of 1941 and the Squadron returned to Bomber Command control at Wattisham on 26 May 1941.

4 Jun 1941	139 Sqn P/O W Baser Sgt A W Simpson RNZAF Sgt C E Triggs	Blenheim IV + + +	R3903 DX- T/o 1900 Horsham St. Faith. Believed shot down by Uffz Nöcker, 3./JG1, W of Bergen-aan-Zee, Holland.	Op: De Kooy

	139 Sqn P/O I A Lees Sgt T C Osborne Sgt C Meredith	Blenheim IV + + +	Z5744 XD- T/o 1900 Horsham St. Faith. Believed shot down in the circumstances previously described. Both crews are commemorated on the Runnymede Memorial.	Op: De Kooy

	214 Sqn Sgt Leeke Sgt Cooper	Wellington IC	R1611 BU-X Crashed and burnt out after colliding with trees near Manea Station, 5 miles SE of March, Cambridgeshire, on the main Cambridge to	Training

Peterborough railway line. Details of this accident are omitted from the Squadron records, but it is reliably reported that moments before the crash, the Wellington had passed low over a field, frightening some farm workers. Sgt Cooper was the aircraft's wireless operator.

	405 Sqn	Wellington II	W5487 LQ- Destroyed by fire 0144 at Driffield, following	Ground

an air raid. This was the first bomber to be written off from an RCAF squadron and a note appended to 405 Squadron RCAF records states that W5487 had been allotted to Sgt Arthur Walroth RCAF.

7 Jun 1941	105 Sqn P/O L S Clayton Sgt A J Stiddard P/O V E G Phillips	Blenheim IV + + +	V6316 GB- T/o 1755 Swanton Morley to patrol Beat 8. Shot down by Me 109s off Terschelling. All are commemorated on the Runnymede Memorial.	Op: Anti-shipping

	107 Sqn Sgt H F Fordham P/O T B Grenon Sgt R G L Morley	Blenheim IV + + +	T1921 OM- T/o 0915 Great Massingham. Lost without trace. P/O T B Grenon was the son of a vicar, the Revd N E Grenon.	Op: Anti-shipping

	107 Sqn Sgt F S B Knox Sgt G A Kaye Sgt M V Berry	Blenheim IV + + +	T2047 OM- T/o 0915 Great Massingham. Lost without trace. Sgt Berry was the son of the Revd A M Berry. Neither crew have any known graves.	Op: Anti-shipping

8 Jun 1941	139 Sqn Sgt C F Matthews P/O G A Prosser Sgt G Mason	Blenheim IV + + +	T1795 XD- Failed to return from a practice bombing exercise. All are commemorated on the Runnymede Memorial.	Training

8-9 Jun 1941	51 Sqn Sgt G Stubbs P/O J R Pertwee Sgt W C G Roper Sgt C F Ranson F/S J Cousins	Whitley V + + + + +	Z6663 MH-D T/o 2240 Dishforth. Crashed 0500 and exploded in a quarry in the Cleveland Hills near Ingleby Greenhow, 4 miles ESE of Stokesley, Yorkshire.	Op: Dortmund

8-9 Jun 1941	78 Sqn	Whitley V		Z6571 EY- Op: Dortmund

8-9 Jun 1941

78 Sqn — **Whitley V** — **Z6571 EY-** — **Op: Dortmund**

Sgt D R Simm	+
Sgt J S Tomkinson	+
P/O A V Snelling	+
Sgt J B Stevens	+
F/S G Billing	+

T/o 2300 Middleton St. George. Crashed while descending through cloud and burst into flames in a small wooded valley near Ellingstring, 4 miles NW of Masham, Yorkshire.

9 Jun 1941

9 Sqn — **Wellington IC** — **R1758 WS-** — **Op: Reconnaissance**

W/C R G C Arnold MiD	+
Sgt J M Pinkham	pow
F/O D Bruce	pow
Sgt H A Wink	pow
Sgt R H Barratt	pow
F/O T A Bax	pow

T/o 1530 Honington for an armed reconnaissance off the French and Belgian coasts. Intercepted NE of Calais by Me 109s and shot down into the sea off Zeebrugge, Belgium. W/C Arnold is buried in Blankenberge Communal Cemetery. While in captivity, Sgt Barratt exchanged identity with Rifleman G S Godden of the Rifle Brigade.

9 Sqn — **Wellington IC** — **T2620 WS-G** — **Op: Reconnaissance**

F/O D F Lamb DFC	+
Sgt C J Partington	+
Sgt D J Mansfield	+
Sgt D A Humphrey	+
Sgt R S Bunce	+
Sgt W A Eccles	pow

T/o 1536 Honington. Lost in circumstance similar to those just described. Sgt Mansfield rests in the Canadian War Cemetery at Adegem, Belgium, while at Vlissingen in Holland can be found the grave of Sgt Partington, whose parents lived in Buenos Aires. The rest of those who died are commemorated on the Runnymede Memorial.

18 Sqn — **Blenheim IV** — **V6427 WV-B** — **Op: Anti-shipping**

Sgt L B Box	+
P/O P Molloy	+
Sgt G K Bass	+

T/o 1516 Oulton. Last seen 1543 entering a fog bank off the Dutch coast. At 0100 on 3 July 1941 the MV Maso recovered the body of Sgt Box. He now rests in Bergen op Zoom War Cemetery; his crew being commemorated on the panels of the Runnymede Memorial.

18 Sqn — **Blenheim IV** — **V6428 WV-M** — **Op: Anti-shipping**

F/S I A Bullivant	+
F/S S D Gallery	+
F/S R F Hind	+

T/o 1518 Oulton. Shot down 1705 by a Me 110 in position 5335N 0622E. F/S Bullivant is buried in Anjum (Friesland) Protestant Cemetery; his crew have no known graves.

11 Jun 1941

107 Sqn — **Blenheim IV** — **V6367 OM-** — **Op: Anti-shipping**

Sgt P J Walker	+
P/O R G Sammons	+
Sgt V A Lewis	+

T/o 0913 Great Massingham. Recalled due to lack of cloud cover, but disappeared without trace. All are commemorated on the Runnymede Memorial.

11-12 Jun 1941

40 Sqn — **Wellington IC** — **R1323 BL-J** — **Op: Düsseldorf**

S/L M E Redgrave	pow
Sgt A F Potter RNZAF	pow
Sgt C Rofe	evd
Sgt P Rockingham	pow
Sgt R Alldrick RCAF	pow
Sgt J A S Abernethy	pow

T/o 2340 Alconbury. Shot down by Marine flak and crash-landed 0121 on a sand bank off Hellevoetsluis, Holland.

40 Sqn — **Wellington IC** — **R1464 BL-L** — **Op: Düsseldorf**

P/O R F Payne	+
Sgt M S Soames	+
P/O L J Moore	+
Sgt N S Wilson	+
Sgt G L Tompson	+
Sgt E W Tyler	+

T/o 2340 Alconbury. Shot down by a night-fighter (Lt Gerhard Loos, I./NJG1) and crashed 0132 at Meerlo (Limburg) 16 km NNW of Venlo, Holland, where the crew were first buried. Since 1945, their remains have been taken to Jonkerbos War Cemetery.

51 Sqn — **Whitley V** — **Z6657 MH-A** — **Op: Duisburg**

F/S H Hannay MiD	+
P/O P E Snyder RCAF	+
Sgt J E Gittins	+
Sgt C G Humble MiD	+
Sgt J Bradshaw	+

T/o 2306 Dishforth. Shot down by a night-fighter (Lt Reinhold Knacke, I./NJG1) and crashed 0316 at Borkel (Noord Brabant), 6 km SW of Valkenswaard, Holland. All are buried in Eindhoven (Woensel) General Cemetery.

11-12 Jun   **61 Sqn**   Hampden I   **AD727 QR-**   **Op: Gardening**
1941

F/O P H H Pritchard	+	T/o 2245 Hemswell to lay mines in Kiel Bay.
P/O F A Caunter-Jackson	+	Shot down by flak. F/O Pritchard was found
F/S P J Breene	+	in the area of Maglehoj Strand, Lolland Island,
Sgt J Bestwick	+	Denmark, where he is buried in Kappel Cemetery.

Sgt Bestwick rests in Kiel War Cemetery, while
the remainder of the crew are commemorated on the Runnymede Memorial.

99 Sqn   Wellington IC   **P9281 LN-**   **Op: Düsseldorf**

Sgt J A Barron	+	T/o Waterbeach. Shot down by a night-fighter.
Sgt W W Hall	pow	Both survivors were wounded, Sgt Harley being
Sgt D H Harley	pow	the most seriously hurt with shrapnel embedded
Sgt J A S Reid	+	in his back. Those who died are buried in
Sgt A E Hibbin	+	Uden War Cemetery.
Sgt J Beattie	+	

Note. In 1989 Sgt Hall wrote a brief report of this action, followed by an
account of his time spent as a prisoner of war. His book was published by
Merlin Books Limited under the title, Flyer's Tale.

99 Sqn   Wellington IC   **W5680 LN-**   **Op: Düsseldorf**

Sgt D G Woodward	+	T/o Waterbeach. All are buried in the Reichswald
Sgt P H H Bratley	+	Forest War Cemetery.
Sgt R C Scott	+	
Sgt J K Cassels	+	
Sgt W McL Ritchie	+	
Sgt A J Arnold	+	

149 Sqn   Wellington II   **W5439 OJ-X The Wizard of Oz**   **Op: Düsseldorf**

Sgt W Harrison	pow	T/o 2343 Mildenhall. Hit by flak and crash-
Sgt G A Johnstone	pow	landed at Het Broek (Gelderland), 3 km NW of
Sgt C Morgan	pow	Berghagen, Holland.
F/S M T Kenny	pow	
F/S V G Anderson	pow	
W/O T E Schofield RNZAF	pow	

300 Sqn   Wellington IC   **W5666 BH-H**   **Op: Düsseldorf**

F/O S T Sedzik	pow	T/o 2306 Swinderby. Ditched, sometime after
Sgt L Maciej	pow	being fixed in position 5230N 0300E. Sgt Kruk-
P/O W A Sojka	pow	Schuster was repatriated to the United Kingdom
Sgt Z Chowanski	pow	on 5 February 1945.
Sgt W Weinberg	pow	
Sgt Kruk-Schuster	pow	

12 Jun   **305 Sqn**   Wellington IC   **R1017 SM-K**   **Training**
1941

F/L T Stefanicki	+	Crashed 1140 following a mid-air collision with
Sgt K Mruk	+	an Oxford from 2 SFTS over Elton, 12 miles E of
P/O S Kowalcze	+	Nottingham. The Oxford struck the Wellington in
Sgt J Krawczyk	+	the area of the astro dome and carried away the
P/O J M Wojtowicz	+	tail unit. Both aircraft crashed from 900 feet
F/O A Zirkwitz	+	and fell about 700 yards apart.

Note. The names and initials of the above have been checked against the
entries made in the Register of Service Burials for Newark Cemetery. In
this same document, the name of LAC William Robson Lawton appears and he
was the pilot of the Oxford aircraft referred to above.

12-13 Jun   **10 Sqn**   Whitley V   **Z6721 ZA-**   **Op: Schwerte**
1941

P/O M Littlewood	T/o 2302 Leeming. Turned back at the Dutch coast
Sgt A Poupard	with the port engine failing, but ditched 0135.
P/O Stevens-Fox	The crew launched the dinghy, but this capsized
Sgt Wilkinson	in the heavy swell, though after a long struggle
Sgt Harrison	the crew managed to haul themselves onto their
	upturned raft. At 0700 a He III overflew the

downed airmen and recognising their plight, the German pilot flew off and found
an RAF ASR launch, which he directed towards the near exhausted bomber crew.
All were rescued and brought to safety at Yarmouth.

2-13 Jun 1941	35 Sqn	Halifax I

35 Sqn   **Halifax I**
Sgt L W Bovington DFM
Sgt Meredith
P/O G A Eperon
Sgt Hammond
Sgt Rudlin
Sgt Coleman
Sgt Willingham

L9498 TL-T   **Op: Hüls**
T/o 2237 Linton-on-Ouse. Overshot the runway on return to base and crashed 0030. No serious injuries reported. Sgt Bovington gained his award while serving with 51 Squadron.

44 Sqn   **Hampden I**
F/S C T C Mercer   +
Sgt R K Main   +
F/S A Kossick   +
Sgt J R Park   +

P4310 KM-   **Op: Soest**
T/o 2250 Waddington. All are buried in the Reichswald Forest War Cemetery.

44 Sqn   **Hampden I**
F/L P J S Shaughnessy   pow
   DFC
Sgt J Wardrop   +
Sgt C W Townsend   pow
Sgt J E Hughff   pow

AE127 KM-   **Op: Soest**
T/o 2300 Waddington. Came down in the sea. Sgt Wardrop is commemorated on the Runnymede Memorial.

77 Sqn   **Whitley V**
Sgt D K McFarland   +
Sgt K R Wainwright RCAF   +
P/O G V Heslop   +
Sgt L S Dyer   +
Sgt D H J Pingel   +

T4279 KN-F   **Op: Schwerte**
T/o 2312 Topcliffe. Shot down by a night-fighter (Oblt Egmond Prinz zur Lippe Weissenfeld, 4./NJG1) and crashed 0110 on land owned by Mr Schmitt of Medemblikkerweg H54, Medemblik (Noord Holland), 15 km NW of Enkhuizen. All are buried in Bergen op Zoom War Cemetery.

102 Sqn   **Whitley V**
Sgt J Chapman   +
P/O R W Dawson   +
Sgt K R Winter   +
Sgt J M B Tunnah   +
Sgt J Hall   +
Sgt J F James RAAF   +

Z6489 DY-   **Op: Schwerte**
T/o 2306 Topcliffe. Shot down by a night-fighter (Lt Reinhold Knacke, I./NJG1) and crashed 0318 on land belonging to Mr De Bie Gagelse Akkers at Waalre (Noord Brabant), 7 km SSW of Eindhoven. All are buried in Woensel General Cemetery.

102 Sqn   **Whitley V**
Sgt N B Berndsson
P/O D N Sampson
Sgt P S Thompson
Sgt C Higson
Sgt G W Griffin
Sgt H Young

Z6565 DY-   **Op: Schwerte**
T/o 2348 Topcliffe. Returned safely to base at 0623 but written off with unspecified damage.

103 Sqn   **Wellington IC**
F/O R S Chisholm   +
P/O A V J Hardcastle   +
F/O W C Taffender   +
F/S A Greensides   +
Sgt A G Burbridge   +
F/S J K E Horniman   +

T2996 PM-C   **Op: Osnabrück**
T/o 2300 Newton. Shot down by a night-fighter (Ofw Hans Rasper, 4./NJG1) and crashed 0037 on land owned by Mr Langendijk, Z22A Zwaagdijk Werv-ershoof (Noord Holland), 10 km W of Enkhuizen. Most are buried at Jonkerbos War Cemetery, with one grave in Bergen General Cemetery.

115 Sqn   **Wellington IC**
Sgt Robson
Sgt Keating
Sgt Tilson
Sgt Bennett
Sgt Green
Sgt G S Aikenhead   inj

R1721 KO-R   **Op: Hamm**
T/o 2342 Marham. Returned to base with failing engines and crashed 0305 after colliding with trees near the airfield. Sgt Aikenhead died from his injuries on 15 June. He is buried in Marham (Holy Trinity) Churchyard.

301 Sqn   **Wellington IC**
F/O Pozyczka   inj
P/O Plawski
F/O Voelmagel
Sgt K Brzozowski
Sgt Pchalek
Sgt Zuk

R1348 GR-   **Op: Osnabrück**
T/o 2307 Swinderby. Overshot and crashed 0201 on return to base, colliding with a Wellington that had landed some thirty-four minutes earlier.

| 12-13 Jun 1941 | 301 Sqn | Wellington IC | GR-K | Ground |

Landed safely at Swinderby from operations at 0127, after which it was hit and damaged beyond repair by another Wellington which had overshot the runway.

| 13-14 Jun 1941 | 44 Sqn | Hampden I | AE129 KM- | Op: Gardening |

Sgt S P C Saunders +
Sgt J R Miller +
Sgt R Greenaway +
Sgt T J Dickson +

T/o 2330 Waddington. Crashed 0050 at Southrey, 8 miles WSW of Horncastle, Lincolnshire.

| | 102 Sqn | Whitley V | Z6510 DY- | Op: Schwerte |

Sgt K P Glassborow +
F/O S V Alderton +
Sgt I P Hunter +
Sgt C T F Baldwin +
Sgt A C Fletcher +
Sgt J R Fraser +

T/o 2257 Topcliffe. Shot down by flak and crashed at Kirchhellen, 20 km NNW of Essen. All are buried in the Reichswald Forest War Cemetery.

| 14 Jun 1941 | 110 Sqn | Blenheim IV | V6334 VE- | Op: Circus 12 |

F/L P Windram +
P/O P R G Howes +
Sgt R L Cox +

T/o Wattisham to bomb the airfield at St-Omer. Presumed lost over the sea. F/L Windram is buried in Boulogne Eastern Cemetery; P/O Howes rests in Bergen op Zoom War Cemetery, while Sgt Cox is commemorated on the Runnymede Memorial.

| 15 Jun 1941 | 76 Sqn | Halifax I | L9514 MP- | Training |

P/O A E Lewin

Landed on the secondary runway at Middleton St. George, but veered to right and the starboard undercarriage unit collapsed when the wheel dug into the soft ground. This was the first aircraft written off by the Squadron since reforming as a bomber unit at Linton-on-Ouse on 12 April 1941.

| | 105 Sqn | Blenheim IV | V6319 GB- | Op: Anti-shipping |

F/O P H Watts +
F/S D D Milroy +
Sgt P B Murray +

T/o 1844 Swanton Morley to patrol Beat 10. Shot down while attacking a flotilla of 10 E-boats off Scheveningen. F/O Watts has no known grave, but his crew are buried at Hoek van Holland.

| | 110 Sqn | Blenheim IV | V6375 VE- | Op: Anti-shipping |

F/S A E Guesford +
Sgt C F Shearn +
Sgt L P C Rolfe +

T/o 1827 Manston to patrol Beats 9 and 10. Crashed in the North Sea. Sgt Shearn has no known grave; the rest of the crew are buried in Kirkeby Cemetery, Denmark.

| 15-16 Jun 1941 | 35 Sqn | Halifax I | L9506 TL-X | Op: Hannover |

F/O J W Murray DFM
P/O D S S Wilkerson
Sgt Nixon
Sgt Constable
Sgt Mennie
Sgt Martin
Sgt Colgan

T/o 2325 Linton-on-Ouse. Badly shot about in the target area by a night-fighter and later crash landed at Bircham Newton airfield, Norfolk. No injuries reported.

| | 106 Sqn | Hampden I | AD863 ZN- | Op: Köln |

P/O D G Dickie +
Sgt A L Glaves +
Sgt P Somers +
Sgt E R Hall +

T/o 2300 Coningsby. Lost without trace. All are commemorated on the Runnymede Memorial. P/O Dickie was a New Zealander serving with the RAF.

| 16 Jun 1941 | 18 Sqn | Blenheim IV | V6512 WV-K | Op: Anti-shipping |

P/O I W Watson +
P/O E K Aires +
Sgt T Dean +

T/o 1523 Oulton to patrol Beat 10. Shot down by ship's flak off Hoek van Holland. All are commemorated on the Runnymede Memorial.

5 Jun
941

21 Sqn   **Blenheim IV**   **V6034 YH-D**   **Op: Anti-shipping**

F/S E A R Leavers DFM	+
Sgt I Overhue DFM, RNZAF	+
Sgt J W H Phelps	+

T/o 1319 Watton. Crashed into the sea off the Frisian Islands after colliding with the mast of the ship being attacked. Thus died a crew that had gained a reputation for showing outstanding courage in low level attacks on enemy shipping. F/S Leavers is buried in Baflo (Den Andel) Protestant Cemetery, Holland; his observer has no known grave, while Sgt Phelps rests in Sage War Cemetery, Oldenburg.

139 Sqn   **Blenheim IV**   **T1832 XD-**   **Op: Anti-shipping**

F/O R R Langley DFC	+
Sgt I D Scourfield	+
Sgt H Gretton	+

T/o 1521 Horsham St. Faith to patrol Beat 9. Shot down by Me 109s. Sgt Gretton is buried in Esbjerg (Fourfelt) Cemetery; the rest of the crew are commemorated on the Runnymede Memorial.

139 Sqn   **Blenheim IV**   **V6332 XD-**   **Op: Anti-shipping**

F/O K M Laird	+
Sgt L J G Wakefield	+
Sgt Robinson	inj

T/o 1522 Horsham St. Faith. Hit by flak and crashed 1740 while trying to force-land in a hayfield at Dakenham Hall Farm, Rackheath, 5 miles NE of Norwich, the Blenheim colliding with a large tree which totally wrecked the bomber.

5-17 Jun
941

9 Sqn   **Wellington IC**   **L7871 WS-B**   **Ground**

Burnt out at Honington while preparing to leave for operations. The unnamed crew escaped injury, but those aircraft waiting their turn to enter the runway had to be cancelled.

51 Sqn   **Whitley V**   **Z6479 MH-M**   **Op: Köln**

Sgt T J Baston	+
P/O C E Crichton	+
P/O K N Holland	pow
Sgt J L Evans	+
F/S D J Jefferis	+

T/o 2243 Dishforth. Shot down by a night-fighter (Ofw Reinhard Kollak, I./NJG1) and crashed 0226 at Houthalen (Limburg), 11 km NNE of Hasselt, Belgium. Three of those who died are buried in the Canadian War Cemetery at Adegem, while P/O Crichton has no known grave.

78 Sqn   **Whitley V**   **Z6492 EY-K**   **Op: Köln**

P/O D S W Lake	+
Sgt H T Ivory	+
Sgt R C Rae	+
Sgt H Bailey	+

T/o 2232 Middleton St. George. Lost without trace. All are commemorated on the Runnymede Memorial.

103 Sqn   **Wellington IC**   **N2849 PM-**   **Op: Duisburg**

S/L D D A Kelly	+
Three times MiD	
Sgt J D MacVicar RCAF	+
F/S S F Marais	+
Sgt L Beaumont	+
Sgt G Houghton	+
Sgt W Connell	+

T/o 2300 Newton. All are buried in Heverlee War Cemetery.

405 Sqn   **Wellington II**   **W5522 LQ-Q**   **Op: Köln**

Sgt W F MacGregor	+
P/O G H S Pullen	+
Sgt R T Martin	+
Sgt S N Harvey	+
Sgt J L Angell	+
F/S L V Goode	+

T/o 2303 Pocklington. Last heard on w/t at 0303. Presumed crashed in the sea midway between the Dutch coast and Ordford Ness, Suffolk. All are commemorated on the Runnymede Memorial. First crew lost flying with an RCAF bomber squadron.

7 Jun
941

115 Sqn   **Wellington IC**   **R1517 KO-Z**   **Air Test**

P/O A Y Evans	+
Sgt R O Docking RCAF	+
P/O A B Brown	+
F/S J R Hurt	+
Sgt H Brown	+
AC2 A Smith	+
Sgt D O Williams	inj

T/o 1555 Marham and climbed slowly to 500 feet, whereupon the Wellington turned through 180 degrees and dived back towards the ground. At about fifteen feet the bomber suddenly levelled out, but then crashed and burst into flames at Palgrave Farm, Sporle, 2 miles NE of Swaffham, Norfolk.

17-18 Jun	**58 Sqn**		**Whitley V**	**N1462 GE-V** **Op: Köln**
1941	P/O D F Walker	+		T/o 2255 Linton-on-Ouse. Shot down by a night-
	Sgt E E Weldon	+		fighter (Oblt Wolfgang Thimming, 2./NJG1) and
	Sgt F A Hatton	+		crashed 0234 some 2 km N of Best (Noord Brabant)
	Sgt J B Jones	pow		10 km NNW of Eindhoven. Those who died are buried
	Sgt D R Black	+		in Woensel General Cemetery.

144 Sqn		**Hampden I**	**AD926 PL-** **Op: Köln**
Sgt Caesar-Gordon			T/o Hemswell. Overshot and crashed 0430 on
P/O Pringle			return to base, finishing up just beyond the
Sgt Horton			airfield perimeter. No injuries reported.
Sgt E W Thompson			

18 Jun	**12 Sqn**	**Wellington II**	**W5354 PH-** **Ground**
1941			Destroyed by fire following a refueling
			accident at Binbrook airfield, Lincolnshire.

50 Sqn		**Hampden I**	**P4389 VN-** **Air Test**
Sgt L R Hinde	+		T/o 1850 Lindholme but crashed almost immediately
Sgt A Campbell	+		in a field beyond the airfield.
Cpl M E Balkin	+		
LAC H Barton	+		
AC2 P C Kemp	+		

18-19 Jun	**10 Sqn**		**Whitley V**	**Z6671 ZA-** **Op: Bremen**
1941	Sgt W R Bradford	+		T/o 2213 Leeming. Last heard on w/t at 0250 and
	Sgt E J Conry RCAF	+		it is believed the Whitley crashed seven minutes
	Sgt D W Griffiths	+		later into the sea off Ameland. The entire crew
	F/S W Kelly	+		are commemorated on the Runnymede Memorial.
	Sgt R O Rintoul	+		

78 Sqn		**Whitley V**	**Z6560 EY-** **Op: Bremen**
F/S V H Marks	+		T/o 2303 Middleton St. George. Lost without
Sgt J G Woolley	+		trace. All are commemorated on the Runnymede
Sgt W P Herman	+		Memorial.
Sgt J H Harris	+		

78 Sqn		**Whitley V**	**Z6661 EY-** **Op: Bremen**
P/O T C Richards	+		T/o 2300 Middleton St. George. Crashed at
F/S H R George	+		Lorup, 45 km SW of Oldenburg, Germany. All
Sgt C F Cook	+		are buried in the Reichswald Forest War
F/S R C Berwick	+		Cemetery. During the Battle of Britain,
			F/S Berwick had served with 25 Squadron.

300 Sqn		**Wellington IC**	**W5665 BH-M** **Op: Bremen**
Sgt W Paleniczek	+		T/o 2202 Swinderby. Believed shot down by
Sgt J Domanski	+		a night-fighter (Ofw Paul Gildner, 4./NJG1)
P/O W Cebrzynski	pow		and crashed 0257 into the Waddenzee, near
Sgt S Winek	pow		Ameland. Sgt Domanski and Sgt Bankowski were
Sgt W Sieczka	+		first buried in the Roman Catholic Cemetery at
Sgt P R Bankowski	+		Nes, but both now lie in Jonkerbos War Cemetery.

301 Sqn		**Wellington IC**	**R1365 GR-** **Op: Bremen**
P/O J P Krassowski	+		T/o 2224 Swinderby. Shot down by a night-
Sgt R Bonkowski	+		fighter (Ofw Paul Gildner, 4./NJG1) and crashed
F/O K Bernas	+		0234 into the sea off Terschelling.
Sgt S Franaszczuk	+		
Sgt M Manasia	+		
Sgt A Wagner	+		

305 Sqn		**Wellington IC**	**R1696 SM-** **Op: Bremen**
Sgt S Lewek	pow		T/o Syerston. Shot down by a night-fighter
Sgt E Olenyn	pow		(Oblt Egmont Prinz zur Lippe Weissendfeld,
P/O K Jaklewicz	pow		4./NJG1) and crashed 0058 in the Polder Het
Sgt K Debkowski	pow		Grootslag at Hoogkarspel (Noord Holland),
F/O K Zebebecki	+		6 km WSW of Einkuizen. F/O Zebebecki is
Sgt H Rogowski	+		buried in Bergen General Cemetery, while
			Sgt Rogowski rests in the Polish Field of
			Honour at Breda in the province of Noord Brabant.

19 Jun 1941	44 Sqn	Hampden I	AD747 KM-	Ferry

44 Sqn — **Hampden I** — **AD747 KM-** — **Ferry**

19 Jun 1941

P/O Lauderdale — inj
Sgt Drakeford — inj
LAC Wall — inj

T/o Ternhill after collecting the Hampden from 24 MU and crashed 1210 at Audleys Cross, 2 miles E of Market Drayton, Shropshire. All three crew members were badly burnt about the face and hands and were admitted to RAF Hospital Cosford for treatment. In addition to his burns, P/O Lauderdale sustained a fracture to the lumber section of his spine. This was his second accident in an aircraft of this type.

44 Sqn — **Hampden I** — **AD904 KM-** — **Ferry**

Sgt C F Greig — +
Sgt J O Walshe — +
Sgt T K Boardman — +

T/o Ternhill and witnessed the above crash. While circling the scene, the pilot lost control and dived into the ground.

49 Sqn — **Hampden I** — **P2068 EA-** — **Training**

Sgt J L Alden — inj

T/o Scampton and crash-landed 1530 at Weeton Cliff Farm, near the airfield. The cause of the accident, in which three crew members were hurt, was engine failure.

226 Sqn — **Blenheim IV** — **Z7282 MQ-** — **Training**

F/O M W Waddington
Sgt Thompson
Sgt Palmer

Ditched 5453N 0132E while on a training exercise over the North Sea. The crew were rescued and taken to Blyth, Northumberland.

19-20 Jun 1941

51 Sqn — **Whitley V** — **Z6563 MH-T** — **Op: Düsseldorf**

P/O A J Brewster — pow
Sgt P J M Thomas — pow
Sgt J B Whitworth — pow
Sgt A S Tarry — pow
Sgt Mann — pow

T/o 2303 Dishforth. It is believed that Sgt Mann was repatriated during one of the prisoner of war exchanges.

99 Sqn — **Wellington IC** — **R1537 LN-** — **Op: Köln**

S/L B J Rogers AFC — +
P/O J McB Kerr RNZAF — pow
Sgt R I Gemmill RCAF — pow
Sgt R H Davis — pow
Sgt H Mahoney — pow
Sgt H H Bedard RCAF — +

T/o Waterbeach. The two airmen who died are buried in the Reichswald Forest War Cemetery.

20 Jun 1941

105 Sqn — **Blenheim IV** — **V6336 GB-** — **Training**

Sgt D O Beacham — +
Sgt P G Griffiths — +
Sgt N W Appleby — +
LAC R C Ballard — +
AC1 G McFadzean — +

Spun and crashed 1400 at East End Farm, Billingford, 15 miles NW of Norwich and to the N of Swanton Morley airfield.

20-21 Jun 1941

218 Sqn — **Wellington IC** — **R1339 HA-J** — **Op: Kiel**

Sgt G G Jillett RNZAF — +
Sgt R H Burr — +
Sgt N R P Goodenough — +
Sgt B J Mees — +
Sgt W A J Davis — +
Sgt A G Venn — +

T/o 2220 Marham. Last heard on w/t at 0335 calling for assistance. At the time of the transmission, the Wellington was plotted 60 miles off the enemy coast. The names of the crew are commemorated on the Runnymede Memorial.

218 Sqn — **Wellington IC** — **R1713 HA-V** — **Op: Kiel**

Sgt M J Fraser RNZAF — +
Sgt J A Donald — +
Sgt D A Dacre RNZAF — +
Sgt W J Baird — +
Sgt D H Harrison — +
Sgt H Hutchinson — +

T/o Marham. Heard on w/t asking for help, after which the bomber disappeared without trace. All are commemorated on the Runnymede Memorial.

21 Jun 1941

21 Sqn — **Blenheim IV** — **V6450 YH-L** — **Op: Circus**

Sgt P Brown — +
Sgt L R Wilson — +
Sgt M D Brooker — +

T/o 1315 Watton. Shot down by Me 109s in the vicinity of St-Omer airfield. All are buried in Longuenesse Souvenir Cemetery at St-Omer.

21 Jun 1941	99 Sqn	Wellington IC	X9643 LN-	Training
	F/O A G Allen	+	\-	
	P/O F Rendall	+		
	Sgt W Bennett	+		
	Sgt J C Stewart	+		
	Sgt W H Lewis	+		
	Cpl C P Eva	+		

Crashed 2 miles ENE of Waterbeach airfield, Cambridgeshire and burst into flames. The accident was caused by the dinghy breaking loose and fouling the elevators.

	207 Sqn	Manchester I	L7310 EM-H	Air Test
	Sgt L Syrett	inj		
	S/L C J F Kydd	+		
	F/S J W Arnott	inj		

T/o Waddington and crashed almost immediately at Dunstan Pillar, just beyond the airfield. The accident was attributed to a loose tappet leading to a valve blockage, which resulted in engine failure. F/S Arnott died from his injuries on 20 July 1941, and it is believed that Sgt Syrett's injuries were so severe that he never returned to operational flying.

21-22 Jun 1941	207 Sqn	Manchester I	L7314 EMY-Y	Op: Boulogne
	F/O J D G Withers DFC	+		
	Sgt A M James	+		
	F/S W Brown DFM	+		
	F/S M V Browne	+		
	F/S A Malone	+		
	Sgt S Veitch	+		
	Sgt J A Maville RCAF	+		

T/o Waddington. Shot down by a Beaufighter from 25 Squadron and crashed 0155 at Wollaston, 9 miles ENE of Northampton. Apart from Sgt Veitch, who is buried in Mere Knolls Cemetery, Sunderland, the crew rest in Lincoln's Newport Cemetery.

Chapter 6

Mounting Losses

22 June to 8-9 July 1941

Almost a year to the day since forcing the French to accept their terms of armistice at Versailles, Germany attacked the Soviet Union. The Non-Aggression Pact signed by the two nations prior to the invasion of Poland was over and the Second World War was entering a new phase of turmoil.

In many ways the alliance between the two nations had been a strange one. Germany was held in the grip of its Fascist dictator, Hitler, while the Russian people cowered beneath the iron rule of Joseph Stalin and communism. It is difficult to imagine two such contrasting ideologies sharing a common aim and, in truth, it was merely a marriage of convenience settled between one despot and another. Furthermore, there is evidence to suggest that Hitler hoped that once he had begun his drive towards Moscow, Britain would respond by joining him in his crusade against the Soviets. If this is true, then he had seriously miscalculated the judgement of Churchill, who, within hours of the start of the invasion, broadcast his support of the Russians. Germany was irrevocably committed to a war on two fronts. Britain, and later America, was committed to supplying Russia with enormous quantities of aid, while at the same time having to bear the brunt of Stalin's frequent outbursts of undisguised hostility towards the west for failing to meet his demands for an early invasion of Europe.

Bomber Command's rôle was hardly affected by this latest German venture. On the actual day of the attack, 2 Group mounted a Circus operation in the direction of Hazebrouck. Six Blenheims, all drawn from 139 Squadron, participated and none were lost, though late in the day Group headquarters at Castlewood House was informed that a Fortress bomber from the recently reformed 90 Squadron had crashed in Yorkshire, killing seven airmen. This was the first loss of one of these new four-engined high-altitude American bombers on which many hopes had been pinned. The sole survivor, a Medical Officer attached to the Squadron from Farnborough, stated that the Fortress had flown into cumulus cloud at 33000 feet and within seconds of entering the cloud mass the airframe had begun to shake violently from the air turbulence.

Control was lost shortly afterwards as the bomber entered a steep dive, and at 25000 feet, approximately, structural failure of the bomber commenced. First, the port wing detached, followed by a gradual break up of the fuselage with the rear portion falling quite slowly. It was from this section of the doomed aircraft that the Medical Officer made good his escape.

The news was disquieting and though much time and effort was put into the programme, the Fortress in its present form proved to be unsuited for Bomber Command operations and the type was withdrawn in the autumn of 1941.

Night raiding towards the end of June 1941 continued to concentrate on shipping targets and industrial centres in the Ruhr Valley.

Relatively small forces were used and it was during an attack on Bremen by less than eighty bombers, that the Command suffered its most serious night losses of the war so far. The Whitley squadrons of 4 Group came off worst with eleven crews missing. 10 Squadron, based at Leeming, and 102 Squadron operating from Topcliffe, each reported four aircraft failing to return, while the rest of the Group's casualties came from another Topcliffe based unit, 77 Squadron. Most were down in the sea off the German coast, but the Royal Navy did manage to reach four survivors from one crew drifting 100 miles off the Yorkshire coast.

Three Wellington bombers were also missing and their loss brought the total for the night to fourteen aircraft.

Serious losses were sustained two nights later when Bremen was paid a return visit, but it was the news that four Stirlings had failed to return from a minor excursion to Hamburg that caused the most concern. Until now, Stirling losses had been minimal, but on this occasion the night-fighters got in amongst the force, claiming three of their number. A couple of Wellingtons were also casualties from the Hamburg raid, which, apart from the above average loss rate, was very successful. Fires were concentrated and much damage was caused, thus adding to that inflicted during the recent raids.

July got off to a brisk start with half-a-dozen Stirlings being sent out by day to try for targets of opportunity in north-west Germany. 7 Squadron had already lost one crew during a similar operation on 28 June when three of their number joined forces with a trio from 15 Squadron and headed for the inland port of Bremen. On that occasion the bombers were chased back across the sea by Me 109s, which succeeded in shooting down the 7 Squadron machine off Flamborough Head. Now a second crew was to perish in similar circumstances.

In general, these daylight raids by the heavy bombers produced few tangible results and the limited damage caused could in no way compensate for the loss of well trained crews. 2 Group, as so often has been told, was bearing the brunt of day operations and on the last day of June its squadrons tried to hit Bremen. Flying under the rather odd name of Operation Wreckage, twenty-eight Blenheims participated with seventeen crews reporting bombing at Kiel, Norderney and Sylt, as well as at the primary target.

Results were disappointing and on 4 July it was decided to repeat the exercise. The dubious honour of being chosen to lead the attack fell to 105 Squadron, based at Swanton Morley. Nine crews were selected, headed by their Australian born CO, Wing Commander H I Edwards, plus six from 107 Squadron led by Wing Commander L V E Petley. The formation, with Edwards in the lead, took off well before breakfast and flew at minimum height across the North Sea to make their landfall below Cuxhaven. Three bombers had already dropped out with technical problems, but the remainder now turned south and, still maintaining a good formation, pressed on towards their objective.

The weather was perfect; clear skies and almost unlimited visibility.

Reaction to the raid by the defenders was immediate and soon the sky was filled with light flak and tracer fire. At fifty feet, or less, the Blenheims made easy targets, but none turned about, despite repeated hits and near collisions with balloon cables and telegraph wires. Casualties, however, were inevitable and four aircraft were shot down, two from each squadron which included the CO of 107 Squadron.

The outstanding leadership displayed by Wing Commander Edwards was duly recognised by the award of an immediate Victoria Cross.

During the same day as this heroic Bremen operation, 226 Squadron flew a diversionary sweep towards Norderney with the purpose of drawing fighters away from the main raid. Light flak hit the leading Blenheim, which was piloted by the Squadron Commander, and moments later his aircraft exploded in a welter of flame and smoke. This was not the end of their suffering, for later in the day another crew was lost during a Circus raid on a chemical plant at Choques.

Further light bomber losses were recorded on the 6th and 7th July, with four Blenheims in total being shot down in the course of anti-shipping operations along the Dutch coast. Flak and fighters were probably responsible for three of the casualties, but one crew plunged into the sea after their aircraft hit the mast of a ship.

Nonetheless, despite the dreadful toll in human lives, the anti-shipping campaign was regarded as a success and, certainly, the night bombing of centres such as Hamburg, Bremen and Kiel had paid dividends. Brest too, had sustained severe damage to its port facilities and it was during a raid here on 1-2 July, that the Prinz Eugen took a direct hit which killed over sixty members of her crew.

Attention was also being given towards attacks on armament industries and Essen was visited on 3-4 July by a small force of Wellingtons and Whitleys. Bombing results were very disappointing, mainly due to thick amounts of cloud that covered most of the Ruhr. Four bombers failed to return and two more were written off in crashes.

Getting to grips with the industrial heart of Germany was never easy and very little was to be achieved in the summer of 1941.

| 22 Jun | 90 Sqn | Fortress I | AN522 WP- | Air Test |
| 1941 | F/O J C M Hawley | + | | |

T/o 1430 West Raynham. Crashed 1800 after flying into cumulus cloud at 33000 feet, followed by structural failure. Wreckage was scattered over a wide area of moorland, 10 miles N of Catterick, Yorkshire. F/L Steward escaped without serious injury.

Lt Bradley USAAC	+	
F/L J B W Humpherson DFC	+	
S/L D A H Robson MB, CH.B	+	
Sgt H P Black	+	
F/S G J Garwood	+	
Sgt T J Wills RCAF	+	
F/L Steward AFC		

| 22-23 Jun | 51 Sqn | Whitley V | T4237 MH-A | Op: Wilhelmshaven |
| 1941 | P/O G L Mattey | | | |

T/o 2304 Dishforth. Ditched 0415 approximately 30 miles off the Yorkshire coast. Sgt Grubb was unable to inflate his Mae West and he drowned before the crew could right the dinghy, which had capsized in the heavy swell. During this time, Sgt Jakeman tried to support Sgt Grubb,

Sgt Reimer		
Sgt Jakeman		
Sgt J H Grubb	+	
Sgt Troughton		

but in the conditions he was unable to maintain a grip on his unconscious colleague. The survivors were rescued at 0900 on 24 June by HMS Patrol Vessel Dane, which in turn put them aboard a fishing vessel making for Scarborough.

	83 Sqn	Hampden I	AD969 OL-X	Op: Bremen
	P/O R J Heavens	+		

T/o 2255 Scampton. Crashed near Bevern, Germany. All are buried in Becklingen War Cemetery, Soltau.

Sgt W G Price	+	
F/S E W Sponder	+	
F/S N E Byres	+	

22-23 Jun	301 Sqn	Wellington IC	R1026 GR-	Op: Bremen

22-23 Jun 1941

301 Sqn   Wellington IC   R1026 GR-   Op: Bremen

P/O S Pietruszka   +
Sgt Poplawski
F/O Sawlewicz
Sgt Florczak
Sgt C Tegowski   +
Sgt Sulgut

T/o 2158 Swinderby. Crashed 0400 following a fire in the starboard engine, which resulted in the propeller falling off. The Wellington came down at Winkburn, 6 miles NW of Newark-on-Trent, Nottinghamshire. The two airmen who died are buried in the Polish Plot at Newark Cemetery.

311 Sqn   Wellington IC   T2990 KX-T   Op: Bremen

F/S B Bufka   pow
F/S A Rozum   +
P/O V Konstacky   +
P/O L Smrcek   +
Sgt J Hejna   +
F/S K Valach   +

T/o 2316 East Wretham. Allegedly shot down by a night-fighter (Oblt Egmont Prinz zur Lippe Weissenfeld, 4./NJG1) and crashed 0213 in the Kostverloren Polder at Niewe Niedorp (Noord Holland), 14 km NE of Alkmaar. Those who died are commemorated on the Runnymede Memorial.

23 Jun 1941

107 Sqn   Blenheim IV   V5517 OM-   Op: Circus 20

F/O E T Fairbank   pow
Sgt R Buckingham   pow
P/O Harrison   pow

T/o 1858 Great Massingham to attack Mardyck airfield. Shot down by fighters over Dunkerque.

107 Sqn   Blenheim IV   V6195 OM-   Op: Circus 20

F/O M V Redfearn-Smith   +
Sgt J A Rudkin   +
Sgt K T Noakes   +

T/o 1858 Great Massingham. Shot down by fighters off Dunkerque. All are buried in the Eastern Cemetery at Boulogne.

23-24 Jun 1941

76 Sqn   Halifax I   L9492 MP-   Op: Kiel

P/O W K Stobbs   +
Sgt A Turner   +
Sgt J L Cullum   +
F/S G H Barnard   +
Sgt J S Lipton   pow
Sgt R S Adair   +

T/o 2309 Middleton St. George. Shot down by a night-fighter (Oblt Reinhold Eckardt, II./NJG1) and crashed 0232 at Eilendorf, 1 km S of Buxtehude, 20 km SW of Hamburg. Those who died are buried in Becklingen War Cemetery, Soltau. This was the first Halifax to be reported missing from air operations.

115 Sqn   Wellington IC   T2963 KO-A   Op: Kiel

P/O Sharpe
Sgt F E Tingley   inj
Sgt Brittan
Sgt Steele
Sgt Chandler

T/o 2259 Marham. On return the pilot tried to land by aid of a Lorenz Beam, but due to faulty equipment and diminishing fuel reserves, an emergency landing was made at Debach, 3 miles NW of Woodbridge, Suffolk. In doing so, the Wellington collided with Moat House council dwellings. Sgt Tingley died from his injuries on 25 June.

24-25 Jun 1941

57 Sqn   Wellington IC   R1608 DX-   Op: Kiel

Sgt H Ward   +
Sgt W R Sutherland RCAF   +
Sgt G L Bentley   +
Sgt R Straugham   +
Sgt A C Frost   +
Sgt T Jones   +

T/o 2215 Feltwell. Believed crashed in the sea near the target. Five bodies were identified and buried on 3 July in the Naval Garrison Cemetery, but since 1945 their remains have been moved to Kiel War Cemetery. Sgt Ward is commemorated on the Runnymede Memorial.

214 Sqn   Wellington IC   R1609 BU-   Op: Emden

Sgt G T Jones   +
P/O J Dodds-Forrest   +
Sgt G T Hunt   +
Sgt J C E Black   +
Sgt K J Barton RCAF   +
Sgt G A D Cotton   +

T/o 2359 Stradishall. Lost without trace. All are commemorated on the Runnymede Memorial. Sgt Cotton had survived a crash-landing earlier in the month on return from Berlin.

305 Sqn   Wellington IC   W5723 SM-F   Op: Boulogne

S/L M K Kielich   +
Sgt W Januszkiewicz   +
P/O Z Idzikowski
Sgt Z S Lewoniec   +
Sgt S Witczac   +
Sgt T Frankowski

T/o Syerston. Hit by flak over Boulogne and from a flak ship anchored off Calais, which damaged the port engine. On nearing Clacton, the order to bale out was given and the tail gunner landed safely on land. The rest of the crew fell into the sea and four were drowned. The bodies of S/L Kielich and Sgt Januszkiewicz were recovered from the water and taken to Newark Cemetery for burial.

25 Jun 1941	18 Sqn	Blenheim IV	V6259 WV-W	Op: Circus 23
	Sgt W H Mounser	+	T/o 1510 Oulton to bomb St-Omer airfield. Hit	
	Sgt G K Richards	+	by flak and crashed in the target area. Two of	
	Sgt W L Waite	+	the crew are buried in Longuenesse Souvenir	
			Cemetery; Sgt Richards has no known grave.	

	21 Sqn	Blenheim IV	V6381 YH-N	Op: Circus 22
	Sgt L J Richards		T/o 1117 Watton to bomb Hazebrouck marshalling	
	Sgt Oderbolz		yards. Crashed 1330 while landing at Southend	
	Sgt Field		airfield, Essex.	

Note. Since the beginning of March, 21 Squadron had lost sixteen Blenheims from which not one airman had survived until this, the seventeenth casualty.

25-26 Jun 1941	49 Sqn	Hampden I	X3060 EA-	Op: Gardening
	P/O D B Falconer		T/o 2320 Scampton to lay mines off the Frisians.	
	Sgt Stuart		Overshot on return to base at 0430 and cart-	
	Sgt Knowling		wheeled into a field. No serious injuries	
	Sgt Drinkwell		reported.	

Note. In due course P/O Falconer gained the DFC and AFC, rising in rank to Wing Commander before being killed on operations on 30 December 1944. He is buried in Rheinberg War Cemetery.

	49 Sqn	Hampden I	AD788 EA-V	Op: Kiel
	Sgt S N Hind	pow	T/o Scampton. Shot down in the target area,	
	Sgt C L Ray	+	either by flak or a night-fighter. Those who	
	Sgt P E Whiting	+	died are buried in Kiel War Cemetery.	
	Sgt C W Hancock	+		

	99 Sqn	Wellington IC	R1372 LN-	Op: Bremen
	Sgt J B Hancock	+	T/o 2338 Waterbeach. Lost without trace.	
	Sgt W R Welch	+	All are commemorated on the Runnymede Memorial.	
	P/O S R Andrews DFM	+	Both Melville's were of Scottish ancestry.	
	Sgt R S Peck	+		
	Sgt W W Melville	+		
	Sgt A Melville	+		

26-27 Jun 1941	40 Sqn	Wellington IC	R1406 BL-C	Op: Köln
	P/O D W Horrocks	+	T/o 2330 Alconbury. Crashed at St.-Laureins	
	P/O K F Glock	+	(Oost Vlaanderen), 7 km NW of Eeklo, Belgium.	
	P/O W G Green	+	Three of the crew are buried in the Canadian	
	Sgt L C Page	+	War Cemetery at Adegem; the remainder are	
	Sgt J S Clover	+	commemorated on the Runnymede Memorial.	
	Sgt T Morris	+		

	61 Sqn	Manchester I	L7304 QR-	Op: Kiel
	F/O K G Webb	+	T/o 2301 Hemswell. Crashed near Brunsbüttel,	
	P/O L J Glover	+	Germany. All are buried in Kiel War Cemetery.	
	F/S F Woodruff	+		
	F/S J Woodward	+		
	Sgt F S Haslemore RNZAF	+		
	P/O C McC Bateman	+		

Note. At this time, 61 Squadron had received only a few Manchesters and for several months to come would continue to use their Hampdens on operations.

	97 Sqn	Manchester I	L7374 OF-	Op: Kiel
	F/O F E Eustace DFC	+	T/o 2336 Coningsby. A w/t message was received	
	Sgt C K McKenzie RNZAF	+	indicating Sgt Penberthy had been killed during	
	F/S J J Clinch DFM	+	an engagement with a night-fighter. Later, the	
	F/S J Elkington	+	bomber crashed into the sea off Westerhever.	
	P/O A A Morgan	+	Four bodies were recovered and now lie buried	
	Sgt P V McLaren DFM, RNZAF	+	in Kiel War Cemetery. The rest are commemorated	
	Sgt C P Penberthy	+	on the Runnymede Memorial.	

26-27 Jun 1941	115 Sqn Sgt Skillen	Wellington IC	R1501 KO-X		Op: Köln

T/o Marham but the pilot retracted the under-carriage prematurely and the Wellington crashed through the boundary fence. No injuries reported.

150 Sqn	Wellington IC	R1644 JN-L	Op: Düsseldorf
P/O J W Sievers DFC	+		
P/O C R C Herbert	+		
P/O A G St J Ross	+		
Sgt W J Grieve	+		
Sgt H G Burgess	+		
Sgt F J Hart RCAF	+		

T/o 2305 Newton. Hit by flak and crashed 0400 at Grubbenvorst (Limburg), on the W bank of the Maas, 6 km NNW of Venlo, Holland. All were laid to rest in Venlo Military Cemetery, but since the ending of hostilities, their remains have been taken to Jonkerbos War Cemetery.

27 Jun 1941	311 Sqn	Wellington IC	R1594 KX-	Unknown

Destroyed by fire. The circumstances in which this Wellington was destroyed are not known. No accident card has been raised, but confirmation of its demise has been traced to Form 78, which indicates that the aircraft was consumed by fire.

27-28 Jun 1941	10 Sqn	Whitley V	P5016 ZA-	Op: Bremen
	Sgt A H Knape	+		
	Sgt D P Walker	+		
	P/O R V C Bolster	+		
	F/S E P Lewis	pow		
	Sgt A S Carson	+		

T/o 2230 Leeming. Those who died in the initial crash are buried in Hamburg Cemetery, Ohlsdorf. It is reported that F/S Lewis escaped from captivity in March 1944, but was recaptured in the July. It is further stated that he was handed over to the SS and was shot on 1 August 1944. His grave is now located in Poland at the Commonwealth War Cemetery in Malbork.

10 Sqn	Whitley V	P5055 ZA-	Op: Bremen
Sgt A G Rickcord	+		
Sgt C S Thomson	+		
Sgt G L Gane	+		
F/S R G Jones	+		
F/S L Hird	+		

T/o 2220 Leeming. All are buried in Hamburg Cemetery, Ohlsdorf.

10 Sqn	Whitley V	T4179 ZA-	Op: Bremen
Sgt J S Shaw	+		
P/O D V Bingham-Hall	+		
Sgt J M McAlonan	+		
Sgt D W Banham	+		
Sgt E Lawley	+		

T/o 2231 Leeming. All are buried in Becklingen War Cemetery, Soltau.

10 Sqn	Whitley V	Z6561 ZA-	Op: Bremen
Sgt N J Gregory	pow		
Sgt D D W Nabarro DCM	pow		
P/O J D Margrie	pow		
P/O G M Frame	pow		
P/O A K Watson	+		

T/o 2232 Leeming. Hit by flak over Kiel and abandoned 0030 over Kiel Bay. Miraculously, four were rescued some six hours later, but P/O Watson was pronounced dead when taken from the water. He is buried in Kiel War Cemetery. Sgt Nabarro escaped from captivity in November 1941, and eventually returned to the United Kingdom.

12 Sqn	Wellington II	W5391 PH-A	Op: Bremen
S/L G A Kitching	+		
F/S B A Rutterford	+		
F/O H Helmore	+		
F/S J M Pickering	+		
Sgt A A Bunker	+		
F/S C G Landon	+		

T/o 2300 Binbrook. Lost without trace. All are commemorated on the Runnymede Memorial.

57 Sqn	Wellington IC	R1794 DX-	Op: Bremen
Sgt M R Ross RAAF	+		
Sgt G H Tett RCAF	+		
Sgt W C Shepherd	+		
Sgt W F Towlson RCAF	+		
Sgt J O'Donnell	+		
Sgt C D Asher	+		

T/o 2300 Feltwell. Last heard on w/t at 0130. All are commemorated on the Runnymede Memorial.

27-28 Jun
1941

77 Sqn		Whitley V	Z6568 KN-B	Op: Bremen

Sgt B C C Harpur
F/O Dean
P/O I A Kayes
Sgt S R Mayston
Sgt Thuell

T/o 2238 Topcliffe. Hit by flak and later ditched approximately 100 miles E of Flamborough Head. During the rescue operation, a Lindholme dinghy was dropped near the crew and Sgt Harpur transferred to this, only to die on 29 June, shortly before the navy reached their position. His body was recovered and was later buried in his home village of Glemsford, Suffolk, where his father, the Reverend A C Harpur, was the Rector.

77 Sqn		Whitley V	Z6630 KN-	Op: Bremen

P/O R E Tidswell + T/o 2241 Topcliffe. Shot down by a night-
Sgt R B Edwards + fighter (Oblt Reinhold Eckardt, II./NJG1).
Sgt J L Ransson + All are buried in Hamburg Cemetery, Ohlsdorf.
Sgt L Dobinson +
Sgt G B Roberts +

77 Sqn		Whitley V	Z6647 KN-	Op: Bremen

P/O P Singleton + T/o 2232 Topcliffe. All are buried in
Sgt J C Goodwin + Becklingen War Cemetery, Soltau.
Sgt H G Chorlton +
Sgt J Humphries +
Sgt A N Williams +

102 Sqn		Whitley V	T4269 DY-	Op: Bremen

Sgt A P Nicoll + T/o 2236 Topcliffe. Crashed at Brunsbüttel,
P/O M N F Jones + Germany, where the crew were first buried.
P/O A Bleakley + Since the war, their remains have been taken
Sgt E G Whitehead + to Kiel War Cemetery.
Sgt R D Davidson +
Sgt A Pratt +

102 Sqn		Whitley V	T4297 DY-	Op: Bremen

Sgt J M Culley pow T/o 2231 Topcliffe. Shot down by a night-
Sgt W M Featherstone pow fighter.
Sgt B R Wallace pow
Sgt J N D Bailey pow
Sgt B N Booth pow

102 Sqn		Whitley V	Z6572 DY-	Op: Bremen

S/L W C McArthur DFM + T/o 2230 Topcliffe. Believed to have crashed
Sgt D M Philp + off the Weser/Elbe estuaries. Four bodies were
Sgt E J J Raper + recovered from the water and buried in various
Sgt W J Clarke + Germany cemeteries. Sgt Clarke has no known
F/S S S Carlile + grave.

Note. S/L McArthur was a veteran bomber pilot who, as a Sergeant pilot, had flown on 102 Squadron's first operation of the war, a Nickel raid by three aircraft over the Ruhr. His DFM had been Gazetted on 17 May 1940.

102 Sqn		Whitley V	Z6759 DY-	Op: Bremen

Sgt G D Jackson + T/o 2238 Topcliffe. Ditched in the sea.
Sgt N J Ranson pow Sgt Jackson is commemorated on the Runnymede
P/O R G Poulter pow Memorial.
Sgt J Urquhart pow
Sgt E W G Dickey pow

142 Sqn		Wellington II	W5386 QT-	Op: Bremen

P/O R A Lomax + T/o 2257 Binbrook. All are buried in Hamburg
Sgt H E Meadows + Cemetery, Ohlsdorf.
P/O A F Struthers +
Sgt P B N Cleburne +
Sgt H Nykerk +
Sgt P T Relf +

28 Jun 1941	7 Sqn	Stirling I	N6007 MG-	Op: **Bremen**

7 Sqn   Stirling I   N6007 MG-   Op: **Bremen**
F/L J K Collins +
Sgt W Hardie +
Sgt G T Webb RCAF +
Sgt C Kelly +
Sgt A T Cole +
F/S D W E Chapple +
Sgt F C Williams +

T/o 1358 Oakington. Shot down 1622 into the North Sea, 20 miles off Flamborough Head, following a running fight with Me 109s from I./JG52. The Stirling was observed to strike the water nose first and with such force that the fuselage broke into two sections. All are commemorated on the Runnymede Memorial.

---

29 Jun 1941   61 Sqn   **Manchester I**   L7315 QR-   **Training**
P/O C G Colborne +

Due to a con-rod failure an engine caught fire and the Manchester crashed in the vicinity of Grantham, Lincolnshire. The wireless operator, who was the sole crew member apart from the pilot, baled out and landed unhurt.

29-30 Jun 1941   7 Sqn   Stirling I   N3664 MG-Z   Op: **Hamburg**
F/O V R Hartwright DFM +
Sgt T G Young +
P/O H D Brander RCAF +
F/S J R Dale +
F/S D H G Poole DFM +
F/S A G Reading +
F/S C W D Brown +

T/o 2309 Oakington. Shot down by a night-fighter (Oblt Helmut Lent, 6./NJG1) and crashed at Zeven, 36 km NE of Bremen. All are buried in Becklingen War Cemetery, Soltau. Details of F/O Hartwright's DFM had appeared in the London Gazette on 7 June 1940, while F/S Poole gained his award for service with 115 Squadron.

---

7 Sqn   Stirling I   N6001 MG-   Op: **Hamburg**
S/L W T C Seale +
Sgt R L Barrett RAAF +
Sgt M G Brown +
F/S B W Grocock +
Sgt R E Walls +
Sgt L Whittle +
Sgt H T Archer +

T/o 2257 Oakington. Shot down by a night-fighter (Oblt Helmut Lent, 6./NJG1) and crashed Wesermünde-Bremerhaven. All are buried in Becklingen War Cemetery, Soltau.

---

15 Sqn   Stirling I   N6015 LS-A   Op: **Hamburg**
P/O C S Renshaw +
Sgt C R Batchellor +
Sgt J K Woodhams +
Sgt D G Brown +
Sgt A M Metaxa +
Sgt W P Grant RCAF +
Sgt S T O'Mara +

T/o 2320 Wyton. Shot down by flak and crashed into the sea off Kiel. Sgt Metaxa, Sgt Woodhams and Sgt Grant RCAF are buried in Kiel War Cemetery; the rest are commemorated on the Runnymede Memorial.

---

15 Sqn   Stirling I   N6016 LS-G   Op: **Hamburg**
Sgt R C Smith +
Sgt D Rees pow
Sgt D B Annesley RNZAF pow
Sgt T S Thorkilsen pow
Sgt W B Louch pow
Sgt L B McCarthy RNZAF pow
F/S R S Storie +

T/o Wyton. Shot down by a night-fighter and crashed at Ellerbek, 14 km NW of Hamburg. The two airmen who died are buried locally at Ohlsdorf.

---

40 Sqn   **Wellington II**   W5456 BL-P   Op: **Hamburg**
F/L A B Baird RNZAF +
P/O J H Walls +
F/S J N Lister +
Sgt A S Rowan +
Sgt S E Bird +

T/o 2245 Alconbury. Lost without trace. All are commemorated on the Runnymede Memorial.

---

50 Sqn   **Hampden I**   X3133 VN-   Op: **Kiel**
Sgt W D Hughes DFM +
Sgt C T Chipperfield +
Sgt A P Drane +
Sgt C R Wells +

T/o 2235 Lindholme. Shot down by a night-fighter (Oblt Reinhold Eckardt, II./NJG1) and crashed 0255 at Haseldorf, 24 km WNW of Hamburg, where all are buried in the Ohlsdorf district.

29-30 Jun 1941	78 Sqn	Whitley V	Z6664 EY-	Op: Bremen

29-30 Jun 1941

78 Sqn **Whitley V** **Z6664 EY-** **Op: Bremen**

Sgt R S Green	+
Sgt E R Ingram	+
Sgt K I Jones	+
Sgt A W Adams	+
F/S L Hird	+

T/o 2243 Middleton St. George. Presumed lost over the sea. Apart from F/S Hird, the crew are commemorated on the Runnymede Memorial.

106 Sqn **Hampden I** **AD895 ZN-** **Op: Bremen**

F/O M R F Baker	+
Sgt J H Bevans	+
Sgt M Ford	+
Sgt G E Smith	+

T/o 2315 Coningsby. Shot down by a night-fighter (Oblt Reinhold Eckardt, II./NJG1) and crashed 0255 to the S of Uetersen, 23 km NW of Hamburg. All are buried in Sage War Cemetery.

115 Sqn **Wellington IC** **R1509 KO-P** **Op: Hamburg**

P/O A F McSweyn RAAF	pow
P/O S W Wild	pow
P/O W Hetherington	pow
Sgt T L Davidson	pow
Sgt E A Gibbs	pow
Sgt J V Gill	inj

T/o 2306 Marham. Hit by flak over Bremen and soon afterwards the Wellington was raked by fire from a Me 110. The bomber was successfully abandoned, but Sgt Gill, who had been badly wounded when the fighter struck, landed in a tree and when he released his parachute harness, he fell forty feet to the ground. Critically injured, he died the next day in hospital. P/O McSweyn RAAF evaded capture for three days and was eventually arrested on a Luftwaffe base in the act of trying to steal a Me 110. He later escaped from captivity and returned safely to England, where he was awarded a Military Cross.

115 Sqn **Wellington IC** **R1508 KO-T** **Op: Hamburg**

| Sgt F S Payne |
| Sgt G G Soames |
| Sgt Ashcroft |
| Sgt H Vernon |
| Sgt H Tucker |
| Sgt Charlton |

T/o Marham. Crash-landed at Manby airfield, Lincolnshire, on return.

115 Sqn **Wellington II** **W5459 KO-L** **Op: Bremen**

F/L J A J Bailey DFC	+
P/O G W Tetlow	+
P/O J H Purser RCAF	+
Sgt E T Panes	+
Sgt F R Nichols	+
F/S R M Gray DFM	+

T/o 2314 Marham. Shot down by a night-fighter (Hptm Walter Ehle, II./NJG1) and crashed 0152 at Altenwarder, 4 km SW of Hamburg. All are buried in Becklingen War Cemetery, Soltau.

218 Sqn **Wellington IC** **T2806 HA-T** **Op: Bremen**

P/O F E Bryant	+
Sgt A E R Barton RAAF	+
P/O E E Ellner	+
Sgt J J Jordan	+
Sgt D C Smallbone	+
F/S T R Marshall	+

T/o 2250 Marham. All are buried in Becklingen War Cemetery, Soltau.

300 Sqn **Wellington IC** **R1640 BH-A** **Op: Bremen**

| Sgt P Nowakowski |
| Sgt Wielondek |
| F/O Dej |
| Sgt H Kudelko |
| Sgt Socha |
| Sgt Sosinski |

T/o 2212 Swinderby. Came down in the North Sea some 40 miles off Grimsby, Lincolnshire.

301 Sqn **Wellington IC** **R1373 GR-L** **Op: Bremen**

F/L L Kozlowski	pow
Sgt A O Weiss	pow
F/L E Hubicki	pow
Sgt H Korab-Brzozowski	+
Sgt J Bujak	pow
Sgt M Hasinski	pow

T/o 2135 Swinderby. Sgt Korab-Brzozowski is buried in Becklingen War Cemetery, Soltau.

30 Jun 1941	35 Sqn	Halifax I	L9499 TL-Q	Op: Kiel

35 Sqn — Halifax I — L9499 TL-Q — Op: Kiel

F/L T D I Robison	+
Sgt L Hancock	+
Sgt P Ingham	+
Sgt E J Harding	pow
F/S A J Davie	+
Sgt R N Hares	+
Sgt R Dunn	+

T/o 1010 Linton-on-Ouse. Shot down by fighters while returning to base. The Halifax was last seen on fire but still resisting strongly and it is believed that the gunners shot down at least one of the fighters before going down out of control. Those who died are buried in Kiel War Cemetery.

107 Sqn — Blenheim IV — R3801 OM- — Op: Westerland

Sgt T A H Drysdale	+
Sgt S T F Edwards	+
Sgt H Challis	+

T/o 1030 Great Massingham. Crashed into the sea. All were initially buried in Westerland Cemetery, Sylt, but since 1945 their bodies have been taken to Kiel War Cemetery.

107 Sqn — Blenheim IV — V6139 OM- — Op: Westerland

Sgt C M Chown	pow
Sgt M Kelly	pow
Sgt A E W Smith	pow

T/o 1029 Great Massingham. Believed to have been hit by flak, after which the Blenheim was put down in the sea.

30 Jun-1 Jul 1941 — 10 Sqn — Whitley V — P5018 ZA-Q — Op: Duisburg

P/O J Barrett	+
P/O W M W Fowler	pow
Sgt W J P Rice	+
Sgt J W Davidson	pow
Sgt H H Josliu	pow

T/o 2347 Leeming. The two airmen who died are buried in the Reichswald Forest War Cemetery.

10 Sqn — Whitley V — Z6584 ZA- — Op: Duisburg

Sgt A R Beveridge	+
Sgt Bassett	
Sgt Lawson	
Sgt G A Alcock	+

T/o 2240 Leeming. On return, and soon after passing over Honington airfield, the Whitley was attacked by an intruder. Both engines caught fire and the bomber crashed 1 mile NE of Thetford, Norfolk.

49 Sqn — Hampden I — X3134 EA-C — Op: Düsseldorf

Sgt B Woolston	
Sgt P McKay	
Sgt E B Chandler	
Sgt G Wood	

T/o 2310 Scampton. Ditched 0230 in the North Sea from where the crew were picked up by an ASR launch eight and a half days later, exhausted but in good shape after their long ordeal.

83 Sqn — Hampden I — AD916 OL-Z — Op: Düsseldorf

F/L N H Svendsen DFC	pow
P/O D Irving	+
P/O S Carter	pow
Sgt L C Coldwell	pow

T/o 2315 Scampton. Hit by flak and crashed at Düren on the E bank of the Rur river. P/O Irving is buried in Rheinberg War Cemetery.

102 Sqn — Whitley V — T4233 DY-K — Op: Duisburg

F/O A L Pullen	+
Sgt J Bruckshaw	+
Sgt F G Coulby	+
Sgt D Sills	+
Sgt J C Newlands	+

T/o 2258 Topcliffe. Shot down by a night-fighter (Hptm Werner Streib, I./NJG1) and crashed 0119 near Diergaarde (Limburg), 12 km SSW of Roermond, Holland. All are buried in Jonkerbos War Cemetery.

1 Jul 1941 — 7 Sqn — Stirling I — N6013 MG- — Op: Borkum

F/O J Kinnane MiD, RAAF	+
P/O J G Elliott RCAF	+
Sgt F G Taylor	+
P/O T E Bolton	+
Sgt K Huntley	+
F/S B K Nicholls	+
Sgt W G Marsh	+

T/o 1200 Oakington. Last seen NW of Texel circling a dinghy and trying to fight off an attack from a pair of Me 109s from II./ZG76. Presumed shot down 1515 in this area. Three of the crew are buried in Esbjerg (Fourfelt) Cemetery, Denmark; the rest are commemorated on the Runnymede Memorial.

21 Sqn — Blenheim IV — V6396 YH-W — Op: Kiel Canal

S/L H D H Cooper DFC	pow
F/S J S Robertson DFM	+
F/S J H Simpson	+

T/o 0830 Watton. F/S Robertson managed to get out of the aircraft, but his parachute opened prematurely and he became caught up in the tail unit. Along with F/S Simpson, he is buried at Hamburg. Details of his award were Gazetted on 28 May 1940.

1 Jul 1941	139 Sqn	Blenheim IV	V6258 XD-	Op: Oldenburg
	Sgt K Fenton	pow	T/o 0848 Horsham St. Faith. Believed shot	
	Sgt A A Fuller	pow	down by Fw Bachmann, 1./JG53 and ditched 60	
	Sgt R W McDonald	pow	km NW of Vlieland in the Dutch Frisian islands.	

1-2 Jul 1941	149 Sqn	Wellington IC	R1343 OJ-B	Op: Brest
	P/O S L St. Vincent-Welch	+	T/o 2238 Mildenhall. Crashed in the target	
	RAAF		area. All are buried in Brest (Kerfautras)	
	Sgt W M Symmons RAAF	+	Cemetery. Sgt Harrison flew in Blenheims	
	Sgt W J Megran	+	with 219 Squadron during the Battle of Britain.	
	Sgt R H Crafts RCAF	+		
	Sgt C C Reidmuller	+		
	Sgt A R J Harrison	+		

Note. This may have been the Wellington reported to have crashed alongside the Prinz Eugen, causing over sixty casualties to her crew.

	149 Sqn	Wellington IC	R1408 OJ-J	Op: Brest
	P/O J E Horsfield	+	T/o 2241 Mildenhall. Crashed at Plouzane	
	Sgt B D J Kennedy RNZAF	+	(Finistère), 10 km W of Brest. All are	
	P/O G F Burbridge	+	buried in Plouzane Churchyard.	
	Sgt F T Kearney	+		
	Sgt J C Robertson	+		
	P/O J F Philpott	+		

	311 Sqn	Wellington IC	R1516 KX-U	Op: Cherbourg
	Sgt O Helma	+	T/o 2202 East Wretham. Shot down by an Allied	
	Sgt A Plocek	+	night-fighter in the vicinity of Mere,	
	P/O R Hapala	+	Wiltshire, and crashed at Lower Park Farm,	
	Sgt A Dolejs	+	near the town.	
	Sgt J Petrucha	+		
	Sgt J Lancik	+		

2 Jul 1941	226 Sqn	Blenheim IV	V6085 MQ-	Op: Circus 29
	F/S A R Carvell	pow	T/o 1120 Wattisham to bomb a power station at	
	Sgt A R Blatch	+	Lille. Crashed in the vicinity of Melville	
	Sgt J T Melvin	+	(Nord), where the two airmen who died are	
			buried in the Communal Cemetery Extension.	

	226 Sqn	Blenheim IV	Z7440 MQ-	Op: Circus 29
	F/S J W Stanley	+	T/o 1120 Wattisham. Crashed in the vicinity	
	Sgt D A Huntley	+	of Melville (Nord), where the crew are buried	
	F/S L H W Smith	+	in the Communal Cemetery Extension.	

2-3 Jul 1941	12 Sqn	Wellington II	W5419 PH-H	Op: Bremen
	F/L W B Baxter	+	T/o 2235 Binbrook. Presumed crashed in the	
	P/O P D Farragut	+	sea. F/S Crocker is buried in Sage War	
	F/S G D Mansel	+	Cemetery, Oldenburg; the remainder of the	
	Sgt P I Ferebee	+	crew are commemorated on the Runnymede	
	F/S B Crocker	+	Memorial. P/O Farragut served under this	
	F/S E F Porter	+	name, though he was born P D MacAlister,	
			son of Sir George and Lady MacAlister.	

	78 Sqn	Whitley V	Z6558 EY-	Op: Köln
	Sgt A Jepson	+	T/o 2324 Middleton St. George. Shot down by	
	P/O G M Kennedy	+	a night-fighter (Lt Reinhold Knacke, II./NJG1)	
	Sgt G A Avory	+	and crashed 0103 at Itteren (Limburg), 5 km N of	
	Sgt J F Hollingworth	+	Maastricht, Holland. All are buried in Jonkerbos	
			War Cemetery.	

	106 Sqn	Hampden I	AD862 ZN-	Op: Duisburg
	P/O R A Walker	pow	T/o 2310 Coningsby. Shot down by a night-	
	P/O B D Campbell	pow	fighter (Lt Reinhold Knacke, II./NJG1).	
	Sgt J Diggory	+	Sgt Diggory is buried in Heverlee War Cemetery,	
	Sgt J Henderson	pow	Belgium.	

2-3 Jul 1941	106 Sqn F/L J F Sharp Sgt R A Reid RCAF Sgt D C K Dunne Sgt W F McKay	Hampden I + + + +	AD873 ZN- Op: Duisburg T/o 2305 Coningsby. Crashed at Grosskönigsdorf, 4 km NNW of Frechen on the rail line between Düren and Köln. All are buried in Rheinberg War Cemetery.
3 Jul 1941	83 Sqn Sgt Adams Sgt J E Foster	Hampden I inj +	X3059 OL-A Training T/o 1010 Scampton. Crashed 1120 while flying 2 miles S of the airfield.
	90 Sqn	Fortress I	AN528 WP- Ground Destroyed by fire 2315 while undergoing ground engine running at Polebrook airfield, Northamptonshire.
	139 Sqn Sgt J A Cormack RAAF Sgt A M Smith Sgt J A G Forsyth	Blenheim IV + + +	V6452 XD- Op: Circus 30 T/o 1022 Horsham St. Faith to bomb a target at Hazebrouck. All are buried at St-Omer in the Longuenesse Souvenir Cemetery.
3-4 Jul 1941	57 Sqn Sgt W J H Hoskins Sgt J C B Irwin F/S E D Evans Sgt R S Sparkes Sgt P H Reay Sgt Poulton	Wellington IC + + + + + inj	R1589 DX- Op: Essen T/o Feltwell. Crashed 0008 at Larman's Fen off Southery Road, Feltwell, Norfolk. The cause of the crash was attributed to instrument failure. Southery Road was closed for several days after the accident while unexploded bombs were removed from the wreckage.
	75 Sqn Sgt I L Reid RNZAF P/O J W Greening RAAF Sgt J R Nation RNZAF Sgt H Jones Sgt R E Haycock Sgt R H Hartstone RNZAF	Wellington IC + + + + + +	W5621 AA- Op: Essen T/o Feltwell. Lost without trace. All are commemorated on the Runnymede Memorial.
	99 Sqn P/O J R L Dunn Sgt S R Mayor Sgt F J Day RCAF Sgt G Kilburn Sgt H M Robertson RCAF Sgt W Stogdale	Wellington IC + + + pow pow pow	T2984 LN- Op: Essen T/o 2328 Waterbeach. Crashed near Molenbeersel (Limburg), 10 km NNW of Maaseik, Belgium. The airmen who died at the time of the crash are buried in Molenbeersel Churchyard, while Sgt Robertson RCAF rests in Poznan Old Garrison Cemetery, Poland, after being shot while trying to escape from Sagan on 29 April 1942.
	102 Sqn Sgt D F Gibson Sgt B A Cotton Sgt A Lakin Sgt W K H Bowden Sgt N W Davies	Whitley V + pow pow pow pow	P5014 DY-J Op: Essen T/o 2306 Topcliffe. Shot down by a night- fighter and crashed 0117 at Arcen (Limburg), on the E bank of the Maas, 12 km N of Venlo, Holland. Sgt Gibson is buried in Jonkerbos War Cemetery.
	102 Sqn Sgt A Davis Sgt R H Burr Sgt G R Davidson Sgt E M Cooke	Whitley V	T4330 DY- Op: Essen T/o 2308 Topcliffe. Crashed 0440 while making an emergency landing on Mill Common at Bacton, 9 miles SE of Cromer, Norfolk. No injuries reported.
	102 Sqn S/L O R C Moseley Sgt H W Fish RCAF P/O H H Wells Sgt P J W Ennis Sgt R M Milligan	Whitley V + + + + +	Z6573 DY- Op: Essen T/o 2314 Topcliffe. Shot down by a night- fighter. All are buried in Rheinberg War Cemetery.
	144 Sqn F/S G C Marsh Sgt D M Napier Sgt E R Foster Sgt W Cross	Hampden I + + + +	AD866 PL- Op: Bremen T/o Hemswell. Presumed lost over the sea. F/S Marsh is buried in Nes General Cemetery, Ameland; his crew are commemorated on the Runnymede Memorial.

3-4 Jul 1941	300 Sqn	Wellington IC	R1642 BH-X	**Op: Bremen**
	F/O K Kula	+	T/o 2246 Swinderby. Those who died are buried	
	P/O W Krupowicz	pow	in Sage War Cemetery, Oldenburg.	
	Sgt M Przybylski	pow		
	Sgt J R Mieczkowski	+		
	Sgt W Urbanowicz	+		
	Sgt O Herman	+		

	301 Sqn	Wellington IC	R1492 GR-	**Op: Bremen**
	F/O Butkiewicz	pow	T/o Syerston. Shot down by a night-fighter	
	G/C B Stachon	+	(Oblt Helmut Lent, 4./NJG1) and crashed 0034	
	F/O J Palka	pow	at Eerste Exloërmond (Drenthe), 18 km NNE of	
	Sgt A Dydo	pow	Emmen, Holland. G/C Stachon was attached to	
	Sgt D Dziegiel	pow	SHQ Swinderby and he is buried in the Polish	
	Sgt Z Hzikowski	pow	Field of Honour at Breda.	

4 Jul 1941	105 Sqn	Blenheim IV	Z7426 GB-	**Op: Bremen**
	Sgt W A Mackillop	+	T/o 0521 Swanton Morley. Hit by flak and	
	Sgt E G Nethercott	+	crashed onto a factory in the target area.	
	Sgt G F Entwistle	+	All are buried in Becklingen War Cemetery.	

	105 Sqn	Blenheim IV	Z7486 GB-	**Op: Bremen**
	F/O M M Lambert	+	T/o 0521 Swanton Morley. Last seen heading	
	Sgt R Copeland	+	away from Bremen and burning fiercely. All	
	Sgt F W R Charles	+	are buried in Becklingen War Cemetery, Soltau.	

	107 Sqn	Blenheim IV	V6020 OM-	**Op: Bremen**
	W/C L V E Petley	+	T/o 0510 Great Massingham. Shot down by	
	F/L R A Bailey DFC	+	flak and crashed in the target area. All	
	Sgt W M Harris	+	are buried in Becklingen War Cemetery, Soltau.	

	107 Sqn	Blenheim IV	V6193 OM-	**Op: Bremen**
	F/L F Welburn	pow	T/o 0515 Great Massingham. Shot down by	
	Sgt D A Duprée	+	flak and crashed in the target area. Those	
	Sgt A E Routley	+	who died were buried in the Hollefriedhot on	
	W/O S J Magee	+	7 July, though since 1945 their remains have	
			been taken to Becklingen War Cemetery, Soltau.	

Note. W/O Magee's Service Number indicates he joined the RAF circa 1925. No
aircrew status has been appended against his name in the cemetery register.

	226 Sqn	Blenheim IV	V6365 MQ-	**Op: Circus 32**
	Sgt A Smith	+	T/o Wattisham to bomb a chemical plant at	
	Sgt F J Hynes	pow	Choques. Crashed 1513 near Dunkerque, where	
	Sgt W R Mathias	+	those who died are buried locally.	

	226 Sqn	Blenheim IV	Z7291 MQ-	**Op: Norderney**
	W/C R G Hurst	+	T/o 0530 Wattisham. Hit by flak and crashed	
	F/S T C Davies DFM	+	into the sea off Norderney. All are buried in	
	F/S R W J Green DFM	+	Sage War Cemetery. Both NCOs were Squadron	
			veterans who had flown throughout the French	
	campaign of 1940.		Their decorations were Gazetted on 25 June 1940.	

4-5 Jul 1941	51 Sqn	Whitley V	Z6741 MH-	**Op: Brest**
	P/O R E Kerr MiD	+	T/o 2310 Dishforth. Crashed near Brest,	
	Sgt G G Duckers	+	where the crew are buried in Kerfautras	
	Sgt K A King	+	Cemetery.	
	Sgt E Wood	+		

	106 Sqn	Hampden I	L4185 ZN-S	**Op: Dortmund**
	P/O G F E Greenhalgh	+	T/o 2300 Coningsby. Crashed at Half Acre Creek	
	P/O G F Wadeson	+	in the Thames Estuary after calling for help on	
	Sgt R A Gilbert	+	w/t.	
	Sgt G G Hutson	+		

4-5 Jul 1941 — 106 Sqn   Hampden I   **AD914 ZN-**   Op: **Dortmund**

F/S N E Bowering MiD   +
F/S D S Bagnall   +
Sgt W H Lapsley MiD   +
Sgt I L T Reis   +

T/o 2300 Coningsby. Shot down near Heesch (Noord Brabant) in the southern outskirts of Oss, Holland. All are buried in Eindhoven (Woensel) General Cemetery.

---

106 Sqn   Hampden I   **AD986 ZN-**   Op: **Dortmund**

Sgt A E Brownbill   +
P/O L S Christman RCAF   +
Sgt S Lindley   +
Sgt S C Morse   +

T/o 2300 Coningsby. Crashed near Brackwede, 6 km SW of Bielefeld. All are buried in the Reichswald Forest War Cemetery.

5-6 Jul 1941 — 10 Sqn   Whitley V   **Z6793 ZA-**   Op: **Münster**

P/O R Goulding   +
Sgt D Morrison   +
Sgt R H Jordan   +
F/S R I H Aird   +

T/o 2248 Leeming. Shot down by a night-fighter (Oblt Helmut Lent, 6./NJG1) and crashed at Coevorden (Overijssel), 5 km NE of De Krim, Holland. All are buried in Hardenberg (Lutten) General Cemetery.

---

49 Sqn   Hampden I   **AD739 EA-A**   Op: **Osnabrück**

P/O A J Henderson   +
F/S I M T Fisher   +
Sgt H Aldridge   +
F/S K Coney   +

T/o Scampton. Lost without trace. All are commemorated on the Runnymede Memorial.

---

61 Sqn   Hampden I   **AD806 QR-**   Op: **Osnabrück**

Sgt T A Holden   +
F/S A A Horn   +
Sgt D A Johnson   +
F/S H Mainey   +

T/o 2300 Hemswell. Lost without trace. All are commemorated on the Runnymede Memorial.

---

6 Jul 1941 — 107 Sqn   Blenheim IV   **T1824 OM-**   Op: **Anti-shipping**

Sgt L G Dicks   pow
Sgt D W Macalister   pow
Sgt D T Brett   +

T/o 0934 Great Massingham to patrol Beat 10. Presumed ditched after attacking a flak ship in the Scheldt Estuary. Sgt Brett has no known grave.

---

226 Sqn   Blenheim IV   **Z7272 MQ-**   Op: **Anti-shipping**

P/O C MacK Stickney   +
F/S R Morgan   +
F/S H K V Wyatt   +

T/o Wattisham. Crashed in the sea off the Dutch coast after colliding with the mast of a ship. The crew have no known graves.

6-7 Jul 1941 — 12 Sqn   Wellington II   **W5360 PH-U**   Op: **Brest**

S/L A G G Baird   +
Sgt C H Robson RNZAF   +
F/O W F Ward   +
F/S T O Burgess DFM   +
F/S K C Amy   +
F/O S P Watkins   +

T/o 2325 Binbrook. Crashed at Guilers (Finistère), 7 km NW of Brest. All are buried in Guilers Churchyard. F/S Burgess gained his DFM while serving as an LAC, details being Gazetted on 21 June 1940.

---

40 Sqn   Wellington IC   **N2843 BL-L**   Op: **Münster**

P/O J E MacK Steeds RNZAF   +
Sgt F C Pocock   +
Sgt D M Evans   +
Sgt A Macaskill   pow
Sgt A E Varnsverry   +
Sgt A G Oliver   +

T/o 2335 Alconbury. Believed crashed in the sea off Texel. Sgt Oliver is buried on the island of Vlieland; the rest of those who died are commemorated on the Runnymede Memorial.

---

49 Sqn   Hampden I   **AD856 EA-P**   Op: **Brest**

Sgt J Flint   inj
Sgt A S Beningfield   inj
Sgt J D Fitch   inj
Sgt E C Atkinson   inj

T/o 2350 Scampton. Shot down while returning to base by an intruder flown by Ofw Wilhelm Beier, I./NJG2 and ditched off Cromer, Norfolk. All were injured during the attack and Sgt Fitch died within a few minutes of the Hampden entering the sea. Sgt Flint rescued his badly wounded navigator and he was subsequently awarded the George Medal and the Distinguished Flying Medal in recognition of his devotion to his crew and his outstanding airmanship. Sadly, Sgt Beningfield, died from his injuries.

6-7 Jul	77 Sqn	Whitley V	Z6642 KN-	**Op: Dortmund**
1941	Sgt N C Bizley	pow	T/o 2238 Topcliffe. Crashed 0355 at Epe	

6-7 Jul 1941

77 Sqn   **Whitley V**   **Z6642 KN-**   **Op: Dortmund**

Sgt N C Bizley — pow
Sgt W J Haslam RCAF — pow
Sgt G C Carter — pow
Sgt W Petch — pow
Sgt W H E Harwood — pow

T/o 2238 Topcliffe. Crashed 0355 at Epe (Gelderland), 16 km NNE of Apeldoorn, Holland. Sgt Harwood received a severe facial injury, caused either by the wire from the trailing aeriel or from a part of his parachute harness.

77 Sqn   **Whitley V**   **Z6752 KN-**   **Op: Dortmund**

P/O J E Simmonds — pow
Sgt E H Alderton — pow
Sgt S A Evans — pow
Sgt D Bradley — pow

T/o 2240 Topcliffe. Shot down by flak and crashed 0200 at Heeze (Noord Brabant), 8 km SE of Eindhoven. Sgt Alderton was slightly wounded in the chest by shrapnel.

106 Sqn   **Hampden I**   **AD861 ZN-**   **Op: Brest**

Sgt J Field — inj
Sgt C Bedell — inj
F/S R McCormack — +
Sgt J Wright — +

T/o Coningsby borrowed by 97 Squadron. Crashed 0242 in Plymouth Sound after colliding with barrage balloon cables.

115 Sqn   **Wellington IC**   **R1063 KO-D**   **Op: Münster**

Sgt O A Matthews RNZAF — +
Sgt J W Bent — +
Sgt C S R Edwards RCAF — +
Sgt K G MacLeay — +
Sgt A Webster — +
Sgt W A Strachan RCAF — +

T/o 2326 Marham. Shot down by a night-fighter (Oblt Helmut Woltersdorf, 4./NJG1) and crashed 0217 into the North Sea off Schiermonnikoog in the Dutch Frisian islands. It is believed the crew tried to make a controlled ditching as a w/t message was received indicating this intent.

144 Sqn   **Hampden I**   **AD871 PL-**   **Op: Brest**

Sgt T Porteous — +
Sgt N V Edwards — +
Sgt L C Crook — +
Sgt J T Leitch — +

T/o Hemswell. Lost without trace. All are commemorated on the Runnymede Memorial.

405 Sqn   **Wellington II**   **W5490 LQ-D**   **Op: Dortmund**

F/O R J Fraas — inj
P/O W S O'Brien — inj
Sgt M G A McKernan RCAF — inj
Sgt T Brown — inj
Sgt T J Doyle — inj
F/S J Luckhurst — +

T/o 2240 Pocklington. Returned to base with one engine out of action and crashed 0406 while circling the airfield in readiness to land. F/O Fraas died from his injuries two days after the accident.

7 Jul   **57 Sqn**   **Wellington IC**   **W5616 DX-**   **Air Test**
1941

Sgt E K Cameron — inj
Sgt R B Turner — +

Crashed 1215 while making a single-engine approach to Methwold airfield, Norfolk. The Wellington undershot the runway, struck a tree and burst into flames, injuring five members of the crew and killing the tail gunner instantly.

105 Sqn   **Blenheim IV**   **V5502 GB-**   **Op: Anti-shipping**

S/L A A McD Scott — +
Sgt R G J Dewin — +
F/S P Conlon — +

T/o 1127 Swanton Morley. Presumed lost off IJmuiden, Holland. F/S Conlon is buried in Westduin General Cemetery at Den Haag. The rest are commemorated on the Runnymede Memorial.

139 Sqn   **Blenheim IV**   **V6084 XD-**   **Op: Anti-shipping**

F/L H C Hilton — +
Sgt J Sykes — +
Sgt J Clayton — +

T/o 1142 Horsham St. Faith. Hit by flak and crashed off Scheveningen, Holland. Two are buried in Dutch cemeteries; F/L Hilton has no known grave.

139 Sqn   **Blenheim IV**   **Z7424 XD-**   **Op: Anti-shipping**

Sgt J A Causon — +
Sgt R Spencer — +
Sgt W B Cundill — +

T/o 1142 Horsham St. Faith. Believed shot down by Lt Ruettger, 3./JG52 and crashed in the sea off Zandvoort, Holland. Two are buried in Dutch cemeteries, but Sgt Causon's body has never been identified and he is commemorated on the Runnymede Memorial.

7-8 Jul **1941**	**9 Sqn** Wellington IC	**R1040 WS-** Op: **Köln**

7-8 Jul
1941

9 Sqn   Wellington IC
P/O D J Jamieson RNZAF   +
Sgt W G Jesson RNZAF   +
P/O G K Coates RCAF   +
Sgt N W Harding   +
Sgt C G Blandon   +
Sgt J S Burnside   +

R1040 WS-   Op: **Köln**
T/o 2340 Honington. Shot down by a night-fighter and crashed 0115 near Maastricht (Limburg), Holland. All are buried in Jonkerbos War Cemetery.

10 Sqn   Whitley V
Sgt H Black   +
Sgt H R Heighton   +
F/S O R Lucas   +
F/S R H Thompson   +

Z6816 ZA-   Op: **Osnabrück**
T/o 2242 Leeming. Last heard on w/t at 0444 after which it is presumed to have crashed in the sea off Flamborough Head. All are commemorated on the Runnymede Memorial.

35 Sqn   Halifax I
F/O P Langmead   pow
Sgt W T Hogan   pow
Sgt F H Brown   pow
Sgt Roberts   pow
Sgt R F Jackson   pow
Sgt Cattran   pow
Sgt K Hartland   pow

L9502 TL-R   Op: **Frankfurt**
T/o 2301 Linton-on-Ouse.

58 Sqn   Whitley V
Sgt P W Goodwin   +
F/S J V Clegg   +
Sgt B E Sale   +
Sgt A H Bird   +
Sgt C Wilkinson   +

Z6644 GE-O   Op: **Osnabrück**
T/o 2240 Linton-on-Ouse. Shot down by a night-fighter (Oblt Hans-Karl Kamp, III./NJG1) and crashed 0119 some 3 km S of Dreierwalde, 8 km NE of Rheine. All are buried in the Reichswald Forest War Cemetery.

61 Sqn   Hampden I
P/O J G N Braithwaite   pow
Sgt G Owens   +
F/S R Wordsworth   +
Sgt J F Walton   +

AD937 QR-   Op: **Mönchengladbach**
T/o 2300 Hemswell. Shot down by a night-fighter (Lt Reinhold Knacke, I./NJG1) and crashed 0017 at Meerssen (Limburg), 6 km NE of Maastricht, Holland. Those who died are buried at Nijmegen in the Jonkerbos War Cemetery.

77 Sqn   Whitley V
F/L C R McL Petley DFC   +
Sgt G Lightley   +
Sgt K W M Christopher   +
Sgt R L Luce   pow
Sgt J H Wilson   +

Z6799 KN-   Op: **Osnabrück**
T/o 2230 Topcliffe. Shot down by a night-fighter (Oblt Helmut Lent, 4./NJG1) and crashed 0055 into a wood near Orvelte (Drenthe), 17 km SSE of Assen, Holland. Those who died are buried in Westerbork General Cemetery.

99 Sqn   Wellington IC
F/L E A Masters   pow
P/O J D Agrell   pow
P/O Elliott   pow
Sgt W Kershaw   pow
Sgt F A Hard   pow
Sgt M J Platz RCAF   pow

T2880 LN-   Op: **Köln**
T/o 2323 Waterbeach.

106 Sqn   Hampden I
Sgt R Wotherspoon   pow
F/S P Hudson DFM   +
Sgt H Tait   +
F/S K C J Botsford   +

AD735 ZN-R   Op: **Mönchengladbach**
T/o Coningsby borrowed by 97 Squadron. Shot down by a night-fighter (Oblt Heinrich Griese, I./NJG1) and crashed 0210 NE of s'Hertogenbosch (Noord Brabant), Holland. Those who died are buried in Uden War Cemetery.

214 Sqn   Wellington IC
F/O R M P Jenkyns   +
P/O J McAnally   +
P/O D N R Armstrong RAAF   +
Sgt E H King   +
Sgt A Evans   +
Sgt G F Roughton   pow

T2992 BU-   Op: **Köln**
T/o 2204 Stradishall. Crashed at Genk-Bodem (Limburg), Belgium. Those who died are buried in As-en-Campine Communal Cemetery.

8 Jul 1941	7 Sqn	Stirling I	N6034 MG-	Op: Mazingarbe

7 Sqn · Stirling I · N6034 MG- · **Op: Mazingarbe**

P/O R D Morley	+
Sgt G S Edwards RCAF	pow
Sgt W Ross	+
P/O J Bailie	+
Sgt R H Lomas-Smith	+
Sgt L N Chappell	pow
F/S W G Williams	+

T/o 0453 Oakington. Hit by flak which damaged the starboard inner engine. Soon afterwards, the bomber crashed near Bethune (Pas-de-Calais), France. Those who died are buried in Longuenesse Souvenir Cemetery, St-Omer.

8-9 Jul 1941 · 9 Sqn · Wellington IC · T2973 WS-G · **Op: Münster**

Sgt B G Pitt	+
Sgt J A Grady RNZAF	+
Sgt H T Barrett	+
Sgt F Gilby	+
Sgt M E Burtis RCAF	+
Sgt D R Rawlings	+

T/o 2331 Honington. Crashed at Neuss, Germany. All are buried in Rheinberg War Cemetery.

---

10 Sqn · Whitley V · Z6627 ZA- · **Op: Hamm**

F/S G B Lewis	+
P/O F Wilson	+
Sgt R V Butcher	+
F/S C J Bevan	+

T/o 2229 Leeming. Lost without trace. All are commemorated on the Runnymede Memorial.

---

35 Sqn · Halifax I · L9521 TL-Z · **Op: Merseburg**

Sgt L W Bovington DFM	pow
Sgt T A Parkes	+
Sgt A R Kiddey	pow
F/S G D Barry	pow
F/S A E Hammond	+
Sgt H S Bradbeer	pow
Sgt N E H Coleman	+

T/o 2233 Linton-on-Ouse. Shot down by a night-fighter (Lt August Geiger, III./NJG1) and crashed onto the home of the Arts family at Rijksweg 187, Mook (Limburg), 10 km SSE of Nijmegen. It is reported that four Dutch civilians died. Sgt Bradbeer was very seriously injured and it was necessary for one of his legs to be amputated. Those who died are buried in Uden War Cemetery.

---

44 Sqn · Hampden I · AD840 KM- · **Op: Hamm**

Sgt A W Wilson	+
Sgt L A Soutar	+
F/S S J Lytle	+
Sgt H D Mackenzie	+

T/o Waddington. All are buried in the Reichswald Forest War Cemetery.

---

44 Sqn · Hampden I · AE153 KM- · **Op: Hamm**

F/S E D Tyler	+
Sgt M Livis RCAF	+
F/S K G Betts	+
Sgt F W Black	+

T/o Waddington. Lost without trace. Sgt Black's body was found in the water on 18 August 1941 and following identification, he was committed back to the sea. Thus, all are commemorated on the Runnymede Memorial.

---

58 Sqn · Whitley V · Z6666 GE-E · **Op: Hamm**

Sgt A W Rigling	pow
Sgt L E Carden	pow
Sgt J S Cameron	pow
Sgt J Gutteridge	pow
Sgt W M Caine	+

T/o 2245 Linton-on-Ouse. Crashed 0240 onto a road near Velden (Limburg), 5 km N of Venlo, Holland. Sgt Caine fell to his death when his parachute failed to open. He is buried in Jonkerbos War Cemetery.

---

78 Sqn · Whitley V · T4209 EY-W · **Op: Hamm**

Sgt W M McQuitty RAAF	+
P/O E A Scott	+
Sgt J F Hafferden	
Sgt D J Clow	+
Sgt W Forster	+

T/o 2300 Middleton St. George. Badly damaged by flak and subsequently ditched 0429 off the east coast. The sole survivor swam 9 miles to shore and raised the alarm, but despite an immediate search of the area, no survivors were found.

---

78 Sqn · Whitley V · Z6555 EY- · **Op: Hamm**

Sgt O W McLean RAAF	+
Sgt C MacK Martin RCAF	+
P/O H H Mountain	+
Sgt K Noddle	+
Sgt L Byrne	+

T/o 2303 Middleton St. George. Crashed 0251 in the North Sea. Sgt Noddle is buried in Kirkeby Cemetery on the Danish island of Romo but the rest of the crew are commemorated on the Runnymede Memorial.

8-9 Jul **1941**	**78 Sqn** P/O Wright Sgt Jones F/S R Jopling Sgt R Boucher Sgt A D Wills	**Whitley V**	**Z6625 EY-L**	**Op: Hamm** T/o 2257 Middleton St. George. Port engine failed while returning over the North Sea and while making an emergency landing the Whitley collided with a haystack and crashed 0405 at Shernborne near Bircham Newton airfield, Norfolk.

83 Sqn   **Hampden I**   **X3139 OL-V**   **Op: Hamm**

F/S R C Brutey	+
Sgt M T Matthews	+
Sgt A MacPherson	+
Sgt V W Kent	pow

T/o 2240 Scampton. Shot down by a night-fighter (Ofw Paul Gildner, 4./NJG1) and crashed 0056 in the sea off Vlieland. Sgt MacPherson is buried in Winsum General Cemetery, but the rest of those who died have no known graves.

Chapter 7

A New Directive

9 July to 22-23 July 1941

The order releasing Bomber Command from four months of almost non-stop aggression against naval targets arrived at High Wycombe early in July 1941. On the 9th, a new directive was brought to the attention of Air Marshal Sir Richard Peirse. In this, the Air Council directed him to concentrate his attention on dislocating the German transportation system of both rail and water networks. Targets in the Ruhr predominated, but industrial cities in the south also featured, along with the key ports of north-west Germany which had been bombed with reasonable success since the start of the anti-shipping campaign.

The general planning of night raiding was not greatly affected by this latest change in emphasis. Maximum effort throughout the new moon periods would continue, while less favourable weather conditions allowed the Commander-in-Chief the discretion to send his bombers to the more distant targets, or to those areas where geographical features assisted in target recognition.

But, of pressing concern to Sir Richard in the summer of 1941 was the disturbing rise in casualties and the continuing technical problems effecting the heavy bomber units. The two Manchester squadrons were the most troublesome in this respect and both 207 and 97 Squadrons received issues of Hampdens in July 1941 in order to remain operational. A third unit, 61 Squadron, had begun converting to the type in June 1941 but the process was slow and Hampdens remained in use until well into the autumn.

Sufficient deliveries of Halifaxes and Stirlings by the spring of 1941 allowed for the reformation of 76 Squadron equipped with the former type, while 15 Squadron converted from Wellingtons to Stirlings in quick order and had resumed operations within weeks of taking delivery of their first aircraft.

All four Polish squadrons were operational in 1 Group, while the arrival of RCAF and RAAF personnel had reached sufficient numbers to allow for the formation of their own bomber units within the structure of the existing bomber groups.

On paper, this looked very encouraging, but the statistical increase in strength of Bomber Command was immediately offset by the rate at which aircraft were being lost.

In recent weeks, losses had risen sharply. One hundred and thirty-three bombers, at least, been lost during the period covered by the previous chapter which was well short of a month of operations. From this quite alarming total, fewer than ten had been the result of ground or training incidents while the remainder were directly attributable to enemy action.

Without exception, these casualties were spread throughout the five bomber groups, but some squadrons were taking higher losses than others. Taking the first six months of the year as a guide, 115 Squadron had lost a total of eighteen aircraft, while one of its sister 3 Group units, 75 Squadron, showed five Wellingtons written off over the same period.

Amongst the Blenheim squadrons of 2 Group, losses were high amongst all their units, with only a handful of personnel surviving in captivity.

Casualty returns from 4 Group and 5 Group showed a steady haemorrhaging of Whitley and Hampden crews. From the former Group, 51 Squadron reported twenty aircraft lost while Hampden casualties from 50 Squadron amounted to eighteen aircraft.

Losses amongst the 1 Group squadrons were less severe, due mainly to the continuing training programme necessary in the wake of converting from Battles to Wellingtons.

However, it is a provable fact that losses amongst the four Polish squadrons were, on average, much lower than their RAF counterparts.

Addressing the problem was not going to be easy. Within the enemy camp it was fully appreciated that while the Allied bombing campaign was not making any serious impact on war production, the incursion by bomber forces over the Third Reich had to be effectively countered. Responsibility for organising an effective defence of the homeland rested mainly on the shoulders of General Josef Kammhuber. Kammhuber was a vigorous character and during 1941 he established a number of measures that were to result in the Luftwaffe gaining increasing control of the night skies over Europe. For Sir Richard Peirse, the remaining months of his command at High Wycombe were marked with growing losses matched, in general, by poor bombing results.

But, these disappointments lay some way off as the Command grappled with the task of implementing the new directive. Aachen, a good sized town close to the German borders with Holland and Belgium, was raided on 9-10 July and good results were obtained for the minimal loss of a Hampden and a Whitley, but raids on the Ruhr were virtually ignored for the rest of July, except for a disappointing showing at Duisburg in the middle of the month when four Wellingtons from a force of less than forty aircraft failed to return and a fifth was totally destroyed when it crashed during a heavy rainstorm in the Brandon area of Suffolk. This particular loss came in the middle of a string of a dozen Wellington casualties in the space of forty-eight hours.

On 16 July, the long suffering 2 Group was ordered to carry out a low-level strike on shipping at Rotterdam. Thirty-six crews were briefed and four were shot down as they pressed home their attacks in the face of a terrible flak barrage.

And so the losses continued for the rest of this period. Mostly, the casualties came in small numbers but like an open wound, the flow of blood was not to be stemmed.

9-10 Jul 1941	40 Sqn	Wellington IC	R1770 BL-C	Op: Osnabrück
	F/O G C Conran	pow	T/o 0005 Alconbury. P/O Edwards is buried in
	P/O P B G Edwards	+	Hannover War Cemetery, while Sgt Davies is at
	Sgt B Kay	pow	rest in the Reichswald Forest War Cemetery.
	Sgt S D Swindells	pow	This suggests one of the two deceased may have
	Sgt G E Davies	+	survived, albeit mortally wounded, for a few
	Sgt J A Tracey	pow	hours following the crash but long enough to
			be taken to a hospital away from the area.

Note. It is believed the Wellington was shot down by Oblt Helmut Lent, 4./NJG1

	77 Sqn	Whitley V	Z6743 KN-	Op: Aachen
	Sgt P J McLean	+	T/o 2229 Topcliffe. Crashed at Snaaskerke
	P/O G G Whitting	+	(West Vlaanderen), 5 km SE of Oostende.
	Sgt A Evans	+	All are buried in Coxyde Military Cemetery.
	Sgt R Brearley	+	

	144 Sqn	Hampden I	AD924 PL-	Op: Aachen
	P/O B J A Rennie	evd	T/o Hemswell. Crashed near Dilsen (Limburg),
	Sgt G F Bottomley	pow	9 km SSW of Maaseik, Belgium, where the two
	Sgt E R Berkey RCAF	+	airmen who died are buried in the local
	Sgt T H Marquiss	+	churchyard.

	305 Sqn	Wellington IC	R1762 SM-G	Op: Osnabrück
	Sgt J Mikszo	pow	T/o 2312 Syerston. F/O Okonski is buried in
	Sgt W Sieminski	pow	the Reichswald Forest War Cemetery.
	F/O M Marcola	pow	
	Sgt J Debiec	pow	
	F/O B P Okonski	+	
	Sgt M Minta	pow	

10 Jul 1941	7 Sqn	Stirling I	N6017 MG-	Op: Chocques
	F/O C V Fraser DFC	+	T/o 1030 Oakington to attack a power station.
	P/O L B O'Reilly	+	Shot down by flak into the sea between Boulogne
	Sgt R J Clifton	+	and le Touquet in the Pas-de-Calais. Most of
	Sgt E H Rogers	+	the crew are buried in Boulogne Eastern Cemetery
	Sgt S Bridges	+	but F/O Fraser rests in Bergen op Zoom War
	Sgt W Wilcox	+	Cemetery, Holland, while Sgt Wood has no known
	Sgt K R Wood	+	grave.

	21 Sqn	Blenheim IV	V6398 YH-A	Op: Circus
	S/L H J C Tudge	pow	T/o 1040 Watton to bomb the docks at Cherbourg.
	Sgt C G Penn	pow	
	Sgt W D Barker	pow	

10-11 Jul 1941	9 Sqn	Wellington IC	W5729 WS-J	Op: Köln
	Sgt S C Retter	+	T/o 0005 Honington fourteen minutes late due to
	Sgt H T M Ainscough	+	problems with the rear turret. Last heard on
	Sgt J E Drew RCAF	inj	w/t at 0411, after which the bomber crashed
	Sgt J Pryde	pow	near Pihen-lès-Guines (Pas-de-Calais), 10 km
	Sgt W J Tidey	+	SW of Calais. It is believed Sgt Drew RCAF was
	Sgt D R Greig	pow	found in a critically injured state and died
			while being treated in hospital. He is buried

in Longuenesse Souvenir Cemetery at St-Omer, while the rest of those who died have been laid to rest in Pihen-lès-Guines Communal Cemetery.

10-11 Jul	300 Sqn	Wellington IC	R1184 BH-B	Op: Köln

10-11 Jul 1941   **300 Sqn**   **Wellington IC**   R1184 BH-B   **Op: Köln**

P/O J Kuflik	pow	T/o 2249 Swinderby.
P/O J Janicki	pow
P/O M Kozinski	pow
Sgt M Sztul	pow
Sgt J Artymuik	pow
Sgt A Suczynski	pow

11 Jul 1941   **15 Sqn**   **Stirling I**   N3661 LS-Q   **Op: Lille**

P/O D F Legatte		T/o Wyton. On return to base the undercarriage
Sgt J D Jeffrey		collapsed and the Stirling was damaged beyond
Sgt R B Strachan		economical repair.
Sgt G K Henson RCAF	
Sgt F Smith	
Sgt H G Dickson RCAF	
Sgt V N Taylor	

11-12 Jul 1941   **144 Sqn**   **Hampden I**   AE119 PL-   **Op: Wilhelmshaven**

Sgt E W Smith	inj	T/o Hemswell. Flew into high ground after
Sgt J Nicoll	+	breaking from cloud near Tunstallon, 13 miles
Sgt S J Easton	inj	ENE of Hull, Yorkshire.
Sgt R Saunders	

12 Jul 1941   **82 Sqn**   **Blenheim IV**   V6524 UX-   **Training**

Sgt J N Hallam RCAF	+	Lost during a training exercise over the North
Sgt H Hastings	+	Sea. Sgt Hallam RCAF is buried in Kiel War
Sgt W L Hiscock	+	Cemetery; his crew have no known graves.

107 Sqn   **Blenheim IV**   Z7487 OM-   **Op: Anti-shipping**

W/C A F C Booth	+	T/o 1120 Great Massingham to patrol Beat 9.
Sgt T Scott	pow	Hit by flak and crashed 1235 into the sea off
F/S C G Goodfellow	+	IJmuiden. W/C Booth's body was found on 7
		August 1941, washed onto German soil. He is
buried in Kiel War Cemetery.		F/S Goodfellow has no known grave.

Note. W/C Booth was the Squadron's second CO to be lost in less than two weeks of operations.

12-13 Jul 1941   **49 Sqn**   **Hampden I**   AD910 EA-Y   **Op: Bremen**

Sgt Batchelor		T/o 2245 Scampton. Ran short of fuel on
Sgt Williams		return and forced-landed 0745 some 5 miles
Sgt Calvert		NE of Pocklington airfield, Yorkshire. The
Sgt Betts		crew escaped injury.

50 Sqn   **Hampden I**   AE226 VN-   **Op: Bremen**

P/O E D Vivian	+	T/o 2230 Lindholme. Shot down by a night-
Sgt J K Lord	+	fighter (Oblt Helmut Lent, 4./NJG1) and crashed
Sgt J Guest BEM	+	0055 at Veendam (Groningen), 30 km ESE of
Sgt H Jackson	+	Groningen, Holland. Sgt Jackson's true
		identity was Israel Jacobovitch.

50 Sqn   **Hampden I**   AE230 VN-   **Op: Bremen**

Sgt J Austin	inj	T/o 2220 Lindholme. Shot down by a night-
Sgt D Onions	+	fighter (Lt Heinz-Martin Hadeball, 7./NJG1)
F/S W McL Crichton	+	and crashed 0105 some 2 km E of Weltrup,
Sgt P A O W Mitchell	+	Germany. Sgt Austin is thought to have
		survived the crash as his date of death
is shown as 16 July.		Along with the rest of the crew, he is buried in
the Reichswald Forest War Cemetery.	

13-14 Jul 1941   **75 Sqn**   **Wellington IC**   X9634 AA-   **Op: Bremen**

Sgt F T Minikin	inj	T/o Feltwell and was climbing on course when the
Sgt Gilding	inj	starboard engine cut as the bomber crossed the
Sgt E Fox	+	east coast at 6000 feet. The pilot immediately
Sgt F J E Price	+	turned about but was unable to prevent the
P/O J T Leacock	+	Wellington from crashing into the sea near
Sgt H P Clarkson	+	Corton, 2 miles N of Lowestoft, Suffolk.
		Both pilots were picked up from the water
at 0215, some two hours after the crash, and taken to Louth Hospital.	

13-14 Jul 1941	115 Sqn	Wellington IC		R1502 KO-W	Op: **Bremen**

13-14 Jul	115 Sqn Wellington IC	R1502 KO-W Op: **Bremen**
1941	Sgt W J Reid pow	T/o 2303 Marham. Shot down by a night-fighter
	Sgt F B Tipper +	(Oblt Egmont Prinz zur Lippe Wiessenfeld, 4./NJG1)
	Sgt G T Buckingham pow	and crashed 0028 between Abbekerke and Onderdijk
	Sgt M B Wallis pow	(Noord Holland), two small communities 7 km and
	Sgt M G Dunne pow	4 km SSE of Medemblik. Sgt Tipper is buried in
	Sgt T W Oliver pow	Bergen General Cemetery.
14 Jul	139 Sqn Blenheim IV	R3704 XD- Op: **Anti-shipping**
1941	P/O R S Wilson +	T/o 0625 Oulton. Shot down by fighters off le
	Sgt R T Stephens +	Havre, where the crew are buried in Ste. Marie
	P/O F W Turner +	Cemetery.
	139 Sqn Blenheim IV	V6253 XD- Op: **Anti-shipping**
	P/O R B Galt +	T/o 0625 Oulton. Lost in circumstances similar
	Sgt S Vardy +	to those previously described. Sgt Vardy is
	Sgt C F J Parslow +	buried in Dunkerque Town Cemetery; the rest of
		the crew have no known graves.
14-15 Jul	7 Sqn Stirling I	N6022 MG-D Op: **Hannover**
1941	F/O D T Witt DFM	T/o 2300 Oakington. Abandoned and left to crash
	Sgt L D A Bolton	0340 at Shotesham Park, Newton Flotman, 7 miles
	Sgt J T Prentice inj	SSE of Norwich. Sgt Prentice broke his back but
	P/O D K Deyell DFM inj	made a good recovery and was later commissioned,
	Sgt A E Burrows	rising to the rank of W/C. F/O Witt gained his
	Sgt L E J Davenport	award for service with 10 Squadron, while P/O
	F/O J L A Mills	Deywell was similarly honoured following a tour
		of operations with 38 Squadron.
	7 Sqn Stirling I	N6033 MG- Op: **Hannover**
	F/S B K Madgwick +	T/o 2300 Oakington. Damaged by flak and on
	Sgt C H Tourville	return to base the Stirling ran out of petrol.
	Sgt W H Robinson	Abandoned and crashed 0415 into Gold Street,
	Sgt M Roach RCAF	Northampton. Tragically, F/S Madgwick slipped
	Sgt A Chambers	out of his parachute harness and fell to his
	Sgt J M Donlan	death. Later, Oakington received a telephone
	Sgt H Macrae	call from the Chief Constable of Northampton-
		shire registering a protest about the crash in
	his county. He is reputedly to have remarked "I can´t have this".

104 Sqn   Wellington II   W5513 EP-P   Op: **Hannover**
P/O W G Rowse   +   T/o 2252 Driffield. Shot down by a night-fighter
Sgt F A Harmer   +   (Oblt Helmut Lent, 4./NJG1) and crashed 0050
P/O J T Monks   +   near the Dextrine factory of K & J Wilkens of
Sgt R J Reynolds   +   Boven Oosterdiep, Veendam (Groningen), 25 km
Sgt W Everest   +   SE of Groningen, Holland. All are buried in
Sgt L D Coogan   +   Veendam General Cemetery.

Note. This was the first loss of a 104 Squadron aircraft since reforming as
a bomber squadron at Driffield on 1 April 1941.

149 Sqn   Wellington IC   T2737 OJ-A   Op: **Bremen**
P/O P L Dixon RAAF   pow   T/o 2305 Mildenhall.
Sgt M E Adams   pow
Sgt J N Grace RNZAF   pow
Sgt A Lawson   pow
Sgt F J Woods   pow
Sgt F W Price   pow

214 Sqn   Wellington IC   R1613 BU-G   Op: **Bremen**
P/O J G Crampton   pow   T/o Stradishall. Shot down by a night-fighter
F/S R Instone   pow   and crashed at Brookstreek in the vicinity of
P/O J C Jenkins   +   Quakenbrück, Germany, where P/O Jenkins was
Sgt R Kent   pow   buried in the Evangelical Cemetery. Since 1945,
F/S H E Jones   pow   his remains have been taken to Rheinberg War
Sgt M A Johnson RCAF   pow   Cemetery.

Note. It is believed that Brookstreek may be a corruption of Brokstrasse,
as no such locality as Brookstreek has been traced.

14-15 Jul	214 Sqn	Wellington IC	R1614 BU-H	Op: Bremen

14-15 Jul 1941

214 Sqn   Wellington IC   **R1614 BU-H**   **Op: Bremen**

P/O V K Brown	+
Sgt M R Collins RCAF	+
Sgt J Taylor	+
Sgt J S Else	+
Sgt R D Hull	+
F/S W G Lewis	+

T/o 2315 Stradishall. Presumed lost over the North Sea. P/O Brown is buried in Holland at Bergen op Zoom War Cemetery, but the bodies of F/S Lewis and Sgt Hull were washed onto English beaches. The rest are commemorated on the Runnymede Memorial.

304 Sqn   Wellington IC   **R1002 NZ-**   **Op: Bremen**

P/O J Ostrowski	
Sgt Trzebski	
P/O Siuda	
Sgt Paskiewicz	
Sgt Szewczyk	
Sgt Gebicki	

T/o 2240 Syerston. Returned early with engine trouble and crashed 0238 in a wood S of Stiffkey some 2 miles NW of Langham airfield, Norfolk, where the crew were hoping to land. No serious injuries reported, though four airmen had to be treated for shock.

305 Sqn   Wellington IC   **W5726 SM-**   **Op: Bremen**

F/O J Janota-Bzowski	+
Sgt J Ostrowski	+
F/O A Lisinski	+
Sgt S Mitkowski	+
Sgt B Burak	+
Sgt C Kaczalski	+

T/o Syerston. All are buried in Becklingen War Cemetery at Soltau.

405 Sqn   Wellington II   **W5534 LQ-N**   **Op: Hannover**

Sgt D B Thrower	pow
P/O R G M Morgan	pow
Sgt V R J Slaughter	pow
Sgt E Jones	pow
Sgt J N Kirk RCAF	pow
Sgt W C Dossetter	pow

T/o 2230 Pocklington. Sgt Kirk was the first Canadian, serving in the RCAF, to be taken into captivity while serving with an RCAF bomber squadron.

15-16 Jul 1941

57 Sqn   Wellington IC   **N2784 DX-N**   **Op: Duisburg**

Sgt S R Rishworth	+
Sgt S W Jackson	+
Sgt W F Archer	+
Sgt H W Hardie	+
Sgt J M Smith	+
Sgt S D Lane	+

T/o 2255 Feltwell. Crashed 0340 while trying to land, coming down 800 yards from the Q site at Brandon, Suffolk, 5 miles NW of Thetford, Norfolk. Heavy rain was a contributory factor in the cause of this accident.

57 Sqn   Wellington IC   **R1624 DX-**   **Op: Duisburg**

Sgt G D Osborne RNZAF	+
Sgt P Wilson	+
Sgt H E Robinson RCAF	+
Sgt C P Blackburn	+
Sgt A W Evans	+
Sgt G C Caesar	+

T/o 2300 Feltwell. A garbled w/t message was received from this aircraft, after which nothing further was heard. All are buried in Heverlee War Cemetery, Belgium.

75 Sqn   Wellington IC   **R3171 AA-**   **Op: Duisburg**

Sgt R E E Fotheringham RNZAF	+
Sgt E V K Higgins RAAF	+
Sgt J H C Roberts RCAF	+
Sgt S A Dyer RNZAF	+
Sgt P E Hare RNZAF	+
Sgt D M MacKinnon RNZAF	+

T/o Feltwell. Presumed crashed in the sea off the Dutch coast. Sgt Fotheringham RNZAF is buried in Bergen op Zoom War Cemetery, while at the New Eastern Cemetery in Amsterdam can be found the grave of Sgt Roberts RCAF. The rest of the crew are commemorated on the Runnymede Memorial.

Note. The composition of this crew was unusual in that not a single RAF airman was included.

115 Sqn   Wellington IC   **R1222 KO-H**   **Op: Duisburg**

F/S N C Cook	+
Sgt R Palmer	+
Sgt W J H Hartry RCAF	+
Sgt K P Campbell	+
Sgt W T McDonald	+
Sgt F Fullard	+

T/o 2301 Marham. Shot down by a night-fighter (Hptm Werner Streib, I./NJG1) and crashed 0145 near Nederweert (Limburg), 4 km NE of Weert, Holland. All are buried in Jonkerbos War Cemetery at Nijmegen.

15-16 Jul 1941	218 Sqn	Wellington IC	R1536 HA-G	Op: Duisburg

	F/L J Stokes	+
	P/O L W Parfitt	+
	Sgt J H Storey	+
	Sgt F Wood	+
	Sgt A Glover	+
	Sgt K D P Dyer RNZAF	+

T/o 2315 Marham. Shot down by a night-fighter (Hptm Werner Streib, I./NJG1) and crashed 0055 at Roggel (Limburg), 10 km NW of Roermond, Holland. The crew were first laid to rest at Venlo, but since the war their remains have been taken to Jonkerbos War Cemetery.

16 Jul 1941	18 Sqn	Blenheim IV	V6267 WV-M	Op: Rotterdam

	W/C T N Partridge DFC	+
	Sgt G A Dvorjetz	+
	F/O J O N Smith DFM	+

T/o 1517 Horsham St. Faith. Hit by flak and crashed 1700 in the Noordsingel at Rotterdam. All are buried in the local Crooswijk General Cemetery. Since the war, a memorial to the crew has been placed near the crash site and this has been adopted by a local school.

	18 Sqn	Blenheim IV	Z7496 WV-W	Op: Rotterdam

	Sgt R J B Rost RAAF	inj
	Sgt J Hughes	+
	Sgt S W Winter	+

T/o 1517 Horsham St. Faith. Crashed 1706 near Ypenburg airfield (Zuid Holland) between Delft and Den Haag. Sgt Rost RAAF is reported to have lived for a few hours following the crash and he died in a hospital at Delft. All are buried in Westduin General Cemetery.

	21 Sqn	Blenheim IV	V6240 YH-B	Op: Rotterdam

	Sgt J E S Bevan	+
	P/O R M Slade	+
	Sgt L R Mynott	+

T/o 1535 Watton. Hit by flak and crashed in the Waalhaven, in the heart of Rotterdam's dockland. Two bodies were recovered and taken for burial in Crooswijk General Cemetery, but nothing could be found of Sgt Mynott and he is commemorated on the Runnymede Memorial.

	139 Sqn	Blenheim IV	Z7362 XD-V	Op: Rotterdam

	S/L E Sydney-Smith	pow
	P/O R A White	pow
	F/S E G Caban DFM	pow

T/o 1600 Oulton. Shot down by flak and crashed in the Waalhaven district of Rotterdam. Details of F/S Caban's award were Gazetted on 7 March 1941, following service with 18 Squadron.

16-17 Jul 1941	40 Sqn	Wellington IC	X3220 BL-H	Op: Hamburg

	S/L R G Weighill	+
	Sgt R D Hesketh	+
	Sgt W E Gibb RCAF	+
	Sgt D A Price	+
	Sgt V H Leng	+
	P/O A W Wilkinson	+

T/o 2305 Alconbury. Crashed 2330 at West Caister, 3 miles NNW of Great Yarmouth, Norfolk. It is believed the crash was caused through the pilot becoming dazzled by searchlights. At the time of the accident, the Wellington was flying at 500 feet, leaving little margin for recovery.

Note. In the summer of 1984, the crash site was excavated and a number of propaganda leaflets were recovered.

	40 Sqn	Wellington IC	X9630 BL-J	Op: Hamburg

	Sgt A W P Bird RNZAF	+
	Sgt B F T Johnson	+
	P/O J R Jamieson RCAF	pow
	Sgt L J Harrison	+
	Sgt B Hassall	+
	Sgt O I S Platt RCAF	+

T/o 2320 Alconbury. Crashed into the sea off the Dutch coast. Three bodies were recovered and buried in Den Burg General Cemetery, while the names of Sgt Johnson and Sgt Platt RCAF can be seen on the panels of the Runnymede Memorial.

	50 Sqn	Hampden I	AD844 VN-	Op: Hamburg

	P/O H M Owens	+
	P/O R G Mitchell	+
	F/S D E Russell	+
	Sgt R W Owen	+

T/o 2250 Lindholme. Two bearings were sent to this aircraft and an IFF plot was obtained at 0114, after which the Hampden and its crew vanished without trace. All are commemorated on the Runnymede Memorial.

	150 Sqn	Wellington IC	R1495 JN-B	Op: Hamburg

	P/O E Bethridge-Topp	+
	Sgt A R Harris RNZAF	+
	P/O K F Glenn	+
	Sgt W R Norman	+
	Sgt R A Galbraith	+
	P/O K C Edwards	pow

T/o 2215 Snaith. Those who died are buried in Hamburg Cemetery, Ohlsdorf.

| 16-17 Jul 1941 | 311 Sqn | Wellington IC | R1718 KX-N | Op: Hamburg |

	Sgt G Nyc	pow	T/o 2307 East Wretham. Shot down by a night-
	Sgt K Stastny	pow	fighter (Ofw Paul Gildner, 4./NJG1) and crashed
	F/O J Zafouk	pow	0327 into the IJsselmeer off Tacozijl. Sgt Mares
	P/O O Cerny	pow	is buried in Lemmer General Cemetery.
	Sgt F Knap	pow	
	Sgt J Mares	+	

| 17 Jul 1941 | 35 Sqn | Halifax I | L9490 TL- | Ground |

Damaged beyond repair on this date and struck from effective charge. Connection between its demise and the report that follows has not been proven.

| | 35 Sqn | Halifax I | L9495 TL- | Training |
| | S/L J B Tait DSO, DFC | | Crash-landed at Linton-on-Ouse following undercarriage failure. No injuries reported. |

| 17-18 Jul 1941 | 149 Sqn | Wellington IC | N2853 OJ-R | Op: Köln |

	Sgt D C Stewart RNZAF	inj	T/o 2341 Mildenhall. Hit by flak and on return
	Sgt Jordan	inj	the pilot decided to make an emergency landing.
	Sgt Brookes	inj	While doing so, he was blinded by a searchlight
	Sgt P Gibbins	+	team stationed at Cockfield, 9 miles NNE of
	Sgt Main	inj	Sudbury, Suffolk. With his night vision lost,
	Sgt J M Dixon RCAF	inj	Sgt Stewart RNZAF crashed 0105 through a line

of trees, near the Moat, between Oldhall Green and Cross Green, bursting into flames on impact.

| | 301 Sqn | Wellington IC | N2840 GR- | Op: Rotterdam |

	F/O B Kuzian	+	T/o 2258 Syerston borrowed by 304 Squadron.
	Sgt J Tomaszewski	+	Shot down by an intruder and crashed 0240 at
	F/O B Klatt	+	Cowtham House Farm, Balderton, 2 miles SE of
	Sgt J Sylwestrowicz	+	Newark, Nottinghamshire. All are buried in
	Sgt J Podziemski	+	the Polish Plot at Newark Cemetery.
	Sgt M Czerniejewski	+	

| 18 Jul 1941 | 15 Sqn | Stirling I | N6030 LS-P | Op: Wesel |

	F/O S D Marshall RAAF	+	T/o Wyton in an attempt to raid Wesel using cloud
	Sgt A J Higgison RNZAF	+	cover. Turned back, due to clearing skies and
	Sgt K G H Davies	+	subsequently crashed in the North Sea. Four
	P/O J D W McCallum	+	bodies are buried in various cemeteries in
	Sgt G H Mayor	+	Holland, while the rest are commemorated on
	F/S C G White AFM	+	the Runnymede Memorial. In civilian life, F/O
	Sgt A W D Frost	+	Marshall RAAF was the yachting correspondent for

the Sydney Telegraph

| | 21 Sqn | Blenheim IV | V5595 YH-P | Op: Anti-shipping |

	Sgt J R M Kemp	pow	T/o 1115 Manston for Channel Stop duties. Shot
	Sgt E A Goold	pow	down by ship's flak off Gravelines.
	Sgt F J Soal	pow	

| | 21 Sqn | Blenheim IV | V6369 YH-N | Op: Anti-shipping |

	Sgt Maguire		T/o 1115 Manston. Landed at 1150 and believed
	Sgt Bangor Jones		damaged to the extent that the Blenheim never
	Sgt Haskins		flew again.

| | 21 Sqn | Blenheim IV | Z7502 YH-R | Op: Anti-shipping |

	S/L D Graham-Hogg	pow	T/o 1115 Manston. Shot down off Cap Gris-Nez.
	Sgt J Marsden	pow	F/S Wyatt is commemorated on the Runnymede
	F/S D W Wyatt	+	Memorial.

| 19 Jul 1941 | 15 Sqn | Stirling I | N6018 LS-C | Op: Lille |

	S/L T W Piper	pow	T/o Wyton. Hit by flak while trying to bomb a
	Sgt D H Jeeves	+	secondary target at Dunkerque. The port inner
	Sgt M O Orchard	+	engine caught fire and shortly afterwards the
	P/O A Hipps	+	bomber dived vertically into the ground at
	Sgt P H Eve	+	Killem (Nord), 2 km SW of Hondschoote, France.
	Sgt S R Symondson	+	
	Sgt G Armstrong RCAF	pow	
	P/O J R Bushell	+	

Date	Squadron	Aircraft	Serial/Code	Operation

9 Jul 941

50 Sqn		Hampden I	AD897 VN-	Training

Sgt E R Bousfield +
Sgt J E S Burke +
F/S J H Tittley +
AC1 H L Reed +

Crashed 1100, inverted, between Lindholme and Finningley after getting into difficulties while practicing formation flying.

105 Sqn		Blenheim IV	V6039 GB-	Op: Anti-shipping

Sgt R W Taylor RNZAF +
Sgt R F G Withrington +
Sgt S Sparkes +

T/o 1122 Swanton Morley. Hit by flak and crashed into the sea off the Dutch coast. All are buried in various cemeteries in Holland.

105 Sqn		Blenheim IV	Z7371 GB-	Training

Sgt W V Hinds

T/o 1450 Swanton Morley and crashed almost immediately.

105 Sqn		Blenheim IV	Z7439 GB-	Op: Anti-shipping

Sgt V G Farrow +
F/S O H Robinson +
Sgt E C Saunders +

T/o 1122 Swanton Morley. Shot down into the sea off Scheveningen, Holland. Two of the crew are buried in Westduin General Cemetery at Den Hagg, but F/S Robinson has no known grave.

311 Sqn		Wellington IC	R1804 KX-	Air Test

F/O J Stransky

T/o 1145 East Wretham but developed an uncontrolled swing and crashed into a steam roller, ripping off the starboard wing and badly crushing the forward fuselage. The wreckage caught fire, but the crew escaped serious injury.

9-20 Jul 941

51 Sqn		Whitley V	Z6487 MH-G	Op: Hannover

P/O A R Thomas +
P/O A W MacKay pow
P/O P A Leuw pow
Sgt F McMullen pow
Sgt J A Walker pow

T/o 2214 Dishforth. P/O Thomas is buried in Sage War Cemetery, Oldenburg.

311 Sqn		Wellington IC	R1371 KX-F	Op: Hannover

Sgt V Netik +
Sgt M Jindra +
P/O J Partyk +
Sgt J Ctvrtlik +
Sgt V Vales +
Sgt P Babacek +

T/o 2252 East Wretham. Crashed in the Waddenzee. Sgt Netik is buried in Oldebroek General Cemetery and Sgt Jindra rests in Uithuizermeeden General Cemetery, Holland. P/O Partyk is buried in Sage War Cemetery, Germany, while the remainder are commemorated on the Runnymede Memorial.

0 Jul 941

18 Sqn		Blenheim IV	V6038 WV-H	Op: Anti-shipping

F/L W Hughes MiD +
Sgt J Hunter +
Sgt M Wilding +

T/o 1530 Horsham St. Faith. Clipped the mast of the ship being attacked and crashed into the sea off le Touquet. All are commemorated on the Runnymede Memorial.

139 Sqn		Blenheim IV	V6069 XD-	Training

Sgt J Evans +

T/o Oulton but stalled and crashed near the airfield boundary.

139 Sqn		Blenheim IV	Z7499 XD-	Op: Anti-shipping

Sgt N Baron DFM +
Sgt K W Hopkinson +
Sgt R W Ullmer DFM +

T/o 1324 Oulton. Hit by flak and crashed into the sea off le Touquet. Sgt Baron is buried in Blankenberge Communal Cemetery, Belgium, while the graves of his crew can be found at Boulogne in the town's Eastern Cemetery. Details of the awards made to Sgt Baron and Sgt Ullmer had appeared in the London Gazette fourteen days previous.

1 Jul 941

76 Sqn		Halifax I	L9533 MP-	Training

P/O L R Blackwell +
Sgt K N Hudgell +
Sgt A J Grenyer +
Sgt J W R Boggis +
Sgt A J Howes +

Crashed 1245 while avoiding a Hurricane which flew across the path of the bomber as it made ready to land at Middleton St. George.

| 21-22 Jul 1941 | 44 Sqn | Hampden I | **AD983 KM-** | **Op: Gardening** |

21-22 Jul 44 Sqn   Hampden I   **AD983 KM-**   **Op: Gardening**
1941   Sgt D M Bruce   +   T/o 2255 Waddington to lay mines off the Frisian
           Sgt W R B Relyea RCAF   +   Islands. Crashed 0400 on the Greenstones, staff
           Sgt J A Connolly   +   residence for Lindum Hall School for Girls at
           Sgt P J Lynch   +   Lincoln. Miss Fowler, the senior French mistress,
                                                  died after being trapped in the burning building.

           115 Sqn   Wellington IC **Z8788 KO-H**   **Op: Mannheim**
           Sgt N L Johnston RCAF   +   T/o 2239 Marham. All are buried in Coxyde
           Sgt F S Payne   +   Military Cemetery, Belgium.
           Sgt R S Saunders   +
           Sgt H Tucker   +
           Sgt H Vernon   +
           Sgt B W O'Hara   +

22 Jul   214 Sqn   Wellington IC T2819 BU-   Unknown
1941   Burnt out. The circumstances leading to
           the loss of this aircraft are not known. No accident card exists, but
           its demise has been established by Form 78.

hapter 8

Three Daylight Raids

3 July to 28 August 1941

n 23 July a reconnaissance mission returned howing that the Scharnhorst had slipped her oorings at Brest and had sailed some 200 iles south-east and was now anchored at la allice. The implications of this move were erious and Bomber Command was ordered to ount an attack on her new berth forthwith. The news also caused deep concern within he operational planning department at High ycombe where staff were finalising orders or a major daylight raid scheduled for the ext day on Brest. A security leak could not e discounted, but it was decided that the ttack should proceed.

Attention was now focused on preparing a esponse to the latest request. The hour was oo late for a full scale attack and in the vent Oakington and Wyton were ordered to espatch a total of six Stirlings, though echnical failure reduced the 15 Squadron ontribution to two aircraft.

The remainder reached La Pallice where ood bombing was reported, but on the return light, one Stirling got into difficulties nd crashed in the sea off Milford Haven.

This was not the only casualty of the day. he Blenheims of 18 Squadron and 21 Squadron pent a torrid late morning and early after-oon attacking shipping off the Dutch and elgian coasts, losing six from an overall orce of seventeen. A high price to pay for he handful of ships attacked.

Overnight, the Command organised small aids over Frankfurt and Mannheim, as well s sending thirty Whitleys from 4 Group to aintain a presence over La Pallice. One ampden from 50 Squadron failed to return rom Frankfurt, last being heard from as it pproached the east coast on return and a 77 quadron Whitley crew were hurt when their omber crashed near Swindon as they tried to inpoint their position after breaking out f low cloud.

And so to the 24th, the day earmarked for he planned assault on Brest.

Some modification was necessary following he departure of the Scharnhorst and instead f the 150 bombers originally envisaged, the aid was scaled down to accommodate a force omprising of seventy-nine Wellingtons drawn rom 1 and 3 Groups, supported by eighteen ampdens and a trio of the new Fortresses of 0 Squadron.

The revised plan now featured an attack on a Pallice by fifteen Halifaxes, while a iversionary strike on Cherbourg by 2 Group as included as a foil for the Wellingtons eading for Brest.

A strong fighter escort was provided for the Blenheims attacking Cherbourg and for the small Hampden contingent operating to Brest. The Wellingtons would have to trust in their own fire power, while the distance to La Pallice made it impossible for any fighter cover to be provided.

By mid-morning the various raids were well under way. At all targets the visibility was excellent and the bombers encountered fierce opposition, though at Cherbourg the Blenheims pressed home their attacks without meeting any fighters. But, if the Luftwaffe had been conspicuous by its absence from Cherbourg, it more than compensated for this at Brest and at La Pallice.

Approaching from the sea, both raids were immediately subjected to a fierce barrage of heavy flak, while at the same time being forced to fight off repeated attacks from the hordes of Me 109s.

Heroism on a grand scale was displayed by attacker and defender alike. The bombers held to their course as they flew into the unremitting barrage of shells. Aircraft were hit repeatedly, often resulting in quite dreadful wounds to their crews and, braving the same gauntlet of fire the fighter pilots closed with their adversaries, breaking away only at the last minute.

At La Pallice, it is reported, the running battle was maintained for a full fifteen minutes. The ground fire was murderous throughout, while above the Halifaxes the Me 109s waded into the attack, exchanging a hail of fire with the air gunners.

Five Halifaxes were shot down, but through the courage of the bomber pilots, at least five bombs hit the Scharnhorst.

At Brest, too, crews claimed good bombing results with several sticks of bombs explod-ing on, or near the Gneisenau. As a measure of the determination by the bombers to get to their aiming points, eight Wellingtons are believed to have crashed within the port area, while a ninth aircraft, captained by the CO of 405 Squadron, crashed near the village of Ploudaniel, a few kilometres to the north-east of Brest.

Losses from the Hampden force were light with two crews missing and overall the raid was judged to have been a success. Within hours of the bombers returning, the German High Command ordered the Scharnhorst to make once more for Brest. The immediate threat to our convoys plying the Atlantic had been lifted.

We now move ahead to August, and the 12th, on which day a near suicidal raid took place against two electricity power stations near

Köln. This time the Blenheim squadrons of 2 Group were the star players with fifty-four crews briefed for Operation 77. The bulk of the force, thirty-eight bombers in all, were ordered to attack Knapsack, lying south-west of the city, with the remaining eighteen going to Quadrath, which lay almost directly west of Köln. Each aircraft was armed with two 500lb bombs and the crews were ordered to fly at low level throughout the course of the raid. The feelings of those charged to carry out this daring operation can be left to the imagination.

In the summer of 1941, Knapsack had the largest steam driven generators in Europe, capable of producing an estimated 600,000 kilowatts, while the smaller Quadrath unit produced somewhere in the region of 200,000 kilowatts of electricity. Both were prime targets and it was hoped that if substantial damage could be caused to these facilities, Hitler might be forced to withdraw some of his fighters from the Russian front and thus relieve the pressure on the Soviets.

Careful planning went into Operation 77, not least being a series of diversionary attacks on targets in northern France and high-altitude raids by single Fortresses on De Kooy airfield in Holland and the German port of Emden. Fighter Command was asked to provide escort cover for all raids, except those involving the Fortresses.

Timing was of the essence and the time-table was adhered too throughout.

Four squadrons, 18, 107, 114 and 139, were assigned to Knapsack with 21 Squadron and 82 Squadron each providing nine crews for the attack on Quadrath.

Both forces were airborne shortly after 9 o'clock, the crews acutely aware that when they crossed the Dutch coast, ahead of them lay the better part of three hours flying over enemy territory.

By and large, the raids went as expected. Flak claimed one of the 82 Squadron aircraft as it crossed the Hoekse Waard polder, outbound, but the rest of the force arrived at Quadrath in good order and carried out their attacks as ordered, before withdrawing hotly pursued by light flak. 21 Squadron lost one Blenheim near the power station and another as it tore towards the North Sea near Texel; three gone from eighteen.

The Knapsack contingent also carried out a brisk attack but were far less fortunate losing seven of their number, though only two are thought to have crashed in the target area, the rest being shot down while clearing the Dutch coast.

Two Blenheims, both from 226 Squadron, were lost while acting as navigation leaders for the escorting fighters, bringing the total casualty count to twelve bombers.

The general consensus of opinion was that the Group had got away lightly!

One more audacious daylight raid remained to be flown in August 1941. This came on the 28th when eighteen Blenheims carried out an evening strike on shipping in the Dutch port

of Rotterdam. Two squadrons of long-range Spitfires accompanied the bombers and the force swept in low from off the sea between the Goeree and Voorne polders. Rotterdam was a few minutes flying time away.

With the Blenheims still down on the deck, the escorting fighters climbed to give top cover. Moments later the leading Blenheims, flying in three compact boxes, encountered a hail of defensive fire which continued all the way into the Waalhaven district.

Banking to the left, the Blenheims flew on through the flak. One, either an 88 Squadron machine, or a 226 Squadron aircraft, hurtled into a warehouse and exploded. The survivors pressed on, their bomb-loads scoring several hits amongst the tightly packed shipping and fires broke out in their wake.

Seven crews failed to return, making this one of the costliest raids flown so far by 2 Group.

Since the war, much has been written about the exploits of the Dam Busters and one of the points frequently expressed is that the raid, flown in May 1943, gave a tremendous boost to the general morale of the country. Without in anyway belittling the bravery of the aircrews of 617 Squadron in carrying out a most hazardous raid at terrible cost, the daylight attacks flown in the summer of 1941 were every bit as important for the confidence of our nation to stand firm in the face of adversity.

In between the three operations discussed, 2 Group lost a further twenty-three aircraft on anti-shipping raids, while Circus attacks in the Lille area on the 18th of August resulted in two more Blenheims being written off.

Night raids, also, were taking an increasing toll as the Command tried to inflict maximum damage on the transportation systems and the industrial base of Germany. Hamburg and Hannover were raided on 25-26 July; nine aircraft became casualties from these two targets, while a minor excursion to Berlin by a handful of heavies resulted in the loss of two Stirlings and a Halifax.

During the early part of August, serious fires were started at Hamburg and production at a celluloid factory in Mannheim was badly effected. Frankfurt, Karlsruhe and Köln were all visited around this period, while Essen was attacked by over one hundred aircraft during the night of 7-8 August. Damage was slight, but on the other side of the Ruhr the marshalling yards at Hamm received a pounding with crews reporting many fires and dense smoke rising to over 10000 feet.

Throughout the late spring and summer, the Command had done its utmost to carry the war into the enemy camp twenty-four hours a day. The seeds of round-the-clock bombing, as it came to be known, were sewn in the spring and high summer of 1941 and not, as it is popularly believed, with the arrival of the United States Army Air Corps in 1943.

But, by late August 1941, the multitude of operations being flown by 2 Group had to be caled down. A combination of high losses in en and equipment, plus the ever pressing emands from other theatres of operations, ere the determining factors. From as early s May 1941, the Group had detached crews to he Mediterranean and there was no respite rom this quarter as autumn approached. This is not to imply that daylight raiding

ceased completely. 2 Group would be actively employed for the remainder of the year, while other Groups were called upon from time to time to supply aircraft for Circus style operations and the like. In general, however, the main thrust lay with the night-bombing campaign and here the results were being viewed as increasingly disappointing.

3 Jul 1941	15 Sqn	Stirling I	N6038 LS-R	Op: la Pallice
	F/O R B Campbell RAAF	+		
	Sgt A J Mitchell	+		
	Sgt G T Friend	+		
	P/O D A Lewis RNZAF	+		
	Sgt W Cockburn	+		
	P/O J H E Warner	+		
	Sgt A R N Whitcher	+		

T/o Wyton to attack the Scharnhorst. Believed damaged by enemy action and subsequently crashed in the sea some 50 miles from Milford Haven in Pembrokeshire. Apart from P/O Lewis RNZAF, the crew are commemorated on the Runnymede Memorial.

18 Sqn	Blenheim IV	R3666 WV-K	Op: Anti-shipping
Sgt W M G Dunham RCAF	+		
Sgt R W Adamson	+		
Sgt N L Harding	+		

T/o 1145 Horsham St. Faith. Shot down by Me 110s from 5./ZG76 and crashed off Den Helder. Two of the crew are commemorated on the Runnymede Memorial, while Sgt Adamson's grave may be found in Westerschelling General Cemetery on Terschelling.

18 Sqn	Blenheim IV	V6250 WV-Z	Op: Anti-shipping
Sgt P D Baker	+		
Sgt W C K Bounds	+		
P/O L F Evans	+		

T/o 1145 Horsham St. Faith. Lost in circumstances similar to those described above. All are commemorated on the Runnymede Memorial.

21 Sqn	Blenheim IV	V6035 YH-O	Op: Anti-shipping
P/O P B Ashley	+		
P/O G F Lowes	pow		
P/O G H Seeley	+		

T/o 1400 Manston. Shot down by a flak ship off Oostende. The two airmen who died are buried here in the New Communal Cemetery.

21 Sqn	Blenheim IV	V6225 YH-W	Op: Anti-shipping
F/L H Waples DFC	+		
Sgt N J Giblin DFM	+		
Sgt A W Handley	+		

T/o 1400 Manston. Crashed in the sea off the Dutch coast. Sgt Giblin's award was Gazetted six days after his death; he is buried in the Northern Cemetery at Vlissingen. The rest of the crew are commemorated on the Runnymede Memorial.

21 Sqn	Blenheim IV	V6321 YH-Z	Op: Anti-shipping
Sgt H P Hartridge RCAF	+		
Sgt C D Phillips	+		
Sgt K B Minty	+		

T/o 1400 Manston. Crashed in the Scheldt estuary after attacking a convoy off the Belgian port of Oostende. All are buried in Vlissingen Northern Cemetery, Holland.

21 Sqn	Blenheim IV	Z7438 YH-D	Op: Anti-shipping
F/L F L Campbell-Rogers	pow		
Sgt J P Sullivan	+		
Sgt D E Bingham	pow		

T/o 1400 Manston. Shot down off Oostende. Sgt Sullivan has no known grave.

3-24 Jul 1941	50 Sqn	Hampden I	AD843 VN-	Op: Frankfurt
	Sgt H T Holme	+		
	Sgt L M Megginson	+		
	Sgt R Evans	+		
	Sgt W M Watt	+		

T/o 2220 Swinderby. Last heard on w/t while over the sea and is presumed lost E of Cromer, Norfolk, as two bodies were recovered from the water in this area.

77 Sqn	Whitley V	Z6643 KN-	Op: la Pallice
F/L F A Dury	inj		
Sgt D R Brown	inj		
Sgt D V Flavell	inj		
Sgt Whittam	inj		

T/o 2157 Topcliffe. Crashed 0450 on sloping ground near Aldbourne, 8 miles SE of Swindon, Wiltshire.

24 Jul
1941

12 Sqn	Wellington II	W5380 PH-L	Op: Brest

Sgt H Heald +
Sgt R K Godfrey +
F/S F J Hardiman +
F/S C R Preece +
Sgt A W Felton +
Sgt J R Mason +

T/o Binbrook. Lost without trace. All are commemorated on the Runnymede Memorial.

35 Sqn	Halifax I	L9512 TL-U	Op: la Pallice

F/S S D Greaves pow
Sgt J N Gibson pow
Sgt J H F Ogden pow
Sgt W C Walters pow
Sgt A Henery pow
Sgt E W Constable pow
Sgt A Gillbanks pow

T/o 1036 Stanton Harcourt. Hit by flak and finished off by a Me 109. Abandoned and left to crash in the sea just to the N of the Ile de Ré opposite la Rochelle.

Note. On 24 July 1981, a Piper Lance landed at Linton-on-Ouse. From the aircraft, which was piloted by ex-W/O Greaves, stepped the crew reported above. A fitting end to an operation begun exactly forty years previous.

35 Sqn	Halifax I	L9527 TL-M	Op: la Pallice

F/S C A Godwin +
Sgt G G Esnouf +
Sgt C H Newstead +
P/O G A Eperon pow
Sgt E O T Balcomb pow
Sgt R T Rudlin +
F/S S H J Shirley +

T/o 1040 Stanton Harcourt. Shot down at Angles (Vendee), 15 km WSW of Lucon, France. Those who died are buried in Angles Communal Cemetery.

40 Sqn	Wellington IC	T2986 BL-A	Op: Brest

Sgt M Evans DFM, RNZAF +
Sgt H T Ellis +
Sgt S G Kybird +
Sgt F Lowrey +
F/S C S Beresford +
Sgt J Hoban +

T/o 1030 Alconbury. Hit by flak and crashed in the town. All are buried in the Kerfautras Cemetery. Sgt Evans was awarded his decoration for outstanding airmanship during operations over Rotterdam. Details of the award were promulgated in the London Gazette on 8 July.

44 Sqn	Hampden I	AD962 KM-	Op: Brest

F/O J F Clayton DFM pow
P/O J M Grant RCAF +
Sgt A J Clarke pow
Sgt W F O'Brien pow

T/o 1100 Coningsby. Shot down into the sea off Brest by fighters. P/O Grant RCAF failed to leave the aircraft and he is commemorated on the Runnymede Memorial.

75 Sqn	Wellington IC	N2854 AA-	Op: Brest

Sgt D F Streeter RNZAF +
Sgt W Owen RCAF +
Sgt R P Carling +
Sgt R J Turner +
Sgt G S Walker RNZAF +
Sgt R S C Craig +

T/o Feltwell. Lost without trace. All are commemorated on the Runnymede Memorial.

76 Sqn	Halifax I	L9494 MP-	Op: la Pallice

S/L W R Williams pow
P/O J G Ireton pow
Sgt A H J Turner pow
Sgt L J Butler pow
Sgt N Kershaw pow
Sgt S Jones pow
Sgt J R Wedderburn pow

T/o 1055 Stanton Harcourt. Hit by flak and finished off by a Me 109. Ditched off la Rochelle, from where the crew were picked up by a French fishing vessel, which in turn transferred the crew to a Kriegsmarine craft which had witnessed the rescue. First time that a Halifax had been successfully ditched.

76 Sqn	Halifax I	L9517 MP-	Op: la Pallice

P/O J F P J McKenna +
Sgt R F S Ford-Hutchinson +
Sgt G Summers +
Sgt V A Davis +
Sgt J M Pilbeam +
Sgt L T Rice +
F/S R W J Hill +

T/o 1057 Stanton Harcourt. Shot down by flak and crashed into the sea off la Rochelle. Four bodies were recovered from the water and taken for burial in local cemeteries. Sgts Ford-Hutchinson, Summers and Rice are commemorated on the Runnymede Memorial.

4 Jul 941	76 Sqn	Halifax I	
	F/L A E Lewin		+
	Sgt W H J Gourley RAAF		+
	F/S C H Horner		+
	Sgt B Phillips		pow
	Sgt P J Vickery		+
	Sgt W A Finlayson		pow
	F/O N W McLeod		pow

L9529 MP-   **Op: la Pallice**
T/o 1034 Stanton Harcourt. Believed shot down by fighters at l'Aiguillon-sur-Mer (Vendee), 14 km SW of Lucon, France. Three of the crew are buried at l'Aiguillon-sur-Mer Communal Cemetery.

101 Sqn	Wellington IC	
F/L F H Craig MiD		+
Sgt A E Sainsbury		+
Sgt D Love		+
Sgt E J Hesmondhalgh		pow
Sgt W H Price		+
Sgt F M Smith		pow

R1702 SR-F   **Op: Brest**
T/o 1136 Oakington. Shot down in the target area by Me 109s. This was the first aircraft lost by the Squadron since converting from Blenheims. Those who died are commemorated on the Runnymede Memorial.

103 Sqn	Wellington IC	
Sgt J S Bucknole		+
Sgt G J Beckwith		+
F/O R Shaw		+
F/S F Barker		+
F/S R Critchley		+
Sgt E C McDonald RNZAF		+

N2770 PM-   **Op: Brest**
T/o 1100 Elsham Wolds. Crashed in the sea off Brest. Sgt Beckwith is buried in the Kerfautras Cemetery; the rest of the crew are commemorated on the Runnymede Memorial.

104 Sqn	Wellington II	
P/O M S Nicholls		+
P/O J C Broadhurst		+
F/S W E Chappell		+
Sgt P D Simpson		+
Sgt A G Tatham		+
F/S J R Powell		+

W5438 EP-E   **Op: Brest**
T/o 1138 Driffield. Last seen 1555 flying at 5000 feet NE of Brest and being attacked by at least four fighters. Other aircraft in the formation say that P/O Nicholls made two runs over Brest in order to be certain of placing his bombs on the target. All are commemorated on the Runnymede Memorial.

144 Sqn	Hampden I	
F/L R B Barr		pow
P/O P G Anderson		+
Sgt J E Wiggall		pow
Sgt A B Cooper		+
Sgt D Parkin		+

AE225 PL-   **Op: Brest**
T/o North Luffenham. Shot down by fighters near Ploudalmézeau (Finistère), 21 km NW of Brest. Those who died are buried in Ploudalmézeau Communal Cemetery.

218 Sqn	Wellington IC	
P/O M Jolly RNZAF		+
Sgt A C Moss		+
Sgt W L Jacobsen RCAF		pow
Sgt J D Knott		pow
Sgt H R Barton		+
P/O L P Kolitz		+

R1726 HA-O   **Op: Brest**
T/o 1126 Marham. Crashed in the sea off Brest. Those who died are commemorated on the Runnymede Memorial.

405 Sqn	Wellington II	
P/O R V Trueman		+
Sgt J C Crump RCAF		+
Sgt A G L Mitchell		+
Sgt J A Fawkes		+
Sgt C Tatton		+
Sgt J L B Martin RCAF		+

W5537 LQ-O   **Op: Brest**
T/o 1153 Pocklington. Lost without trace. All are commemorated on the Runnymede Memorial.

405 Sqn	Wellington II	
W/C P A Gilchrist DFC		evd
Sgt J S Paton		evd
P/O W Mackay RCAF		pow
Sgt R H Westburg		pow
Sgt M H J Dalphond RCAF		evd
F/O R G M Whigham		+

W5551 LQ-U   **Op: Brest**
T/o 1130 Pocklington. Shot down at Ploudaniel (Finistère), 15 km NE of Brest. F/O Whigham, the Squadron's Gunnery Leader, is buried in Lesneven Communal Cemetery. He was the son of General Sir R D Whigham, GCB, KCMG, DSO.

24 Jul 1941	405 Sqn	Wellington II	W5581 LQ-V Op: Brest

24 Jul 1941   405 Sqn   Wellington II   W5581 LQ-V   Op: Brest

Sgt J W Craig   inj   T/o 1134 Pocklington. Ditched 1635 some
Sgt H S McNeill   inj   300 yards off Torpoint, Devon. The tail
Sgt Leonard   gunner, Sgt Higgins, was wounded when the
Sgt Bain   Wellington was savaged by fighters, but
Sgt J J Hughes   he remained at his post and claims to have
Sgt G K Higgins   inj   destroyed one of the attackers.

24-25 Jul 1941   57 Sqn   Wellington IC   R1369 DX-   Op: Kiel

Sgt F L Green   +   T/o 2220 Feltwell. Crashed in the sea off
Sgt C D Lynch   +   the Frisian Islands. Three of those who died
Sgt R E Drake RCAF   +   are buried in Sage War Cemetery, Oldenburg.
Sgt M D Hennessy   pow   Sgt C D Lynch has no known grave and his name
Sgt L W Collins   pow   is commemorated on the Runnymede Memorial.
Sgt H P Lynch   +

58 Sqn   Whitley V   T4285 GE-O   Op: Emden

Sgt H A Williams   T/o 2306 Linton-on-Ouse. Crashed 2320 with
F/S Knight   its bomb load intact into the River Ouse.
P/O Rees   No injuries reported.
Sgt Horne
Sgt Fenton

61 Sqn   Hampden I   AE189 QR-   Op: Kiel

F/O M Parry   +   T/o 2304 North Luffenham. Shot down by
P/O G P Wise DFM   +   a night-fighter and crashed 0105 into the
F/S A F Hill   +   sea off the Dutch port of Den Helder. F/S
Sgt I F Waugh RNZAF   +   Hill is buried in Westerschelling General
     Cemetery, Terschelling and Sgt Waugh RNZAF
lies in Kiel War Cemetery. The rest of the crew have no known graves.

103 Sqn   Wellington IC   R1397 PM-   Op: Brest

Sgt M S Lund RNZAF   +   T/o 2340 Elsham Wolds. Lost without trace.
Sgt A E Owen   +   All are commemorated on the Runnymede Memorial.
Sgt J J Cox   +
Sgt R P Williams   +
Sgt A J Le Poidevin   +
Sgt F G Walker   +

304 Sqn   Wellington IC   X9620 NZ-   Op: Emden

F/O L J Karczewski   +   T/o 2305 Lindholme. Shot down by a night-
Sgt Z Witkowski   +   fighter (Oblt Egmont Prinz zur Lippe Weissenfel
F/O S W Rzepa   +   4./NJG1) and crashed 0224 at Opperdoes (Noord
F/O Z Zuwala   +   Holland), 3 km SW of Medemblik. Sgt Rzepa is
Sgt B Salamon   +   buried in Bergen General Cemetery; the rest
F/O J H G Musial   +   have been interned at Hoek van Holland.

25 Jul 1941   301 Sqn   Wellington IC   T2576 GR-D   Training

F/O W Rebuszynski   +   T/o Hemswell but crashed almost immediately
F/O Bernasinski   into trees bordering the airfield. The pilot,
     who was the only fatality, is buried in the
     Polish Plot at Newark Cemetery.

1419 Flt   Whitley V   Z6727   Air Test

F/L A D Jackson   inj   Engines failed while testing secret equipment
     and in the force-landing that followed, the
Whitley collided with a telegraph pole and crashed 1525 near Newmarket,
Cambridgeshire, injuring the eight persons on board.

25-26 Jul 1941   7 Sqn   Stirling I   N6035 MG-A   Op: Berlin

F/L M C G Sherwood   pow   T/o 2250 Oakington. Crashed at Oudorp (Noord
Sgt W P Wood   pow   Holland), 2 km W of Alkmaar.
Sgt B A A Fowler   pow
F/L G M Fuller   pow
Sgt R I Stone   pow
Sgt T F M Williams   pow
Sgt D C Allan RNZAF   pow

| 25-26 Jul
1941 | 10 Sqn | Whitley V | T4231 ZA-A | Op: Hannover |

25-26 Jul 1941

10 Sqn — Whitley V — T4231 ZA-A — Op: Hannover

P/O W McN Spiers MiD	+
Sgt W Puttick	+
P/O H J Daniels	+
Sgt C W F D E Lawson	+
Sgt D B Beverley	+

T/o 2228 Leeming. Crashed at Koersel (Limburg), 15 km NNW of Hasselt, Belgium. P/O Daniels had received a Commendation of Gallantry. All are buried in Koersel Communal Cemetery.

10 Sqn — Whitley V — Z6624 ZA-O — Op: Hannover

S/L P W F Landale DFC	+
P/O G Pringle	+
Sgt G Wells RNZAF	+
Sgt A W Earp	+
F/S G Christie	+

T/o 2221 Leeming. Crashed in the North Sea. Sgt Wells RNZAF was washed ashore at km-paal on Texel on 25 August 1941; he is buried in Den Burg General Cemetery. The graves of P/O Pringle and F/S Christie are in Kiel War Cemetery, while the rest of the crew are commemorated on the panels of the Runnymede Memorial.

15 Sqn — Stirling I — N6029 LS-K — Op: Berlin

F/L F Thompson RAAF	pow
F/L T H B Tayler	pow
Sgt J T Day	pow
Sgt B Beecroft	pow
Sgt F Smith	pow
Sgt L C Titterton	pow
Sgt H N Guymer RNZAF	pow

T/o Wyton. Badly shot about by a Ju 88 which caused significant damage to the Stirling's fuel tanks. Subsequently, the bomber ditched 0540 in the North Sea, roughly 40 km off the Dutch coast. The crew drifted for six days before their dinghy came ashore in the area of Zandvoort.

35 Sqn — Halifax I — L9507 TL-W — Op: Berlin

P/O E R P S Cooper	+
Sgt J M R Cruickshank	+
Sgt E Short MiD	+
F/S R V Collinge MiD	+
F/S A J Heller DFM	+
Sgt D J Mennie	+
F/S R A Bates	+

T/o 2242 Linton-on-Ouse. All are buried in the 1939-1945 War Cemetery at Berlin. Details of F/S Heller's DFM appeared in the London Gazette on 31 May 1940.

49 Sqn — Hampden I — X3151 EA-T — Op: Hannover

P/O Cooke	
P/O King	
Sgt Evans	
Sgt Newall	

T/o 2225 Scampton. Crash-landed 0514 on return to base, coming down 2 miles S of the airfield. No reported injuries.

50 Sqn — Hampden I — AE234 VN- — Op: Hannover

Sgt C G Montgomery	+
Sgt R H Rampton	+
Sgt W Ellsley	+
Sgt A E Medden	+

T/o 2240 Swinderby. Believed to have crashed near Thurlby, 7 miles SSW of Lincoln. All are buried in Thurlby (St. Germain) Churchyard.

83 Sqn — Hampden I — AD835 OL-G — Op: Hannover

Sgt P H Draper	pow
Sgt J N B Tate	+
Sgt E Marsden	+
Sgt F L T Ireson	+

T/o 2205 Scampton. Shot down by a night-fighter (Lt Lothar Linke, II./NJG1) and crashed 0357 off Schiermonnikoog. The three airmen who died are buried in Vredenhof Cemetery.

102 Sqn — Whitley V — Z6576 DY- — Op: Hannover

S/L E A Verdon-Roe	+
P/O W L Rees	+
Sgt A R Holmes	+
Sgt W A McGinley	+
Sgt L Netherclift	+

T/o 2224 Topcliffe. Shot down by a night-fighter and crashed in the North Sea 10 km W of De Kooy airfield, Holland. All are commemorated on the Runnymede Memorial.

102 Sqn — Whitley V — Z6866 DY- — Op: Hannover

Sgt H G Benfield	pow
P/O I P B Denton	pow
Sgt K S Carter	pow
Sgt W R Gibson	pow
Sgt R V Harnett	pow

T/o 2230 Topcliffe. Hit by flak and crashed 0235 at Maurik (Gelderland), 14 km ENE of Culemborg, Holland.

25-26 Jul	300 Sqn	Wellington IC	R1178 BH-L		Op: Hamburg

25-26 Jul 1941   **300 Sqn**   **Wellington IC**   **R1178 BH-L**   **Op: Hamburg**
P/O Klecha
P/O Gostomski
F/O Zurawski
Sgt Wize
Sgt Chanecki
Sgt Tomasziewski

T/o 2259 Hemswell. Ditched 9 miles NE of Cromer, Norfolk, while returning to base. All were rescued, unharmed.

300 Sqn   **Wellington IC**   **X9639 BH-E Assam Bomber I**   **Op: Hamburg**
Sgt M Sloma   +
P/O W Jakimowicz   +
P/O T Srzednicki   +
Sgt A Horak   +
Sgt F Zemmler   +
Sgt J Danielewicz   pow

T/o 2258 Hemswell. Those who died are buried in the Reichswald Forest War Cemetery.

27-28 Jul 1941   **44 Sqn**   **Hampden I**   **P4406 KM-**   **Op: Gardening**
Sgt P C Gammon   +
Sgt B Winchester   +
F/S G R Slater   +
Sgt N H Whittaker   +

T/o 2315 Waddington for a mining sortie off Lorient. Hit by flak and crashed in the sea. Sgt Whittaker is buried at Gavres Communal Cemetery, France; the rest have no known graves.

28 Jul 1941   **21 Sqn**   **Blenheim IV**   **P6954 YH-**   **Training**
P/O M Forster   +
F/S E E Sturgeon   +
F/S J Rennie   inj

Crashed at Swanton Morley, Norfolk, after colliding with an 88 Squadron machine. P/O Forster had previously served as a 2Lt in The Green Howards (Yorkshire Regiment).

88 Sqn   **Blenheim I**   **L1342 RH-**   **Training**
S/L P R Barr   inj
F/S H W Bennett   inj

Crashed in circumstances similar to those described above.

90 Sqn   **Fortress I**   **AN534 WP-**   **Air Test**
F/S H C G Brook   +
F/S R G Bradley   +
Sgt R Henderson   +
F/S R C A Muir   +
Sgt R Smith   +
Sgt P S Pugh   +

T/o 1700 Polebrook. Crashed shortly after 1700 while conducting a high altitude test. The Fortress entered very severe turbulence and this was followed by structural failure of the starboard wing. The bomber came down in the vicinity of Wilbarston, 4 miles W of Corby, Northamptonshire.

28-29 Jul 1941   **50 Sqn**   **Hampden I**   **AD902 VN-**   **Op: Gardening**
P/O Christophers
Sgt Glenn
Sgt Thompson
Sgt Bullin
crash-landed 0430 at base. No

T/o 2200 Swinderby to lay mines in Kiel Bay. Encountered severe electrical storms, which led to partial failure of the instruments and radio equipment. The mine was jettisoned in safe condition NE of Hull and the Hampden injuries reported.

50 Sqn   **Hampden I**   **AE159 VN-**   **Op: Gardening**
P/O W B Burrows   +
P/O J M Graham   +
F/S C J Jolin   +
Sgt C D Rose   +

T/o 2220 Swinderby to lay mines in Kiel Bay. Lost without trace. All are commemorated on the Runnymede Memorial.

29 Jul 1941   **78 Sqn**   **Whitley V**   **Z6838 EY-**   **Training**
Sgt Turnbull RCAF
cause of the accident was attributed to jammed ailerons.

T/o Middleton St. George and crashed almost immediately just beyond the airfield. The

30 Jul 1941   **18 Sqn**   **Blenheim IV**   **L9240 WV-G**   **Op: Kiel Canal**
Sgt H D Cue   pow
Sgt J M Jarrell RCAF   pow
Sgt P C Brewer   pow

T/o 1300 Horsham St. Faith.

Note. This Blenheim was a survivor of AASF operations in May 1940 and at the time of its demise had flown at least fifty-three operational sorties.

30 Jul 1941	82 Sqn	Blenheim IV	R3803 UX-N	Op: **Kiel Canal**

Sgt P Stocks +
Sgt G G Lee +
P/O E S Hale +

T/o 1243 Bodney. Crashed in the sea. Sgt Stocks has no known grave; his crew are buried in Fourfelt Cemetery, Esbjerg, Denmark.

82 Sqn   Blenheim IV   V6513 UX-S   Op: **Kiel Canal**

P/O J Bell +
Sgt J Tague +
Sgt E G Martin +

T/o 1243 Bodney. Lost in the vicinity of Heligoland. All are commemorated on the Runnymede Memorial.

106 Sqn   Hampden I   AD970 ZN-   **Air Test**

Sgt Lockyer
Sgt S E Thurston +
AC1 Sissons

T/o 1035 Coningsby. Stalled while flying low over the sea and crashed to the S of Skegness Pier, Lincolnshire. Sgt Thurston is commemorated on the Runnymede Memorial.

139 Sqn   Blenheim IV   V6176 XD-   Op: **Anti-shipping**

Sgt L H Gruer +
Sgt J M Blundell +
Sgt D G Dennis-Smithers +

T/o 1400 Oulton. Presumed lost over the sea. Sgt Blundell is buried in Fourfelt Cemetery, Esbjerg; the rest have no known graves.

139 Sqn   Blenheim IV   V6266 XD-   Op: **Anti-shipping**

Sgt G R Menish +
P/O P Brown +
Sgt R Haley +

T/o 1400 Oulton. Shot down by Me 110s from ZG76 and crashed 180 km N of Texel. All are commemorated on the Runnymede Memorial.

139 Sqn   Blenheim IV   V6322 XD-   Op: **Anti-shipping**

P/O P G Shillitoe +
Sgt P J Walder +
P/O E C Elder +

T/o 1400 Oulton. Presumed lost over the sea. P/O Elder is buried at Esbjerg in the Fourfelt Cemetery; the rest have no known graves.

139 Sqn   Blenheim IV   V6439 XD-   Op: **Anti-shipping**

Sgt W S Campbell +
Sgt R G McRobert +
Sgt S R B Severn +

T/o 1400 Oulton. Lost to Me 110s from ZG76, approximately 180 km N of Texel. All are commemorated on the Runnymede Memorial.

30-31 Jul 1941   44 Sqn   Hampden I   AD755 KM-   Op: **Köln**

Sgt J G Armstrong
Sgt C R Morley RCAF
Sgt J Flint
Sgt S C Edwards

T/o 2340 Waddington. Crash-landed 0115 at Carlton-le-Moorland, 9 miles SSW of Lincoln. No injuries reported.

61 Sqn   Hampden I   P4399 QR-   Op: **Köln**

Sgt Baker
F/S R J W Geater +
Sgt W Chambers +
Sgt W Butler +

T/o 2306 North Luffenham. Crashed 0400 at Deast Hill, Dartford, Kent, after the pilot lost control while flying in a violent electrical storm.

61 Sqn   Hampden I   AE266 QR-   Op: **Köln**

P/O P J N Adshead +
F/S Scott inj
F/S R R B Durtnall DFM +
Sgt K M Fillmore +

T/o 2318 North Luffenham. Crashed 0450 while trying to land at Upwood. F/S Durtnall, it will be recalled, had survived a very serious crash at the beginning of the year and at the time of his death, he was nearing the end of his tour of operations. On 18 February 1946, Sgt Fillmore's brother, F/L E G Fillmore DFC, died while on service and he is buried in the same grave as Sgt Fillmore at Sudbury Cemetery.

77 Sqn   Whitley V   T4212 KN-   Op: **Boulogne**

P/O D Iveson
Sgt W G Carter
Sgt Lloyd
Sgt E W Burgess
Sgt Morgan

T/o 0025 Topcliffe. Shortly after leaving the runway, the bomber stalled and crashed, bursting into flames on impact. The crew escaped with little more than a bad shaking.

Note. P/O Iveson continued his tour and soon became an outstanding bomber pilot. In late 1943 he took over command of 76 Squadron and when the war ended he remained in the RAF, eventually converting to jets and flying the Victor V-bomber with 10 Squadron in the late 1950s.

30-31 Jul 1941	99 Sqn	Wellington IC	T2957 LN-	Op: Köln

99 Sqn   Wellington IC   T2957 LN-   Op: Köln

P/O G N Bevan MiD +   T/o 0018 Waterbeach. All are buried in
Sgt T I Hicks +   the Canadian War Cemetery at Adegem, Belgium.
P/O B C Curtis +
Sgt W H Wyatt +
Sgt W G Herrod +
Sgt F L Molteni +

142 Sqn   Wellington II   W5364 QT-H   Op: Köln

F/S H A V Vidler +   T/o 0001 Binbrook. Crashed 0256 on heath
Sgt V R Sutton +   land in the Ashdown Forest near Nutley, 5
Sgt W S Brooks +   miles NNW of Uckfield, Sussex. The bomber
F/S A E Cave +   struck the ground at a slight nose down
Sgt T S Hathaway +   angle and with the port engine feathered.
Sgt L Saunders +

Note. Shortly after this tragic accident, the mother of Sgt Sutton arranged for the erection of a white wooden cross at the scene of the crash in memory of her son and his crew. In 1954, a stone cross and plaque were placed on the site and a sandstone wall was added in 1971. Since the late 1970s, Remembrance Day services have been held at this memorial to the six airmen who died in the service of their country, half a century ago. The inscription reads:

> To the glorious memory of
> Sgt P V R Sutton, Aged 24 years
> 142 Bom Sqdn RAF
> Also, his five companions
> who lost their lives here
> through enemy action,
> 31-7-41   Mother

144 Sqn   Hampden I   AD784 PL-   Op: Köln

P/O D Brook RNZAF +   T/o North Luffenham. Crashed in the sea off
Sgt P T Giblett +   the coast of Holland. P/O Pratt is buried in
P/O C D Hewson RCAF +   Bergen op Zoom War Cemetery; the rest are
P/O F E Pratt +   commemorated on the Runnymede Memorial.

144 Sqn   Hampden I   AE252 PL-   Op: Köln

Sgt G Harvey +   T/o North Luffenham. Crashed in the vicinity
Sgt J G Rogers RCAF +   of Cambrai (Nord), France, where the crew are
Sgt R B Chrisp +   buried in the Route de Solesmes Communal
Sgt R W Smale +   Cemetery.

150 Sqn   Wellington IC   W5719 JN-S   Op: Köln

Sgt P H C Parrott +   T/o 2325 Snaith. Returned early due to
Sgt J A Haswell +   adverse weather and crashed 0405 into high
Sgt J D Evelle RCAF +   ground at Upper Tor near Edale, Derbyshire.
Sgt D A Monk +
Sgt F K Webber +

1 Aug 1941   44 Sqn   Hampden I   AD966 KM-R   Air Test

Sgt G M Le Blanc Smith +   Crashed 1710 near South Park, Lincoln.
Sgt G D Dodds RCAF +   AC1 Clarke is described in the CWGC burial
Sgt A Forsythe +   register for Crowle Cemetery as being a
AC1 T B Jeffcote +   pilot under training.
AC1 A D Clark +

107 Sqn   Blenheim IV   N3568 OM-   Op: Anti-shipping

S/L H F Thomson +   T/o 1119 Great Massingham. Crashed in the sea
P/O A C Macpherson +   off Vlissingen, Holland, where the crew are
Sgt L C Williams +   buried in the town's Northern Cemetery.

107 Sqn   Blenheim IV   Z7498 OM-   Op: Anti-shipping

Sgt C E Powell +   T/o 1119 Great Massingham. Presumed crashed in
Sgt M Roberts pow   the sea. Sgt Powell has no known grave.
Sgt H E Hunt pow

2 Aug 1941	**82 Sqn**	**Blenheim IV**	**V6026 UX-M**	**Op: Anti-shipping**

W/C K O Burt DFC   +
Sgt W T Ellis DFM   +
F/S A D W Curr DFM   +

T/o 1315 Bodney to patrol Beat 9. Shot down by ship's flak off Den Helder. W/C Burt is buried in Bergen op Zoom War Cemetery; Sgt Ellis rests in Kiel War Cemetery, while F/S Curr's body was found near Esberg harbour, Denmark, and he was buried on 5 September 1941 in the Fourfelt Cemetery.

2-3 Aug 1941	**7 Sqn**	**Stirling I**	**N3663 MG-**	**Op: Berlin**

P/O C I Rolfe   pow
Sgt L R Burrows   +
Sgt D S Merrells   pow
Sgt C A Tout   pow
Sgt E R Amos   +
Sgt J N Alder   +
Sgt M A Young   +

T/o 2218 Oakington. Shot down by a night-fighter and crashed at Werder, Germany. Sgt Burrows was mortally wounded during the attack and he is buried, along with the rest of those who died, in the 1939-1945 War Cemetery at Berlin.

83 Sqn   **Hampden I**   **AE154 OL-H**   **Op: Kiel**

S/L F Newall
P/O S Monkhouse
P/O G M Bishop
Sgt H Dickerson

T/o 2240 Scampton. Ditched 0703 after running out of fuel some 40 miles E of Flamborough Head. The crew were rescued eleven hours later.

101 Sqn   **Wellington IC**   **R1088 SR-O**   **Op: Hamburg**

P/O Bundey
P/O Reynolds
Sgt Lewis
Sgt Hayter
Sgt France
Sgt Thompson

T/o 2234 Oakington. Crash-landed 0523 at Rodgerous Field, Park Farm, Brabourne, 6 miles ESE of Ashford, Kent. The bomber caught fire, but the crew escaped injury.

101 Sqn   **Wellington IC**   **R1800 SR-T**   **Op: Hamburg**

Sgt W R Davey   +
Sgt W Watson   +
Sgt L Hill   +
Sgt G A Smith   +
Sgt W H Walker   +
Sgt T C Quinlan   +

T/o 2248 Oakington. Shot down by a night-fighter (Fw Siegfried Ney, 4./NJG1) and crashed in the IJsselmeer. Two bodies were recovered from the water; Sgt Walker rests at Leeuwarden and Sgt Quinlan is buried at Scharl. The rest have no known graves.

103 Sqn   **Wellington IC**   **X3204 PM-**   **Op: Hamburg**

Sgt Kelsey

T/o 2230 Elsham Wolds. Ditched 0706 some 40 miles NE of Spurn Head.

Note. The page in the 103 Squadron ORB reporting this incident is barely readable, hence the exclusion of the rest of the crew.

104 Sqn   **Wellington II**   **W5580 EP-K**   **Op: Berlin**

P/O R H McGlashan   +
Sgt D G Hodge   +
F/O P B Verver   +
Sgt A E Simpkin   +
Sgt H P S White   +
Sgt E J Stevenson RCAF   +

T/o 2207 Driffield. Ditched in the North Sea and it is known that at least some, if not all of the crew, managed to get into the dinghy. On 10 August, following severe westerly gales, the dinghy, containing the bodies of P/O McGlashan and Sgt Simpkin, was washed ashore near Dikjendeel. Both were buried in Westerland Cemetery, Sylt, while seventeen days later the sea gave up the remains of F/O Verver and he was laid to rest in List Church Cemetery, Sylt. Since 1945, all have been reinterned in Kiel War Cemetery. Their companions are commemorated on the Runnymede Memorial.

405 Sqn   **Wellington II**   **W5483 LQ-J**   **Op: Berlin**

F/L T R Kipp RCAF   pow
F/L R F Terry RAAF   pow
Sgt R S Skan   pow
Sgt J W Murfin   pow
Sgt G A Pruette   pow
F/S W Menzies RCAF   pow

T/o 2210 Pocklington.

| 2-3 Aug
1941 | 405 Sqn | Wellington II | W5527 LQ-F | Op: Hamburg |

2-3 Aug 1941 — 405 Sqn — Wellington II — W5527 LQ-F — Op: Hamburg

P/O R Cox   +
P/O J R Horn RAAF   +
P/O A O Learmonth RCAF   +
F/S R M Thomas   +
Sgt J M Reed   +
Sgt H B McKenzie   +

T/o 2235 Pocklington. Crashed in the North Sea. The body of Sgt McKenzie was washed onto a sand dune at Husby Klit on 23 August; he is buried in Lemvig Cemetery, Denmark. The rest of the crew are commemorated on the Runnymede Memorial.

---

3 Aug 1941 — 21 Sqn — Blenheim IV — V6384 YH- — Training

Sgt L Cornish RCAF   inj
Sgt Relph   inj
Sgt Robson   inj

Crashed 1745 while trying to make an emergency landing 1 mile N of Portisham, 6 miles SW of Dorchester.

3-4 Aug 1941 — 218 Sqn — Wellington IC — X9747 HA-E — Op: Hannover

P/O J A Maxwell RCAF   +
P/O T G Cottier RCAF
P/O G F Jacobsen RCAF
F/S G P Hoult
Sgt G M Siddal
P/O G J L Crabb   +

T/o 2228 Marham. Due to severe turbulence and partial instrument failure, the crew were ordered to bale out. Four had complied, when the bomber crashed 2300 at Salthouse, 7 miles NE of Norwich.

218 Sqn — Wellington IC — Z8781 HA-S — Op: Hannover

W/C J L H Fletcher   +
Sgt F C Dodd   +
F/S R J Alexander   pow
F/S T A E Bridewell   +
F/S F Grail   +
Sgt E S Spong   pow

T/o 2254 Marham. Those who died are buried in Becklingen War Cemetery, Soltau.

---

5 Aug 1941 — 18 Sqn — Blenheim IV — V6519 WV- — Training

P/O T G Jefferson

Crashed 1623 while trying to land at Horsham St. Faith. No injuries reported.

5-6 Aug 1941 — 12 Sqn — Wellington II — W5421 PH-G — Op: Aachen

F/L R B Langlois   pow
Sgt J W McLarnon   pow
Sgt H J E Burrell   pow
F/S R A Copley   pow
Sgt R D Porteous RNZAF   pow
Sgt J L Newton   evd

T/o 2225 Binbrook. Landed on Antwerpen-Deurne airfield, where the crew set fire to the Wellington in order to prevent it from falling into enemy hands.

50 Sqn — Hampden I — AE137 VN- — Op: Karlsruhe

Sgt D G Fothergill   +
Sgt S O Hirschfield   +
Sgt H Smith   +
Sgt A Davies   +

T/o 2205 Swinderby. Crashed at Essen, where the crew were initially laid to rest in the Süd-West Friedhof. All have since been taken to the Reichswald Forest War Cemetery.

51 Sqn — Whitley V — Z6803 MH-J — Op: Frankfurt

P/O M W Tilley   +
Sgt O L M Williams   +
Sgt K A Dean   +
Sgt L W J Hart RCAF   pow

T/o 2210 Dishforth. Crashed in the vicinity of Liège, where those who died are buried in St. Walburg Communal Cemetery.

76 Sqn — Halifax I — L9516 MP- — Op: Karlsruhe

Sgt T A Byrne   pow
Sgt C B Flockhart   pow
Sgt J H Pitt   pow
Sgt L A Thompson   pow
Sgt G W S Taylor   pow
Sgt R Brown   +
F/L T B Leigh   pow

T/o Middleton St. George. Believed to have crashed near Glabbeek (Brabant), 8 km N of Tienen, Belgium, though Sgt Brown is buried in Durnbach War Cemetery, Germany. F/L Leigh, an Australian serving with the RAF, was shot by the Gestapo on 30 March 1944, after taking part in the mass break out from Sagan. He is buried in Poznan Old Garrison Cemetery, Poland. Sgt Flockhart made a successful escape from captivity.

5-6 Aug 1941	77 Sqn	Whitley V		Z6826 KN- Op: Frankfurt

5-6 Aug 1941

77 Sqn   **Whitley V**   **Z6826 KN-**   **Op: Frankfurt**

P/O D G Baber — pow
Sgt A Day RCAF — evd
P/O I A Kayes — pow
Sgt W F Thuell — pow
Sgt M B C Delaney RCAF — pow

T/o 2207 Topcliffe. After bombing Koblenz as an alternative target, the Whitley was hit by flak and subsequently abandoned near Meulebeke (West Vlaanderen), 6 km SSW of Tielt, Belgium. Sgt Day RCAF was assisted by the Comète organisation.

103 Sqn   **Wellington IC**   **W5656 PM-**   **Op: Frankfurt**

Sgt D M Greey — +
Sgt J P Taylor RCAF — +
Sgt J Moules — +
Sgt F W Alleway — +
Sgt R M G Griffin — +
Sgt C Deges — +

T/o 2245 Elsham Wolds. Reported crashed at Château Ledquent, Marquise (Pas-de-Calais), 15 km SW of Calais.

104 Sqn   **Wellington II**   **W5485 EP-J**   **Op: Karlsruhe**

P/O B W M Jones — +
Sgt W S Denby RAAF — +
P/O H Brant — +
F/S R J David — +
Sgt R N Barcroft — +
Sgt G F Lister — +

T/o 2234 Driffield. All are buried in Durnbach War Cemetery.

104 Sqn   **Wellington II**   **W5517 EP-**   **Op: Saarbrücken**

Sgt W T R Stephenson RCAF
Sgt Nowlan
Sgt Moore
Sgt K Hutchinson
Sgt Storer
Sgt Clynes

T/o 2235 Driffield. Hit by flak over the target and on return crash-landed at Horsham St. Faith airfield, Norfolk, where the bomber was declared beyond economical repair.

106 Sqn   **Hampden I**   **AE120 ZN-**   **Op: Mannheim**

Sgt W L Knowles RNZAF — +
Sgt J M Macilwraith — +
F/S A P Price DFM — +
Sgt C Rhodes — +

T/o 2225 Coningsby. Shot down by a night-fighter and crashed onto a house in Gendringen (Gelderland), 30 km ESE of Arnhem. Two people living in the house were killed; the crew are buried in Gendringen Roman Catholic Cemetery.

115 Sqn   **Wellington IC**   **R1471 KO-T**   **Op: Mannheim**

F/L F L Litchfield — pow
Sgt R H Hilton-Jones — pow
Sgt D A Boutle — pow
Sgt A S Lawson — pow
Sgt E F Lambert — pow
Sgt Walker — pow

T/o 2247 Marham. Sgt Boutle sustained a fractured skull and, it is reported, Sgt Walker broke his leg. The remainder escaped serious injury.

149 Sqn   **Wellington IC**   **R1524 OJ-P**   **Op: Mannheim**

Sgt F D Fowler — +
Sgt E A R Thomson — +
Sgt H Hale RCAF — +
Sgt V Scholey — +
Sgt B A J Richardson — +
Sgt S Morris — +

T/o 2211 Mildenhall. Crashed at St. Martens-Voeren (Liège), 18 km NNW of Verviers, Belgium. All are buried in St. Martens-Voeren (Fouron-St. Martin) Churchyard.

305 Sqn   **Wellington II**   **W5593 SM-**   **Op: Frankfurt**

S/L S Scibior — pow
Sgt M Kowalski — evd
Sgt W Rybak — +
F/O M Saferna — +
F/O J J S Sukiennik — +
Sgt S Tomicki — evd

T/o Lindholme. Those who died are buried in Charleroi Communal Cemetery, Belgium.

6 Aug 1941

77 Sqn   **Whitley V**   **Z6740 KN-**   **Training**

P/O Ogston — +
P/O J A Quick — +
P/O A W Tomlinson — +
Sgt H J Gibbs — +

Crashed 1345 at Alveston, 2 miles NE of Stratford-upon-Avon, Warwickshire, following an in flight fire which resulted in structural failure of the mainplanes.

6-7 Aug 1941	11 OTU	Wellington IC	Z8807	Op: Nickel

11 OTU   Wellington IC   **Z8807**   Op: **Nickel**

Sgt J A Walker RCAF   pow
Sgt R Charlesworth   pow
Sgt T Humphery   pow
Sgt R C Mackenzie RAAF   pow
Sgt L E Sparks   pow
Sgt S J Pryor   pow

T/o Bassinbourn to drop leaflets over France. Believed to have been the first bomber OTU aircraft reported missing from a flight over enemy occupied territory.

44 Sqn   Hampden I   **X2917 KM-R**   Op: **Calais**

Sgt C S Bradbury   +
Sgt W J McQuade RCAF   +
F/S S D Yeomans   +
Sgt D H Howe   +

T/o 2235 Waddington. Encountered bad weather over East Anglia and, after clipping the tops of trees, crashed just inside the perimeter of Barton Bendish airfield, then a satellite base for Marham, Norfolk.

51 Sqn   Whitley V   **Z6488 MH-W**   Op: **Frankfurt**

Sgt R J Allen   pow
Sgt A R B Ward   pow
P/O F T Clayton   pow
Sgt G Haines   inj
Sgt P E Tripp   pow

T/o 2200 Dishforth. Shot down by a night-fighter (Ofw Reinhard Kollak, I./NJG1) and crashed 0221 at Ginder Farm, Heeze (Noord Brabant), 8 km SE of Eindhoven. Sgt Haines died within a few hours of the crash and he is buried in Woensel General Cemetery.

51 Sqn   Whitley V   **Z6808 MH-N**   Op: **Frankfurt**

P/O G E Pinney
Sgt Ganley
P/O Gallaher
Sgt Keen
Sgt Bradshaw

T/o 2208 Dishforth. Abandoned over Swanton Morley airfield due to severe icing. Moments later the Whitley crashed at East Bradenham, 5 miles SW of East Dereham, Norfolk and was burnt out. Norfolk Civil Defence files show the crash occurring at 0300.

57 Sqn   Wellington IC   **Z8704 DX-**   Op: **Mannheim**

Sgt B Cleaver   pow
Sgt M P Whitworth   pow
Sgt E Lloyd   pow
Sgt R Parish   pow
Sgt N C Davies   pow
Sgt D McCaig   pow

T/o 2225 Feltwell. Last heard on w/t at 0555, at which time the Wellington was plotted over French territory.

58 Sqn   Whitley V   **Z6835 GE-Q**   Op: **Frankfurt**

P/O A A Law
Sgt C O Steggall
Sgt Kemp
Sgt Cartledge
P/O Harris

T/o 2235 Linton-on-Ouse. Overshot on return to base and crashed 0557 into a hangar. No serious injuries reported.

75 Sqn   Wellington IC   **R1648 AA-**   Op: **Mannheim**

Sgt L I A Millett   pow
Sgt R G Morgan RNZAF   pow
Sgt D Polley   pow
Sgt C Simpson   pow
Sgt J W Bottomley   +
Sgt W N K Mellon   +

T/o Feltwell. Ditched in the North Sea. Sgt Bottomley was killed when the aircraft hit the water and Sgt Mellon drowned as the Wellington sank. Both are commemorated on the Runnymede Memorial.

78 Sqn   Whitley V   **T4158 EY-**   Op: **Frankfurt**

P/O Atchison
Sgt Harwood
Sgt McMullan
Sgt Elliott
Sgt J Bell

T/o Middleton St. George. Ditched 12 km N of Dunkerque. The crew were picked by HSL145, out from Dover, in the face of heavy gunfire from enemy coastal batteries.

144 Sqn   Hampden I   **AD903 PL-A**   Op: **Calais**

Sgt P A Hammond   +
Sgt R T Clark   +
Sgt J H H Cutmore   +
Sgt E F Reeve   +

T/o North Luffenham. Lost without trace. All are commemorated on the Runnymede Memorial.

| 6-7 Aug 1941 | 144 Sqn | Hampden I | AE140 PL- | Op: **Karlsruhe** |

144 Sqn   **Hampden I**   **AE140 PL-**   **Op: Karlsruhe**

6-7 Aug 1941

P/O S W S Beedie RNZAF +
Sgt H E Fear RCAF +
Sgt J R Cook +
Sgt F T Prest +

T/o North Luffenham. Lost without trace. All are commemorated on the Runnymede Memorial.

149 Sqn   **Wellington IC**   **X9633 OJ-R**   **Op: Mannheim**

Sgt J T Farmer +
Sgt F S Ellis +
Sgt D E G Denier RAAF +
Sgt G Lickley +
Sgt V B Quinlan RCAF +
Sgt A Yoxall +

T/o 2239 Mildenhall. Crashed at Thorembais St. Trond (Brabant), 15 km SE of Wavre, Belgium. All are buried in Thorembais St. Trond Communal Cemetery.

150 Sqn   **Wellington IC**   **W5721 JN-Z**   **Op: Frankfurt**

P/O C Landreth +
P/O A C Anderson RNZAF +
P/O A F Bruce +
Sgt J H Bolton +
Sgt W J Culley +
P/O A W Lambert +

T/o 2235 Snaith. All are buried in the Reichswald Forest War Cemetery. P/O Lambert's father served in the 3rd Bn The Rifle Brigade, dying from his wounds, in France, on 19 February 1915.

214 Sqn   **Wellington IC**   **X9750 BU-**   **Op: Mannheim**

P/O C McD Didsbury RNZAF +
Sgt R G Burnett +
Sgt W J V Crowsley +
Sgt N E Mills +
Sgt E J Page +
P/O G D E Stack RCAF +

T/o Stradishall. Lost without trace. All are commemorated on the Runnymede Memorial.

300 Sqn   **Wellington IC**   **X9676 BH-M**   **Op: Frankfurt**

F/L H J Cichowski +
F/O S Jasinski +
F/O T Chrostowski +
Sgt F Jezierski +
Sgt C Szczukowski +
F/O E Jura +

T/o 2212 Hemswell. Crashed in the North Sea. Two bodies, those of F/L Cichowski and F/O Jura, were recovered from the water and taken for burial in the Polish Plot at Newark Cemetery.

7 Aug 1941   **7 Sqn**   **Stirling I**   **N3636 MG-A**   **Ground**

Mainplanes twisted after slipping from its jacks at Oakington. The airframe was later converted for instructional purposes as 3056M. This particular Stirling had been delivered to the Squadron on 24 September 1940, but only flew one operation and had been grounded since late June 1941.

107 Sqn   **Blenheim IV**   **R3816 OM-**   **Training**

P/O H A T Lind +
Sgt N W Paples +

T/o 1755 Manston but crashed almost immediately after the starboard elevator tab jammed.

7-8 Aug 1941   **15 Sqn**   **Stirling I**   **N3658 LS-E**   **Op: Essen**

P/O F J Needham +
S/L J Vivian +
Sgt G W Jeffrey RCAF +
Sgt S H Broyd +
Sgt J T Corbett +
F/S R A Ross +
Sgt K L Rowley +

T/o Wyton. Shot down by a night-fighter and crashed at Overasselt (Gelderland), 8 km SSW of Nijmegen. All are buried in Uden War Cemetery.

83 Sqn   **Hampden I**   **X3118 OL-J**   **Op: Essen**

F/S F J Wood +
P/O J E Cunning +
Sgt E C Matthewman +
Sgt W J Mackay +

T/o 2330 Scampton. Crashed into the sea off the Dutch coast. Three bodies were recovered and taken for burial in various cemeteries, but P/O Cunning has no known grave.

97 Sqn   **Hampden I**   **AE303 OF-**   **Op: Essen**

P/O B B H Rodwell +
Sgt G P Imison +
F/S M C Harvey +
F/S R R Bell +

T/o Coningsby. Crashed in the North Sea. F/S Bell is buried in Westerschelling General Cemetery on Terschelling; his companions are commemorated on the Runnymede Memorial.

8 Aug	114 Sqn	Blenheim IV	R3743 RT-	Training

1941   F/L Patterson

Crash-landed 0953 on marshes near North Wootton, 3 miles NNE of King's Lynn, Norfolk. Shortly before the crash, the Blenheim had hit the sea during bombing practice.

114 Sqn	Blenheim IV	V6522 RT-	Training

P/O S R O Richmond RNZAF inj
Sgt J D Mackay   +

Crashed in circumstances similar to those previously described, though this particular aircraft came down near the railway station.

139 Sqn	Blenheim IV	N3627 XD-	Training

Sgt J A Gibbs   +
Sgt J P Shaw   +
Sgt D Beale

Crashed 0944 near North Barningham church at Barningham Park to the NW of Matlaske, Norfolk. Two of the crew baled out, but Sgt Shaw, a Canadian serving in the RAF, had only one hook of his parachute fastened and this fatally delayed the canopy from deploying.

8-9 Aug	10 Sqn	Whitley V	Z6815 ZA-	Op: Kiel

1941
P/O M Littlewood   +
Sgt E Bayley   +
P/O J E Evans   +
Sgt R T Timms   +
Sgt N Moores   +

T/o 2154 Leeming. Crashed in the target area. P/O Evans has no known grave, but the rest of the crew are buried in Kiel War Cemetery. P/O Littlewood was a Canadian and his brother was also killed on active service.

50 Sqn	Hampden I	AE124 VN-	Op: Gardening

P/O Milnes
P/O R F B Temperley
Sgt Graver
Sgt Bigby

T/o Swinderby for a mining operation off the Frisian Islands, but the port engine cut and the Hampden crashed near the airfield. No serious injuries reported.

61 Sqn	Hampden I	X3127 QR-	Op: Kiel

P/O J W W Graham   pow
Sgt L R Biddlecombe   pow
Sgt W D Hughes   pow
Sgt A C Nuttall RNZAF   +

T/o 2218 North Luffenham. Believed crashed near Kiel. Sgt Nuttall RNZAF is reported to have been killed in the air; he is buried in Kiel War Cemetery.

61 Sqn	Hampden I	AE259 QR-	Op: Kiel

P/O Metcalfe
P/O McCulloch
Sgt Ashurst
Sgt McKeown

T/o 2216 North Luffenham. On return the crew passed over an Allied convoy off Spurn Head and were promptly fired upon. Damaged, the Hampden crash-landed 0530 near Fosdyke on the N bank of the Welland, close to where the river enters The Wash, some 6 miles SSE of Boston, Lincolnshire.

61 Sqn	Hampden I	AE263 QR-	Op: Kiel

Sgt T Craven   +
Sgt V E Baker   +
Sgt G S Lodington   +
F/S E N R Robertson   +

T/o 2225 North Luffenham. Lost without trace. All are commemorated on the Runnymede Memorial.

78 Sqn	Whitley V	Z6655 EY-	Op: Kiel

Sgt J W Bell
Sgt Pindon
Sgt Buttell
Sgt R Boucher
Sgt Porter

T/o 2219 Middleton St. George. Hit by flak over the target and severely damaged. Unable to make the English coast, the crew ditched 78 miles NE of Blyth, Northumberland.

301 Sqn	Wellington IC	T2625 GR-B	Op: Hamburg

F/O M Liniewski   +
F/O J L M Wiszniewski   +
P/O S Cioch   +
Sgt Z Baderski   pow
Sgt E Kozlowski   +
Sgt I Gacon   pow

T/o 2226 Hemswell. Shot down by a night-fighter (Oblt Ludwig Becker, 4./NJG1) and crashed 0025 just inside German territory opposite the Dutch town of Nieuwe Schans (Groningen), 12 km ENE of Winschoten. Those who died are now buried in Hannover War Cemetery.

10 Aug 1941	114 Sqn	Blenheim IV	L8751 RT-	Training

10 Aug 1941

114 Sqn   Blenheim IV   L8751 RT-   **Training**
Sgt F V Clarke   inj
Sgt J M O'Grady   +
Crashed 1615 while trying to make an emergency landing at West Raynham airfield, Norfolk.

226 Sqn   Blenheim IV   V5854 MQ-L   Op: **Anti-shipping**
S/L M W Waddington   +
F/S I N Forsyth   +
F/S D Palmer   +
T/o Wattisham. Hit by flak while leading an attack on a convoy and seen to crash in the sea. All are commemorated on the Runnymede Memorial.

226 Sqn   Blenheim IV   Z7280 MQ-M   Op: **Anti-shipping**
Sgt J M Osborne RCAF   +
Sgt K A McManus RCAF   +
Sgt W Roberts   +
T/o Wattisham. Shot down by Me 109s into the Strait of Dover. Two are commemorated on the Runnymede Memorial, but the body of Sgt Osborne RCAF was eventually washed onto German territory and his grave may be found in Kiel War Cemetery.

12 Aug 1941

18 Sqn   Blenheim IV   V6423 WV-P   Op: **Köln-Knapsack**
P/O G H Hill   pow
P/O R Chadwick   pow
Sgt L A F Parrish   pow
T/o 0920 Horsham St. Faith. Crashed at Diest (Brabant), Belgium. P/O Chadwick received very severe leg injuries and was later repatriated.

18 Sqn   Blenheim IV   V6437 WV-C   Op: **Köln-Knapsack**
P/O M T K Walkden   +
P/O B F W Matthews   +
Sgt A C Cutler   +
T/o 0920 Horsham St. Faith. Crashed in the sea off the Dutch coast. Sgt Cutler is buried in Vlissingen Northern Cemetery; his companions are commemorated on the Runnymede Memorial.

18 Sqn   Blenheim IV   V6497 WV-U   Op: **Köln-Knapsack**
S/L A F H Mills RCAF   pow
F/O W A Staniland   pow
Sgt L C Mitchell   pow
T/o 0925 Horsham St. Faith. Ditched in the North Sea, after clearing the Dutch coast, homebound.

21 Sqn   Blenheim IV   V5874 YH-P   Op: **Köln-Quadrath**
P/O J W Corfield   +
P/O A L A Williams   +
P/O M F Williams   +
T/o 0928 Watton. Crashed into the sea off Texel, where the crew are buried in Den Burg General Cemetery.

21 Sqn   Blenheim IV   Z7451 YH-D   Op: **Köln-Quadrath**
Sgt G J Langston   pow
Sgt D J Roberts   pow
Sgt K V Attew   +
T/o 0930 Watton. Hit by flak, which killed Sgt Attew, and crashed at Köln-Porz. Sgt Attew is buried in Rheinberg War Cemetery.

82 Sqn   Blenheim IV   T2437 UX-Y   Op: **Köln-Quadrath**
P/O G C Rolland   +
P/O H M Clark   +
Sgt E Bainbridge   +
T/o Bodney. Hit by flak and crashed 1210 at Strijensas in the Hoekse Waard polder, 10 km SW of Dordrecht, Holland. All are buried in Strijen Protestant Cemetery.

114 Sqn   Blenheim IV   Z7281 RT-P   Op: **Köln-Knapsack**
Sgt D J Wheatley   +
Sgt J L West   +
Sgt J Stead   +
T/o 0910 West Raynham. Hit by flak and crashed in the Westerschelde off Vlissingen. Sgt Stead has no known grave, but his two companions were taken northwards by the tides and both rest in Sage War Cemetery.

139 Sqn   Blenheim IV   V5725 XD-   Op: **Köln-Knapsack**
Sgt H Ingleby RCAF   +
Sgt D F J Phillips   +
F/S G H Appleyard   +
T/o 0949 Oulton. Crashed at Berrenrath, 12 km SW of Köln. All are buried in Rheinberg War Cemetery.

139 Sqn   Blenheim IV   V6261 XD-   Op: **Köln-Knapsack**
F/L A G Herbert RNZAF   +
P/O C C O George   +
Sgt G Benton   +
T/o 0949 Oulton. Shot down off the Dutch coast by fighters. Two are buried in Bergen General Cemetery; P/O George has no known grave.

139 Sqn   Blenheim IV   Z7448 XD-   Op: **Köln-Knapsack**
Sgt G Coast   pow
P/O K J Mackintosh   pow
Sgt D A Wilson   +
T/o 0949 Oulton. Crashed at Hücheln, 11 km WSW of Köln. Sgt Wilson is buried in Rheinberg War Cemetery.

12 Aug 1941	226 Sqn	Blenheim IV	V5859 MQ-	Op: Fighter Support

F/L G I Lewis +
F/S N S Cardell +
F/S J C Woods +

T/o 1000 Martlesham Heath. Hit by flak and crashed near Philipoine (Zeeus Vlaanderen), Belgium. All are buried in Vlissingen Northern Cemetery, Holland.

| 226 Sqn | Blenheim IV | Z7352 MQ- | Op: Fighter Support |

F/L H S Young +
P/O A C Rossiter +
Sgt J A Anderson +

T/o 1000 Ipswich. Shot down by Me 109s and crashed in the Westerschelde off Zoutelande. F/L Young is buried in Noordwijk General Cemetery; his crew have no known graves.

| 12-13 Aug
1941 | 9 Sqn | Wellington IC | R1341 WS-Z | Op: Hannover |

Sgt E Lewin +
Sgt G B Smith RCAF +
Sgt J A Lennard +
F/S C W A Wells +
Sgt H F Barron +
Sgt R R Passmore RNZAF +

T/o 2120 Honington. Shot down at Rotenburg, 24 km NE of Verden, Germany. All were buried at Rotenburg but since 1945 their remains have been taken to Becklingen War Cemetery, Soltau.

| 9 Sqn | Wellington IC | R1513 WS- | Op: Kiel |

F/L K R Ball MiD +
Sgt S Wintersgill +
Sgt E Cullen +
Sgt C H Chandler +
Sgt A T Hatton RCAF +
Sgt T E McGeragle RCAF +

T/o 2129 Honington. Crashed in the River Weser. Four bodies were recovered and since the end of hostilities have been laid to rest in Becklingen War Cemetery. Sgt Cullen and Sgt Hatton RCAF have no known graves and both are commemorated on the Runnymede Memorial.

| 15 Sqn | Stirling I | N3656 LS-H | Op: Berlin |

P/O J E M Conran
P/O S P Edgehill
Sgt Spicer
P/O H V D Bonney
F/S Munns
Sgt Ward
Sgt McMahon

T/o Wyton. Badly damaged by enemy action and on return crash-landed at Honington airfield, Suffolk, with unserviceable hydraulics and a propeller shot away. Written off as beyond economical repair.

| 15 Sqn | Stirling I | N3659 LS-N | Op: Berlin |

Sgt J D Jeffrey pow
Sgt G T Taylor +
Sgt R B Strachan +
Sgt G K Henson RCAF +
F/S W E Barrett +
Sgt H G Dickson RCAF +
Sgt V N Taylor pow

T/o Wyton. Shot down by a night-fighter and crashed at Berxen, 30 km SSE of Bremen. Those who died are buried in Hannover War Cemetery.

| 35 Sqn | Halifax I | L9497 TL-K | Op: Berlin |

P/O J McGregor-Cheers
Sgt Burns RCAF inj
Sgt W N Collins
Sgt A A S Heggie
Sgt J Fuller
Sgt J B Anderson RCAF
P/O V M Markham

T/o 2125 Linton-on-Ouse. Hit by flak in the port outer engine, which later failed completely. Crash-landed 0445 at Ashcroft Farm, Hindolveston, 7 miles E of Fakenham, Norfolk. Both pilots were thrown from the aircraft, Sgt Burns RCAF sustaining a broken ankle.

| 76 Sqn | Halifax I | L9531 MP-R | Op: Berlin |

Sgt C E Whitfield +
Sgt J J Berry +
Sgt K R F Kenworthy pow
P/O V D Durham +
Sgt A Critchlow +
Sgt N F Brotherton +
F/S W A I Bone pow

T/o 2134 Middleton St. George. Shot down by a night-fighter (Lt Hans Autenrieth, 6./NJG1) and crashed 500 metres E of Wittstedt, 15 km SSE of Bremerhaven. All baled out, but fate intervened and five fell into a swamp and drowned. Of the two survivors, F/S Bone was killed on 19 April 1945, when Allied fighters shot up the prisoner of war column in which he was marching. He is buried in the 1939-1945 War Cemetery at Berlin, while the rest of those who died are interned in Becklingen War Cemetery, Soltau.

12-13 Aug 1941	76 Sqn	Halifax I	

76 Sqn   Halifax I   **L9530 MP-L**   **Op: Berlin**

F/L C C Cheshire   pow
Sgt P H T Horrox   pow
Sgt R C Wash   pow
F/S G J Smalley   pow
Sgt E C Gurmin   pow
Sgt A T Niven   +
F/S W Woods   +

T/o 2135 Middleton St. George. Shot down by flak near Parnewinkel, a small town roughly midway between Bremerhaven and Hamburg. The two airmen who died are buried in Becklingen War Cemetery, Soltau. F/L Cheshire was the brother of Leonard Cheshire VC, who later commanded 76 Squadron.

76 Sqn   Halifax I   **L9562 MP-**   **Op: Berlin**

Sgt J McHale   +
Sgt R J McInnes RCAF   +
Sgt C Austin   +
Sgt S C Mayes   +
Sgt E P Hogan   +
Sgt L E Brown RCAF   +
F/S J G S West DFM   +

T/o 2129 Middleton St. George. Crashed 0525 on return to base. The Halifax stalled on its approach to land and on impact burst into flames. An examination of the wreckage suggested the bomber may have been damaged by enemy action.

97 Sqn   Manchester I   **L7424 OF-**   **Op: Berlin**

F/O J A Little   pow
F/O M G Geoghegan   pow
Sgt G R Tiley   pow
F/S R G W Hodgkinson   pow
Sgt L Robinson   pow
Sgt G L Scott RNZAF   pow
F/S R W Jones   pow

T/o 2102 Coningsby. Last heard on w/t at 0228 indicating the crew were about to bale out. Subsequently, the Manchester crashed near Münster, where Sgt Scott RNZAF was admitted to hospital with a broken leg.

99 Sqn   Wellington IC   **R1503 LN-**   **Op: Boulogne**

P/O G S Eccles

T/o Waterbeach but due to poor trimming, the Wellington failed to gain height and, after flying into tree tops, crashed 2 miles ENE of the airfield, injuring three of the crew.

104 Sqn   Wellington II   **W5443 EP-T**   **Op: Berlin**

Sgt R C Holyman   +
Sgt R E C Hudson   +
Sgt G Cox   +
Sgt W Maxwell RCAF   +
F/S T Herrington   +
Sgt T Bell   +

T/o 2136 Driffield. All are buried in Hannover War Cemetery.

104 Sqn   Wellington II   **W5461 EP-R**   **Op: Berlin**

S/L H Budden DFC   pow
Sgt J D Morgan   pow
Sgt C K Mousley   pow
Sgt L G Smalley   pow
Sgt D Storer   pow
F/S D F Sugden RCAF   pow

T/o 2125 Driffield. Sgt Morgan broke an ankle after landing heavily, while Sgt Smalley was the sole survivor from a 102 Squadron Whitley which crashed on 29 August 1940. Their skipper, S/L Budden, joined 51 Squadron prior to the outbreak of war and completed his first tour of operations by early July 1940.

115 Sqn   Wellington IC   **T2563 KO-D**   **Op: Essen**

P/O Wood
Sgt R A Hodges   inj
P/O A J A Day RAAF   inj
Sgt C D Tavener   inj
Sgt S W Morton RCAF   inj
Sgt B G Evans RNZAF   +

T/o 2134 Marham. Shot down by a Ju 88C intruder (Ofw Peter Laufs, I./NJG2) and crashed 0220 at Smith's Farm, Scottow, 4 miles SSW of North Walsham, Norfolk.

115 Sqn   Wellington IC   **Z8835 KO-U**   **Op: Essen**

Sgt J T Wallace RNZAF   +
Sgt R Keighley   +
Sgt J Porthouse   +
Sgt R G F Aldersley RCAF   +
Sgt A W Morgan   +
Sgt D J Nolan   +

T/o 2127 Marham. Sgt Keighley has no known grave; the rest of the crew are buried in Becklingen War Cemetery, Soltau.

12-13 Aug 1941	142 Sqn	Wellington II	W5433 QT-	Op: **Berlin**

F/L A D Gosman — pow
P/O J R Gibbon — pow
F/L R McD Durham — pow
Sgt L Frith — pow
Sgt K S Holman — pow
Sgt J Jackson RNZAF — pow

T/o 2046 Binbrook. Last heard on w/t indicating the port engine had failed and the Wellington was being abandoned.

---

149 Sqn Wellington IC R1024 OJ-V Op: **Hannover**

P/O F H Beemer RCAF — +
Sgt P E H Dangerfield — +
P/O F W J Scott RCAF — +
Sgt J R Littlefield — +
Sgt C F Young — +
Sgt E W Hall — +

T/o 2116 Mildenhall. Crashed in the sea off Sylt. Both Canadians are buried in Kiel War Cemetery; the remainder of the crew have no known graves and their names are commemorated on the Runnymede Memorial.

---

149 Sqn Wellington IC T2716 OJ-W Op: **Hannover**

P/O Fox
Sgt Woodhouse
Sgt G Morris RCAF — inj
F/S Batten
Sgt A N Hampson — +
Sgt N Jones

T/o 2114 Mildenhall. Hit by flak, which killed Sgt Hampson, and further damaged by a night-fighter. On return to base, the Wellington crash-landed 0520 at Elvedon, Suffolk, 3 miles SW of Thetford, Norfolk, fatally injuring Sgt Morris RCAF.

---

207 Sqn Manchester I L7377 EM-G Op: **Berlin**

S/L G R Taylor DFC — +
P/O J J Nottidge — +
F/S T Beattie DFM — +
F/S G R Birt DFM — +
F/S W Wetherill — pow
Sgt D H McPhail — inj

T/o Waddington. Hit by flak and crashed 0200 at Grossbeeren, 5 km SE of Teltow, Germany. Sgt McPhail survived the crash, but died on 14 August while undergoing treatment for his burns. Along with the rest of those who died, he is buried in the 1939-1945 War Cemetery at Berlin.

---

207 Sqn Manchester I L7381 EM-R Op: **Berlin**

F/O W M R Smith DFC — +
F/S A R Cotterell — +
P/O E A Reeman — +
Sgt J Allen — +
F/S A Halfpenny DFM — +
Sgt A E Coakes — +

T/o Waddington. Shot down by a night-fighter (Oblt Ludwig Becker, 4./NJG1) and crashed 0125 at the Lange Dijk at Slochteren (Groningen), 16 km E of Groningen, Holland. All are buried in the Canadian War Cemetery at Holten.

13-14 Aug 1941 83 Sqn Hampden I AD935 OL-U **Training**

P/O E R Davis — +
Sgt G A Newbold — +
Sgt W Wells — inj

T/o 2020 Scampton. Crashed 0040 after colliding with trees at Badsey, 2 miles ESE of Evesham, Worcestershire.

---

14 Aug 1941 110 Sqn Blenheim IV V6515 VE- Op: **Anti-shipping**

Sgt E S Elmes — +
Sgt A W Kirby — +
Sgt H D Higgins — +

T/o Wattisham. Shot down while attacking a convoy off Norway. All are commemorated on the Runnymede Memorial.

14-15 Aug 1941 7 Sqn Stirling I N6041 MG- Op: **Magdenburg**

W/C H R Graham
Sgt R W Taylor RAAF
F/S J R Walker
Sgt J L Martin
F/S H Watson
Sgt M T Coon
Sgt G E Mitchell DFM, RCAF
F/L S G Stock

T/o 2056 Oakington. Overshot and crashed 0446 on return to base. F/S Mitchell RCAF was later to lose his life on operations with 75 Squadron on 6 April 1942.

---

7 Sqn Stirling I N6042 MG- Op: **Magdeburg**

P/O W N Crebbin
Sgt W R Butterfield
Sgt R Ferguson
Sgt R W Cotton
Sgt J McCarley
Sgt T J Ryder
F/S J Lowe

T/o 2114 Oakington. Landed 0410 at Graveley airfield, Huntingdonshire, on return and ran into an unmarked obstruction, causing damage that was deemed uneconomical to repair.

14-15 Aug 1941	7 Sqn	Stirling I	W7434 MG-E	Op: Hannover

7 Sqn — Stirling I — W7434 MG-E — Op: Hannover

F/O D T Witt DFC, DFM
Sgt S G Matkin
Sgt D White
Sgt J R Alverson
F/S M G Gardiner
Sgt L A Penn
P/O A H Piper

T/o 2100 Oakington. Crashed on return to base and while trying to land in poor visibility. A week after this incident, the London Gazette carried news of the award of a DFM to F/S Gardiner.

12 Sqn — Wellington II — W5536 PH-M — Op: Rotterdam

Sgt Cameron
Sgt Cook
Sgt Price   inj
Sgt K Harrison   +
Sgt A Wakeford   inj
Sgt Thorpe

T/o 2130 Binbrook. Shot down by a Ju 88C intruder (Ofw Robert Lüddeke, I./NJG2) and crashed 0230 near the Humber river. The two injured airmen were admitted to Grimsby and District General Hospital, where Sgt Wakeford died from his wounds.

15 Sqn — Stirling I — N6043 LS-G — Op: Hannover

S/L J F Foulsham
Sgt Hayes
Sgt D Ferguson
Sgt R N Chancellor
Sgt W A Conn   +
Sgt Griffiths
Sgt P G Osman

T/o Alconbury but lost power from the port inner engine. Unable to maintain height, the Stirling crashed just to the N of Ramsey St. Mary's, 10 miles NNE of Huntingdon.

15 Sqn — Stirling I — W7435 LS-W — Op: Magdeburg

P/O E J D Guild
Sgt E P De Ville
Sgt T H B Jones
Sgt W C Mackenzie RCAF
Sgt A Needham
Sgt A D Wallace
Sgt F C Snead RCAF

T/o 2210 Alconbury but crashed almost immediately after developing a swing which could not be controlled.

15 Sqn — Stirling I — W7437 LS-L — Op: Magdeburg

Sgt R R Stewart   pow
Sgt J M Johnson   pow
Sgt J Brown   pow
Sgt J B L Bunce   pow
Sgt J D Aitken   pow
Sgt G H Burland   pow
Sgt E C Haynes   pow

T/o Alconbury. Ditched in the North Sea.

35 Sqn — Halifax I — L9500 TL-H — Op: Magdeburg

P/O R Lisle   +
Sgt M G Garner   +
Sgt H T McQuigg   +
Sgt K R Sewell   +
F/S J J Rogers   +
F/S J A A Cox   +
Sgt W L Berry RCAF   +

T/o 2206 Linton-on-Ouse. Crashed at Andervenne, 18 km ESE of Lingen-Ems, Germany, where the crew were first buried in the Neuer Friedhof. Since 1945, their remains have been taken to the Reichswald Forest War Cemetery.

49 Sqn — Hampden I — AE262 EA- — Op: Braunschweig

Sgt Owen
Sgt Donald
Sgt A Kettlewell
Sgt Drinkwell

T/o 2058 Scampton. Overshot and crashed 0320 on return to base. Visibility was poor and this was a contributory factor. No injuries reported.

51 Sqn — Whitley V — Z6819 MH-X — Op: Hannover

Sgt P R Griffin   +
Sgt F B H Wildgoose   +
Sgt S P Donoghue   +
Sgt F Gill   +
Sgt G E Bagshaw   +

T/o 2148 Dishforth. Shot down by a night-fighter (Oblt Helmut Lent, 4./NJG1) and crashed 0320 off Schiermonnikoog in the Dutch Frisian Islands. Three bodes were washed ashore, but Sgt Wildgoose and Sgt Bagshaw have no known graves.

14-15 Aug	83 Sqn	Hampden I	AE131 OL-W	Op: Braunschweig

14-15 Aug   83 Sqn   Hampden I   **AE131 OL-W**   Op: **Braunschweig**
1941   P/O P H Slater-Eiggert   +   T/o 2110 Scampton. Hit by flak and crashed at
            F/S L S Thorrowgood   +   Pattensen, 12 km S of Hannover. All are buried
            P/O W C Rasbary   +   in Hannover War Cemetery.
            Sgt F Stephens   +

            102 Sqn   Whitley V   **Z6746 DY-**   Op: **Hannover**
            Sgt J Reid   T/o 2203 Topcliffe. Overshot and crashed 0501
            Sgt G F J Hoben   on return to base. Visibility was extremely
            P/O S R Whipple   poor at the time. No injuries reported.
            Sgt R C Perriam
            Sgt J Griffiths

            102 Sqn   Whitley V   **Z6829 DY-**   Op: **Hannover**
            Sgt G K Powell   +   T/o 2218 Topcliffe. Shot down by a night-
            Sgt F W Penn RAAF   pow   fighter (Ofw Paul Gildner, 4./NJG1) and crashed
            P/O W W Bell-Towers RAAF   +   0448 in the Waddenzee, S of Terschelling. Those
            Sgt R T Philp   +   who died are buried on the island in the
            F/S L E D Lindsay   +   Westerschelling General Cemetery. Sgt Penn RAAF
            Sgt T A Vermiglio   pow   needed treatment for his wounds.

            102 Sqn   Whitley V   **Z6842 DY-**   Op: **Hannover**
            F/L D N Sampson   pow   T/o 2202 Topcliffe. Shot down by a night-
            Sgt J D Hamilton   pow   fighter (Oblt Ludwig Becker, 4./NJG1) and
            Sgt E Alderton   pow   crashed 0117 at Terwispel (Friesland),
            Sgt W J Scott   pow   10 km SSW of Drachten, Holland.
            Sgt K G Lewis   pow

            102 Sqn   Whitley V   **Z6877 DY-**   Op: **Hannover**
            Sgt A W Hawkes   pow   T/o 2210 Topcliffe. Shot down by a night-
            P/O G W Cole   pow   fighter and crashed 0145 near Jögel, Germany.
            Sgt K P Marlow   pow   Sgt Hampson RCAF is buried in the Reichswald
            Sgt A Nicholas   pow   Forest War Cemetery.
            Sgt D E J Hampson RCAF   +

            Note. The location Jögel has not been traced.

            104 Sqn   Wellington II   **W5486 EP-H**   Op: **Hannover**
            P/O J Drewsen   +   T/o 2140 Driffield. All are buried in
            Sgt R S Herring   +   Becklingen War Cemetery, Soltau.
            Sgt D E Phare   +
            Sgt P J Davey   +
            Sgt H Kay   +
            Sgt E H Reels   +

            115 Sqn   Wellington IC   **R1500 KO-K**   Op: **Hannover**
            Sgt C G Alway   +   T/o 2110 Marham. Crashed in the North Sea.
            Sgt D A Clabburn-Detrez   +   Sgt Alway and Sgt Duke are buried in Sage War
            Sgt D H Allan   +   Cemetery, Oldenburg; the rest of the crew are
            Sgt R W J Smalldon   +   commemorated on the Runnymede Memorial.
            Sgt J G Park RCAF   +
            Sgt R W Duke   +

            150 Sqn   Wellington IC   **R1016 JN-A**   Op: **Hannover**
            Sgt J D Elder   pow   T/o 2145 Snaith. Crashed near Leeuwarden
            Sgt H H M Barton   +   (Friesland), Holland, where Sgt Barton is
            Sgt E W McConchie RNZAF   pow   buried in the Northern General Cemetery.
            Sgt H Dodsworth   pow
            Sgt C Davies   pow
            Sgt J W Whittingham   pow

            150 Sqn   Wellington IC   **R1394 JN-V**   Op: **Hannover**
            Sgt A P Perry-Keane   +   T/o 2140 Snaith. Lost without trace. All
            Sgt D R Sherwin   +   are commemorated on the Runnymede Memorial.
            Sgt E P Beckwith   +
            Sgt S C Tottle   +
            Sgt A R McEldon   +
            Sgt J H Keen   +

14-15 Aug 1941	218 Sqn	Wellington IC	R1008 HA-A	Op: Hannover

P/O A P Mitchell	+
Sgt K E Smith	+
Sgt C J Matthews	+
P/O E Wakefield	+
Sgt A R Bell	+
Sgt K F Lewis	+

T/o 2216 Marham. Last heard on w/t at 0057 indicating a successful attack. All are buried in Becklingen War Cemetery at Soltau.

218 Sqn   Wellington IC   X9753 HA-G   Op: Hannover

P/O W C Wilson	+
Sgt J C Cottingham	+
Sgt G A Munro	+
Sgt P Prosser	+
Sgt A I P Anderson	+
Sgt R Barnard	pow

T/o 2118 Marham. Presumed to have crashed in the sea off the French coast, having last been heard on w/t at 0402. Those who died are buried in the Canadian War Cemetery at Leubringhem, Calais.

405 Sqn   Wellington II   W5496 LQ-M   Op: Hannover

P/O G H Fleming RCAF	+
Sgt J F B Dawson RCAF	+
Sgt A R Lesley RCAF	+
Sgt J E Stott	+
Sgt E Stansfield	+
Sgt J P Molloy RCAF	+

T/o 2203 Pocklington. Lost without trace. All are commemorated on the Runnymede Memorial.

15 Aug 1941   50 Sqn   Hampden I   P4408 VN-   Op: Air Sea Rescue

F/O J A Whitecross DFC	+
Sgt M O Fisher	+
F/S N Gray DFM	+
Sgt R Taylor	+

T/o Swinderby. Presumed lost over the North Sea shortly after signalling at 1530 that the engines were failing. F/S Gray and Sgt Taylor are buried in Sage War Cemetery, Oldenburg; the rest are commemorated on the Runnymede Memorial.

Note. F/O Whitecross had only recently returned to the Squadron following his successful evasion from France, where he had landed following a mining sortie on 28-29 April 1941.

16 Aug 1941   90 Sqn   Fortress I   AN523 WP-D   Op: Brest

P/O Sturmey	
P/O Franks	
P/O Mulligan	
F/S Goldsmith	inj
Sgt H Needle	+
F/S S Ambrose	+
Sgt M J Leahy	+

T/o 0903 Polebrook. Attacked by fighters at 32000 feet, the highest interception of an Allied bomber yet recorded, and severely shot about. On return, the Fortress was crash-landed on Roborough airfield, Plymouth, where it burst into flames. Those who died were killed during the air engagement.

16-17 Aug 1941   10 Sqn   Whitley V   Z6586 ZA-F   Op: Köln

P/O H H Pearson	+
Sgt S A Loveday	+
P/O D W H Walker	+
Sgt J Welsh	+
Sgt S F B Bott RCAF	+

T/o 2202 Leeming. Crashed near Martenslinde (Limburg), 16 km SE of Hasselt, Belgium. All are buried in Heverlee War Cemetery.

10 Sqn   Whitley V   Z6794 ZA-   Op: Köln

Sgt E H Lager	+
Sgt S S Shapiro RCAF	pow
Sgt J W Meyers RCAF	pow
Sgt V Y H Sewell RCAF	+
Sgt J E Fulkerson RCAF	pow

T/o 2209 Leeming. It is reported that at least four of the crew baled out, but Sgt Sewell's parachute failed to deploy. He is buried, along with Sgt Lager, in the Reichswald Forest War Cemetery.

10 Sqn   Whitley V   Z6805 ZA-   Op: Köln

Sgt B S Craske	pow
Sgt H P Calvert MiD	pow
Sgt King	pow
Sgt Robertson	pow

T/o 2203 Leeming. Sgt Calvert is reported to have been involved in a mass escape bid from Stalag IIIE in May 1942, and was shot by civil police at Dresden on 20 May 1942. He is buried in the 1939-1945 War Cemetery at Berlin.

16-17 Aug 1941	12 Sqn	Wellington II	
	F/L C N McVeigh		inj
	F/O B M J Vincent		+
	F/S E H Nancarrow		+
	Sgt Purslow		inj
	F/S C G C Frost		+
	F/S D Murray		inj

W5444 PH-T Op: Köln

T/o 2135 Binbrook. Crashed 0130 while making an emergency landing near Melton Constable, 8 miles ENE of Fakenham, Norfolk, during which the Wellington smashed into a bridge. The injured were admitted to the Norwich and Norfolk General Hospital.

44 Sqn	Hampden I	
Sgt J G Armstrong		+
Sgt C R Morley RCAF		+
Sgt J Flint		+
Sgt S C Edwards		+

AE239 KM- Op: Düsseldorf

T/o 2315 Waddington. Lost over the North Sea. Sgt Edwards is buried in Kiel War Cemetery; the rest of the crew have no known graves. All had been involved in a crash at the end of July.

58 Sqn	Whitley V	
Sgt B A Hammond		pow
Sgt R D Wagstaff		pow
Sgt J B Mackerson		pow
Sgt S E Davidson		pow
Sgt T A Nichols		pow

Z6729 GE-T Op: Köln

T/o 2344 Linton-on-Ouse. Shot down by a night-fighter (Oblt Willi Dimter, I./NJG1) and crashed 0420 near the Diacomessen Hospital at Breda (Noord Brabant), Holland. Earlier, at 0254 the bomber was heard on w/t asking for a bearing but Bircham Newton's reply was not acknowledged.

78 Sqn	Whitley V	
Sgt T A Sherman RCAF		+
Sgt G L Olsen RCAF		+
F/S R Jopling		+
Sgt D A Wilson		+
Sgt D F Hawkes		+

Z6577 EY-F Op: Köln

T/o 2252 Middleton St. George. Crashed 0247 at Ohé en Laak (Limburg) on the W bank of the Juliana Kanaal, 14 km SW of Roermond, Holland. All are buried in Jonkerbos War Cemetery.

78 Sqn	Whitley V	
Sgt J H Malet-Warden		+
Sgt J C Beardmore		+
Sgt A J R Millard-Tucker		+
Sgt G H P Buchanan RCAF		+
F/S A Brown		+

Z6754 EY- Op: Köln

T/o 2305 Middleton St. George. Crashed 0350 at Buggenum (Limburg), 5 km NNW of Roermond, Holland. All are buried in Jonkerbos War Cemetery.

78 Sqn	Whitley V	
F/L J A Cant		pow
P/O J L Asprey RAAF		+
Sgt W E Kerr		pow
Sgt A D Wills		+
Sgt J Geary		pow

Z6823 EY-B Op: Köln

T/o 2256 Middleton St. George. Crashed 0315 at Velddriel (Gelderland), 6 km SE of Zaltbommel, Holland. P/O Asprey RAAF is buried in Jonkerbos War Cemetery, Sgt Wills rests at Eindhoven in the Woensel General Cemetery.

97 Sqn	Manchester I	
F/L J L Nunn		pow
Sgt P W Ratcliff		pow
F/S W Wood		pow
W/O J N Ashmore DFC		pow
Sgt H Currie MiD		pow
Sgt A G Smith RNZAF		inj
F/S P Williams		+

L7384 OF- Op: Düsseldorf

T/o 2250 Coningsby. Shot down by a Me 110 flown by Hptm Werner Streib, I/NJG1. F/L Nunn crash-landed the Manchester, just inside the border with Belgium, as Sgt Currie had been wounded and was unable to bale out. He was taken to Aachen, where he died from his injuries. His body rests in Rheinberg War Cemetery, while F/S Williams, who was killed after baling out, is buried in the Canadian War Cemetery at Adegem, Belgium.

99 Sqn	Wellington IC	
P/O G L Wells RAAF		+
P/O N Dotchin		+
P/O W A Casey RCAF		+
Sgt F W York		+
Sgt R M Williams		pow
Sgt G Crane		+

X9700 LN-B Op: Duisburg

T/o 2334 Waterbeach. Shot down by a night-fighter (Lt Hans-Dieter Frank, I./NJG1) and crashed 0215 near Roggel (Limburg), 9 km NW of Roermond, Holland. Those who died were buried at Venlo, but since 1945 their bodies have been taken to Jonkerbos War Cemetery.

104 Sqn	Wellington II	
Sgt W T R Stephenson RCAF		+
Sgt J W Nolan		+
F/S S C Steward		+
Sgt K Hutchinson		+
Sgt I H A Henderson		+
P/O P J Murphy		+

W5532 EP-M Op: Köln

T/o 2327 Driffield. Crashed 0002 at South Leverton, 6 miles SSW of Gainsborough, Lincolnshire. PC Hollingsworth of East Retford Police Station narrowly escaped death when the bomb-load exploded as he helped organise a rescue attempt.

16–17 Aug	106 Sqn	Hampden I	AD756 ZN-	Op: Düsseldorf
1941	P/O G G Watts	+		
	Sgt L Acres	+		
	Sgt G V Lynn	pow		
	Sgt J H Cook	pow		
	P/O J Grant	+		

T/o 2205 Coningsby. Shot down by a night-fighter (Oblt Redlich, I./NJG1) and crashed 0244 near Gembloux (Namur), Belgium. P/O Grant had been given permission to accompany the crew in order to obtain operational experience. He is buried, along with the rest of those who died, in the Communal Cemetery at Gembloux.

	106 Sqn	Hampden I	AE134 ZN-	Op: Düsseldorf
	P/O T M Robinson	pow		
	Sgt R G Woodwards	pow		
	Sgt J Harker	pow		
	Sgt H Birtwhistle	pow		

T/o 2220 Coningsby. Shot down by a night-fighter (Oblt Wolfgang Thimmig, I./NJG1) and crashed 0138 near Meijl (Limburg), 16 km NE of Weert, Holland. P/O Robinson died in captivity on 10 October 1941 and is buried at Hannover.

	207 Sqn	Manchester I	L7311 EM-F	Op: Düsseldorf
	P/O H G Keartland	pow		
	Sgt A Ross	pow		
	F/S A Wappett DFM	pow		
	Sgt E G Ball	pow		
	Sgt J R Currie DFM	pow		
	Sgt W Hart	pow		

T/o Waddington. Shot down by a night-fighter (Hptm Werner Streib, I./NJG1) and crashed at Oberkrüchten, Germany. Sgt Hart was quite seriously wounded by shell splinters which entered his back.

	305 Sqn	Wellington II	W5463 SM-E	Op: Köln
	Sgt S Przeclawski	+		
	Sgt J Plachta	+		
	F/O A B Miondlikowski	+		
	Sgt S Stankiewicz	+		
	Sgt E Majewski	+		
	Sgt F Wardenski	+		

T/o 2119 Lindholme. Presumed lost over the North Sea. Four members of the crew are buried in cemeteries in Belgium and Holland, while Sgt Przeclawski and Sgt Wardenski have no known graves. On 18 August, a pigeon from this bomber returned to Lindholme at 0830, but no message was attached that may have indicated the fate of this Wellington and its crew.

17–18 Aug	50 Sqn	Hampden I	AE185 VN-	Op: Bremen
1941	P/O E C Maskell	pow		
	P/O H Law	+		
	Sgt P F B Orwin	+		
	Sgt G A Cowell	+		

T/o 2255 Swinderby. Shot down by a night-fighter (Oblt Ludwig Becker, 4./NJG1) and crashed 0144 at Paterswolde (Groningen), 8 km S of Groningen, Holland. Those who died are buried in Haren General Cemetery.

	83 Sqn	Hampden I	AD837 OL-E	Op: Bremen
	Sgt G S Linacre			
	Sgt J Harrison			
	Sgt W Hunt			
	Sgt R H Calder			

T/o 2145 Scampton. Ditched 0840 some 10 miles off Holy Island, Northumberland. A local patrol boat rescued the crew.

18 Aug	18 Sqn	Blenheim IV	V6175 WV-G	Op: Circus 78
1941	Sgt Vickers	inj		
	Sgt Lowe	inj		
	Sgt V A Stevens	+		

T/o 1715 Manston. Hit by flak, which killed Sgt Stevens, and crash-landed 1845 just to the SE of Tollgate cottage, East Guldeford, 1 mile NE of Rye, Sussex.

	110 Sqn	Blenheim IV	V5491 VE-	Op: Circus 78
	Sgt N W Berg	+		
	Sgt J R G Harvey	+		
	Sgt J S Fazakerley	+		

T/o Wattisham. Hit by flak and crashed into the channel. Two bodies were washed onto the south coast; Sgt Fazakerley is commemorated on the Runnymede Memorial.

18–19 Aug	10 Sqn	Whitley V	Z6564 ZA-Z	Op: Köln
1941	P/O W A S Evill	+		
	Sgt K M Tompkins	+		
	Sgt C P O'Dell	+		
	Sgt D MacL Duffy RCAF	+		
	Sgt T H Park RCAF	+		

T/o 2223 Leeming. Crashed near Rekem (Limburg), 14 km ESE of Genk, Belgium. All are buried in Rekem Communal Cemetery. Sgt Park RCAF was an American from Jersey city.

18-19 Aug	**10 Sqn**	**Whitley V**	**Z6672 ZA-**	**Op: Köln**
1941	S/L M M Kane	pow	T/o 2214 Leeming. Crashed near Lanaye (Limburg),	
	P/O E E Manison	+	on the Belgian/Dutch border some 16 km ENE of	
	Sgt H le Q Mourant	pow	Tongeren. P/O Manison is buried in Lanaye	
	Sgt H L Crich RCAF	+	Communal Cemetery, while the rest who died	
	Sgt S Norcross	+	are interned in Heverlee War Cemetery.	

51 Sqn	**Whitley V**	**Z6566 MH-Q**	**Op: Köln**
Sgt W B James DFM, MiD	pow	T/o 2144 Dishforth. Hit by flak fifteen	
Sgt D A Switzer RCAF	pow	minutes after leaving the target and crash-	
P/O C D Roberts	pow	landed near Maastricht (Limburg), Holland.	
Sgt A G Lowe DFM	pow	It is reported that Sgt James ordered his	
Sgt H R James	pow	crew to bale out, giving up his parachute	

to one of the wireless operators, whose own
'chute had been rendered unusable by shrapnel. News of this unselfish act
reached the Allied authorities and Sgt James was subsequently awarded the
DFM. Tragically, he contracted consumption, was repatriated and died on
10 November 1944.

51 Sqn	**Whitley V**	**Z6569 MH-S**	**Op: Köln**
P/O H B Robertshaw	pow	T/o 2151 Dishforth. Shot down by a night-	
P/O A G Trites RCAF	pow	fighter, which fatally wounded Sgt Evetts,	
Sgt J L Ives RCAF	pow	and crashed near Vliermaalroot (Limburg),	
Sgt L A Evetts	+	9 km SE of Hasselt, Belgium. Sgt Evetts is	
Sgt R A C Hooper	pow	buried in the Canadian War Cemetery, Adegem.	

51 Sqn	**Whitley V**	**Z6731 MH-A**	**Op: Köln**
P/O W J Loney RCAF	+	T/o 2129 Dishforth. Crashed 0315 on the	
Sgt J L Gilman	+	B1116 road near Crouches Farm at Laxfield,	
Sgt R E Bennett	+	11 miles NW of Leiston, Suffolk, due to a	
Sgt J Taylor	+	fire in the wireless compartment.	
Sgt E J Lowater RAAF	+		

51 Sqn	**Whitley V**	**Z6811 MH-D**	**Op: Köln**
Sgt J A B Jamieson	+	T/o 2134 Dishforth. Crashed 0200 near Malden	
P/O F W Shorrock RCAF	+	(Gelderland), 5 km S of Nijmegen. It is thought	
Sgt A Milne RAAF	+	the Whitley may have collided with an enemy	
Sgt F W Coles	pow	night-fighter. Those who died are buried in	
Sgt H R F Johnston RCAF	+	Uden War Cemetery.	

106 Sqn	**Hampden I**	**AD919 ZN-**	**Op: Köln**
Sgt Field	inj	T/o 2310 Coningsby. Force-landed 2315, due	
P/O Finlayson	inj	to engine failure, at Chapel Hill, 10 miles	
Sgt Norman	inj	NW of Boston, Lincolnshire.	
Sgt Wright	inj		

149 Sqn	**Wellington IC**	**X9704 OJ-B**	**Op: Duisburg**
P/O J C Lynn	+	T/o 2329 Mildenhall. Shot down by a night-	
Sgt W J R Culpan RNZAF	pow	fighter, which fatally wounded P/O Mendoza,	
P/O R R Henderson RCAF	pow	and crashed at Haelen (Limburg), 5 km NW of	
Sgt C G Jones	pow	Roermond, Holland. Those who died are buried	
Sgt K K Sterrett	pow	in Jonkerbos War Cemetery, though originally	
P/O M I A Mendoza	+	they were laid to rest at Venlo.	

149 Sqn	**Wellington IC**	**X9746 OJ-A**	**Op: Duisburg**
P/O Gregory		T/o 2307 Mildenhall. Attacked by a Ju 88 after	
Sgt Reed	inj	being coned in searchlights near Venlo. Sgt	
P/O Raffaelli	inj	Reed was wounded in the groin and the navigator	
F/S Beach		received a superficial head injury. A fire	
Sgt Beckett		broke out in the rear fuselage, but this was	
Sgt Billington		extinguished by Sgt Billington. The Wellington	

landed safely at 0449, but following a technical
inspection, it was deemed to be beyond economical repair and it was struck off
charge on 29 September 1941.

18-19 Aug 1941	218 Sqn	Wellington IC		N2844 HA-M	Op: Duisburg
	Sgt K C Shearing		+		
	Sgt R G Boswell		+		
	Sgt L J George RCAF		+		
	Sgt A MacG Wilson RAAF		+		
	Sgt S A Maguire		+		
	P/O E D Pockney		+		

N2844 HA-M   Op: Duisburg
T/o 2348 Marham. Shot down by a night-fighter (Fw Siegfried Ney, 4./NJG1) and crashed 0206 in the IJsselmeer. Three bodes, those of Sgt Wilson RAAF, Sgt Boswell and P/O Pockney, were found and taken for burial in various Dutch cemeteries. The rest have no known graves.

218 Sqn   Wellington II

Sgt H G Huckle   pow
Sgt R K Pridham   pow
Sgt A J Condon RAAF   pow
Sgt A Learmonth   pow
Sgt R S McKinnell   +
Sgt L Stephens   pow

W5457 HA-Z   Op: Köln
T/o 2343 Marham. Sgt McKinnell is reported to have been killed in the aircraft. He is buried in Rheinberg War Cemetery.

300 Sqn   Wellington IC

Sgt K Ceglinski   +
Sgt S Kuropatwa   +
Sgt Wybaniec   inj
F/O A Paszkowski
Sgt Kordys
Sgt Glucklick

R1641 BH-Z   Op: Duisburg
T/o 2335 Hemswell but crashed almost immediately due to premature retraction of the undercarriage and burst into flames. Shortly afterwards, the bomb-load exploded. Those who died are buried in Newark Cemetery.

19 Aug 1941   114 Sqn   Blenheim IV

W/C J L Nicol DSO   +
F/S E T W Jones   +
F/O H J Madden DFC   +

V6236 RT-D   Op: Anti-shipping
T/o 1720 West Raynham to patrol Beat 9. Shot down by fighters from 5./ZG76 some 35 km NW of Vlieland. F/S Jones is buried in Sage War Cemetery; the rest have no known graves.

114 Sqn   Blenheim IV

P/O R U McCracken RNZAF   +
P/O H R Bentley   +
Sgt A Clague   pow

V6366 RT-N   Op: Anti-shipping
T/o 1715 West Raynham. Lost in circumstances similar to those described above. Those who died are commemorated on the Runnymede Memorial.

114 Sqn   Blenheim IV

Sgt R K Clarke   +
P/O R A Stratton   +
Sgt P A Davies   +

Z7347 RT-U   Op: Anti-shipping
T/o 1720 West Raynham. Lost in circumstances similar to those previously described. Sgt Clarke has no known grave; his crew are buried in cemeteries on Ameland and in Germany.

304 Sqn   Wellington IC

F/O Morawski

R1761 NZ-   Training
Landed at Madley airfield, Worcestershire, but when the pilot realised he was likely to run into a gang of workmen, he opened up the throttles and tried to go round again. In doing so the Wellington failed to gain height and crashed into trees, just beyond the runway. No injuries reported.

19-20 Aug 1941   9 Sqn   Wellington IC

Sgt C T Everitt   +
Sgt P J Brady   +
Sgt H B S Johnston   +
Sgt T Whalley   +
Sgt T Armstrong   +
Sgt H E Temple   +

R1455 WS-D   Op: Kiel
T/o 2114 Honington. Believed hit by flak and crashed 0035 in the tidal area some 2 km S of Hojer Sluse off the Danish coast. All were buried with full military honours in Tonder Cemetery on 23 October 1941, with a Wehrmacht band in attendance, as well as Danish personnel.

83 Sqn   Hampden I

P/O R J Potts   +
Sgt I W R Ilsley   +
Sgt G D Clark   +
Sgt G T Shirley   +

AD907 OL-K   Op: Kiel
T/o 2110 Scampton. Crashed into the sea 6 miles E of Bridlington, Yorkshire.

101 Sqn   Wellington IC

Sgt W R Fisher   +
Sgt J G Richardson   +
Sgt J A Nichols   +
Sgt J Bainbridge   +
Sgt R Willis   +
Sgt D McIntyre   +

W5715 SR-N   Op: Kiel
T/o 2049 Oakington. Lost without trace. All are commemorated on the Runnymede Memorial.

19-20 Aug 1941	104 Sqn F/L W W Burton Sgt K M Woodhead RAAF Sgt J Haney Sgt H E Johnson Sgt D C Marshall RCAF P/O J G Rogers RCAF	Wellington II + + + + + +	W5416 EP-	Op: Kiel

T/o 2240 Driffield. Last heard on w/t at 0318 trying to raise Bircham Newton. Presumed lost over the North Sea. The body of Sgt Haney was washed ashore on 19 September 1941 at Norderpiep and was laid to rest at Büsum. Since 1945, he has been taken to Kiel War Cemetery. The rest are commemorated on the Runnymede Memorial.

20 Aug 1941	82 Sqn F/L Gibbs Sgt E L Cash Sgt Pascoe	Blenheim IV +	V6445 UX-E	Op: Anti-shipping

T/o 1217 Bodney to patrol Beat 7. Collided with the mast of a ship and subsequently crashed at 1645 while trying to make an emergency landing at Acklington airfield, Northumberland. Sgt Cash died from his injuries and he is buried in Chevington Cemetery.

21 Aug 1941	102 Sqn Sgt I C Hay P/O P B Detlor RCAF SGT D J McK Bush Sgt N G Williams Sgt C S Neveu	Whitley V + + + + inj	Z6862 DY-	Training

T/o 1450 Topcliffe, but after climbing steeply, stalled and crashed near the airfield.

22 Aug 1941	150 Sqn S/L A B Olney	Wellington IC	T2622 JN-D	Training

Crash-landed 1200 at Snaith airfield, following a flapless approach, which resulted in the bomber overshooting the runway. No injuries reported.

22-23 Aug 1941	10 Sqn P/O K W Liebeck RCAF Sgt G Fletcher Sgt R Silver Sgt M McLaughlin Sgt R Speer	Whitley V + + inj inj inj	T4234 ZA-	Op: le Havre

T/o 2002 Leeming. Crashed 0141 into high ground on Widdale Fell, 2031 feet asl, 2 miles NE of Dent, an isolated Westmoreland village, 12 miles ESE of Kendal.

	106 Sqn P/O A F McGruer RNZAF P/O J P Early DFC, RCAF Sgt A L P Rawlinson Sgt J W Goddard	Hampden I + + + +	AE220 ZN-	Op: Mannheim

T/o 2140 Coningsby. Shot down by flak near Plankstadt, 5 km W of Heidelberg, Germany. All are buried in Durnbach War Cemetery.

23 Aug 1941	104 Sqn Sgt F R Richardson RAAF P/O Murdoch Sgt R J Mountier Sgt Scott Sgt B W Robbens Sgt A D F Craig	Wellington II inj inj inj inj inj inj	W5477 EP-	Transit

Crashed 1145 while trying to land at Driffield on return from Martlesham Heath.

	114 Sqn P/O N F Thompson Sgt G H Macnamara P/O J M Dobson P/O H J Fuller	Blenheim IV + + + +	V6179 RT-	Training

Crashed after colliding with a house at Canons Park, Edgware, Middlesex. Visibility in the area was extremely poor at the time of the accident.

24-25 Aug 1941	35 Sqn P/O J McGregor-Cheers Sgt T P McHale Sgt W N Collins Sgt A A S Heggie Sgt J Fuller Sgt J B Anderson RCAF P/O V M Markham	Halifax I + + + + + + +	L9572 TL-G	Op: Düsseldorf

T/o 2053 Linton-on-Ouse. All attempts to raise this aircraft on w/t failed, the last being made at 0312. Presumed to have crashed near Chièvres (Hainaut), Belgium, where the crew are buried in the Communal Cemetery. It will be recalled that apart from the Sgt McHale, the crew had recently experienced a bad crash on return from Berlin.

	49 Sqn Sgt O B McMahon Sgt G Upton Sgt J MacKinnon Sgt E Welbourne	Hampden I + + + +	AD967 EA-H	Op: Düsseldorf

T/o Scampton. Collided in the air at 0250 with an 83 Squadron Hampden, both aircraft falling near Whale Jaws Farm, Hackthorn, 7 miles NNE of Lincoln.

24-25 Aug 1941	51 Sqn	Whitley V	Z6505 MH-F	Op: Düsseldorf

Sgt J C W King	pow	T/o 2059 Dishforth. Shot down by a night-fighter
F/S C J Powell RCAF	pow	(Lt Hans-Dieter Frank, I./NJG1) and crashed 0130
F/O E R Templer	pow	at De Millert at Eind (Limburg), 5 km SE of
Sgt V Thompson	pow	Nederweert, Holland.
F/S A R Lacharite RCAF	pow	

78 Sqn	Whitley V	Z6466 EY-A	Op: Düsseldorf
Sgt W G Rogers	+	T/o 2009 Middleton St. George. Crashed near
Sgt E C Findon	+	Wavre (Brabent), 27 km SE of Brussels. All
Sgt J Hadfield	+	are buried in Wavre Communal Cemetery.
Sgt W D Edge	+	
Sgt B Douglas	+	

78 Sqn	Whitley V	Z6742 EY-	Op: Düsseldorf
P/O Fransden		T/o 2017 Middleton St. George. Abandoned, on
Sgt D A Sinclair RCAF	+	fire, and crashed 0227 near Mistley, Essex, on
Sgt Becker		the S bank of the Stour. Sgt Sinclair RCAF
Sgt Young		was found in the wreckage and he is buried in
Sgt Gale		Ipswich Cemetery.

83 Sqn	Hampden I	X3121 OL-F	Op: Düsseldorf
F/L A J G Mills DFC	+	T/o 2030 Scampton. Collided in the air with a
Sgt J A A Somerville	+	49 Squadron aircraft and crashed in similar
Sgt B V Mason	+	circumstances to those described previously.
F/S D I Sharp	+	

83 Sqn	Hampden I	AE223 OL-V	Op: Wesel
P/O V C O R Maybury	+	T/o 2030 Scampton. Landed 0225 but a few
P/O T G M Macintyre	+	minutes later there was an explosion and the
Sgt E J Clarke	+	Hampden burst into flames. In addition to
Sgt R Scholes	+	the crew, four members of the ground staff
Cpl W Inkpen	+	died in the explosion, caused, it is believed,
LAC L S Rayment	+	by a bomb falling from the aircraft as the
AC1 W R Stevenson	+	bomb-doors were opened for inspection of the
AC2 C Ogden	+	bay.

25-26 Aug 1941	7 Sqn	Stirling I	N6020 MG-B	Op: Karlsruhe

F/O K O Blunden	+	T/o 2102 Oakington. Reported crashed at Trier,
P/O J D Wright	+	Germany, due to a combination of enemy action
Sgt G Nicholson	+	and adverse weather. Those who died are buried
Sgt J D Edworthy RCAF	+	in Rheinberg War Cemetery.
Sgt W E Allan RCAF	+	
P/O E F Drew	+	
Sgt D A Lloyd	pow	

40 Sqn	Wellington IC	T2514 BL-D	Op: Karlsruhe
Sgt D F Youldon	+	T/o 2043 Alconbury. All are buried in Rheinberg
Sgt W H Cole	+	War Cemetery.
Sgt T Appleby	+	
Sgt J D Duthie	+	
Sgt W Fisher	+	
Sgt E C Shea	+	

40 Sqn	Wellington IC	X9749 BL-J	Op: Karlsruhe
S/L A C Martin	+	T/o 2045 Alconbury. Crashed near Handzame
P/O T R Fyles	+	(West Vlaanderen), 10 km ESE of Diksmuide,
P/O R R Reynolds	+	Belgium. All are buried in Handzame Communal
Sgt G Knight	+	Cemetery.
Sgt R J F Perras RCAF	+	
F/O W Wright	+	

50 Sqn	Hampden I	AE320 VN-	Op: Mannheim
Sgt R J Fisher	+	T/o Swinderby. All are buried in Rheinberg
P/O R F B Temperley	+	War Cemetery. P/O Temperley had survived a
Sgt L R E Sciville	+	crash while setting out on a mining operation
Sgt K Fyvie	+	earlier in the month.

25-26 Aug 1941	144 Sqn	Hampden I	Sgt D A Whiting + / P/O A E Hayward pow / Sgt G C Smith + / Sgt J Christie +

25-26 Aug 1941 — **144 Sqn** — **Hampden I** — **AD918 PL-** — Op: **Mannheim**

Sgt D A Whiting +
P/O A E Hayward pow
Sgt G C Smith +
Sgt J Christie +

T/o North Luffenham. Crashed in the vicinity of Brussels, where those who died are buried in the Town Cemetery.

---

144 Sqn — **Hampden I** — **AE265 PL-** — Op: **Mannheim**

P/O I G St C Pringle pow
Sgt J R Blake pow
Sgt J Erskine pow
Sgt S C Brown pow

T/o North Luffenham. Force-landed on Ypenburg airfield, Holland. In captivity, Sgt Erskine exchanged identity with Marine A Hydes.

---

26 Aug 1941 — **21 Sqn** — **Blenheim IV** — **Z7483 YH-N** — Op: **Anti-shipping**

Sgt A S Oman +
Sgt T Parkinson +
Sgt R Hamilton +

T/o 1155 Watton. Hit by flak and crashed off Bergen-aan-Zee, Holland. All are commemorated on the Runnymede Memorial.

---

82 Sqn — **Blenheim IV** — **R3767 UX-R** — Op: **Heligoland**

Sgt R J Greenough +
Sgt A A Matthews +
Sgt H Bonnett +

T/o 1022 Bodney. Shot down by fighters from 3./JG52. All are commemorated on the Runnymede Memorial.

---

82 Sqn — **Blenheim IV** — **T2165 UX-W** — Op: **Heligoland**

S/L F A G Lascelles DFC +
F/S W J Ordway +
F/S C P Weir +

T/o 1032 Bodney. Believed shot down by Lt Dähne, 2./JG52 in the vicinity of Heligoland. All are buried in Sage War Cemetery, Oldenburg.

---

82 Sqn — **Blenheim IV** — **V6435 UX-V** — Op: **Heligoland**

F/L H R Shuttleworth +
Sgt M C Hind +
Sgt O W J Bishop RNZAF +

T/o 1053 Bodney. Shot down by fighters from 3./JG52. All are commemorated on the Runnymede Memorial.

---

82 Sqn — **Blenheim IV** — **Z7277 UX-P** — Op: **Heligoland**

Sgt A R J Dick +
P/O K C Judd +
P/O W F Race +

T/o 1032 Bodney. Shot down by fighters from 3./JG52. P/O Race is buried in Becklingen War Cemetery; the rest have no known graves.

---

88 Sqn — **Blenheim IV** — **L8788 RH-N** — Op: **Anti-shipping**

P/O G B Dunn +
P/O J R A Jones +
F/S B D Davies +

T/o 1030 Attlebridge to patrol Beat 7. Shot down off IJmuiden, Holland. All are commemorated on the Runnymede Memorial.

Note. This was the Squadron's first operational loss since joining 2 Group, a month previous. P/O Dunn had served as a Captain in The Highland Light Infantry.

---

226 Sqn — **Blenheim IV** — **Z7305 MQ-T** — Op: **Anti-shipping**

Sgt G V Smith +
Sgt S Burdon +
Sgt C C Topping RCAF +

T/o 1154 Wattisham. Hit by flak and crashed off IJmuiden, Holland. Sgt Burdon is buried in Bergen General Cemetery; the rest have no known graves.

26-27 Aug 1941 — **9 Sqn** — **Wellington IC** — **W5703 WS-** — Op: **Köln**

S/L H E Bufton evd
Sgt J T Stickles RCAF pow
Sgt W F Crampton evd
Sgt S Murray pow
Sgt R P Wright pow
Sgt K B Read evd

T/o 2235 Honington. Last heard on w/t at 0312, having sent an SOS at 0207 indicating engine trouble on leaving the target area. Believed to have crash-landed in France.

---

106 Sqn — **Hampden I** — **AE301 ZN-** — Op: **Gardening**

F/O M J C Harwood DFC +
F/S N Lusher +
F/S N T Powell pow
F/S W A Oastler MiD +

T/o 2200 Coningsby to lay mines in the Western Baltic. Shot down by a flak ship E of Aalborg, Denmark and crashed 0330 into the Limfjorden. Those who died are buried at Frederikshavn.

---

106 Sqn — **Hampden I** — **AE302 ZN-** — Op: **Köln**

Sgt H V Wilkinson +
Sgt K V Runcorn +
Sgt A P J Grundy +
Sgt A Mitchell +

T/o 2245 Coningsby. Lost without trace. All are commemorated on the Runnymede Memorial.

27-28 Aug 1941

50 Sqn	Hampden I	X2991 VN- **Op: Mannheim**
P/O Ferrie		T/o 2250 Swinderby but failed to gain height
Sgt Redwood		and crashed near the airfield. No injuries
Sgt Holland		reported.
Sgt Hawkins		

78 Sqn	Whitley V		Z6508 EY- **Op: Mannheim**
P/O K W Davies		+	T/o 0135 Middleton St. George. Crashed in
Sgt S E Rowed RCAF		+	the sea off Dunkerque, where Sgt Harper and
Sgt G T Harper		+	Sgt Gennon RNZAF are buried in the local War
Sgt J W Bills		+	Cemetery. The rest of the crew have no known
Sgt P Gennon RNZAF		+	graves.

78 Sqn	Whitley V		Z6872 EY- **Op: Mannheim**
Sgt H A Woodhatch		inj	T/o 2002 Middleton St. George. Hit by flak
Sgt Childs		inj	after bombing Bruges as an alternative. On
Sgt Olley		inj	return to base, the Whitley crashed at 0045
Sgt Davidson		inj	and burst into flames.

115 Sqn	Wellington IC	R1468 KO-Q **Op: Mannheim**
P/O Foster		T/o 2045 Marham. Crashed 0330 while trying
Sgt Soames		to land at West Raynham in conditions of heavy
Sgt Lewis		rain and poor visibility. A fire broke out,
Sgt McKay		but no serious injuries are reported.
Sgt Gregory		
Sgt Nuttall		

115 Sqn	Wellington IC	W5710 KO-J **Op: Mannheim**
S/L Sidnall		T/o 2005 Marham. Abandoned near Cromer,
P/O Wood		Norfolk, after encountering poor visibility.
Sgt Hart		
P/O Drummond		
Sgt Brooks		
F/S Johnson		

115 Sqn	Wellington IC	X9672 KO-F **Op: Mannheim**
P/O Pooley		T/o 2008 Marham. Crashed 0310 after being
Sgt Taylor		abandoned near Honing, a small village midway
P/O Foster		between North Walsham and Stalham, Norfolk.
Sgt Taylor		
Sgt Heslop		
Sgt Cork		

150 Sqn	Wellington IC	W5722 JN- **Op: Mannheim**
Sgt E R Nicholson		T/o 2045 Snaith. On return, the crew tried
		to land at Martlesham Heath, Suffolk, but

were unable to do so due to poor visibility. Subsequently, three baled out, after which the pilot force-landed near Levington Reach on the River Orwell, 5 miles SE of Ipswich.

28 Aug 1941

21 Sqn	Blenheim IV		V5825 YH-R **Op: Rotterdam**
P/O W L MacDonald		pow	T/o 1445 Watton. Crashed in the target area.
Sgt R J Somerfield		+	Sgt Somerfield is commemorated on the Runnymede
P/O W Beckingham		pow	Memorial.

21 Sqn	Blenheim IV		V6436 YH-L **Op: Rotterdam**
P/O F K Orme RCAF		+	T/o 1447 Watton. Hit by flak and crashed at
P/O S F M Gunnis		+	Maassluis (Zuid Holland), 14 km WSW of Rotterdam.
P/O A H Collins		+	All rest in Hoek van Holland General Cemetery.

21 Sqn	Blenheim IV		Z7435 YH-S **Op: Rotterdam**
Sgt K Hayes		+	T/o 1446 Watton. Crashed at Rozenburg (Zuid
Sgt A A C Shaddick		+	Holland), 16 km WSW of Rotterdam. All are
Sgt R F Brian		+	buried in Hoek van Holland General Cemetery.

28 Aug
1941

21 Sqn   Blenheim IV   **Z7447 YH-A**   **Op: Rotterdam**
S/L R A Shuttleworth   inj   T/o 1446 Watton. Crashed off the Dutch coast.
F/S D J Mackan   +   S/L Shuttleworth was still alive when a rescue
F/S G Brittain   +   craft reached the scene, but he died shortly
after being admitted to the Wilhelmina Hospital
at Amsterdam. He is buried here in the Eastern Cemetery; his crew rest in
Hoek van Holland General Cemetery.

44 Sqn   Hampden I   **AD917 KM-P**   **Transit**
Sgt B W Johnson   inj   Landed 0330 Horsham St. Faith after a mining
Sgt S Mallen   +   operation, and crashed 1000 while returning to
F/S W H Saville   inj   Waddington, the Hampden coming down on a Q site
Sgt E A Windsor   +   near the airfield.

88 Sqn   Blenheim IV   **L9379 RH-**   **Op: Rotterdam**
P/O T G Edwards   +   T/o 1740 Attlebridge. Crashed at Rozenburg
P/O F A Letchford   +   (Zuid Holland), 16 km WSW of Rotterdam. All
F/S F Tweedale   +   are buried in Hoek van Holland General Cemetery.

88 Sqn   Blenheim IV   **Z7445 RH-**   **Op: Rotterdam**
F/O J O Alexander   +   T/o 1739 Attlebridge. Crashed at Schiedam in
F/S A J Hardy   +   the target area. All are buried in the city's
F/S J L Briggs   +   Crooswijk General Cemetery. F/O Alexander, son
of Major-General R O Alexander of Victoria, BC,
was awarded a medal of the Royal Humane Society for saving a life at sea.

110 Sqn   Blenheim IV   **Z7441 VE-**   **Training**
P/O D J J Ritchie   inj   Crashed 1250 on Sand's Marsh, N of the River
Ant at Wayford Bridge, 1 mile W of Stalham,
Norfolk.

226 Sqn   Blenheim IV   **Z7289 MQ-R**   **Op: Rotterdam**
P/O F M V Johnstone   pow   T/o 1430 Wattisham. Crashed in the Maashaven
Sgt R Evans   pow   docks area of Rotterdam.
Sgt R G Drake   pow

226 Sqn   Blenheim IV   **Z7299 MQ-F**   **Op: Rotterdam**
Sgt R J O'Connell RCAF   T/o 1450 Wattisham but swung out of control
Sgt Saunders   and crashed.
P/O Robertson

Note. 88 Squadron ORB indicates their aircraft took off circa 1430, but were
recalled. This suggests the raid on Rotterdam turned out to be a split affair
with 88 Squadron going in alone, during the early evening. Other sources do
not support this and it is possible the first entry was a clerical error.

Chapter 9

Doubts and Disappointments

8-29 August to 7 November 1941

Two major problems confronted Sir Richard Peirse in the autumn of 1941. Bomber wastage was one, the second was the inescapable fact that much of the night-bombing was failing to find its mark.

The root cause of both problems was the growing sophistication of the enemy defences and the inadequate technical advances within Bomber Command to overcome the inherent weaknesses within the present bomber fleet.

On moonlit nights, interception from night fighters was on the increase, while raids carried out in marginal weather produced negligible bombing results and a sharp rise in crashes as tired crews fought the twin elements of fatigue and nature.

First, a brief comment on the now serious wastage problem. At the end of March 1941, bomber losses amounted to 181 Aircraft. By the end of June, this figure had increased to 541, while casualty returns at the end of the third quarter showed that losses had more than tripled over the previous three months and now stood at just over 1170.

Most of this attrition rate was caused by enemy action, but training accidents still took their toll. At a conservative estimate, over 5500 airmen were either missing, or had been involved in crashes ranging from merely frightening to fatal.

Within the OTUs, nearly 300 bombers had been lost in the first nine months of the year. Grim statistics that could not be ignored.

The second problem facing the Commander-in-Chief was the inability of his squadrons to deliver consistently accurate raids on Germany's industrial base.

There were many reasons for these shortcomings in bombing performance, a serious lack of adequate radio and navigational aids being just two. Trials with a navigation device known as Gee were showing promise. Three ground stations were ready by the end of June, and service testing of the new equipment by 115 Squadron was also showing positive results. During early August, Gee trials were extended over the North Sea and during the night of 11-12 August, two of the squadron's Wellingtons successfully bombed Monchengladbach.

Generally, however, the bombing campaign was not going well at all, and this disquiet was siezed upon by Lord Cherwell, Chief Scientific Advisor to the Prime Minister, Winston Churchill. At Cherwell's instigation DM Butt, a senior civil servant working in the War Cabinet Secretariat, was ordered to conduct a detailed analysis of night-bombing photographs for the months of June and July. Butt received his brief in early August and his report was in Cherwell's hands by the 18th. The conclusions of his investigations made unpalatable reading.

Even in good weather, bombing results were judged to be poor with only a small percentage of bombs falling anywhere near their intended target.

When the report was circulated amongst the Air Council, doubts were expressed as to the accuracy of Butt's findings, but it was also freely acknowledged that the present state of affairs were less than satisfactory.

Little else about the report needs to be said at this stage. Sir Richard's position at High Wycombe was safe for the time being, but there could be no escaping the fact that improvements were being sought, and sought quickly.

At squadron level, life continued much as before. Duisburg, Frankfurt, Mannheim, Köln and Essen were visited in what remained of August. Noteworthy amongst this quintet of attacks was the raid on Frankfurt. For the first time, Bomber Command despatched over 100 aircraft to the city and included in the 143 sorties was a Hampden from 455 Squadron RAAF. This was the first occasion that an Australian bomber unit had participated in the campaign, and though 455 Squadron was destined to transfer to Coastal Command in the spring of 1942, the honour of being the first fell to this unit which had formed at Williamstown in New South Wales on 23 May 1941.

Inclement weather marred the operation and in addition to the couple of Hampdens and a Whitley that failed to return, four bombers were lost in crashes, mainly as a result of running low on fuel.

A return visit took place on 2-3 September and, again, bombing results were poor. The capital city of Berlin was attacked during the same night and minor raids were flown against the channel ports, as well as mining operations. Officially, only twelve bombers from a total of 201 sent to all targets were missing. In reality, over twice that number were written off, illustrating only too painfully the growing casualties now being regularly experienced. It is interesting to note that the CO of 61 Squadron put his name to the Battle Order for Berlin and he was accompanied by Group Captain Barrett, North Luffenham's station commander. It is said that both officers went on the raid to give the crews a morale booster. Sadly, their Manchester became one of the night's many casualty statistics, having been shot down by flak over the city with total loss of life.

Five nights later, the bombers were once again over Berlin, this time in considerable strength. Visibility was good and returning crews were confident that a good attack had been delivered. Dockyard facilities at Kiel and at Boulogne were also attacked with good fires started at both locations.

Rounding off a busy night, eight Hampden crews from 5 Group dropped mines off the Frisian Islands.

Twenty-five bombers were written off, thus equalling the casualties recently referred too. Sandwiched between these two nights of heavy raiding was an attack on a chemical plant at Hüls in the Ruhr. From a mixed force of just eighty-eight aircraft, nine Whitleys and two Wellingtons were lost. The first week of September had been costly, to say the least.

Despite these worrying totals, the Command was able to operate at near maximum strength when over 200 crews were involved in raids against Hamburg and Le Havre in the middle of the month. The trip to Hamburg was well worth the effort. In the face of intense searchlight activity from the multitude of batteries ringing the city and with a fierce flak barrage in attendance, the bomber crews pressed home an excellent attack.

Huge fires sprang up in several areas and quite substantial damage was caused in the Wandsbek district where a 4000 pound block-buster exploded with terrifying force. The blast totally demolished an apartment block and the rescue services were at full stretch for several hours as they strove bravely to extricate the few survivors from the rubble.

Eight bombers failed to return, at least two of these falling to night-fighters. But flak was responsible for the demise of a 75 Squadron Wellington, captained by Sergeant J A Ward VC. James Ward, a New Zealander, had won his Victoria Cross just two months previous while flying as a second pilot on operations to Münster.

In the wake of a night-fighter attack, the Wellington's starboard engine had been set on fire. All efforts at extinguishing the blaze from inside the bomber failed and it was at this stage that Sgt Ward decided to try and stifle the fire using an engine cover.

Attached to a rope, held firmly by other members of the crew, he clawed his way onto the wing and though he was able to force the tarpaulin into the flames, the slip stream took it away before the fire was fully out.

By the time the New Zealander had regained the comparative safety of the fuselage, he was close to exhaustion.

In recognition of this courageous action, James Ward was recommended for an immediate Victoria Cross. This was duly approved and details were promulgated on 5 August 1941, in the London Gazette. Now, he was again in great danger but on this occasion he was unable to leave the stricken bomber before it crashed, burning fiercely, in the target area.

Night operations for the rest of September were flown on a reduced scale, though a long haul to the port of Stettin in the Baltic attracted a force of 139 aircraft. It turned out to be an expensive exercise with eight crews missing and five bombers destroyed in crashes. The Whitley squadrons of 4 Group came off worst; four failed to return and of the five crashes referred too, four were Whitleys.

Daylight activity was restricted to a mixture of anti-shipping sweeps and Circus raids to targets in northern France and the most significant event concerning 2 Group was the ceasing of Fortress operations by 90 Squadron. Since making their debut over Wilhelmshaven on 8 July, servicing problems had hampered their use and the maximum number available at any one time had never exceeded four aircraft.

In retrospect, 90 Squadron had performed quite well. The raid on Wilhelmshaven had been accurate and a study of the twenty operations involving Fortresses reveals that approximately half of the fifty-two sorties despatched were completed satisfactorily.

From these raids, one bomber had been written off in a crash near Plymouth after being extensively damaged by fighters and two had been shot down while trying to reach Oslo on 8 September. Development testing had accounted for two others, both being totally destroyed with heavy loss of life. A sixth Fortress had been destroyed by fire in a ground accident.

October commenced with a series of minor raids on Karlsruhe, Stuttgart and at ports along the channel coast. The Karlsruhe raid was a total failure due to fog descending on the bomber bases and a recall signal was sent.

Weather conditions were only marginally better over the next couple of nights before turning completely foul thus necessitating a halt to both day and night operations.

This inclement state in the autumn weather continued until the night of 10-11 October when raiding restarted with attacks on Essen and Köln. At Essen, where the aiming point was the Krupps armaments complex, thick fog prevailed and bombing was widely scattered across the Ruhr. Conditions at Köln were hardly better and, again, the attack petered out leaving only minor damage in its wake.

The cost to the Command was high with at least sixteen bombers written off, including two Wellingtons missing from a visit to the port of Boulogne.

Then, on 12-13 October, a new record in the number of sorties despatched was set, 373 in total. Three targets were selected, Nürnberg, Bremen and Hüls, with the former being chosen as the primary.

This was the first time that the Command had flown to Nürnberg in strength and post war research suggests that only a few of the

52 crews involved actually reached their objective. Most of the bombing fell over open countryside and several small villages suffered as a consequence.

Cloud cover at Bremen was almost total and a similar picture emerges at Hüls, where the chemical factory attacked in early September was the principal target.

Sixteen bombers were lost, a high casualty figure for what was a disappointing night's work.

Slightly better results were achieved at Nürnberg on 14-15 October, and raids on Kiel and Hamburg towards the end of the month were also deemed reasonably satisfactory.

Day light operations by 2 Group were flown on sixteen days during October. Fourteen Blenheims joined the casualty statistics and anti-shipping sweeps were finally curtailed early in November.

The handful of crews that had come through the last eight traumatic months must have sighed with collective relief. Ill equipped for the task demanded of them, the Blenheim squadrons had performed quite magnificently. Now, with winter fast approaching, the burden of day operations was to fall mainly on the night-bomber force.

28-29 Aug 1941	7 Sqn	Stirling I	N3666 MG-Z

28-29 Aug 1941 — 7 Sqn — Stirling I — N3666 MG-Z — Op: Duisburg

F/L D J H Lay DFC
Sgt C Tourville
Sgt W H Robinson
Sgt M Roach DFM, RCAF
Sgt A Chambers
Sgt J Donlan
Sgt H Macrae

T/o 0117 Oakington. Badly shot about over the North Sea by a Me 110 and on return the bomber landed at Newmarket, where the port undercarriage unit collapsed. Sgt Macrae was wounded during the engagement and he baled out.

7 Sqn — Stirling I — W7438 MG- — Op: Duisburg

P/O J E Chilvers +
Sgt J W Blakey +
Sgt F C Child +
P/O C F Hart RCAF +
F/S A Penn +
Sgt G J Truscott +
Sgt N R Cowin +

T/o Oakington. Crashed at Kaarst, 12 km WSW of Düsseldorf. All are buried in Rheinberg War Cemetery. F/S Penn was a Canadian serving with the RAF.

35 Sqn — Halifax I — L9501 TL-Y — Op: Duisburg

P/O A E C Adkins +
P/O C J Pearson +
Sgt F W Hill +
Sgt H Brelsford +
Sgt A J Manning +
Sgt H Thompson +
Sgt A W Rose +

T/o 0012 Linton-on-Ouse. All are buried in the Reichswald Forest War Cemetery.

40 Sqn — Wellington IC — Z8839 BL-L — Op: Duisburg

P/O J E King +
Sgt J C Bredin RCAF pow
Sgt B T Kearsley +
Sgt A A Cormack +
Sgt A C T Barter pow
Sgt T Arnold pow

T/o 2342 Alconbury. Crashed at Mülheim. Those who died were buried in the Nord Friedhof at Düsseldorf, but since 1945, their remains have been taken to the Reichswald Forest War Cemetery.

49 Sqn — Hampden I — AD971 EA-O — Op: Duisburg

P/O T P Pratt +
P/O H C Tonge +
Sgt C Hodkinson +
Sgt A C Willis +

T/o Scampton. Believed shot down over the North Sea by a night-fighter. Sgt Willis is buried in Harlingen General Cemetery; the rest of the crew have been interned in cemeteries on the islands of Texel and Vlieland.

49 Sqn — Hampden I — AE126 EA-N — Op: Duisburg

P/O B M Fournier +
Sgt D H Barrett +
Sgt E R Palmer +
Sgt D Watson +

T/o Scampton. Shot down by a night-fighter (Oblt Helmut Lent, 4./NJG1) and crashed 0340 into the sea off Ameland, where all are buried in Nes General Cemetery.

28-29 Aug
1941

104 Sqn	Wellington II	W5595 EP-E	Op: Duisburg
Sgt G H Spickett	+		
Sgt A G Geddes RCAF	+		
Sgt H A French	+		
Sgt E S Jones	+		
Sgt J A D Rheaume RCAF	+		
Sgt D C Hayward	+		

T/o 2340 Driffield. All are buried in Rheinberg War Cemetery.

106 Sqn	Hampden I	AE193 ZN-A	Op: Duisburg
Sgt E R H Lyon	pow		
Sgt R J K Woodroofe	pow		
Sgt G B Stanton	pow		
Sgt G Luke	pow		

T/o 2330 Coningsby. Ditched in the North Sea, NW of Texel, from where they were rescued four days later by a Dutch fishing trawler and taken to Zoutcamp. Suffering from exhaustion, the bomber crew decided to surrender, rather than jeopardise the lives of their Dutch saviours.

405 Sqn	Wellington II	W5488 LQ-B	Op: Duisburg
P/O E M Watts	+		
Sgt I B Quinn RCAF	pow		
Sgt D M Hughes RCAF	+		
Sgt J W T Davies	+		
Sgt R J Hollobone	+		
Sgt D S MacLeod	pow		

T/o 2350 Pocklington. Those who died are buried in Rheinberg War Cemetery.

29-30 Aug
1941

50 Sqn	Hampden I	AD839 VN-	Op: Frankfurt
Sgt L C Turner	+		
Sgt J G Procter	+		
Sgt T H Willis	+		
Sgt R V Urpeth	+		

T/o 2145 Swinderby. Crashed in the vicinity of Abbeville (Somme), France, where the crew are buried in the Extension to the Communal Cemetery. Earlier, the bomber had been heard on w/t, in contact with Sealand d/f station.

50 Sqn	Hampden I	AE229 VN-	Op: Frankfurt
F/S I P Mapp	inj		
Sgt K S Furley			
Sgt Welford	inj		
Sgt E R James			

T/o 2135 Swinderby. Crashed 0430 onto a Q site at Bassingham, 8 miles SSW of Lincoln.

58 Sqn	Whitley V	Z6504 GE-K	Op: Frankfurt
Sgt A P A McKenzie	+		
Sgt Kingsford-Smith			
Sgt Fuce			
P/O Ivins			
Sgt D Mole			

T/o 2105 Linton-on-Ouse. Ditched 0014 some 2 miles off Brightlingsea, Essex. The four survivors were rescued within three hours of their aircraft entering the water.

61 Sqn	Hampden I	AE247 QR-	Op: Frankfurt
Sgt H Richmond	+		
Sgt J Spencer	+		
Sgt J Archer	+		
Sgt A G Clarke	+		

T/o 2152 North Luffenham. Lost without trace. All are commemorated on the Runnymede Memorial.

76 Sqn	Halifax I	L9518 MP-	Op: Frankfurt
S/L R Bickford DFC	+		
P/O Jones			
Cpl Randall			
F/S J Flannigan			
Sgt Reilly			
Sgt G W Duckmanton	+		

T/o 2113 Middleton St. George. Abandoned at 2000 feet and crashed 0415 near Pocklington airfield, Yorkshire. S/L Bickford died after his parachute became caught up in the tail assembly. The crash was attributed to the bomber running low on fuel.

102 Sqn	Whitley V	Z6863 DY-	Op: Frankfurt
S/L J O Lalor MiD	inj		
Sgt H J W Newnes	+		
Sgt M R Bowes	+		
Sgt F Potts	pow		
Sgt R C Watchorn	pow		

T/o 2101 Topcliffe. Crashed, grievously wounding the pilot in the legs. The two survivors helped him to a nearby barn, where he died six hours later. Along with Sgt Newnes and Sgt Bowes, he is buried in Rheinberg War Cemetery.

9-30 Aug 941	102 Sqn	Whitley V		Z6951 DY-	Op: Frankfurt

102 Sqn   **Whitley V**

Sgt P E Carreau RCAF   +
Sgt A E Masters   +
Sgt W V Atkinson   +
Sgt F G Kuebler   inj
Sgt C Higson   inj

Z6951 DY-   **Op: Frankfurt**
T/o 2112 Topcliffe. Crashed 0500 at Friar's Thorn Farm near Docking airfield, Norfolk, and burst into flames.

103 Sqn   **Wellington IC**

P/O W R Oldfield   pow
Sgt G P Williams RAAF   +
Sgt A H Figg RCAF   +
Sgt H A Kelly   +
Sgt J Grassom   +
Sgt H Dunn   pow

R1213 PM-   **Op: Mannheim**
T/o 2031 Elsham Wolds. Struck by lightning and crashed in the vicinity of Vlissingen (Zeeland), Holland, where those who died are buried in the town's Northern Cemetery.

115 Sqn   **Wellington IC**

Sgt J K Murdoch   +
Sgt F J McGaw   +
F/S A Forse   +
Sgt W H Blades RCAF   +
F/S J W Boyce RCAF   inj
Sgt W J Cowell   +

X9826 KO-D   **Op: Mannheim**
T/o 2014 Marham. Believed shot down by an intruder and crashed 0212 near Martlesham Heath airfield, Suffolk. F/S Boyce RCAF died from his injuries on 1 September.

214 Sqn   **Wellington IC**

Sgt E W Foxlee RCAF   +
Sgt J H Williamson   +
Sgt J E Jerrard   +
Sgt G Klusky   +
Sgt E Halestrap   +
Sgt K Morris   +

R1604 BU-   **Op: Mannheim**
T/o Stradishall. Crashed 2300 in the vicinity of Vlissingen (Zeeland), Holland, where the crew are buried in the Northern Cemetery. During 1972 the RNethAF excavated wreckage from this bomber, after which it was suggested its demise may have been caused by a lightning strike.

0-31 Aug 941	101 Sqn	Wellington IC

101 Sqn   **Wellington IC**

P/O Reynolds   inj
P/O D L Crichton RAAF   inj
Sgt L A Nauze   inj
Sgt O W Barlow   +
Sgt Myers   inj

Z8860 SR-   **Op: Hamburg**
T/o 2112 Oakington. Crashed at Rampton, 7 miles NNW of Cambridge. P/O Crichton RAAF died from his injuries on 1 September.

1 Aug 941	44 Sqn	Hampden I

44 Sqn   **Hampden I**

P/O P R Owen   +
Sgt D G Forbes   +
AC2 F B Prest   +

AD939 KM-   **Training**
Crashed 1210 near Waddington following a midair collision with a 412 Squadron Spitfire from Digby, captained by P/O W R Hughes RCAF. AC2 Prest was an Initial Training Wing candidate.

1 Aug-Sep 1941	12 Sqn	Wellington II

12 Sqn   **Wellington II**

P/O C P Khosla RIAF   +
P/O R N Dastur RIAF   +
Sgt W B Clark RCAF   +
Sgt P J Lewis   +
Sgt J F Wolff RCAF   +
Sgt R B Russell   +

W5577 PH-U   **Op: Boulogne**
T/o 2115 Binbrook. Crashed in the sea off the French coast. Three bodies were later recovered and their graves are now at the Canadian War Cemetery, Dieppe. The remainder are commemorated on the Runnymede Memorial. P/O Khosla RIAF hailed from Lahore, while his co-pilot came from Bandra, Bombay.

44 Sqn   **Hampden I**

Sgt S A Harvey   +
Sgt H A Taylor RCAF   +
F/S J E Phillips   +
Sgt R K Hayes   +

AD726 KM-   **Op: Köln**
T/o 2040 Waddington. Crashed in the North Sea 25 miles E of Harwich, Essex. Two bodies were washed onto the Belgian coast and both are buried in Oost-Duinkerke Communal Cemetery. The names of Sgt Harvey and F/S Phillips are perpetuated on the panels of the Runnymede Memorial.

83 Sqn   **Hampden I**

Sgt F Dacey   +
Sgt G G Bensley   +
Sgt J A D Clark   +
Sgt H G Tonks   +

AD859 OL-O   **Op: Köln**
T/o 2015 Scampton. Crashed at Munsterbilzen (Limburg), 9 km SSE of Genk, Belgium. All are buried in Heverlee War Cemetery.

31 Aug–	83 Sqn	Hampden I	AD912 OL-Y	Op: **Köln**
1 Sep 1941	F/L E P Willcox DFC	+	
	P/O D B Organ	pow	
	Sgt H C Gabbitas	pow	
	F/S J Lawrence	pow	

T/o 2015 Scampton. Shot down by a night-fighter (Uffz Pahler, I./NJG1) and crashed 0018 at Meijel (Limburg), 16 km NE of Weert, Holland. The pilot is buried in Jonkerbos War Cemetery.

	83 Sqn	Hampden I	AE187 OL-L	Op: **Köln**
	F/S R C Plaistowe	+	
	Sgt A J Somerville-Woodiwis	+	
	Sgt J Hughes	+	
	Sgt R B Scott	+	

T/o 2015 Scampton. Shot down by a night-fighter (Oblt Willi Dimter, 3./NJG1) and crashed 2347 at Deurne (Noord Brabant), 9 km ESE of Helmond, Holland. All are buried in Woensel General Cemetery at Eindhoven.

	99 Sqn	Wellington IC	R1411 LN-N	Op: **Köln**
	P/O G S Eccles	+	
	Sgt D H Hodge	+	
	Sgt A F B Broadribb	+	
	Sgt D R Mallett	+	
	Sgt G E Boxall	+	
	Sgt Stevens	inj	

T/o 2028 Waterbeach. Diverted to Mildenhall on return, where the pilot misjudged his first attempt to land. While making a second circuit, the Wellington was shot down by a Ju 88C intruder flown by Fw Alfons Köster, NJG2, and crashed 0248 in a field at Beck Row, Mildenhall, Suffolk.

	101 Sqn	Wellington IC	R1703 SR-J	Op: **Köln**
	P/O J F Ashton	+	
	Sgt R T Wood RCAF	pow	
	Sgt E R V Lane	+	
	Sgt J B Redden RCAF	+	
	Sgt L A Warburton	evd	
	Sgt J W Hutton	evd	

T/o 2014 Oakington. Crashed at Boxbergheide (Limburg) in the western suburbs of Genk, Belgium. Those who died are buried in Schaffen Communal Cemetery.

	102 Sqn	Whitley V	Z6837 DY-	Op: **Essen**
	P/O E G M Anderson RCAF	+	
	Sgt T H Wood RCAF	+	
	Sgt T C Boyle	+	
	Sgt N C J Carter	+	
	Sgt M S Humphrey RCAF	+	

T/o 1950 Topcliffe. Crashed near Schaffen (Brabant), 3 km NE of Diest, Belgium. All are buried in Schaffen Communal Cemetery.

	102 Sqn	Whitley V	Z6868 DY-	Op: **Essen**
	P/O B B P Roy		
	Sgt L W Carr		
	Sgt P L N Trehearn		
	Sgt P A Taylor		
	Sgt R Gayler		

Destroyed on the ground at Topcliffe by an explosion which totally wrecked the Whitley as it prepared to take off. The crew had a quite remarkable escape, as did the crew of another Whitley which was damaged by the explosion.

	207 Sqn	Manchester I	L7316 EM-U	Op: **Köln**
	P/O T R Gilderthorp	pow	
	P/O P G C Wood	+	
	Sgt L C Parker	pow	
	Sgt B Akrigg	+	
	F/S R W Gray RCAF	+	
	Sgt W M Cadney RCAF	+	

T/o Waddington. Hit by flak on the approach to the target and crashed near Oberkruchen, Germany. Those who died are buried in Rheinberg War Cemetery.

1 Sep	405 Sqn	Wellington II	W5535 LQ-	Training
1941	Sgt Turner		
	Sgt H S McNeil		
	Sgt A N McLennan RCAF		

Crashed 2150 in a field 1 mile N of Pocklington airfield. The accident was caused by a fire in the port engine and though the crew escaped any serious injury, the Wellington was destroyed before the flames could be brought under control.

1-2 Sep	144 Sqn	Hampden I	AD905 PL-	Op: **Köln**
1941	F/O M T H Adams	pow	
	F/S A J Box DFM	+	
	Sgt G J P Hartlett	+	
	Sgt G E Morgan	+	

T/o North Luffenham. Crashed near Köln, where those who died were initially buried in the Süd Friedhof. Since the war, their bodies have been taken to Rheinberg War Cemetery.

Note. F/S Box was on his second tour of operations, having flown in Blenheims with 15 Squadron during the summer of 1940. Details of his award appeared in the London Gazette on 13 September 1940.

Sep **941**	**139 Sqn**	**Blenheim IV**	
	S/L K H Walsh		+
	F/S A G Hole		+
	Sgt G H Brook		+

Z7274 XD-   Op: **Anti-shipping**
T/o 1023 Manston. Hit by flak and crashed into the sea off the Belgian coast. Sgt Brook has no known grave; the rest are buried in cemeteries in Belgium and in Holland.

?-3 Sep **941**	**35 Sqn**	**Halifax I**	
	F/O R James DFC		+
	Sgt S R Arthur		pow
	Sgt A R P Mills		pow
	Sgt H S Oldman		pow
	Sgt J K Young		+
	Sgt R G Mullally		pow
	Sgt T E Allasson		pow

L9508 TL-X   Op: **Berlin**
T/o 2049 Linton-on-Ouse. Last heard on w/t when N of the target. The two airmen who died are buried in the 1939-1945 War Cemetery at Berlin.

---

35 Sqn	**Halifax I**	
P/O D S Fraser		+
Sgt R L B Beare		pow
Sgt N Willingham		+
P/O J P B Cushion		+
Sgt D Slater		+
Sgt A H Stroud		+
Sgt E Wilkinson		pow

L9560 TL-F   Op: **Berlin**
T/o 2050 Linton-on-Ouse. Transmitted a signal indicating the aircraft was on track and about to cross the enemy coast. Those who died are buried at Berlin in the 1939-1945 War Cemetery. P/O Fraser and P/O Cushion were sons of high ranking RAF officers.

---

40 Sqn	**Wellington IC**	
P/O A R Fitch		+
Sgt T Stabler		
P/O A Kinnerburgh		
Sgt A C S Delgada		
Sgt T Robertson		+
Sgt W V Parslow RCAF		

R1030 BL-R   Op: **Oostende**
T/o 2010 Alconbury. Ditched 10 miles off the port of Harwich, Essex. Of the four survivors, P/O Kinnerburgh was wounded. The body of P/O Fitch was eventually washed onto the shores of Belgium and he is buried in Middelkerke Communal Cemetery. P/O Roberston rests in Cupar New Cemetery, Fife, Scotland.

---

40 Sqn	**Wellington IC**	
P/O Baker		
Sgt Robins		
Sgt Holtby		
Sgt A Simpson		
Sgt E Crook		
Sgt MacLachlan		

X9669 BL-F   Op: **Frankfurt**
T/o 2000 Alconbury. Returned to base early and crashed 2330 while trying to land in poor visibility. The bomber caught fire and AC2 Riden was instrumental in helping to rescue the crew and through his devotion to duty, serious injuries were averted.

---

44 Sqn	**Hampden I**	
Sgt Knight		
Sgt Spanner		
Sgt J Stephens		+
Sgt Churchill		

AD913 KM-K   Op: **Frankfurt**
T/o 2025 Waddington. While over the target, the port engine failed and after struggling to return to base on one engine, the Hampden was abandoned at 0245 near Dorking, Surrey. It is believed that Sgt Stephens failed to leave the aircraft as his body was found close to the wreckage.

---

44 Sqn	**Hampden I**	
P/O E A W Thompson		+
P/O H J Cook RCAF		+
Sgt E Dyer DFM		+
Sgt W McBeth		+

AE152 KM-R   Op: **Berlin**
T/o 2045 Waddington. Presumed lost over the North Sea. P/O Thompson is buried in Nes General Cemetery, Ameland; his crew have no known graves.

---

44 Sqn	**Hampden I**	
Sgt L A Robertson		+
Sgt H N Unwin		+
F/S H B Turner		+
Sgt T P A Riddell		+

AE254 KM-W   Op: **Berlin**
T/o Waddington. Crashed at Wittenberg, Germany. All are buried in the 1939-1945 War Cemetery at Berlin.

---

44 Sqn	**Hampden I**	
Sgt D N N de Brath		+
Sgt R L Cole		+
Sgt A Golston		pow
Sgt J Rawson		pow

AE313 KM-C   Op: **Frankfurt**
T/o Waddington. The two airmen who died are buried in Rheinberg War Cemetery.

2-3 Sep
1941

49 Sqn	**Hampden I**	**X3136 EA-K**	**Op: Berlin**

Sgt W C Samuel
Sgt West
Sgt Watchorn
Sgt Tilley

T/o 1943 Scampton. Crash-landed 0550 on scrub land at Thornham Ling Common, Thornham, 4 miles ENE of Hunstanton, Norfolk. Sgt Samuel was lost from operations on 25 June 1942.

49 Sqn	**Hampden I**	**AE203 EA-F**	**Op: Berlin**

Sgt J Flint GM, DFM
Sgt Combes
Sgt Jardine
F/S J D Gadsby

T/o 1950 Scampton. Crash-landed 0657 at Stradbroke, 15 miles NE of Stowmarket, Suffolk. No injuries reported.

50 Sqn	**Hampden I**	**X2919 VN-**	**Op: Berlin**

Sgt Mudd   inj
Sgt Glenn
Sgt Dalgleish   inj
Sgt Pullin

T/o 2035 Swinderby. Crash-landed 0510 between Wansford and Wittering airfield. The two injured airmen were admitted to Stainforth General Hospital.

50 Sqn	**Hampden I**	**AE157 VN-**	**Op: Gardening**

P/O Ferrie
P/O Bartley
Sgt Holland
Sgt Hawkins

T/o 1935 Swinderby. Landed 0320 at Waddington in poor visibility and collided with a Hampden belonging to 44 Squadron. Both machines were extensively damaged and subsequently written off charge.

50 Sqn	**Hampden I**	**AE305 VN-**	**Op: Berlin**

F/S F A Titcomb
Sgt R M Gifford RCAF
Sgt Raynes
Sgt Christy

T/o 2035 Swinderby. Crash-landed 0525 astride the A149 Warham to Stiffkey road on the Norfolk coast, near Wells-next-the-Sea. Before coming to a halt, the bomber passed beneath telephone wires and slid through two hedges. Soon after this incident, both pilots were posted to 408 Squadron RCAF.

57 Sqn	**Wellington II**	**W5434 DX-Y**	**Op: Frankfurt**

Sgt L T Hutchison RAAF   +
Sgt F McNeill   +
Sgt F K Crossley   +
F/S L T Lawson RCAF   +
F/S A C Turgeon RCAF   +
Sgt D E Soles RCAF   +

T/o 2025 Feltwell. Crashed 0320 after hitting a house in Bar Lane, Stapleford. At the time of the crash, visibility was extremely poor.

61 Sqn	**Manchester I**	**L7388 QR-**	**Op: Berlin**

W/C G E Valentine DSO   +
G/C J F T Barrett DSO &   +
  Bar, DFC
F/L A B Harrison DSO   +
Sgt E E Dowse   +
Sgt J E Nicholson   +
Sgt W D Hamer RNZAF   +
F/O L Duckworth   +

T/o 2030 North Luffenham. Shot down by flak over Berlin. All are buried locally in the 1939-1945 War Cemetery. At 43 years of age, it is likely that G/C Barrett served in the First World War.

77 Sqn	**Whitley V**	**Z6648 KN-**	**Op: Frankfurt**

Sgt D W Mercer
Sgt Gardiner
Sgt Armstrong
Sgt Hemming
Sgt Taylor

T/o 2026 Topcliffe. Crash-landed 0530 at Chellaston on the southern outskirts of Derby. The Whitley had run low on fuel and fog was obscuring ground details. No serious injuries reported.

83 Sqn	**Hampden I**	**X3144 OL-N**	**Op: Gardening**

Sgt C W Allen   +
Sgt A W Rowan   +
Sgt H B B T Smith   +
Sgt H Kay   +

T/o 2000 Scampton to lay mines off the Frisians. Presumed lost in the target area. Sgt Rowan is buried on Texel, while Sgt Kay rests in Harlinge General Cemetery. The rest have no known graves

83 Sqn	**Hampden I**	**AD978 OL-C**	**Op: Berlin**

W/C H V Satterley
Sgt K Rogers
Sgt J R Cross
Sgt H Yardley

T/o 2005 Scampton. Crashed 0450 on Stone Pit Hills, near Grimston, 6 miles ENE of King's Lynn Norfolk. The crew escaped with only minor cuts and abrasions.

| 2-3 Sep | 83 Sqn | Hampden I | AE315 OL-X | Op: **Gardening** |
| 1941 | Sgt R B Olliver | pow | | |

T/o 2000 Scampton to lay mines off the Frisians. While flying low in the target area, the Hampden struck a sand-bank and crashed in the sea. Sgt Walshe was repatriated before the end of the war.

	Sgt J F Payne	pow		
	F/S H Logan	pow		
	Sgt J D Walshe	pow		

	102 Sqn	Whitley V	Z6946 DY-	Op: **Frankfurt**
	F/S S T Modeland RCAF	+		
	Sgt D M Bozer RCAF	+		
	P/O J C Nixon RCAF	+		
	Sgt A F Jaggers	+		
	Sgt L M Bowen RCAF	+		

T/o 2056 Topcliffe. Crashed 0355 in Rectory Lane, Kirton, 8 miles SE of Ipswich. A house known as The Haven was badly damaged, as was the front of June Cottage. A 4 year old girl was slightly hurt. The force of the crash also fractured water mains in the area, as well as bringing down electricity cables. Since the war, five pews in Kirton parish church have been named in remembrance of the crew.

| | 104 Sqn | Wellington II | W5435 EP-F | Op: **Frankfurt** |
| | P/O R A Doherty | inj | | |

T/o Driffield. Crashed 2225 at Thewhitts Farm, Boroughbridge, 6 miles SE of Ripon, Yorkshire, while trying to land in poor visibility. The entire crew were admitted to the Harrogate and District Hospital for treatment.

| | 150 Sqn | Wellington IC | Z8815 JN- | Op: **Frankfurt** |
| | Sgt Dickenson | | | |

T/o 2000 Snaith. Crash-landed 0215 near Kenley, Surrey, after the bomber shed its starboard airscrew. No serious injuries reported.

	214 Sqn	Wellington IC	R1717 BU-	Op: **Frankfurt**
	F/L R H May	+		
	Sgt C Hambleton	+		
	F/O J P McKay RCAF	+		
	Sgt L W Price	+		
	Sgt L Black	+		
	Sgt C J Brakeman RCAF	+		

T/o Stradishall. Presumed crashed in the sea off the French coast. All are buried in the Town Cemetery at Dunkerque.

	218 Sqn	Wellington IC	X9810 HA-K	Op: **Oostende**
	S/L Gibbes DFC			
	Sgt Helfer			
	Sgt Adamson			
	Sgt Ross			
	Sgt Purcell			
	Sgt K England			

T/o 2022 Marham. Hit by flak and crashed in the sea off the Belgian coast. The crew came ashore three days later at Westgate, on the western outskirts of Margate, Kent.

	305 Sqn	Wellington II	W5563 SM-Q	Op: **Frankfurt**
	Sgt Molata			
	F/O Drzechowski			
	F/O Jarkewski			
	Sgt Kratowchil			
	Sgt Reng			
	Sgt Czech			

T/o 2013 Lindholme. Hit by flak, while outbound, over Oudenaarde, Belgium, which caused a fire in the starboard engine. The pilot turned about, but the port engine subsequently failed and the Wellington was ditched 7 miles off the South Foreland, Kent. The crew were rescued by HSL147.

| 3 Sep | 44 Sqn | Hampden I | X3025 KM- | Ground |
| 1941 | | | | |

Damaged beyond repair at Waddington after being struck by a 50 Squadron Hampden, landing in bad visibility.

3-4 Sep	58 Sqn	Whitley V	Z6869 GE-T	Op: **Brest**
1941	P/O A A Law	+		
	Sgt W H Trewin RCAF	+		
	Sgt R L Ward RCAF	+		
	Sgt C O Steggall	+		
	P/O E D Comber-Higgs	inj		

T/o 1921 Linton-on-Ouse but recalled at 2030 and ordered to divert to Acklington, where the Whitley crashed 2345 into a field at Turnbull Farm and burst into flames.

Note. It will be recalled that P/O Law had survived a traumatic three days drifting in the North Sea after ditching on return from operations on 17-18 April 1941, while as recently as 7 August he had survived a serious crash at Linton-on-Ouse.

3-4 Sep 1941	115 Sqn	Wellington IC	**W5684 KO-G**	**Op: Brest**

115 Sqn   Wellington IC
P/O Scholes
Sgt Morton
Sgt Batty
Sgt Newark
Sgt Kinsey
Sgt Haynes

W5684 KO-G   **Op: Brest**
T/o 2003 Marham. Believed hit by flak and after running into bad weather on return, the crew baled out in the vicinity of Horrabridge, 3 miles SE of Tavistock, Devon.

---

4 Sep 1941   18 Sqn   Blenheim IV
Sgt D G Adams RAAF   pow
Sgt F Woodcock   +
Sgt M Koransky   +

Z7296 WV-P   **Op: Circus 93**
T/o 1501 Horsham St. Faith to bomb a chemical factory at Mazingarbe. Shot down by Me 109s.

---

6 Sep 1941   10 Sqn   Whitley V
Sgt W Stuart RCAF   +
P/O Austin   +
Sgt P W Bryant   +
Sgt Whitlock   inj

Z6932 ZA-   **Air Test**
Landed at Acklington airfield, Northumberland, after becoming lost in poor visibility. On leaving to return to Leeming, the Whitley flew into h/t cables, crashed and burst into flames.

6-7 Sep 1941   10 Sqn   Whitley V
Sgt A Poupard   +
P/O J F Laurie-Dickson   +
F/S R H Wilson RCAF   +
Sgt R J Garrod   +
Sgt P T Takarangi RNZAF   +

Z6478 ZA-S   **Op: Hüls**
T/o 1949 Leeming. Shot down by a night-fighter (Oblt Ludwig Becker, 4./NJG1) and crashed 2300 on an artillery practice range operated by the Wehrmacht near Oldebroek (Gelderland), Holland. All are buried locally in the General Cemetery.

---

10 Sqn   Whitley V
F/S R M Holder   pow
P/O P R M Runnacles   pow
Sgt J Grounds   pow
Sgt J H Morgan RCAF   pow
Sgt N S Jones RCAF   pow

Z6942 ZA-   **Op: Hüls**
T/o 1953 Leeming.

---

49 Sqn   Hampden I
Sgt Robinson   inj
Sgt Sanderson   inj
Sgt J C Price   inj
Sgt J Mossop   inj

AD744 EA-   **Op: Gardening**
T/o 2150 Scampton to lay mines off Oslo. On return, the Hampden ran out of fuel and crashed 8 miles SW of Banff, Scotland.

---

57 Sqn   Wellington IC
Sgt N J Lake   +
Sgt B A Clark RNZAF   +
Sgt R K Hutt   +
Sgt H M Elder   +
Sgt G W Richardson   +
F/S J A Brooks   +

Z8794 DX-H   **Op: Hüls**
T/o 2110 Feltwell. All are buried in the Reichswald Forest War Cemetery.

---

75 Sqn   Wellington IC
P/O J E Johnson   +
Sgt R S D Johnston   +
Sgt R M Minchin   +
Sgt R Davies   +
Sgt W Bearne   +
Sgt W J Barker   +

X9767 AA-S   **Op: Hüls**
T/o Feltwell. Shot down by a night-fighter (Oblt Emil Woltersdorf, III./NJG1) and crashed 0011 near Borculo (Gelderland), 8 km SE of Lochem, Holland. All are buried in Borculo General Cemetery.

---

77 Sqn   Whitley V
P/O Havelock
P/O Watts
F/S Hancock
Sgt Fitzpartrick
Sgt C H R Ford

Z6654 KN-   **Op: Hüls**
T/o 2000 Leeming. Damaged by a night-fighter and crash-landed 0240 at North Cart Gap on Cromer beach, Norfolk.

---

77 Sqn   Whitley V
Sgt D W Mercer   +
Sgt J H Painter RCAF   +
Sgt D G Kemp   +
Sgt D W Gillies   +
P/O R J Minnis RNZAF   +

Z6668 KN-   **Op: Hüls**
T/o 2004 Leeming. Crashed at Quackenbrück, Germany, where the crew were buried in the Evangelical Cemetery. Since 1945, their remains have been interned in Rheinberg War Cemetery. Sgt Mercer was an American from Omaha, Nebraska.

6-7 Sep **1941**	**77 Sqn**		**Whitley V**	**Z6824 KN-**	**Op: Hüls**
	S/L A J Hannigan	+		T/o 1954 Leeming. Shot down by a night-fighter	
	Sgt D Thomas	pow		(Oblt Hans-Karl Kamp, III./NJG1) and crashed	
	P/O N Woodward RCAF	+		2315 at Borculo (Gelderland), 8 km SE of Lochem,	
	Sgt C M Evans	+		Holland. Those who died are buried in Borculo	
	Sgt E C E Myers RCAF	+		General Cemetery.	

78 Sqn **Whitley V** **Z6864 EY-** **Op: Hüls**
Sgt Jones RAAF
Sgt Jones
Sgt Miller
Sgt Vere
Sgt Rouse

T/o 2025 Middleton St. George. Attacked by an intruder and crash-landed 0315 a few hundred yards SE of Markington church, 4 miles SSW of Ripon, Yorkshire.

78 Sqn **Whitley V** **Z6881 EY-** **Op: Hüls**
P/O F B Thorpe +
Sgt C V Matheson +
Sgt D V Logan RAAF +
Sgt G Carman RNZAF +
Sgt C J Storer +

T/o 2037 Middleton St. George. Shot down by a night-fighter (Oblt Helmut Lent, 4./NJG1) and crashed 0125 at Bergum (Friesland), 12 km ESE of Leeuwarden, Holland. All are buried in Tietjerksteradeel (Bergum) Protestant Churchyard.

83 Sqn **Hampden I** **AE319 OL-J** **Op: Gardening**
P/O J B Leetham pow
Sgt N B Morrison +
Sgt L W Sadezky pow
Sgt H Yardley +

T/o 2030 Scampton to lay mines off Oslo. Shot down by flak in the target area and crashed near Sandvika, Norway. Those who died are buried in Oslo Western Civil Cemetery.

102 Sqn **Whitley V** **Z6574 DY-B** **Op: Hüls**
P/O J R Croucher +
Sgt J R Tugman +
Sgt H L B Morphett RAAF +
F/S A L Halsey RCAF +
F/S J Glover RCAF +

T/o 2034 Topcliffe. Came down in the sea some 60 miles ENE of Bircham Newton, Norfolk. All are commemorated on the Runnymede Memorial.

102 Sqn **Whitley V** **Z6970 DY-R** **Op: Hüls**
Sgt P C Eyre +
Sgt L A Stock RCAF +
Sgt K P Withyman +
Sgt T McGill +

T/o 2105 Topcliffe. Shot down by a night-fighter and crashed 0107 at Sambeek (Noord Brabant), 26 km NE of Helmond, Holland. All are buried in Woensel General Cemetery.

7 Sep
1941 **226 Sqn** **Blenheim IV** **Z7306 MQ-U** **Op: Anti-shipping**
Sgt J D Fieldman +
Sgt F K Phillips +
Sgt J H Carr +

T/o 1130 Wattisham. Hit by flak and crashed off Scheveningen, Holland. Sgt Phillips is buried in Hoek van Holland General Cemetery; his two companions have no known graves.

226 Sqn **Blenheim IV** **Z7312 MQ-N** **Op: Anti-shipping**
F/L C E C Haggitt +
P/O R F Bennett +
F/O C D Ramsay +

T/o 1130 Wattisham. Crashed off Scheveningen, Holland. F/L Haggitt is buried at Amsterdam in the New Eastern Cemetery; but his crew have no known graves.

7-8 Sep
1941 **7 Sqn** **Stirling I** **N6046 MG-** **Op: Berlin**
Sgt A Yardley pow
F/L C M Hall RAAF pow
Sgt D Owens pow
Sgt J H Boulton pow
Sgt J M Sutton pow
Sgt L E J Davenport pow
Sgt A Speakman pow

T/o 2001 Oakington. Shot down by a night-fighter and crashed at Recklinghausen, Germany.

9 Sqn **Wellington IC** **R1499 WS-** **Op: Berlin**
Sgt T F Wilmot
Sgt Anderson
P/O Boyle
Sgt Shepherd
Sgt Cassidy
Sgt Webborn

T/o 2014 Honington. Crash-landed 0445 on return to base, due to a mistaken assumption that the aircraft had run out of petrol. A fire broke out and the Wellington was destroyed. No injuries reported.

7-8 Sep 1941	9 Sqn	Wellington IC	Z8845 WS-	Op: **Berlin**

9 Sqn		Wellington IC	Z8845 WS-	Op: **Berlin**
Sgt J C Saich DFM	+			
Sgt R A Banks	+			
Sgt W B Lowe RCAF	+			
Sgt W R Balls	+			
Sgt E Trott	+			
Sgt A S Macdonald	+			

T/o 2030 Honington. Last heard on w/t at 0050 sending NAP. Believed shot down shortly after this by a night-fighter (Oblt Helmut Lent, 4./NJG1) and crashed at Terwispel (Friesland), 10 km SSW of Drachten, Holland. All are buried in Gorredijk General Cemetery.

Note. The precise meaning of NAP has not been established, but it is thought to allude to the success, or otherwise, of the mission.

12 Sqn		Wellington II	W5598 PH-N	Op: **Berlin**
S/L P F Edinger	+			
Sgt R G Hill	+			
P/O J W McCarthy RCAF	pow			
Sgt W E Stayte	+			
Sgt R C Baumber	+			
Sgt A F Suckling	+			

T/o 2150 Binbrook. Those who died are buried in the Reichswald Forest War Cemetery.

12 Sqn		Wellington II	Z8328 PH-	Op: **Berlin**
S/L S S Fielden	pow			
Sgt T V Johnston RCAF	pow			
F/L W J Peat RCAF	pow			
Sgt R Ledgerwood	pow			
Sgt L R Lanfear	pow			
Sgt A H Smith RAAF	pow			

T/o 2150 Binbrook.

15 Sqn		Stirling I	N6045 LS-U	Op: **Berlin**
F/L R P Wallace-Terry	pow			
Sgt R Harper	pow			
Sgt W C Moir	pow			
Sgt R B Pape	pow			
Sgt C S Aynsley	pow			
Sgt R D Hooley	pow			
Sgt H J Dunnett	pow			
Sgt J E Dodd	pow			

T/o Wyton. Hit by flak and later crashed between Hengelo and Steenderen (Gelderland), 10 km NNW of Doetinchem, Holland. Sgt Pape was repatriated in September 1944, and after the war he wrote a vivid account of his many experiences under the title 'Boldness Be My Friend`.

44 Sqn		Hampden I	X2921 KM-Z	Op: **Gardening**
Sgt A A Watt	+			
Sgt J R Newcombe	+			
Sgt A D Wimbush	+			
Sgt E S Cox	+			

T/o 2115 Waddington but failed to climb away and crashed 2117 at Branston Hall Farm near the airfield. The mine, which they were intending to plant in Kiel Bay, exploded on impact.

49 Sqn		Hampden I	AE236 EA-	Op: **Kiel**
P/O J W T Bromham	+			
Sgt E V Durham	+			
Sgt P J Duffy	+			
Sgt A Kettlewell	+			

T/o Scampton. Crashed in the target area. All are buried in Kiel War Cemetery.

50 Sqn		Hampden I	AE318 VN-	Op: **Kiel**
Sgt D Good	pow			
Sgt D F Endsor	pow			
Sgt R Williamson	pow			
Sgt I A MacDonald	pow			

T/o Swinderby. Crashed near Oldenburg, Germany.

51 Sqn		Whitley V	Z6744 MH-	Op: **Berlin**
Sgt J P Wood	+			
Sgt H B Clark RCAF	+			
Sgt D C Bass	+			
Sgt J Taylor	+			
F/S L S B Younger	+			

T/o 2009 Dishforth. All are buried in Berlin at the 1939-1945 War Cemetery.

51 Sqn		Whitley V	Z6937 MH-	Op: **Berlin**
Sgt J A Reynolds	+			
P/O L C R Wilson	+			
Sgt A A Jessup	inj			
Sgt A E Barrett	+			
Sgt Duke	inj			

T/o 2003 Dishforth. Stalled and crashed 0550 while making a second attempt to land at base. Sgt Jessup survived the crash, but died soon afterwards in Station Sick Quarters. Sgt Duke´s injuries were minor.

7-8 Sep
1941

| 51 Sqn | Whitley V | Z6938 MH- | Op: Berlin |

Sgt Wilson — int
P/O Gibson — int
Sgt Willson — int
Sgt Morgan — int
Sgt Troughton — int

T/o 2007 Dishforth. Hit by flak and damaged so severely that the crew elected to make for neutral Sweden, rather than risk trying to return to base. Subsequently, the Whitley was abandoned near Marieberg, S of Malmo, Sweden. Sgt Troughton broke one of his ankles and he was taken to hospital in Trälleberg for treatment.

| 58 Sqn | Whitley V | Z6836 GE-J | Op: Berlin |

Sgt J Wood — +
Sgt H A Perks — +
Sgt J H Smythe — +
Sgt E K Cartledge — +
F/O A G Inderwick — +

T/o 2014 Linton-on-Ouse. All are buried in Kiel War Cemetery.

| 58 Sqn | Whitley V | Z6947 GE-S | Op: Berlin |

Sgt K McI Newton — +
P/O F R Wilbraham — pow
Sgt B J Kemp — pow
Sgt L E Proctor — pow
Sgt J Ford — pow

T/o 2017 Linton-on-Ouse. Sgt Newton has no known grave. His name is commemorated on the Runnymede Memorial.

| 104 Sqn | Wellington II | W5362 EP-J | Op: Berlin |

Sgt F Richardson RAAF — +
Sgt F G Barrett — +
Sgt W H Anderson — +
Sgt B W Robbens — +
F/S A D F Craig MiD — +
Sgt R J Mountier — +

T/o 2034 Driffield. Lost without trace. All are commemorated on the Runnymede Memorial.

| 106 Sqn | Hampden I | AE299 ZN- | Op: Berlin |

Sgt M C Curties — pow
F/S F J Matkin RCAF — +
Sgt J Plant — +
Sgt H Mann — +

T/o 2125 Coningsby. Crashed near Schwartenek, Germany. Those who died are buried in Kiel War Cemetery.

Note. Despite an extensive search, the location Schwartenek, which is quoted in the Hampden File, has not been identified.

| 115 Sqn | Wellington IC | R1772 KO-M | Op: Kiel |

Sgt R B D Hill — +
Sgt T E F Mutton — pow
Sgt P Fincham — pow
Sgt E E Mason — pow
Sgt K E Squire — pow
Sgt J A Williams — pow

T/o 2023 Marham. Sgt Hill is buried in Kiel War Cemetery.

| 115 Sqn | Wellington IC | R1798 KO-B | Op: Berlin |

Sgt I P McH Gordon — +
F/S J G O´H Keating RCAF — +
P/O R Le M Cox — +
Sgt G A Cook — +
Sgt J G Selley — +
Sgt F A Baty RNZAF — +

T/o 2023 Marham. Shot down by a night-fighter (Oblt Helmut Lent, 4./NJG1) and crashed 0458 near Drachtstercompagnie (Friesland), 4 km NE of Drachten, Holland. All are buried in Smallingerland (Drachtstercompagnie) Protestant Churchyard.

| 144 Sqn | Hampden I | AD936 PL- | Op: Berlin |

P/O P Stevens — pow
Sgt A W Payne — pow
Sgt H Thompson — pow
Sgt I R Fraser — +

T/o North Luffenham. Hit by flak and crashed SE of Amsterdam. Sgt Fraser has no known grave and his name is commemorated on the Runnymede Memorial.

| 144 Sqn | Hampden I | AE304 PL- | Op: Berlin |

P/O R J Roake — +
Sgt B Hemmings — +
Sgt E Horton — +
Sgt S E Taft — +

T/o 2052 North Luffenham. Crashed 2055 on the Empingham to Ketton road, Rutland, to the NE of the airfield, some 4 miles WSW of Stamford, Lincolnshire.

7-8 Sep 1941	149 Sqn	Wellington IC	X9705 OJ-J	Op: **Berlin**
	Sgt G W Fenton	+	T/o 2015 Mildenhall. All are buried in the	
	Sgt W R Malkemus RCAF	+	Reichswald Forest War Cemetery.	
	Sgt M McL Keswick RCAF	+		
	Sgt S D Chamberlain	+		
	Sgt E C Hatton	+		
	Sgt J M Dixon RCAF	+		

	207 Sqn	Manchester I	L7380 EM-W	Op: **Berlin**
	F/L W J Lewis	pow	T/o Waddington. Damaged by a night-fighter,	
	Sgt C S F Powell	pow	while outbound and still over the North Sea.	
	Sgt R B MacLeod RCAF	pow	The crew managed to reach Wilhelmshaven, where	
	Sgt D Kingston	pow	bombs were jettisoned, before turning for home.	
	Sgt C F Hall	pow	Subsequently, the Manchester force-landed N of	
	F/S E S Miller RCAF	pow	Ballum on the Dutch island of Ameland.	

	214 Sqn	Wellington IC	R1784 BU-	Op: **Berlin**
	W/C G L Cruickshanks DFC	+	T/o Stradishall. All are buried in Berlin at	
	S/L W Davies	+	the 1939-1945 War Cemetery.	
	F/O W Esplen	+		
	F/L K J Falconer DFC	+		
	Sgt L T Chapman	+		
	Sgt A N Page	+		

	218 Sqn	Wellington II	W5449 HA-Y	Op: **Berlin**
	S/L H L Price		T/o 2110 Marham. Crash-landed 0430 in a wheat	
	Sgt Webber		field at Hall Farm, Barton Bendish, 7 miles WSW	
	F/S Woodmason		of Swaffham, Norfolk, after flying from the	
	Sgt Riley		Dutch coast with the starboard engine on fire.	
	Sgt Giles			
	Sgt Davidson			

	405 Sqn	Wellington II	W5521 LQ-P	Op: **Berlin**
	Sgt J S Saunders RCAF	pow	T/o 2032 Pocklington.	
	Sgt P S MacNutt RCAF	pow		
	P/O W K Mackey RCAF	pow		
	F/S R Perkin	pow		
	Sgt J S Courtnall	pow		
	Sgt Smith	pow		

8 Sep 1941	90 Sqn	Fortress I	AN525 WP-D	Op: **Oslo**
	F/O D A A Romans DFC	+	T/o 0915 Polebrook to bomb the Admiral	
	P/O F G Hart	+	Scheer in Oslo harbour. Attacked at 25000	
	Sgt P B Corbett	+	feet by two Me 109s and despite sending one	
	Sgt J Brown	+	fighter down, the Fortress was observed to	
	Sgt W G Honey	+	crash at 1127 in mountainous country. All	
	Sgt H Merrill RCAF	+	are buried in Bygland Churchyard in the Otra	
	Sgt R H Beattie	+	Valley some 100 km N of Kristiansand, Norway.	

	90 Sqn	Fortress I	AN533 WP-N	Op: **Oslo**
	S/L A Mathieson	+	T/o 0925 Polebrook. Shot down by Me 109s.	
	Sgt H D P Sleath	+	All are commemorated on the Runnymede Memorial.	
	P/O F J Hogan DFC	+		
	F/S N H Davies	+		
	Sgt C D James	+		
	Sgt R Willis	+		
	Sgt R Allan	+		

Note. The Fortress was withdrawn from operations shortly after this raid.
F/O Romans, captain of AN525, served with distinction on 44 Squadron during
1940, surviving several ditchings and gaining a DFC.

8-9 Sep 1941	44 Sqn	Hampden I	P4285 KM-U	Op: **Kassel**
	P/O Anekstein		T/o Scampton. Crashed 0350 with failing	
	Sgt J G Armstrong	inj	engines, colliding with trees as the crew	
	Sgt Walker	inj	tried to land at Coningsby.	
	Sgt Campbell			

8-9 Sep 1941	49 Sqn	Hampden I		AD805 EA-R Op: Kassel

8-9 Sep 1941

49 Sqn   Hampden I   **AD805 EA-R**   Op: Kassel
P/O Jones
Sgt Thorndyke
Sgt Taylor
Sgt T H Hardisty

T/o 2005 Scampton. Crash-landed 0632 low on fuel at Lenn Farm, North Carlton, 5 miles NNW of Lincoln. No injuries reported, but it is known that Sgt Hardisty died on 8 December 1941.

50 Sqn   Hampden I   **AD854 VN-**   Op: Kassel
Sgt F Rowney   +
Sgt Morgan
Sgt T A Barker   +
Sgt Mitchell

T/o 1950 Swinderby. Crashed 0350 between Woburn and Husborne Crawley, 10 miles NW of Luton, Bedfordshire, after running out of fuel. The two survivors parachuted to safety.

83 Sqn   Hampden I   **AE188 OL-D**   Op: Kassel
Sgt G S Linacre   inj
Sgt C R Speakman
Sgt B G Galloway-Wilson
Sgt R H Calder

T/o 2002 Scampton. Crash-landed 0430 in a field close to Boscombe Down airfield, Wiltshire. Less than a month previous, Sgt Linacre and Sgt Calder had landed in the sea off Holy Island.

10-11 Sep 1941

35 Sqn   Halifax I   **L9526 TL-0**   Op: Torino
P/O Cresswell
Sgt Rowley-Blake
Sgt Stewart
P/O A Abels
Sgt Wing
Sgt Turner
Sgt Lowe

T/o 2240 Stradishall. Force-landed 0622 in a field near Harling Road Station on the rail line between Thetford and Norwich. No one was hurt and the Halifax was not too seriously damaged. However, it never flew again and by mid-1942 the airframe was in use as instructional aid, bearing the serial 3034M.

35 Sqn   Halifax I   **L9566 TL-R**   Op: Torino
F/O G S Williams   pow
Sgt A Osborne   pow
Sgt J E Murrell   pow
Sgt Hedley   pow
Sgt Ryder   pow
Sgt E H Jackson   pow
Sgt A Urquhart   pow

T/o 2235 Stradishall. Last heard on w/t at 0615, plotted N of le Havre. It is believed the crew mistook the Cherbourg peninsula for the English coast and turned towards France, instead of maintaining a northerly track.

101 Sqn   Wellington IC   **R1699 SR-D**   Op: Torino
P/O Allen
Sgt Christensen
Sgt R W A Saxton   evd
Sgt G Campbell   evd
Sgt J R Worby   evd
Sgt H I Hickton   evd

T/o 1938 Oakington. Last heard on w/t at 0145 indicating a force-landing was imminent. A snap bearing fixed the bomber's position as 4910N 0400E, thus placing the crew over France and in the region of Épernay. The fate of P/O Allen and Sgt Christensen has not been established.

103 Sqn   Wellington IC   **R1396 PM-**   Op: Torino
P/O D L Petrie   +
Sgt P M Bennett   +
Sgt G S Rye   +
Sgt C E Wagon   +
Sgt A W Vernon   +
Sgt G R Blackmore RCAF   +

T/o 2004 Elsham Wolds. Lost without trace. All are commemorated on the Runnymede Memorial.

104 Sqn   Wellington II   **W5576 EP-N**   Op: Torino
S/L D M Strong   pow
Sgt Woodruffe   evd
F/L H T Beare RCAF   pow
Sgt J A Chubb   pow
Sgt N S Fisher   pow
Sgt R Ritson   pow

T/o 2130 Stradishall.

11 Sep 1941

102 Sqn   Whitley V   **Z6870 DY-**   Training
S/L J D Reardon DFC   +
Sgt H E Moore RCAF   +
F/S J W R Griffiths   +

Crashed 2250 at Topcliffe during night dual training. The Whitley stalled on finals and burst into flames on impact.

11-12 Sep 1941	10 Sqn	Whitley V	P5109 ZA-	Op: **Warnemünde**

11-12 Sep 1941

10 Sqn   Whitley V   P5109 ZA-   Op: **Warnemünde**

P/O R P Purvis	+
P/O J C Greenfield	+
Sgt R L Fitsell	+
Sgt J Nightingale	+
Sgt K A Irwin RCAF	+

T/o 2047 Leeming. Last heard on w/t indicating they were preparing to ditch some 80 miles off the east coast. All are commemorated on the Runnymede Memorial. P/O Purvis had previously served in The West Yorkshire Regiment (The Prince of Wales' Own).

10 Sqn   Whitley V   Z6867 ZA-   Op: **Warnemünde**

P/O A E Hacking	
Sgt McBride	
Sgt Turner	
Sgt Davidson	
Sgt Mackenzie	inj

T/o 2051 Leeming. Ditched 0555 some 2 miles off Flamborough Head, after running out of fuel. Just over an hour later, the destroyer HMS Wolsey rescued the crew, Sgt Mackenzie suffering from a fractured left arm.

44 Sqn   Hampden I   AD981 KM-A   Op: **Rostock**

Sgt Dedman	
Sgt Birkett	
Sgt Norman	
Sgt Hugh	

T/o 2144 Waddington. Ditched, out of petrol, 20 miles off Cromer, Norfolk. Within thirty-five minutes of alighting, the crew were rescued by HMS Garth.

58 Sqn   Whitley V   Z6498 GE-D   Op: **Warnemünde**

Sgt C R D Browne	pow
P/O R T C O White	pow
Sgt F E Bowen	pow
Sgt A A J Goss	pow
Sgt J Overson	pow

T/o 2053 Linton-on-Ouse. Ditched.

58 Sqn   Whitley V   Z6931 GE-O   Op: **Warnemünde**

P/O G Lambert	
Sgt Cooper	
Sgt Mott	
Sgt Thompson	
Sgt Cairns	

T/o 2049 Linton-on-Ouse. Crashed 0600 near the Majestic Hotel at Harrogate, Yorkshire, after being abandoned. No injuries reported.

75 Sqn   Wellington IC   R1038 AA-   Op: **Kiel**

Sgt K V D Roe	+
Sgt K A Tomlinson	+
Sgt M W S McVety	+
Sgt D F Dunlop	+
Sgt N Tweedie RAAF	+
Sgt T B Hopkins RCAF	+

T/o Feltwell. Lost without trace. All are commemorated on the Runnymede Memorial.

106 Sqn   Hampden I   AE300 ZN-   Op: **Rostock**

Sgt J A Bannister	pow
Sgt R J Dunn	pow
Sgt J A S Philson	pow
Sgt F W Davies	pow

T/o 2140 Coningsby. Last heard on w/t at 0220 and the Hampden crashed five minutes later at Hostrup, 17 km NE of Vejle, Denmark. The crew were arrested within 48 hours of baling out.

144 Sqn   Hampden I   AE118 PL-   Op: **Rostock**

P/O Booker	inj
Sgt A J Pomes RCAF	inj
Sgt S J Binns	
Sgt Crossley	

T/o North Luffenham. Crashed 0615 at Barn Farm, Billesdon, 8 miles E of Leicester.

144 Sqn   Hampden I   AE121 PL-   Op: **Rostock**

Sgt N H Page	+
Sgt J L Longmore	+
Sgt Bailey	
Sgt Bowskill	

T/o North Luffenham. Crash-landed 0600 near Isolation Camp, Empingham, 6 miles E of Oakham, Rutland.

149 Sqn   Wellington IC   X9879 OJ-V   Op: **Kiel**

Sgt D W Bennett RCAF	+
Sgt D J Wyatt	+
Sgt D G Willis	+
Sgt I P Graham RCAF	+
Sgt P M Wakefield	+
Sgt R H Kenvin	+

T/o 2052 Mildenhall. Shot down near Kiel, where the crew are buried in the local War Cemetery.

12 Sep 1941	104 Sqn P/O F N Pope	Wellington II	W5441 EP- Training Crash-landed 1700 at Middleton on Wold, 6 miles SW of Driffield, Yorkshire. The crew escaped injury.

12-13 Sep 1941	40 Sqn S/L J C Atkins + Sgt R C Thompson pow P/O R M Ryder RAAF + Sgt B T Banner pow F/S A E Hough pow Sgt D F Darlow pow	Wellington IC	R1328 BL-T Op: Frankfurt T/o 1955 Alconbury. Last heard on w/t at 2206 indicating the port engine had failed. The two airmen who died are buried in Rheinberg War Cemetery.

	218 Sqn Sgt C F Dare RNZAF pow Sgt L Booth pow Sgt I H Leitch pow Sgt R Purdy pow Sgt K R Birchenough pow Sgt R Moodie pow	Wellington IC	X9670 HA-N Op: Frankfurt T/o Marham.

13 Sep 1941	21 Sqn P/O F N Grant RAAF + Sgt P E Ritter + F/S R E Hall + Sgt T W J Thomas + P/O E J Tuckey + Cpl E Clayton inj	Blenheim IV	V5463 YH- Training T/o 1108 Watton but stalled and crashed into a hangar, bursting into flames. It is believed that some of the casualties may have been working inside the hangar at the time of the accident.

	97 Sqn Sgt G H Hartley Sgt Appleyard Sgt J Canham Sgt Dean Sgt Baker Sgt Mayland Sgt Gross	Manchester I	L7306 OF- Training T/o 2020 Coningsby but crashed following a burst starboard tyre. A fire broke out but the crew scrambled clear with only a few bruises to show for their ordeal.

13-14 Sep 1941	57 Sqn Sgt S D G Gray	Wellington IC	R1792 DX- Op: Brest T/o 2215 Feltwell but the pilot throttled back too soon and the Wellington sank back

to the ground and was damaged beyond repair. No injuries reported.

	76 Sqn P/O R E Hutchin + Sgt Wood Sgt Crowe Sgt Browne F/S J Flannigan Sgt Littlehales Sgt Wallace	Halifax I	L9567 MP- Op: Brest T/o 0142 Middleton St. George. Crashed 0255 near the River Ouse at Water End, Renhold, 3 miles NE of Bedford. One airman is reported to have injured his ankle as he landed by parachute.

	97 Sqn P/O D E Fox Sgt J S Warton + F/S Hall Sgt F W Tewson Sgt J Goldie Sgt B S Robertson	Manchester I	L7383 OF-F Training Crashed 0232 after striking a house in Perch Lane, Westwick, 11 miles NNE of Norwich, trapping several members of the crew in the wreckage. The cause of the accident was attributed to the bomber running low on fuel, necessitating an emergency landing.

	99 Sqn Sgt J S F Watt Sgt Bell Sgt J W Humphrey RCAF Sgt J K Whitfield Sgt H Martin Sgt Bolton	Wellington IC	X9703 LN-G Op: Brest T/o 2222 Waterbeach and crashed almost immediately, bursting into flames. No injures reported, but the five aircraft still waiting to leave had to be cancelled.

13-14 Sep 1941	214 Sqn Sgt Nicholls Sgt Klassen Sgt Jordan Sgt Swan Sgt Gibbons Sgt Trevillian	Wellington IC	**N2802 BU-N** Op: **Brest** T/o 2220 Stradishall. Crashed 0350 near Wantage Hospital, 1 mile NE of Wantage, Berkshire.

15 Sep 1941	18 Sqn	Blenheim IV	**V6425 WV-** Training
	P/O G C Pryor RCAF	inj	Crash-landed 1515 at Hall Farm, North Walsham,
	Sgt Mills	inj	Norfolk, after hitting the sea during low level
	Sgt Buckley	inj	bombing practice.

	207 Sqn	Manchester I	**L7318 EM-K** Transit
	F/O E E G Crump	+	Crashed 1810 and exploded after diving into
	P/O J P A Sawyer	+	the ground in the Waddington circuit. The
	P/O J R Clements RCAF	+	crew, along with a large servicing party,
	Sgt N A Mathison	+	were returning to base after attending to
	LAC L W Carter	+	a Manchester that had landed at Haverigg
	LAC J F Riding	+	airfield, Cumberland.
	LAC H F Winter	+	
	AC1 R Boyd	+	
	AC2 J W Grace	+	
	AC2 J Lister	+	

15-16 Sep 1941	15 Sqn	Stirling I	**N6021 LS-O** Op: **Hamburg**
	P/O E J D Guild	+	T/o Wyton. Shot down by a night-fighter
	P/O H J A Dyer MiD	+	(Uffz Walter Geislinger, 6./NJG1) and crashed
	Sgt T H B Jones	+	at Hemslingen, 13 km ESE of Rotenburg, Germany.
	F/S W C Mackenzie RCAF	+	All are buried in Becklingen War Cemetery at
	Sgt A Needham	+	Soltau. The majority of the crew had been
	Sgt A D Wallace	+	involved in a Stirling crash a month previous.
	Sgt F C Snead RCAF	+	

	35 Sqn	Halifax I	**L9503 TL-P** Op: **Hamburg**
	P/O H J Brown	+	T/o 1955 Linton-on-Ouse. P/O Brown is buried
	S/L J H Barrett	pow	in Kiel War Cemetery.
	Sgt J W Hays	pow	
	F/S J A Arnsby RCAF	pow	
	Sgt H E Greene	pow	
	Sgt R Shaw	pow	
	Sgt S T Fisher	pow	

	44 Sqn	Hampden I	**AD930 KM-L** Op: **Hamburg**
	Sgt C E Musgrave	inj	T/o 1835 Waddington. Crashed 0317 at Harmston,
	Sgt J Endersby	inj	5 miles S of Lincoln, after flying into trees
	Sgt R L Cox	+	on the approach to land.
	F/S J Barry	+	

	51 Sqn	Whitley V	**Z6957 MH-** Op: **Hamburg**
	Sgt J C Gowland	pow	T/o 1905 Dishforth. The two airmen who died
	Sgt J H Davis	pow	are buried in Hamburg Cemetery, Ohlsdorf.
	P/O J I Davies RCAF	pow	
	Sgt J T Evans	+	
	Sgt V Flynne	+	

	57 Sqn	Wellington IC	**X9923 DX-** Op: **Hamburg**
	Sgt A J Witherington	+	T/o 1950 Feltwell. Crashed 0315 at Marham
	Sgt Hudson		airfield, Norfolk, and burst into flames.
	Sgt Morgan	inj	
	Sgt K W C Clark	+	
	Sgt E I L Grego	inj	
	Sgt Cobley		

15-16 Sep 1941	75 Sqn	Wellington IC	X3205 AA-	Op: Hamburg

Sgt J A Ward VC, RNZAF	+	T/o Feltwell. Hit by flak and crashed in
Sgt H G Sloman	+	the target area. Those who died are buried
Sgt R W Toller	+	in Hamburg Cemetery, Ohlsdorf. Sgt Ward VC
Sgt H Watson	pow	gained his decoration for outstanding bravery
Sgt K H Toothill	+	during operations to Münster on 7-8 July 1941.
F/S L E Peterson RCAF	pow	

75 Sqn	Wellington IC	X9759 AA-	Op: Hamburg

Sgt A H R Hawkins RNZAF	+	T/o Feltwell. Those who died are buried in
Sgt R B Blakeway RNZAF	pow	Hamburg Cemetery, Ohlsdorf.
Sgt J G Foulkes	+	
Sgt W E Mullins	pow	
Sgt D P Fawcett	+	
P/O H M Aitchison RCAF	+	

83 Sqn	Hampden I	AE362 OL-S	Op: Hamburg

P/O J Bromiley	inj	T/o 1830 Scampton. Crashed on return to base
P/O W L Rowe		and while trying to land in fog.
Sgt S Isherwood		
P/O E Goodman		

83 Sqn	Hampden I	AE365 OL-N	Op: le Havre

F/O W Cunning		T/o 1830 Scampton. Crashed in circumstances
Sgt J Urquhart		similar to those reported above. No injuries
Sgt T Dalby		reported.
Sgt G Cox		

106 Sqn	Hampden I	P4413 ZN-J	Op: Hamburg

P/O Loftus	inj	T/o 1825 Coningsby. Crashed 0320 astride
Sgt Walley	inj	a road just beyond Pocklington airfield,
Sgt Flowerday	inj	where the crew were trying to land.
P/O Ward	inj	

106 Sqn	Hampden I	AE232 ZN-	Op: Hamburg

Sgt K Richardson	pow	T/o 1830 Coningsby. Shot down by a night-
F/S J J McIntryre RCAF	+	fighter (Oblt Walter Barte, I./NJG1) and crashed
Sgt H D Clapham	pow	2251 at Wilhelmsburg directly S of Hamburg.
Sgt H Kirk	pow	F/S McIntyre RCAF has no known grave. While
		in captivity, Sgt Kirk exchanged identity with

Fus F Robson of the Northumberland Fusiliers, who was being held at Lamsdorf.

305 Sqn	Wellington II	W5526 SM-J	Op: le Havre

W/C J K M Drysdale DSO	+	T/o 1927 Lindholme. Crashed in the target
F/L W R Gardiner	+	area. F/O Jeremy is buried at Honfleur on the
F/S W C Wheatley	+	south bank of the Seine, in the St-Léonard
F/S J D Truscott	+	Communal Cemetery, the rest of the crew now
F/L W C Ward	+	lie in the Ste. Marie Cemetery at le Havre.
F/O I D Jeremy DFC	+	

311 Sqn	Wellington IC	R1015 KX-L	Op: Hamburg

Sgt V Soukup	+	T/o 1955 East Wretham. Crashed at Andervenne,
Sgt J Miklosek	+	17 km ESE of Lingen-Ems, Germany, where the
P/O M Sedlacek	+	crew were initially buried in the Neuer Friedhof.
P/O A Zimmer	+	Since 1945, their bodies have been taken to the
Sgt Z Babicek	+	Reichswald Forest War Cemetery.
Sgt A Jarnot	+	

455 Sqn	Hampden I	AE249 UB-	Op: Hamburg

P/O A J Hibell	pow	T/o 1924 Swinderby. Shot down by a night-
Sgt W N Pratt	+	fighter (Oblt Walter Barte, I./NJG1) and
Sgt H Hobbs	+	crashed 2354 near Winkeldorf, 12 km SSW of
Sgt P H Clayden	pow	Zeven, Germany. The two airmen who died
		are commemorated on the Runnymede Memorial.

This was the first loss on bomber operations by an RAAF bomber squadron.

16 Sep 1941	18 Sqn	Blenheim IV	V6339 WV-C	Op: Anti-shipping

Sgt C A Tracey +
P/O J H Rodgers +
Sgt A H Higgs +

T/o 1230 Horsham St. Faith to patrol Beat B. Crashed in the sea. Sgt Tracey is buried in Den Burg General Cemetery, Texel; his crew are commemorated on the Runnymede Memorial.

139 Sqn	Blenheim IV	Z7363 XD-	Training

P/O P G Brown

Ditched 1145 off Clacton, Essex. The accident happened when the pilot tried to adjust his compass while flying low and, inadvertently, he flew into the sea.

218 Sqn	Wellington IC	R3153 HA-	Unknown

Destroyed by fire in circumstances that are not known. No accident card raised, but Form 78 indicates this Wellington was consumed by fire.

17 Sep 1941	82 Sqn	Blenheim IV	V6086 UX-X	Op: Circus 95

P/O C J Harper +
P/O J B Patterson +
Sgt D A Bartrip +

T/o 1304 Bodney to attack a power station and chemical complex at Mazingarbe.

17-18 Sep 1941	75 Sqn	Wellington IC	X9834 AA-	Op: Karlsruhe

Sgt W B M Smyth +
P/O W J S Smith pow
P/O K E A Savage +
Sgt J W Reid pow
Sgt H C McL Haselden RNZAF +
Sgt A H Heard pow

T/o Feltwell. Crash-landed, on fire, at Holsthum on the River Prüm, 12 km SSW of Bitburg, Germany. Sgt Reid was shot while trying to escape from Lamsdorf on 29 December 1941. He is buried in Cracow Military Cemetery, Poland; those who were killed in the crash are buried in Rheinberg War Cemetery.

18 Sep 1941	88 Sqn	Blenheim IV	V6380 RH-G	Op: Anti-shipping

P/O B E Hislop RAAF +
P/O R M Burlinson RCAF +
Sgt M A Stratton +

T/o 0940 Attlebridge to patrol Beat 9. Presumed crashed in the sea while attacking a convoy off the Belgian coast. Two of the crew are buried in cemeteries in Holland; P/O Hislop RAAF is commemorated on the Runnymede Memorial.

88 Sqn	Blenheim IV	Z7488 RH-F	Op: Anti-shipping

P/O T E Cooper RNZAF +
F/S S R E Hammersley +
Sgt R S Hambly RCAF +

T/o 0940 Attlebridge. Believed shot down by Lt Koenig, 5./ZG76. All are commemorated on the Runnymede Memorial.

405 Sqn	Wellington II	W5492 LQ-K	Air Test

Sgt R J Chandos +
Sgt N W Thompson RNZAF +
Sgt F P Turton +
Sgt G Phillips +
Sgt C H Fletcher +
Sgt J M Maxon RCAF +
Sgt W I Strother +
AC1 H Armitage +

Crashed 1105 at Northfield Farm, 2 miles NNE of Pocklington, Yorkshire. The accident was caused by the dinghy breaking loose from its stowage and fouling the elevators, which in turn sent the Wellington into a steep dive and structural failure occurred, at approximately 5000 feet.

19-20 Sep 1941	58 Sqn	Whitley V	Z6936 GE-Q	Op: Stettin

F/L R E Orchard DFC +
P/O J C Howell +
Sgt J D Robertson RCAF +
Sgt E J Start +
F/S T Wood +

T/o 2055 Linton-on-Ouse. All are buried in the 1939-1945 War Cemetery at Berlin. F/L Orchard came from Otago, New Zealand.

142 Sqn	Wellington II	W5384 QT-	Op: Stettin

P/O I C Burke +
Sgt A Carstairs +
Sgt T G Lister +
Sgt J G Jones +
Sgt D J MacKintosh +
Sgt Rayment

T/o 2258 Mildenhall. Ditched 0325 some 8 miles E of Orford Ness, Suffolk. For most of the return flight, the Wellington had been flying on the starboard engine. Sgt Rayment was rescued unharmed; the remainder, for reasons unknown, failed to get into the dinghy.

9-20 Sep 941	405 Sqn	Wellington II	Z8344 LQ-F	Op: Stettin

9-20 Sep
941

405 Sqn   Wellington II   Z8344 LQ-F   Op: Stettin
Sgt T F Dougall   pow   T/o 2222 Pocklington. Two of the crew, Sgt Lord
P/O W B Towler   pow   and Sgt Clayden, were killed in late April 1945,
Sgt J Lord   pow   probably as the result of erroneous attacks by
Sgt D J Clayden   pow   Allied fighter aircraft on prisoner of war
Sgt J Emsley   pow   columns. Both are buried in Berlin at the
Sgt C W Forman RCAF   pow   1939-1945 War Cemetery.

0 Sep
941

18 Sqn   Blenheim IV   R3843 WV-   Op: Anti-shipping
F/S J M Nickleson RCAF   +   T/o 1237 Horsham St. Faith. Shot down by Marine
Sgt W Meadows   +   flak off Zandvoort, Holland, while attacking a
Sgt J E Pearson   +   convoy. Two of the crew are buried in Dutch
cemeteries, but F/S Nickleson RCAF has no known
grave and his name is commemorated on the Runnymede Memorial.

226 Sqn   Blenheim IV   V6422 MQ-   Op: Anti-shipping
Sgt J C V Colmer   +   T/o Wattisham to patrol Beat 10. Attacked a
Sgt G K Bartlett RAAF   +   convoy off Hoek van Holland and crashed after
Sgt L Trevor   +   being caught in the blast of its own bombs.
Sgt Trevor has no known grave; the rest of the
crew are buried in the New Eastern Cemetery at Amsterdam.

226 Sqn   Blenheim IV   Z7310 MQ-V   Op: Anti-shipping
F/L M H R Namias   +   T/o Wattisham. Hit by flak in the starboard
Sgt K F Hood   +   engine while running into attack a convoy and
Sgt J J Robson   +   seen to crash in the sea. F/L Namias has no
grave and he is commemorated on the Runnymede
Memorial; his crew are buried in Crooswijk General Cemetery at Rotterdam.

0-21 Sep
941

10 Sqn   Whitley V   Z6802 ZA-P   Op: Berlin
Sgt P G Rochford   T/o 1837 Leeming. Hit by flak while bombing
Sgt Owen   Wismar as an alternative target. Subsequently,
P/O Openshaw   the Whitley ran out of fuel and the crew ditched
Sgt Cleere   0500 off Withernsea, Yorkshire. All were picked
Sgt Howells   up two hours later by an HSL out from Grimsby.

57 Sqn   Wellington IC   R1271 DX-   Op: Berlin
Sgt J C McGeach   T/o 1935 Feltwell. Ditched following a fire in
Sgt S H Dunn RCAF   the starboard engine and loss of power from the
Sgt C G Freeman   port motor. The five survivors were taken into
Sgt D J O Pyre   Grimsby, where they were admitted to the local
Sgt J H Sherriff   +   RN Hospital. Sgt Sherriff is commemorated on
Sgt E E Hartland   the Runnymede Memorial.

57 Sqn   Wellington IC   R1706 DX-   Op: Frankfurt
Sgt E R Backhouse   T/o 1925 Feltwell. Returned to base at 0200,
Sgt Greenwood   but it is believed the Wellington was damaged
Sgt H T Smith   and it was struck off charge on 30 September
Sgt M E G Hastings   1941 as beyond repair.
Sgt F R Humphreys RCAF
Sgt G Maher

58 Sqn   Whitley V   Z6865 GE-V   Op: Oostende
P/O L J Pestridge   T/o 1926 Linton-on-Ouse. As the Whitley crossed
P/O Trickett   the East Anglia coast near Orford Ness, trouble
Sgt Taylor   was experienced with the starboard exactor unit.
Sgt Wallace   This was followed by total engine failure and the
Sgt Howarth   crew baled out, leaving the aircraft to crash
2123 on Breckles Heath, 6 miles NE of Thetford,
Norfolk. No injuries reported.

75 Sqn   Wellington IC   R1518 AA-   Op: Berlin
Sgt J A Matetich   T/o 1930 Feltwell. Abandoned and crashed 0430
Sgt Jordan   at Swanton Abbot, 3 miles SSW of North Walsham,
Sgt Lawton   Norfolk, while trying to reach Horsham St.
Sgt F H Worlledge   Faith. Earlier, the crew had been ordered
Sgt A Service   to divert to Coltishall, due to fog at base.
Sgt D F Barkhouse RCAF

20-21 Sep 1941	75 Sqn	Wellington IC	T2805 AA- Op: Berlin

20-21 Sep 1941

75 Sqn   Wellington IC   T2805 AA-   Op: Berlin

P/O A S Raphael	T/o Feltwell. Force-landed 0400 in a sixty
Sgt Machin	acre field at Grove Farm, near Upper Street,
Sgt R G Craig RCAF inj	Horning, 9 miles NE of Norwich. Sgt Craig
Sgt M A Macdonald	RCAF was admitted to the Norfolk and Norwich
Sgt C E J Aichison	Hospital where he died from his injuries the
Sgt J H Godrey	next day.

Note. An account of this crash appears in the book ´A Village At War (Horning 1939-1945)`. P/O Raphael was killed on the Peenemünde raid in August 1943, by which time he was a Flight Commander on 467 Squadron RAAF.

77 Sqn   Whitley V   Z6827 KN-   Op: Berlin

Sgt J W Harwood	T/o 1846 Leeming. Ditched 0350 off Bridlington,
P/O McCarthy	Yorkshire. The crew were rescued within an hour
Sgt Armstrong	of entering the sea.
Sgt Lewis	
Sgt Fitzpatrick	

77 Sqn   Whitley V   Z6934 KN-   Op: Berlin

Sgt L G Sinclair RCAF +	T/o 1843 Leeming. All are buried in Berlin
Sgt R F Archer +	at the 1939-1945 War Cemetery.
P/O S Goulston +	
Sgt C A Foster +	
F/S B G Wilbee RCAF +	

101 Sqn   Wellington IC   X9922 SR-   Op: Oostende

Sgt W R Dil RNZAF inj	T/o 1912 Oakington. Crashed 2300 into trees
P/O D I Evans +	at Preston Deanery, near Northampton. At the
P/O W R Lugar RCAF +	time of the accident, the wireless equipment
F/S D G Chattell RCAF +	was unserviceable and the pilot had descended
Sgt F D Rogers +	in an attempt to establish his position. Sgt
Sgt Rawbathan inj	Dil RNZAF died soon after the crash.

103 Sqn   Wellington IC   L7886 PM-   Op: Frankfurt

P/O K H Wallis	T/o Elsham Wolds. Ran short of fuel and with
	no response from calls for assistance, the

Wellington was abandoned 0410 some 4 miles NNW of Market Rasen, Lincolnshire.

103 Sqn   Wellington IC   R1539 PM-   Op: Frankfurt

Sgt A H Rex +	T/o 1902 Elsham Wolds. Crashed near Holbeach,
Sgt G K Proctor RCAF +	7 miles ENE of Spalding, Lincolnshire, after
P/O A G Stanes +	trying to make an emergency landing in fog.
Sgt E G Paul +	
Sgt E G Lennon +	
Sgt Bennett inj	

103 Sqn   Wellington IC   X9609 PM-   Op: Berlin

F/O T Wardhaugh +	T/o 1910 Elsham Wolds. Crashed in the
S/L J A Ingram DFC pow	Ambt-Delden (Overijssel), 6 km WSW of Hengelo,
Sgt N W Clyde pow	Holland. F/O Wardhaugh is buried in Ambt-
Sgt W D King pow	Delden General Cemetery, but Sgt Thomas has
Sgt J G Wright pow	no known grave.
Sgt C A F Thomas +	

103 Sqn   Wellington IC   X9665 PM-   Op: Berlin

P/O I Murchie +	T/o 1936 Elsham Wolds. All are buried in
Sgt G F Findlay RCAF +	the Reichswald Forest War Cemetery.
Sgt D Blake +	
P/O A G Milne +	
Sgt D P Hawkes +	
Sgt J B Bell +	

144 Sqn   Hampden I   X3030 PL-   Op: Frankfurt

Sgt E Parker +	T/o North Luffenham. Crashed 2205 into h/t
Sgt H D Weaver RCAF +	cables alongside the Morcott to Uppingham road,
Sgt R F Abernethy +	some 2 miles SE of the airfield. The accident
Sgt J Tankard +	happened as the crew were preparing to land.

20-21 Sep 1941	144 Sqn F/O W P Carroll Sgt L Smith Sgt P A Giovetti Sgt C Kellington	Hampden I	+ + + +	AD872 PL- Op: Frankfurt T/o North Luffenham. Crashed 0250 some 4 miles NNE of Coningsby airfield, Lincolnshire. Fog was a contributory factor. Sgt Giovetti was a Portuguese national serving with the RAF.

	144 Sqn Sgt E C W Turner Sgt R J Pulham Sgt R Atkinson Sgt T Pearce	Hampden I	+	AD922 PL- Op: Frankfurt T/o 1920 North Luffenham. Ran out of petrol and abandoned 0420, except for the pilot, near the airfield at Swanton Morley. Moments later, the Hampden crashed at Foulsham, 16 miles NW of Norwich.

	144 Sqn F/O Kingston Sgt De Courcy Sgt Tod Sgt Tobin	Hampden I	AD923 PL- Op: Frankfurt T/o North Luffenham. Crash-landed on Hutton Moor, Yorkshire, while trying to find Dishforth. The crew had been diverted away from base due to poor visibility.

	150 Sqn Sgt Dickenson	Wellington IC	X9811 JN- Op: Frankfurt T/o 1905 Snaith. Crash-landed 0140 on a sand-bank, following a collision off Spurn

Head with a barrage balloon cable. The impact severed the port airscrew and
for the second time in less than a month, Sgt Dickenson was obliged to make
a force-landing, less one of his propellers.

	214 Sqn P/O Barnard Sgt Avent Sgt Emmerson Sgt Harvey Sgt Kitney Sgt Nash	Wellington IC	inj	R1712 BU- Op: Berlin T/o 1931 Stradishall. Hit by flak near Münster and very severely damaged. On return, the crew crash-landed on Manston airfield, Kent. P/O Barnard's injuries proved so severe that he was unable to continue with his flying career.

	214 Sqn Sgt L D Kissack P/O C W Abrey P/O J B Ruston RCAF Sgt J Aitken Sgt I J Green P/O White	Wellington II	+ + + + + inj	W5452 BU-U Op: Berlin T/o 1924 Stradishall. Crashed into trees while trying to make an emergency landing at Manston.

Note. Of the twenty bombers written off this night, seventeen were lost
as a result of accidents.

21 Sep 1941	88 Sqn Sgt O R Smart RNZAF	Boston III	W8285 RH- Training Crashed 1035 while landing on the short runway at Attlebridge airfield, Norfolk.

This was the first Boston to be written off in Bomber Command service.

22 Sep 1941	88 Sqn F/S J R G Ralston	Blenheim IV	Z7454 RH-V Training Crashed 1920 while landing at Attlebridge in poor visibility.

	114 Sqn P/O R Feilden P/O F H Brown RCAF Sgt S S J Collier	Blenheim IV	+ + +	V5490 RT- Training Crashed near Cromer, Norfolk, after colliding with the mast of a ship moored on the nearby practice range.

24 Sep 1941	300 Sqn P/O W Radwanski	Wellington IV	R1510 BH- Training Crashed 1515 while practicing low level circuits at Hemswell. A sudden loss of

engine power was experienced and the pilot tried to make a straight ahead
landing, but was baulked by another aircraft taking off. First loss of a
Wellington IV in Bomber Command service.

26-27 Sep 1941	9 Sqn	Wellington III	X3222 WS-	Op: Emden

Sgt J Gingles — inj
Sgt H W White — +
P/O J B Thompson RCAF — inj
Sgt J A Chisholm — inj
Sgt R G Lifford — +
Sgt J A Lovis

T/o 2002 Honington. Recalled, but crashed 2345 at Rushford, 3 miles ESE of Thetford, Norfolk. P/O Thompson RCAF was rushed to the West Suffolk General Hospital at Bury St. Edmunds, where he died within a few hours of being admitted. This was the first Wellington III written off in Bomber Command.

---

115 Sqn   Wellington IC   R1332 KO-X   Op: Emden

Sgt M E Farnan — +
Sgt J Horabin — +
Sgt R G Wernham — +
F/S A Harkness RCAF — +
P/O C S White RCAF — +
Sgt J S Lappin RCAF — +

T/o 1850 Marham. Last heard on w/t indicating an engine was on was on fire. Subsequently, the Wellington came down in the sea off the Frisian Islands. Sgt Wernham is buried in Sage War Cemetery, Oldenburg; the remainder of the crew are commemorated on the Runnymede Memorial.

---

305 Sqn   Wellington II   W5557 SM-G   Op: Köln

Sgt E Buszko — +
Sgt J S Leyche — inj
Sgt W Wasilenko — inj
Sgt T Korczuk — inj
P/O Barzdo — inj
Sgt Pisarek — inj

T/o 1943 Lindholme. Crashed 0135 on Hatfield Moor, close to Lindholme airfield. Sgt Leyche and Sgt Wasilenko were still alive when pulled from the wreckage, but both died within hours of the accident. Sgt Korczuk succumbed to his injuries the following day.

---

27 Sep 1941   104 Sqn   Wellington II   W5432 EP-H   Air Test

P/O J R Robertson RCAF — +
Sgt L M Rhodes — +
Sgt M W Wright — +
Sgt Dundas — +
Sgt B K G Willmer — +
Sgt V E T Riddiford — +

Crashed 1645 at Pinhoe, 2 miles NE of Exeter, while trying to land at the nearby airfield. The Wellington had landed at Exeter after being damaged by flak over Brest on 4-5 July 1941, and following repairs it was being air tested in readiness for its return to Driffield.

---

28 Sep 1941   15 Sqn   Stirling I   N3660 LS-M   Training

W/C P B B Ogilvie DSO

Crashed while trying to land in poor visibility at Warboys airfield, Huntingdonshire.

---

97 Sqn   Manchester I   L7375 OF-B   Air Test

F/O H S Blakeman

Crashed at Sibsey, 4 miles NNE of Boston, Lincolnshire, when the starboard propeller jammed in fine pitch. Both crew members survived.

28-29 Sep 1941   9 Sqn   Wellington IC   R1279 WS-   Op: Genova

F/S W S Kitson DFM — +
P/O J R Freeland RCAF — +
Sgt R G Gove — +
Sgt J R Palmer — +
Sgt J W Lee — +
Sgt J A McLean — +

T/o 1934 Honington. Last heard on w/t at 0208 indicating engine trouble while over the Alps. All are buried in Milano War Cemetery. F/S Kitson had recently commenced a second tour of operations with 9 Squadron, having completed his first in the summer of 1940.

---

49 Sqn   Hampden I   AD733 EA-B   Op: Frankfurt

F/L J D Mundy DFC — pow
Sgt P C P Darwin — pow
Sgt A S Winton — pow
F/S F R Hibbert DFM — pow

T/o Scampton.

---

49 Sqn   Hampden I   AE376 EA-E   Op: Frankfurt

Sgt A C Walker — +
Sgt T H Smith — +
Sgt R E Greenhalgh — +
Sgt A Raine — +

T/o 0009 Scampton and crashed eleven minutes later at Burton Estate near Lincoln. The Hampden burst into flames on impact.

---

57 Sqn   Wellington IC   Z8789 DX-   Op: Genova

S/L Warfield — inj
P/O Harries — inj
P/O Tettenborn
P/O Blench — inj
Sgt Hughes
Sgt Edinburgh

T/o 1855 Feltwell. Crashed 0535 while trying to land at base in poor weather. The bomber caught fire, but the crew are thought to have escaped serious injury.

28-29 Sep 1941	**57 Sqn**	**Wellington IC**		**Z8868 DX-C** **Op: Genova**

28-29 Sep 1941	57 Sqn	Wellington IC		Z8868 DX-C	Op: Genova
	Sgt J W Paul		+	T/o Feltwell. Presumed lost over the sea.	
	Sgt A H Greenwood		+	Apart from F/S Pastons RCAF, the crew are	
	Sgt H A A North RAAF		+	commemorated on the Runnymede Memorial.	
	F/S R Pastons RCAF		+		
	Sgt G Hudson		+		
	Sgt G L Chapman RCAF		+		

	75 Sqn	Wellington IC		R1177 AA-	Op: Frankfurt
	Sgt S J G Isherwood			T/o 1920 Feltwell. Crashed 0320 at Birds	
	Sgt Climie			Green, Sible Hedingham, 3 miles NW of Halstead,	
	P/O E M Sangster RCAF			Essex, after being abandoned by the crew.	
	Sgt B W Shelnutt RCAF				
	Sgt H A D Stanley RCAF				
	Sgt H Bell				

	99 Sqn	Wellington IC		T2879 LN-	Op: Frankfurt
	Sgt J S Parry RNZAF		+	T/o 1924 Waterbeach. Last heard on w/t some	
	Sgt I J Robertson		+	ten hours after leaving base. Crashed in the	
	P/O W R J Brown RCAF		+	sea. Sgt Robertson and Sgt Macdonald RNZAF	
	Sgt A W M Chapman RAAF		+	are buried in Den Burg General Cemetery; P/O	
	Sgt H McL Macdonald RNZAF		+	Brown RCAF rests in Harlingen General Cemetery;	
	Sgt E Fieldhouse		+	the remainder have no known graves.	

Note. Two Chapman's lost their lives during the night's operations. Both are commemorated on the Runnymede Memorial.

	99 Sqn	Wellington II		W5436 LN-X	Op: Frankfurt
	P/O K H N Rumbo		+	T/o 1917 Waterbeach. Crashed 0200 at Horringer,	
	Sgt V E Waldron		+	2 miles SW of Bury St. Edmunds, Suffolk, while	
	Sgt Paxton		inj	returning to base.	
	Sgt J Darbyshire		+		
	F/S Gill		inj		
	Sgt Cooke		inj		

	99 Sqn	Wellington IC		X9761 LN-	Op: Frankfurt
	Sgt E Coleman		pow	T/o 1914 Waterbeach.	
	Sgt L Birk		evd		
	Sgt J L Trask		pow		
	F/S H G Lewis		pow		
	Sgt R Dyer		evd		
	Sgt J Dicks		evd		

	99 Sqn	Wellington IC		Z8869 LN-	Op: Frankfurt
	Sgt J S F Watt		+	T/o 1911 Waterbeach. Collided with a line of	
	Sgt J D Broadley RNZAF		+	trees, exploded and crashed 0055 at Stone Farm,	
	Sgt J W Humphrey RCAF		+	Great Finborough, 2 miles SW of Stowmarket,	
	Sgt H Martin		+	Suffolk. A large haystack was destroyed in	
	Sgt J K Whitfield		+	the blaze that followed the crash.	
	Sgt D Richardson		+		

29-30 Sep 1941	7 Sqn	Stirling I		W7433 MG-U	Op: Stettin
	W/O A Fletcher		+	T/o 1900 Oakington. Last heard on w/t at 0258	
	Sgt D E Coyle		+	over the North Sea, plotted some 40 miles NE of	
	Sgt J Tucker		+	Lowestoft, Suffolk. Three bodies were eventually	
	P/O W H J Thompson		+	washed onto the Dutch coast; Sgt Burrows was	
	Sgt H H Mansfield		+	recovered from the water and he is buried in	
	Sgt A E Burrows		+	Derby, while W/O Fletcher and Sgts Mansfield	
	Sgt H J Walker		+	and Walker have no known graves.	

	7 Sqn	Stirling I		W7441 MG-Y	Op: Stettin
	Sgt C J Cobbold		pow	T/o 1850 Oakington. Shot down by a night-	
	Sgt E D Tovey		+	fighter and crashed 2215 over the Little Belt,	
	Sgt J J Copley DFM		pow	Denmark. Those who died are commemorated on	
	Sgt D Y Neil		pow	the Runnymede Memorial. The survivors tried	
	Sgt A Donaldson		pow	to avoid capture, but all were arrested in	
	Sgt E J Rodger		+	the early hours of 1 October.	
	Sgt C W Fulbeck		+		

29-30 Sep
1941

| 51 Sqn | Whitley V | Z6474 MH-A | Op: Stettin |

Sgt C A Guan RAAF

T/o 2254 Dishforth and crashed a few minutes later 1 mile SW of the airfield. A fire broke out and it is reported one member of the crew was slightly injured.

| 58 Sqn | Whitley V | Z6939 GE-E | Op: Stettin |

Sgt G B Walters +
Sgt R Hayden +
Sgt J E Turner RAAF inj
Sgt W Cawthorne inj
Sgt G McHugh RCAF

T/o 1854 Linton-on-Ouse. Crashed 0420 on return to base, coming down in a wood just off the airfield. A fire developed and the Whitley was totally destroyed.

| 58 Sqn | Whitley V | Z6944 GE-R | Op: Stettin |

P/O I A N Atchison +
Sgt J R M Vaisey +
Sgt C B McMullan +
Sgt J E Horne +
Sgt S I C Moulds RCAF +

T/o 1852 Linton-on-Ouse. Lost without trace. All are commemorated on the Runnymede Memorial.

| 77 Sqn | Whitley V | Z9147 KN- | Op: Stettin |

Sgt R E Wheatley
Sgt Smith
P/O Birch
Sgt Ladkin
Sgt Warren

T/o 1804 Leeming. Stalled and crashed 0310 on return to base. The Whitley came down in a small copse and one crew member was slightly hurt.

| 77 Sqn | Whitley V | Z9150 KN- | Op: Stettin |

P/O E G Smith +
Sgt A H K Pedley +
Sgt H W McColm RCAF +
Sgt R W Dunkley +
Sgt J C Hiltz RCAF +

T/o 1805 Leeming. All are buried in Kiel War Cemetery.

| 78 Sqn | Whitley V | Z9126 EY- | Op: Stettin |

Sgt R W Bird +
Sgt I McCarthy +
Sgt H B Buttell +
F/S B Ward +
Sgt R R Vosper +

T/o 2139 Middleton St. George. Last heard on w/t while homebound, calling for help. A bearing taken at the time indicated the Whitley was near Sylt. All are commemorated on the Runnymede Memorial.

| 102 Sqn | Whitley V | Z6871 DY-A | Op: Stettin |

P/O D B Delaney
Sgt D K Kibbe RCAF +
Sgt P L N Trehearn
Sgt C Miller inj
Sgt R Gayler inj
Sgt C Carr

T/o 1853 Topcliffe. Crashed 0355 on high ground 1400 feet asl at Danby Head, 10 miles N of Kirbymoorside, Yorkshire.

| 102 Sqn | Whitley V | Z6949 DY- | Op: le Havre |

P/O L B Renolds RNZAF inj
Sgt J R McMackie inj
Sgt J D Charrott inj
Sgt G P Thompson inj
Sgt J E Sumpton inj
Sgt P Hay inj

T/o 2353 Topcliffe. Crashed 0500 while trying to land at Upper Heyford airfield, Oxfordshire. By 1945, P/O Renolds RNZAF had risen in rank to S/L and was commanding C Flight 158 Squadron at Lissett.

Note. The six-man crew composition of the above aircraft is quite unusual and suggests that in addition to the two pilots, each Whitley carried two navigators.

| 115 Sqn | Wellington IC | X9673 KO-B | Op: Hamburg |

Sgt L H Ellis +
Sgt D J McKenzie RAAF +
Sgt A W Petherick +
Sgt A L Roberts +
Sgt A R Cooper +
Sgt J G C Keeble +

T/o 1946 Marham. Shot down by a night-fighter (Fw Kalinowski, 6./NJG1) and crashed 0026 some 500 metres S of Hittfeldt railway station, 10 km S of Harburg, Germany. All are buried in Becklingen War Cemetery, Soltau.

29-30 Sep 1941	115 Sqn	Wellington IC		
	Sgt A R Hulls		+	
	Sgt J H Goodey RAAF		+	
	P/O W K Colfe RCAF		+	
	Sgt T D Griffiths		+	
	Sgt T W Bull		+	
	P/O N R Suttleworth		pow	

X9910 KO-Y — Op: **Hamburg**
T/o 1931 Marham. Shot down by a night-fighter (Oblt Ludwig Becker, 4./NJG1) and crashed 2252 at Blijham (Groningen), 5 km SE of Winschoten, Holland. The five airmen who died are buried in Wedde (Blijham) Protestant Churchyard.

142 Sqn	Wellington II
P/O G W Bull	+
Sgt J M Pattison	+
F/O M Jacoby	+
F/S J Parkin	+
F/S T H Harrower	+
F/O J O W K Ferris	+

W5378 QT-A — Op: **Stettin**
T/o 1910 Binbrook. Shot down near Kiel, where the crew are buried in the local War Cemetery. F/S Harrower had served for a considerable time on the Squadron and had survived a serious training accident at the beginning of the year.

144 Sqn	Hampden I
Sgt McDermott	
Sgt Boucher	
Sgt H Smith	
Sgt Elliott	

AE143 PL- — Op: **Hamburg**
T/o North Luffenham. Crash-landed in the garden of a house at Sunnyside near Driffield airfield Yorkshire, after running out of fuel.

214 Sqn	Wellington IC
Sgt L Hancock	pow
Sgt D F Cooper	pow
Sgt J I Burbridge	pow
Sgt J W B Follitt	pow
Sgt A N Jones	pow
Sgt H Antehley	pow

X9884 BU- — Op: **Stettin**
T/o Stradishall. Crashed near Landsmeer (Noord Holland), 7 km N of Amsterdam.

30 Sep-1 Oct 1941	9 Sqn Wellington III
Sgt A O Humble-Smith	inj
Sgt J J W Hurley	inj
Sgt S F Hall RNZAF	inj
Sgt A S Barron RCAF	inj
Sgt L M Ramsey RCAF	inj
Sgt A Taylor	inj

X3347 WS- — Op: **Hamburg**
T/o 1945 Honington. Crashed 0224 on return to base. The three most seriously injured were taken to the West Suffolk Hospital at Bury St. Edmunds, while the remainder were treated locally in Station Sick Quarters.

57 Sqn	Wellington II
Sgt G H Johnson	pow
Sgt W C Hayman RNZAF	pow
Sgt C D Clark	pow
Sgt L Jones	pow
Sgt C A Sapcote	pow
Sgt A A Norman	pow

W5445 DX- — Op: **Hamburg**
T/o 1915 Feltwell.

1-2 Oct 1941	10 Sqn Whitley V
P/O T W G Godfrey	
Sgt Watt	
P/O Watts	
Sgt W Webster	
Sgt Beare	

Z6941 ZA-O — Op: **Stuttgart**
T/o 1835 Leeming. Ditched 0530 in the Bristol Channel some 22 miles SW of Milford Haven, Pembrokeshire, after straying from course and running out of fuel. The crew were rescued at 0900 and taken to RAF Pembroke Dock.

106 Sqn	Hampden I
Sgt N J Newby	int
Sgt F W Tisdall	int
Sgt J Wakelin	int
Sgt D Reid	int

AD768 ZN- — Op: **Karlsruhe**
T/o 1820 Coningsby. Passed over the United Kingdom on return and was eventually abandoned over the Glendowan Mountains in County Donegal, Eire.

3 Oct 1941	226 Sqn Blenheim IV
F/S B J Faurat RCAF	

Z7292 MQ- — **Training**
Crashed 1415 while landing at Long Kesh airfield, County Down, Northern Ireland.

305 Sqn	Wellington II
Sgt Szybka	inj
Sgt Duda	inj
LAC Jablonski	inj
LAC Matysiak	inj

W5529 SM- — **Air Test**
The port engine failed and the Wellington crashed while trying to make a single engine landing at Lindholme.

3-4 Oct 1941	7 Sqn	Stirling I	N6085 MG-H **Op: Brest**

3-4 Oct 1941   7 Sqn   Stirling I   **N6085 MG-H**   **Op: Brest**

S/L D I McLeod   +
Sgt I Hunter RNZAF
F/S J R Walker   +
P/O J R Alverston
Sgt J A Marshall   +
F/S H Watson   +
F/L S G Stock   +

T/o Oakington. Shot down by a Ju 88C intruder (Fw Alforns Köster, I./NJG2) and crashed 2230 near Bourn, 8 miles WSW of Cambridge. The two survivors baled out at 700 feet and both landed safely. Tragically, Sgt Hunter RNZAF was killed six weeks later when his Stirling crashed on take off for Kiel.

10-11 Oct 1941   12 Sqn   Wellington II   **W5379 PH-O**   **Op: Köln**

P/O D W D Faint   +
P/O W A Wise   pow
P/O G C Frew   +
Sgt K H Price   +
Sgt A J Childs RCAF   +
Sgt W G Morton   pow

T/o 0020 Binbrook. Crashed 0325 at Haamstede (Zeeland), Holland. Those who died are buried in Bergen op Zoom War Cemetery.

---

12 Sqn   Wellington II   **Z8397 PH-**   **Op: Köln**

Sgt F H N Tothill   +
SGT L S Dunlop   +
Sgt R H Todman   +
Sgt A E Cosgrove   +
F/S A A Nordon   +
Sgt A Pilkington   +

T/o 2352 Binbrook. Crash-landed 0130 on the beach 200 yards S of California Gap, Ormesby, 1 mile NW of Caister-on-Sea, Norfolk. As the bomber slid to a halt, so it touched off a mine and exploded. The bodies of the crew were first taken to the nearby Bungalowe Garage for formal identification.

---

44 Sqn   Hampden I   **AE382 KM-A**   **Op: Dunkerque**

Sgt J P A Bonett   pow
Sgt G W Niblett   pow
Sgt F E Wotton   pow
Sgt J A Anderson   pow

T/o 1855 Waddington.

---

57 Sqn   Wellington IC   **X9756 DX-**   **Op: Köln**

Sgt E R Backhouse   +
Sgt D Macdonald RAAF   +
Sgt H T Smith   +
Sgt M E G Hastings   +
F/S F R Humphreys RCAF   +
Sgt G Maher   +

T/o 2359 Feltwell. Crashed near Köln, where the crew were first buried. Since the war, their remains have been taken to Rheinberg War Cemetery.

---

57 Sqn   Wellington IC   **Z8897 DX-**   **Op: Köln**

Sgt M C Young   +
Sgt W E Hearle RAAF   +
Sgt J E Medhurst   +
Sgt C T Harbottle RCAF   +
Sgt J G Hanlin   +
Sgt T Kelly   +

T/o 2355 Feltwell. All are buried in Rheinberg War Cemetery.

---

58 Sqn   Whitley V   **Z9154 GE-T**   **Op: Essen**

F/S A R Robbins   +
Sgt A W Cooper   +
P/O D S McDonald RCAF   +
Sgt T A W Hamilton   +
Sgt W H Sproule RCAF   pow

T/o 0035 Linton-on-Ouse. Believed shot down by Lt Möller, 6./JG53 and crashed 0035 off Callantsoog, Holland. Three members of the crew are buried in Bergen op Zoom War Cemetery. P/O McDonald RCAF has no known grave.

---

58 Sqn   Whitley V   **Z9204 GE-**   **Op: Essen**

Sgt E E Jones
P/O McKenzie
Sgt Carmichael
Sgt Harwood
Sgt Fraser

T/o 0040 Linton-on-Ouse. Ditched 0825 some 11 miles ESE of Skegness, Lincolnshire. At 1135, the Skegness lifeboat, 'Anne Allen', rescued the crew from the water.

---

75 Sqn   Wellington IC   **Z8909 AA-**   **Op: Köln**

Sgt R F Curlewis RAAF   +
Sgt C M Thompson RNZAF   +
Sgt A C Edwards   +
Sgt F Garde   +
Sgt R L Warburton   +
Sgt T R Murphy RNZAF   +

T/o Feltwell. Crashed near Köln, where the crew were first buried at the British War Cemetery 1914-1918 in the Zollstock district. Since 1945, their remains have been taken to Rheinberg War Cemetery.

10-11 Oct 1941	75 Sqn	Wellington IC		Z8945 AA-	Op: Köln

T/o 0012 Feltwell. Landed safely at 0620, but believed to have been damaged. This was reported on 13 October and, subsequently, the Wellington was written off charge three days later.

Sgt Taylor
Sgt Bell
Sgt Harrington
Sgt Roberts
Sgt Monk
Sgt Tasker

78 Sqn   Whitley V   Z6825 EY-   Op: Essen

T/o Middleton St. George only to be hit on the flare-path by another Whitley.

P/O Fransden
Sgt Dennis
Sgt Bowden
Sgt Young
Sgt Taylor   inj

78 Sqn   Whitley V   Z9127 EY-   Op: Essen

T/o Middleton St. George but collided with another Whitley on the flare-path.

P/O Leyland
Sgt Dench   inj
P/O Geddes
Sgt Donaldson
Sgt Vere

83 Sqn   Hampden I   AD911 OL-M   Op: Essen

T/o 2305 Scampton. Crashed in the Waddenzee off Harlingen, Holland. Sgt Brooks is buried in Den Burg General Cemetery on the island of Texel.

Sgt D C Hedley   pow
Sgt G Mitchell   pow
Sgt W A Brooks   +
Sgt E W E Gough   pow

101 Sqn   Wellington IC   R1219 SR-   Op: Köln

T/o 0007 Oakington. Last heard on w/t, at which time the Wellington was plotted over Belgium. Sgt Highfield has no known grave, while Sgt Bowden exchanged identity with a New Zealander, Driver W B Swears.

P/O G A D Imeson   pow
Sgt J R Ritchie RNZAF   pow
Sgt J Parkington   pow
P/O R C Carroll   pow
Sgt G A Highfield   +
Sgt V I Bowden   pow

106 Sqn   Hampden I   AE144 ZN-   Op: Essen

T/o 0010 Coningsby. Crashed at Lippramsdorf-Haltern, 15 km N of Recklinghausen. All are buried in the Reichswald Forest War Cemetery.

P/O G A O Gordon   +
Sgt P R Martin   +
Sgt F Morris   +
Sgt W H A Everson   +

218 Sqn   Wellington IC   R1511 HA-L   Op: Bordeaux

T/o 2200 Marham. Crashed at Villenave d'Ornon (Gironde), 3 km S of Bordeaux. Sgt Judge is buried in Villenave d'Ornon Communal Cemetery. A few minutes prior to the crash, the crew were able to make a w/t call indicating the aircraft was about to be abandoned.

Sgt V G Haley   evd
Sgt W J Bowhill   pow
Sgt H H Judge   +
Sgt A R Langley   pow
Sgt P L Jones   pow
Sgt D MacDiarmid   pow

218 Sqn   Wellington IC   X9677 HA-V   Op: Bordeaux

T/o 2151 Marham. Came down in the sea off St. Alban's Head on the Dorset coast. An extensive search was conducted by the St. Ives lifeboat during which some wreckage was found. This is reported as part of a wing, camouflaged black and blue, and a wheel. At least three members of the crew are commemorated on the Runnymede Memorial; the remainder are assumed to have been saved.

Sgt McLean
Sgt Honeyman
Sgt J D Pugh   +
Sgt R W Stephenson   +
Sgt Bensted
Sgt E W Ireland   +

12 Oct 1941   18 Sqn   Blenheim IV   N3629 WV-   Training

Crashed at Felthorpe Manor, 7 miles NW of Norwich.

Sgt D C Laws   +
P/O G S Willsher   +
Sgt A F Cullen   +

21 Sqn   Blenheim IV   Z9737 YH-   Training

Crashed 1540 after colliding with a tree near Kingesby.

Sgt F Cocking   +
Sgt M J Counter   +
Sgt E J Gill   +

| 12 Oct 1941 | 82 Sqn | Blenheim IV | L4880 UX-Z | Op: **Anti-shipping** |

Sgt F E V Day +
Sgt G A Robbins +
Sgt F V F Lane +

T/o 1155 Bodney. Shot down by a flak ship off IJmuiden, Holland. Sgt Robbins is buried in Westduin General Cemetery; his two companions are commemorated on the Runnymede Memorial.

| | 82 Sqn | Blenheim IV | V5824 UX-C | Op: **Anti-shipping** |

Sgt J J Ashurst +
Sgt T V Steele +
Sgt R J Banks +

T/o 1155 Bodney. Lost in circumstances similar to those previously described. Sgt Banks is buried in Westduin General Cemetery; the rest are commemorated on the Runnymede Memorial.

| 12-13 Oct 1941 | 12 Sqn | Wellington II | W5552 PH- | Op: **Nürnberg** |

Sgt C B Elsdon DFM pow
Sgt K A Cometti RNZAF pow
Sgt C W Lewis RCAF pow
Sgt F G Pett pow
Sgt N Cass pow
Sgt D C Jackson RCAF pow

T/o Binbrook. A report of Sgt Elsdon's award had appeared in the London Gazette as recently as 23 September 1941.

| | 15 Sqn | Stirling I | N3667 LS-T | Op: **Nürnberg** |

F/L I R Ryall
P/O C B Ordish
Sgt D Phillips
Sgt Fisher
Sgt Howard
Sgt D Clarke
Sgt Surette
F/O Martin

T/o Wyton. Returned early with defective pitch and fuel mixture controls on the port engines and crashed while trying to land at base. No injuries reported.

| | 15 Sqn | Stirling I | N6047 LS-P | Op: **Nürnberg** |

P/O V C H Colbourne +
P/O H Mohr-Bell +
Sgt S Bentley +
P/O T E Wootton +
Sgt I L Evans +
Sgt B W Wareham +
Sgt G J Goodwin RCAF +
Sgt F A Lamb +

T/o Wyton. Shot down by a night-fighter and crashed at Mariembourg (Namur), 12 km SSW of Philippeville, Belgium. All are buried at Dinant in the Citadelle Military Cemetery.

| | 35 Sqn | Halifax I | L9579 TL-P | Op: **Nürnberg** |

Sgt Williams
Sgt Stocker
P/O Mason
Sgt Sykes
Sgt Thorpe
Sgt Crocker
Sgt Pennell

T/o 1955 Linto-on-Ouse. Partially abandoned after running low on fuel, after which the pilot crash-landed 0409 roughly 1 mile N of base. The wreckage caught fire, but no one was seriously hurt.

| | 40 Sqn | Wellington IC | X9619 BL-M | Op: **Nürnberg** |

P/O I M V Field RNZAF +
Sgt P F Collis +
F/O E J Sugg RAAF +
Sgt R A Dundon +
F/S T L Duxbury RCAF +
Sgt H R G Chapman +

T/o 1924 Alconbury. Crashed in the vicinity of Dinant (Namur), Belgium, where the crew are buried in the Military Cemetery.

| | 40 Sqn | Wellington IC | X9822 BL-J | Op: **Bremen** |

Sgt G F Bateman +
Sgt P A Milton +
Sgt F Jenkins +
Sgt E R B Magrath +
Sgt H F Eyre +
Sgt H R Legg +

T/o 1926 Alconbury. Shot down by a night-fighter (Oblt Helmut Lent, 4./NJG1) and crashed 0006 at Westergeest (Friesland), 7 km SE of Dokkum, Holland. All are buried in Westergeest Protestant Churchyard.

12-13 Oct 1941	**50 Sqn**	**Hampden I**	**AE367 VN-** Op: **Hüls**

12-13 Oct
1941

50 Sqn   **Hampden I**
P/O J M Waddell RNZAF   +
P/O W E Hinchcliffe   +
Sgt R W Curtis   +
Sgt N R Lawson   +

AE367 VN-   Op: **Hüls**
T/o Swinderby. All are buried in the Reichswald Forest War Cemetery.

57 Sqn   **Wellington IC**
Sgt A W Jeffries   +
P/O H L Myers RCAF   +
SGT P F M Cooke RNZAF   +
Sgt W C Wood   +
P/O L Rickard RCAF   pow
Sgt W H S Byers   +

R1757 DX-   Op: **Nürnberg**
T/o 1900 Feltwell. Crashed into a marsh near Blenkenham (Overijssel) on the NE edge of the Noord-Oost-Polder, Holland. Four of the crew are buried in Emmeloord General Cemetery, but the grave of P/O Myers RCAF is located in the General Cemetery at Kuinre.

58 Sqn   **Whitley V**
Sgt C G Lord RAAF   +
Sgt H E Donson RCAF   +
Sgt J G Rich RAAF   +
Sgt W H Burns RCAF   +
Sgt H C Lee   +

Z9155 GE-G   Op: **Nürnberg**
T/o 1909 Linton-on-Ouse. Crashed 0457 roughly 1 mile S of Pocklington airfield, Yorkshire, while being diverted. A few minutes before the crash, the pilot radioed to say he was almost out of fuel.

75 Sqn   **Wellington IC**
S/L P B Chamberlain   +
Sgt D C Holley   +
P/O J A Robinson RCAF   +
Sgt R G Butt   +
Sgt F E Austin   +
Sgt J R Ashley   +

X9981 AA-   Op: **Nürnberg**
T/o Feltwell. Crashed in the vicinity of Dinant (Namur),Belgium, where the crew are buried in the Military Cemetery.

76 Sqn   **Halifax I**
F/S E B Muttart RCAF   +
P/O N F Trayler   pow
Sgt D Cotsell   pow
Sgt L A Roberts   pow
SGT R W P Alexander   pow
Sgt W H Hunt   pow
Sgt G H Patterson   pow
Sgt J W Duffield   pow

L9561 MP-H   Op: **Bremen**
T/o 1945 Middleton St. George. Shot down by a night-fighter (Lt Leopold Fellerer, 4./NJG1) and crashed 2149 near Wons (Friesland), 10 km S of Harlingen, Holland, where F/S Muttart RCAF is buried in the General Cemetery.

77 Sqn   **Whitley V**
P/O R L Lloyd   +
Sgt W E Mortimer   +
Sgt J Alterson RCAF   +
Sgt C G Taylor RCAF   +
Sgt D G Robb   +

Z6801 KN-   Op: **Nürnberg**
T/o Leeming. Crashed at Daussois (Namur), 7 km WNW of Philippville, Belgium. All are buried in the Citadelle Military Cemetery at Dinant.

102 Sqn   **Whitley V**
Sgt J W Stell RCAF
Sgt J M M Wilson
Sgt D C Wilson
Sgt C Miller
Sgt O T McIlquham

Z6761 DY-   Op: **Nürnberg**
T/o 1839 Topcliffe. Crashed 0513 at Market Deeping, 10 miles SW of Spalding, Lincolnshire, after running out of fuel.

144 Sqn   **Hampden I**
Sgt H E Chamberlain   +
Sgt E W Hawkins   +
Sgt C A J Webster   +
Sgt C M Morris   +

AD965 PL-   Op: **Hüls**
T/o North Luffenham. Shot down by a night-fighter (Oblt Helmut Lent, 4./NJG1) and crashed 0033 into the IJsselmeer. Sgt Chamberlain, who hailed from Southern Rhodesia, is buried in Makkum Protestant Churchyard, while his crew are commemorated on the Runnymede Memorial.

207 Sqn   **Manchester I**
P/O B D Bowes-Cavanagh   +
Sgt R S Stuart   +
F/S J A Cheeseman   pow
Sgt A J Carter   +
Sgt G P Spindler   +
Sgt J W Leason   +
Sgt I H D Passy   +

L7312 EM-L   Op: **Hüls**
T/o Waddington. Shot down by a night-fighter (Ofw Paul Gildner, 4./NJG1) and crashed at Horendonk (Antwerpen), 27 km NNE of Antwerpen. Those who died are buried in Essen (Horendonk) Communal Cemetery.

12-13 Oct	214 Sqn	Wellington IC		X9762 BU-
1941	Sgt J A Key	pow		

12-13 Oct 1941 — **214 Sqn** — **Wellington IC** — **X9762 BU-** — Op: **Nürnberg**

Sgt J A Key — pow
Sgt H R Boyd RCAF — pow
Sgt A Saxton — pow
Sgt R Mutch — pow
Sgt C W G King — pow
Sgt C W Heathman — pow

T/o 1931 Stradishall. Sgt Heathman died on 19 April 1945, when the prisoner of war column, in which he was marching, was mistakenly shot up by Allied fighters. He is buried in the 1939-1945 War Cemetery at Berlin.

218 Sqn — **Wellington IC** — **Z8910 HA-F** — Op: **Nürnberg**

Sgt J R C MgGlashan
Sgt Helfer
P/O Greigg
Sgt R S C Stewart
Sgt J Dobson
Sgt F C Adams

T/o 2005 Marham. Landed 0450 but was involved in an accident with another aircraft and damaged beyond repair.

13 Oct 1941 — **139 Sqn** — **Blenheim IV** — **Z7273 XD-H** — Op: **Circus 108A**

F/L R J Chamberlain DFC — +
Sgt F L C Jewell — +
Sgt D Beale — +

T/o 1215 Oulton. Shot down by Me 109s near Arques (Pas-de-Calais), 4 km SE of St-Omer. All are buried in Boulogne Eastern Cemetery.

13-14 Oct 1941 — **44 Sqn** — **Hampden I** — **AD975 KM-** — Op: **Köln**

Sgt E Owen — +
F/S G H Edmondson RCAF — +
Sgt G Shearer — +
Sgt G R Ramsay — +

T/o 0120 Waddington. Shot down by a night-fighter (Oblt Roderer, I./NJG1) and crashed 2339 at Waasmunster (Oost Vlaanderen), 7 km ENE of Kokeren, Belgium. All are buried in Wassmunster Communal Cemetery.

50 Sqn — **Hampden I** — **AE251 VN-** — Op: **Köln**

F/L E R Abbott DSO, DFM — pow
P/O Chase — pow
Sgt T G Wake — pow
Sgt Barrett — pow

T/o Swinderby. Shot down by flak. F/L Abbott had gained his DFM for service with 50 Squadron, the details being promulgated on 22 October 1940. Notification of his DSO was published in the London Gazette ten days after his capture.

101 Sqn — **Wellington IC** — **T2846 SR-** — Op: **Düsseldorf**

Sgt R L Betts — pow
Sgt L D A Bolton — pow
P/O W Barrett — pow
Sgt J M Atkinson — pow
Sgt L Pearman — evd
Sgt R H Cage — pow

T/o 1838 Oakington.

115 Sqn — **Wellington IC** — **Z8844 KO-S** — Op: **München**

Sgt F H E Deardon — +
Sgt P L Browne RAAF — +
Sgt P W Jarrett — +
Sgt M S Preece — +
Sgt B F Widdecombe — +
Sgt F P Stewart — +

T/o 2304 Marham. All are buried in Durnbach War Cemetery.

207 Sqn — **Manchester I** — **L7321 EM-D** — Op: **Köln**

P/O J Unsworth DFM — +
P/O H B Carroll — evd
P/O W E Simpson RCAF — +
Sgt G T Cox — evd
F/S E Moulding — +
Sgt A F Dickson RCAF — +
P/O F Mason — +

T/o Waddington. Shot down by a night-fighter (Oblt Heinrich Griese, 1./NJG1) and crashed at Hozemont, Belgium. Those who died are buried in Heverlee War Cemetery. P/O Unsworth was awarded his DFM for service with 49 Squadron.

207 Sqn — **Manchester I** — **L7373 EM-T** — Op: **Köln**

P/O L A Paskell DFM — +
Sgt D V Chant — +
F/S K H L Houghton DFM — evd
F/S G H Roberts — +
Sgt A D Smith — pow
Sgt C D G Walter — +
Sgt L J Compton — +

T/o Waddington. Shot down by a night-fighter and crashed 2 km E of Beverlo (Limburg), 18 km NNW of Hasselt, Belgium. Those who died are buried in Schaffen Communal Cemetery. F/S Houghton gained his DFM for service with 83 Squadron. He was later commissioned and died while on service in the Middle East, where he is buried in Ramleh War Cemetery, Israel.

| 4 Oct 1941 | 114 Sqn | Blenheim IV | Z7278 RT- | Training |

Sgt W J Anstey +
Sgt A J Southwood +
Sgt J W Kerrison +

Crashed at Clenchwarton, 2 miles W of King's Lynn, Norfolk, while engaged in a low flying exercise.

| 14-15 Oct 1941 | 15 OTU | Wellington IC | R1275 | Op: Nickel |

Sgt J C Spragge +
Sgt C L Humphrey pow
Sgt E A Tredenick RCAF +
Sgt P B Tomes +
Sgt T J Snell +
Sgt E J Waldron +

T/o Harwell. Crashed in the vicinity of Evreux (Eure), France, where those who died are buried in the Communal Cemetery.

| | 15 OTU | Wellington IC | R1783 | Op: Nickel |

Sgt A E R Beverley +
Sgt W H Box +
Sgt D A Rutherford RCAF +
F/S W S Barclay RCAF +
Sgt D A Cameron +
Sgt W M McGarry +

T/o Harwell. Crashed at Barville (Eure), 18 km E of Lisieux, France. All are buried in Barville Churchyard.

| | 40 Sqn | Wellington IC | X9882 BL-W | Op: Nürnberg |

Sgt J R Hiscock +
Sgt D A Scott RAAF +
Sgt J P B Cambray +
Sgt B C Dymott +
Sgt A J Thomas +
Sgt J H White +

T/o 2322 Alconbury. Lost without trace. All are commemorated on the Runnymede Memorial. At 41 years of age, Sgt Dymott was well above the average age for airmen employed on flying duties of an operational nature.

| | 40 Sqn | Wellington IC | X9926 BL-T | Op: Nürnberg |

P/O G B Buse +
Sgt R C Tyrrell +
Sgt F E Ridler +
Sgt J Chapman +
Sgt R H G Collins +
Sgt S C Hodge +

T/o Alconbury. All are buried in Durnbach War Cemetery.

| | 40 Sqn | Wellington IC | Z8782 BL-E | Op: Nürnberg |

Sgt K D Edis +
Sgt J E Hawkins +
Sgt R E Bates +
F/S R M McIntrye RCAF +
F/S J E Weir RCAF +
F/S I J McDonald +

T/o 2301 Alconbury. Exploded in the air near Karlsruhe, where the crew were first taken for burial. Since 1945, their remains have been interned at Durnbach War Cemetery.

| | 78 Sqn | Whitley V | Z9213 EY- | Op: Nürnberg |

P/O D S King RCAF
P/O Pruden
Sgt Jupp
Sgt Lyndon
Sgt Campbell

T/o 2252 Middleton St. George. Crashed 0615 near Hythe, Kent, after being abandoned, low on fuel. P/O King RCAF was later posted to 76 Squadron and was reported missing from operations to Brest on 30 December 1941.

| | 218 Sqn | Wellington IC | Z8865 HA-O | Op: Nürnberg |

Sgt K G Fisher inj
Sgt Jetten
Sgt Borrowdale
Sgt Clarke
Sgt Smith
Sgt Mewes

T/o 2310 Marham but soon afterwards the port engine failed and the crew made an early return. Approaching to land, the Wellington collided with some trees and crashed 0100 just short of the runway. No serious injuries reported.

| 5 Oct 1941 | 114 Sqn | Blenheim IV | L9382 RT- | Op: Anti-shipping |

P/O W H Davidson RCAF +
Sgt E K Saul +
Sgt D G Peppler +

T/o 0745 West Raynham to patrol the eastern half of Beat 8. Shot down by fighters from 5./ZG76 and crashed 1203 into the sea some 130 km WNW of Den Helder, Holland. No bodies were found and all are commemorated on the Runnymede Memorial.

15 Oct 1941	114 Sqn	Blenheim IV	V5875 RT-	Op: Anti-shipping

Sgt C S Balzer RAAF +
Sgt H L Elliott RCAF +
Sgt V F W Slae +

T/o 0745 West Raynham. Lost in circumstances similar to those previously reported. Two are commemorated on the Runnymede Memorial; the pilot is buried in Harlingen General Cemetery.

139 Sqn   Blenheim IV   V6249 XD-   Op: Anti-shipping
S/L R T Stubbs DFC +
Sgt J W Bradley +
Sgt W P Thom RCAF +

T/o 0758 Oulton. Lost without trace. All are commemorated on the Runnymede Memorial.

139 Sqn   Blenheim IV   Z7300 XD-   Op: Anti-shipping
Sgt E F G Gill +
Sgt A W Humphries +
Sgt D W Marshall +

T/o 0758 Oulton. Lost without trace. All are commemorated on the Runnymede Memorial.

139 Sqn   Blenheim IV   Z7320 XD-   Op: Anti-shipping
F/O T R Paxton +
P/O H M Clarke +
F/O R C Holloway +

T/o 0758 Oulton. Lost without trace. All are commemorated on the Runnymede Memorial.

226 Sqn   Blenheim IV   Z7493 MQ-Y   Op: le Havre
P/O R M Hudson RAAF +
Sgt D Poulston +
Sgt G S Needler +

T/o 1346 Tangmere to attack a tanker reported at le Havre. Shot down by Me 109s in the target area.

226 Sqn   Blenheim IV   Z7494 MQ-Z   Op: le Havre
Sgt S L T Paine +
Sgt R G Banks +
Sgt W J S Wolstenholme +

T/o 1346 Tangmere. Lost in circumstances similar to those previously described.

Note. This was a particularly hard day for the Blenheim squadrons of 2 Group. From a total of twenty-four aircraft despatched on all types of operations, no less than seven had been lost and not a single airman had survived.

15-16 Oct 1941	57 Sqn	Wellington IC	X9978 DX-	Op: Köln

P/O K J Miller RAAF +
Sgt N J Lewery +
Sgt D W Jennings +
Sgt E T Christie +
Sgt G W T Jackson +
Sgt B S Jones +

T/o 1835 Feltwell. Shot down by a night-fighter (Fw Maier, I./NJG1) and crashed 2117 Grevenbicht (Limburg), on the E bank of the Maas, 8 km NW of Sittard, Holland. All were buried at Venlo, but since 1945 their bodies have been taken to Jonkerbos War Cemetery.

75 Sqn   Wellington IC   W5663 AA-   Op: Köln
SGT R C Barker +
P/O T B Robertson RNZAF +
Sgt H D Grimes RAAF +
Sgt D L Beney +
Sgt G F Cole pow
Sgt J B Stephenson RCAF pow

T/o Feltwell. Crashed near Düsseldorf, where those who died were buried in the Nord Friedhof. Since the end of hostilities, their remains have been taken to the Reichswald Forest War Cemetery.

75 Sqn   Wellington IC   X9916 AA-   Op: Köln
Sgt J A Matetich +
Sgt F L R Wood RNZAF +
F/S N H Welsh RNZAF +
Sgt F H Worlledge +
Sgt A Service +
Sgt D F Barkhouse RCAF +

T/o Feltwell. All are buried in Rheinberg War Cemetery. Sgt Service had previously served with 29 Squadron, taking part in the Battle of Britain.

16 Oct 1941	78 Sqn	Whitley V	Z6646 EY-	Training

P/O B O Smith

Crashed 2010 in the circuit of Croft airfield, Yorkshire, injuring at least four members of the crew. The accident was attributed to engine failure.

305 Sqn   Wellington II   W5591 SM-B   Transit
Sgt W Jedrzejczak

Crashed 2110 while trying to land at Lindholme in poor visibility. The Wellington, which was burnt out, was returning to base from Binbrook where Marconi had modified the radio equipment.

6-17 Oct 941	40 Sqn	Wellington IC	Z8862 BL-B	Op: Duisburg

6-17 Oct 941

40 Sqn   Wellington IC

S/L T G Kirby-Green   pow
Sgt J A Lamb   +
Sgt J A Jacques RCAF   +
Sgt A H Harman   +
F/S P L Henningan DFM   +
F/O P C Campbell-Martin   +

Z8862 BL-B   Op: Duisburg
T/o 0106 Alconbury. Those who died at the time of the crash are buried in the Reichswald Forest War Cemetery. S/L Kirby-Green rests in Poznan Old Garrison Cemetery, Poland, after being shot by the Gestapo on 29 March 1944, following the mass escape from Stalag Luft III.

102 Sqn   Whitley V

Sgt L W Carr
Sgt J E Church
Sgt R B Shoebridge
Sgt D Cramp
Sgt R J Horton

Z6958 DY-   Op: Duisburg
T/o 0041 Topcliffe. Landed safely 0745 at base, but with flak damage of such severity that the Whitley was deemed to be beyond worthwhile repair.

103 Sqn   Wellington IC

P/O Jones
P/O Smith
Sgt Mills
Sgt Edwards
Sgt Yates
Sgt Leake

R1217 PM-   Op: Duisburg
T/o 0103 Elsham Wolds. Hit by flak in the port engine, which burned intermittently after clearing the Dutch coast. Base was reached at 0659 and following a technical inspection, the Wellington was declared a write-off.

218 Sqn   Wellington IC

F/L Dunham
Sgt Hinwood
Sgt McKay
Sgt Wheeler
Sgt Murray
Sgt Turner

Z8957 HA-L   Op: Duisburg
T/o 0125 Marham carrying, for the first time by the Squadron, a 4000lb bomb. While crossing the coast, outbound, the port engine failed and the Wellington was abandoned 0210 near Cantley, 10 miles SE of Norwich.

305 Sqn   Wellington II

Sgt S Hildebrandt   +
F/O M B Kosowski   +
F/O A Bryk   +
Sgt T Lang   +
Sgt J Hejnowski   +
F/O J Lucki   +

W5579 SM-L   Op: Dunkerque
T/o 1910 Lindholme. Presumed lost over the sea. Sgt Lang is buried in Blankenberge Communal Cemetery, Belgium; the remainder have no known graves.

Oct 41

88 Sqn   Blenheim IV

F/O P C Nangle RAAF   +
F/S P B Fullerton RCAF   +
Sgt I A Macdonald RCAF   +

L9020 RH-   Training
Crashed at Weston Longville, 9 miles NW of Norwich. All are buried in Swanton Morley (All Saints) Churchyard.

9-21 Oct 41

15 Sqn   Stirling I

Sgt E P De Ville
Sgt Rigby
Sgt Spriggs
Sgt Scott
Sgt Cook
Sgt R L Aiken   +
Sgt Bain

W7431 LS-A   Op: Bremen
T/o Wyton. Crashed 0130 at Catsholm Farm near Methwold airfield, Norfolk. Prior to the crash, five of the crew baled out and Sgt Aiken died as a result of doing so.

50 Sqn   Hampden I

P/O W Laidlaw   +
Sgt K S Furley   +
Sgt W A Saunders   +
Sgt E R James   +

AE383 VN-   Op: Bremen
T/o Swinderby. All are buried in Becklingen War Cemetery at Soltau.

97 Sqn   Manchester I

P/O W G Noble   +
Sgt L L Harrison RNZAF   +
Sgt A F G Redwood   +
Sgt N F Hunt   +
Sgt C C Kolar   +
F/O L A J Mills DFC   +
Sgt R M C Worthington   +

L7462 OF-   Op: Bremen
T/o 1830 Coningsby. Last heard on w/t at 0030 indicating the wireless equipment was causing problems. On 4 November, news came from Coltishall that the body of Sgt Hunt had been recovered from the sea, and a similar message was received from Martlesham Heath in respect of Sgt Redwood. Both are buried in the United Kingdom; the remainder are commemorated on the Runnymede Memorial.

| 20-21 Oct 1941 | 97 Sqn | Manchester I | R5783 OF-V | Op: Bremen |

97 Sqn — **Manchester I** — **R5783 OF-V** — **Op: Bremen**

20-21 Oct 1941

Sgt G H Hartley
Sgt Appleyard
Sgt J Canham
Sgt Dean
Sgt Baker
Sgt Mayland
Sgt Gross

T/o 1822 Coningsby. Force-landed 0030 on marshland at Friskney, 8 miles SW of Skegness, Lincolnshire. This was the second Manchester incident involving this crew in a little over a month. No injuries reported.

99 Sqn — **Wellington IC** — **R3222 LN-** — **Op: Bremen**

Sgt L G Faunt RAAF +
Sgt P Kay +
Sgt J A McDonough +
Sgt R B Allport +
Sgt H E Dance +
Sgt R Pinkerton +

T/o 1843 Waterbeach. Lost without trace. All are commemorated on the Runnymede Memorial.

99 Sqn — **Wellington IC** — **Z8891 LN-** — **Op: Bremen**

Sgt Morgan
Sgt Macauley
P/O Wagstaff
Sgt Price
Sgt Cline
Sgt Bartlett

T/o 1825 Waterbeach. Ditched in the North Sea while returning to base, coming down off the fishing port of Lowestoft, Suffolk. Appropriately, it was a trawler that brought the crew to safety.

106 Sqn — **Hampden I** — **AD746 ZN-** — **Op: Bremen**

Sgt Cooke
Sgt Fry
Sgt Goodwin
Sgt Gowan

T/o 1830 Coningsby. Crashed 0225 on return to base. The crew escaped injury.

106 Sqn — **Hampden I** — **AD984 ZN-** — **Op: Bremen**

Sgt J L Lockwood RCAF +
Sgt G F Williams RNZAF +
Sgt W Alton +
Sgt T G Jones +

T/o 1830 Coningsby. Crashed at Borby, Germany. All are buried in Kiel War Cemetery.

Note. The location Borby has not been traced and it is likely that the name appended in the records has been misspelt.

149 Sqn — **Wellington IC** — **Z8795 OJ-C** — **Op: Bremen**

P/O A C L Hodge +
P/O D W Brubaker RCAF +
Sgt J St G Johnston +
Sgt F L Capstick RCAF +
Sgt J W Horrocks +
Sgt L E Scantlebury +

T/o 1829 Mildenhall. Crashed in the River Schelde. Sgt Brubaker RCAF and Sgt Scantlebury are buried in Schoonselhof Cemetery, Antwerpen, while their companions are commemorated on the Runnymede Memorial.

207 Sqn — **Manchester I** — **L7487 EM-N** — **Op: Bremen**

P/O J C L Ruck-Keene +
P/O G S Macdonald RCAF +
P/O H S Ray RCAF +
F/S J S Cooper +
Sgt D D Taylor RCAF +
Sgt W H Cubbon +
Sgt H C Gardner +

T/o Waddington. Crashed in the North Sea, 18 miles off Great Yarmouth, Norfolk. The body of P/O Macdonald RCAF was eventually washed onto the French coast and he is buried in the Eastern Cemetery at Boulogne. His companions have no known graves. P/O Ruck-Keene was the son of Admiral W G E Ruck-Keene MVO, JP, who lost two sons on active service with the navy.

304 Sqn — **Wellington IC** — **N2852 NZ-** — **Op: Emden**

Sgt N Zykow +
P/O S Borzecki +
F/O A E Gisman +
Sgt H Plis +
Sgt R Klimiuk +
Sgt W Adamik +

T/o 1812 Lindholme. Crashed in the North Sea in the vicinity of Heligoland. Sgt Zykow and F/O Gisman were initially buried at Wilhelmshaven, but since 1945 their remains have been taken to Sage War Cemetery, Oldenburg

0-21 Oct 1941	311 Sqn	Wellington IC		R1046 KX-E	Op: **Bremen**

311 Sqn   Wellington IC   R1046 KX-E   Op: **Bremen**

Sgt V F E Prochazka	pow
Sgt F Petr	pow
F/O E J M Vesely	pow
Sgt F B Valnerova	pow
Sgt J Susa	pow
Sgt J Ziolensy	pow

0-21 Oct 941   **311 Sqn**   Wellington IC   **R1046 KX-E**   Op: **Bremen**

T/o 1855 East Wretham. Last heard on w/t at 2201 asking for help, after which it is believed the Wellington was shot down by a night-fighter and crash-landed on a sandbank 7 km S of Schiermonnikoog in the Dutch Frisian islands.

408 Sqn   Hampden I   **P1212 EQ-T**   Op: **Bremen**

Sgt D G Bradley RNZAF   +
Sgt A T McMillan RCAF   +
Sgt Coles   +
Sgt R A Stansfield   +

T/o 1814 Syerston. Crashed 0045 at Haltham, 4 miles SSW of Horncastle, Lincolnshire, while trying to land at Coningsby. This was the first Squadron loss since commencing operations on 11-12 August 1941.

458 Sqn   Wellington IV   **Z1218 D**   Op: **Antwerpen**

Sgt P J M Hamilton   +
Sgt P G Crittenden RAAF   +
P/O D K Fawkes   +
Sgt T Jackson   +
Sgt A Y Condie   +
Sgt P G E A Brown   pow

T/o 1839 Holme-on-Spalding Moor as part of the Squadron's first operation. Those who died are buried in Charleroi Communal Cemetery, Belgium. Sgt Crittenden RAAF was the first Australian, serving in Bomber Command, to be killed on operations flying with an RAAF squadron.

1 Oct 941   **21 Sqn**   Blenheim IV   **V5580 YH-X**   Op: **Anti-shipping**

F/L F C Powles DFC   +
Sgt J D Life   +
F/S S J Williams   +

T/o 1215 Watton. Crashed in the sea. At least two of the crew were seen to get out of the Blenheim, after it hit the water. All are buried in Sage War Cemetery, Oldenburg.

82 Sqn   Blenheim IV   **V5634 UX-A**   Op: **Anti-shipping**

P/O J H Richardson   +
F/S A J Park   +
F/S G C P Haines   +

T/o 1330 Bodney. Believed shot down off Katwijk aan Zee, Holland, by Fw Ederer, 3./JG53. All are commemorated on the Runnymede Memorial.

82 Sqn   Blenheim IV   **V6146 UX-O**   Op: **Anti-shipping**

P/O B B Barber RAAF   +
P/O H H Pibus RCAF   +
Sgt E W Paine   +

T/o 1330 Bodney. Lost in the same circumstances as previously described. All are commemorated on the Runnymede Memorial.

1-22 Oct 941   **12 Sqn**   Wellington IC   **W5393 PH-**   Op: **Bremen**

Sgt J K Millar   +
Sgt G L McInerny   +
Sgt L W Rogers   +
Sgt P F Tracey   +
Sgt M R Forty   +
Sgt Taylor   inj

T/o 1800 Binbrook. Crashed 0055 into a row of Married Quarters while trying to land at base.

44 Sqn   Hampden I   **AE257 KM-**   Op: **Bremen**

P/O W H Budd   +
P/O D Schafheitlin RCAF   +
Sgt W E Austin   +
Sgt M J Hughes   +

T/o 1835 Waddington. Presumed crashed in the North Sea. Two are buried in cemeteries on the German mainland and two, P/O Schafheitlin RCAF and Sgt Austin, have no known graves.

142 Sqn   Wellington IV   **Z1210 QT-M**   Op: **Bremen**

Sgt T E Parker RCAF   +
Sgt J Forrest   +
F/S J F Gauley RCAF   +
F/S E L Phillips   +
Sgt L W Shearing   +
Sgt B R Thomas   +

T/o 1822 Binbrook. Presumed lost over the sea. Sgt Forrest and F/S Phillips are commemorated on the Runnymede Memorial; the rest of the crew are buried in Sage War Cemetery at Oldenburg.

301 Sqn   Wellington IV   **Z1217 GR-W**   Op: **Bremen**

Sgt L Cieslak   pow
Sgt M Borodej   pow
F/O J Riedl   pow
Sgt A Stalewski   pow
Sgt A Mlodzik   pow
Sgt A Klee-Berg   pow

T/o Hemswell.

22 Oct 1941	51 Sqn	Whitley V	Z9145 MH-K	Training

22 Oct 1941 — **51 Sqn** — **Whitley V** — **Z9145 MH-K** — **Training**
Sgt J L Perrin +
P/O A Baerlein +
Sgt R E Sayer +
Crashed 2355 at Mangles Farm, Givendale, 4 miles NW of Boroughbridge, Yorkshire. Believed to have been the first Whitley from the Squadron to be written off in a non-operational crash during 1941.

22-23 Oct 1941 — **57 Sqn** — **Wellington IC** — **Z8792 DX-** — **Op: Mannheim**
P/O R F L Tong inj
Sgt S Pizzie inj
Sgt R Durham inj
Sgt A J Gillespie inj
Sgt A Frost inj
Sgt M Harris inj
T/o 1815 Feltwell. Crash-landed 0005 at Erwarton on the W bank of the River Orwell, 7 miles SE of Ipswich.

75 Sqn — **Wellington IC** — **X9914 AA-** — **Op: Mannheim**
Sgt C Taylor +
Sgt F A Spark RNZAF +
Sgt S J L Levack +
Sgt J Roberts RAAF +
Sgt W R Steele +
Sgt R H Tasker +
T/o Feltwell. Crashed near Werken (West Vlaanderen), 7 km ESE of Diksmuide, Belgium. All are buried in Werken Churchyard.

83 Sqn — **Hampden I** — **AD934 OL-T** — **Op: Mannheim**
Sgt J Mowatt
Sgt S Brown
Sgt T R Riddell
Sgt G Rex
T/o 1830 Scampton. Crashed 0200 while trying to land at Swanton Morley airfield, Norfolk. No injuries reported. A thick coating of ice on the pilot's windscreen was a contributory factor to the accident.

99 Sqn — **Wellington II** — **W5454 LN-** — **Op: Mannheim**
Sgt T H C Mahon +
Sgt D W Soden +
Sgt J H Kay +
Sgt R D Partridge +
Sgt J D H Lewis +
Sgt S G Westbrook RCAF +
T/o 1758 Waterbeach. Heard on w/t indicating that the aircraft was returning to base after suffering an engine fire. All are commemorated on the Runnymede Memorial.

150 Sqn — **Wellington IC** — **T2967 JN-J** — **Op: Mannheim**
Sgt A L Bradshaw +
Sgt P P F Du Pre +
P/O G C O'Neill RCAF +
Sgt H I S Armes +
Sgt K Carter +
Sgt R L Hunt +
T/o 1815 Snaith. All are buried in Durnbach War Cemetery.

405 Sqn — **Wellington II** — **Z8419 LQ-V** — **Op: le Havre**
Sgt C R Hall RCAF +
Sgt P T W Walker RCAF +
Sgt W L N Johnston RAAF +
Sgt L E Dodge RCAF +
F/S L H Jackson RCAF +
F/S G F Marr RCAF +
T/o 1815 Pocklington. Last heard on w/t at 2100 signalling operation completed 2030. Presumed lost over the sea. F/S Jackson RCAF is buried in Fécamp (le Val aux Clercs); the rest of this all Commonwealth crew are commemorated on the Runnymede Memorial.

408 Sqn — **Hampden I** — **P1218 EQ-Q** — **Op: Mannheim**
F/S F A Titcomb +
Sgt R M Gifford RCAF pow
Sgt P A J Ragg +
F/S R R Walker +
T/o 1845 Syerston. Those who died are buried in Durnbach War Cemetery. It will be recalled that F/S Titcomb and Sgt Gifford RCAF had, until quite recently, served with 50 Squadron.

458 Sqn — **Wellington IV** — **R1765** — **Op: le Havre**
F/L J A H Sargeaunt inj
P/O B P Hickey RNZAF
P/O R Birnie RAAF
Sgt M W Shapir RAAF inj
Sgt A S Austin
Sgt R J Hobbs +
T/o 1830 Holme-on-Spalding Moor. Hit by flak and subsequently the crew were ordered to bale out. Five did so, landing in the vicinity of Aldershot, Hampshire. Sgt Shapir RAAF fractured a leg and he was admitted to the Cambridge Hospital at Aldershot; the body of Sgt Hobbs was found in the wreckage of the bomber.

3 Oct 1941	311 Sqn	Wellington IC	T2624 KX-	**Training**
	Sgt K Hurt	+	Lost over the Irish Sea. Those named are	
	Sgt O Januj	+	commemorated on the Runnymede Memorial.	
	Sgt J Polednik	+		
	Sgt J Rolenc	+		

23-24 Oct 1941	44 Sqn	Hampden I	AE290 KM-	**Op: le Havre**
	Sgt P H Bell	+	T/o 0325 Waddington. Lost without trace.	
	Sgt K A Holmes	+	All are commemorated on the Runnymede Memorial.	
	Sgt R H Atkinson	+		
	Sgt A T Laing	+		

	50 Sqn	Hampden I	AE256 VN-	**Op: Kiel**
	P/O K T Cooper	+	T/o Swinderby. Hit by flak and crashed	
	Sgt R C Blamey	+	in the target area. All are buried in	
	Sgt W C Wright	+	Kiel War Cemetery.	
	Sgt S Barton	+		

24-25 Oct 1941	51 Sqn	Whitley V	Z6874 MH-	**Op: Frankfurt**
	Sgt G M Porrett	pow	T/o 1737 Dishforth. Crashed near Pihen-lès-	
	Sgt J P Magwood RCAF	pow	Guines (Pas-de-Calais), 10 km SW of Calais,	
	Sgt H R Wilson RCAF	evd	where Sgt Wheeler RCAF is buried in the	
	Sgt C E Wheeler RCAF	+	Communal Cemetery.	
	Sgt D G Pinney	pow		

	101 Sqn	Wellington IC	X9828 SR-	**Op: Frankfurt**
	P/O G F Bundey	+	T/o 1809 Oakington. Crashed in the North Sea.	
	F/S A J Page	+	F/S Page is buried in Oostende New Communal	
	Sgt W F W Lewis	+	Cemetery; the rest of the crew have no known	
	F/S J R France	+	graves.	
	Sgt A C Hayter	+		
	Sgt D R Thompson	+		

	103 Sqn	Wellington IC	T2506 PM-	**Op: Frankfurt**
	P/O R G Keefer RCAF	int	T/o 2122 Elsham Wolds. Crash-landed in County	
	SGT L C Draper	int	Clare, Eire.	
	P/O J P S Calder RCAF	int		
	Sgt A C Dalton	int		
	Sgt M B Brown	int		
	Sgt A Virtue	int		

	144 Sqn	Hampden I	AE316 PL-	**Op: Frankfurt**
	F/L I H Kingwell	pow	T/o North Luffenham. Believed to have ditched	
	Sgt F C Stephenson RCAF	+	off the Belgian coast. Sgt Smith is buried at	
	Sgt L A Parker	pow	Dunkerque; Sgt Stephenson RCAF is commemorated	
	Sgt A W Smith	+	on the Runnymede Memorial.	

	150 Sqn	Wellington IC	T2960 JN-	**Op: Frankfurt**
	Sgt Wilkinshaw		T/o 1950 Snaith. Landed 0155 with flak damage	
	Sgt Skrender		of such severity that, following a technical	
	Sgt Wilkinson		inspection, the Wellington was written off	
	F/S Leigh		charge.	
	Sgt Grundy			
	Sgt Sutton			

	405 Sqn	Wellington II	W5489 LQ-A	**Op: Frankfurt**
	P/O Frizzle		T/o 1828 Pocklington. Hit by flak, which caused	
	Sgt Graham		considerable damage to the wing fuel tanks. The	
	P/O Gibson		Wellington returned to base at 0010, but while	
	Sgt Allen		being taxied to its dispersal, a fire broke out,	
	Sgt Jones		completely destroying the aircraft. No injuries	
	Sgt Pickard		reported.	

5 Oct 1941	15 Sqn	Stirling I	N6040 LS-C	**Training**
	P/O S P Edgehill		Crash-landed at Wyton airfield, Huntingdonshire. No injuries reported.	

	50 Sqn	Hampden I	AE184 VN-	**Training**
	Sgt A J Weber		Reported crashed at Ratcliffe near York.	

26 Oct 1941	40 Sqn	Wellington IC	X9974 BL-	Ferry

P/O C G R Saunders RCAF +
Sgt H L Steadman RCAF +
Sgt V J Hale +
Sgt D Y N Crosby RCAF +
Sgt A N Irving RCAF +
P/O A Lodge +
F/S H Higginson +
Sgt E J Beard +
Cpl G I F Davies +
LAC C Robson +

T/o Hampstead Norris bound for Gibraltar, with Malta as its ultimate destination, and crashed almost immediately. A total of sixteen aircraft and crews were involved in the Malta detachment, leaving just a small nucleus of crews at Alconbury to continue bomber operations over Europe.

88 Sqn	Blenheim IV	V6421 RH-Y	Op: **Anti-shipping**

P/O J Rollinson +
P/O A E Day +
Sgt E W Andrews +

T/o 1410 Attlebridge. Hit by flak in the port engine and crashed one minute after attacking a convoy off the Dutch coast. The pilot and his observer were seen to get out of the sinking aircraft, but they are presumed to have drowned as all are commemorated on the Runnymede Memorial.

207 Sqn	Manchester I	L7422 EM-V	Training

S/L K H P Beauchamp

Crashed at Hardings Farm, Linwood, 2 miles SSE of Market Rasen, Lincolnshire. The bomber was carrying a complement of thirteen, including a number of ATC cadets.

26-27 Oct 1941	44 Sqn	Hampden I	AE398 KM-	Training

Sgt M Gruber

Arrived over Coltishall airfield, Norfolk in poor visibility and circled for the next thirty minutes, before an engine failed necessitating an immediate force-landing. In doing so, the Hampden crashed 1730, seriously injuring at least one airman.

57 Sqn	Wellington IC	R1722 DX-	Op: **Hamburg**

P/O J A Watson RCAF +
Sgt Wilson
P/O Scarlett
Sgt Cox
Sgt Andrews inj
Sgt Meek

T/o 1820 Feltwell. Crash-landed 0220 roughly 2 miles S of Berners Heath range, Suffolk. While returning to base, the Wellington had run low on fuel, losing height as a result. The nacelle tanks were switched on, by which time the bomber was below 300 feet and a crash-landing became inevitable.

57 Sqn	Wellington IC	Z8946 DX-S	Op: **Hamburg**

P/O J S Walters pow
Sgt D S Fisk RCAF +
P/O I H Collett RNZAF pow
Sgt T C Bartle pow
Sgt L C Bentley RCAF +
Sgt F W Wade RCAF +

T/o 1810 Feltwell. Last heard on w/t at 2324 after which, according to captured German Marine records held in Copenhagen, the bomber crashed 0020 in the tidal area S of Romo Island, Denmark. The survivors were rescued by a marine vessel and taken to Sylt, while two bodies were recovered from the water and buried in Fourfelt Cemetery, Esbjerg. Sgt Wade RCAF is commemorated on the Runnymede Memorial.

75 Sqn	Wellington IC	Z1168 AA-	Op: **Hamburg**

Sgt S J G Isherwood pow
Sgt D J Pyman RNZAF pow
P/O E M Sangster RCAF pow
Sgt H A D Stanley RCAF pow
Sgt B W Shelnutt RCAF +
Sgt H Bell pow

T/o Feltwell. Sgt Shelnutt RCAF is commemorated on the Runnymede Memorial. While in captivity, Sgt Isherwood exchanged identity with LCpl J F White of the Australian Imperial Force.

106 Sqn	Hampden I	AD785 ZN-	Op: **Hamburg**

Sgt E B Smith +
P/O D R Bowden +
Sgt Halward +
F/S D B Stables DFM +

T/o 1810 Coningsby. Exploded and crashed 0215 onto the Whitby to Scarborough road, Yorkshire. F/S Stables had gained his award for service with 61 Squadron during 1940.

106 Sqn	Hampden I	AE136 ZN-	Op: **Hamburg**

P/O J M Wood pow
Sgt D J Carmichael RCAF +
Sgt E Haste +
Sgt R A Gladen +

T/o 1755 Coningsby. Crashed at Selsingen, 9 km NNW of Zeven, Germany. Those who died are buried in Becklingen War Cemetery at Soltau.

26-27 Oct 1941	304 Sqn	Wellington IC	W5720 NZ-	Op: **Hamburg**

P/O E A Ladro
P/O T Skarzinski
F/O T B Sokolowski
P/O T L Krzywon
F/O S Stenocki   +
P/O L K Assman

T/o 1755 Lindholme. Ditched 2210 approximately
12 miles off Cromer, Norfolk, following failure
of the port engine. Apart from F/O Stenocki,
the crew were rescued by the Sheringham lifeboat
'Forester's Centenary`, seventeen hours after
entering the water.

27 Oct 1941	114 Sqn	Blenheim IV	V5888 RT-	Op: **Anti-shipping**

Sgt J W Bradley   +
P/O R H Batten   +
Sgt E D Kennedy   +

T/o 1305 West Raynham. Shot down by Me 109s from
4./JG53 and crashed 1506 into the sea W of Texel.
Sgt Kennedy is buried in Westerschelling General
Cemetery, Terschelling. His two companions have
no known graves and both are commemorated on the Runnymede Memorial.

	114 Sqn	Blenheim IV	Z7309 RT-G	Op: **Anti-shipping**

P/O W G C Beatson   +
P/O H Jones   +
Sgt J Bradshaw RCAF   +

T/o 1305 West Raynham. Hit by flak and finished
off by fighters from 4./JG53, the Blenheim crashed
1507 into the sea off Den Helder, Holland. All are
commemorated on the Runnymede Memorial.

28-29 Oct 1941	15 Sqn	Stirling I	W7429 LS-X	Op: **Plzen**

P/O A W I Jones
Sgt G Mackie
Sgt East
Sgt Sinclair
Sgt Strang
Sgt Barrass
Sgt Sykes
Sgt Bennett

T/o Wyton. Landed Warboys with the port engines
unserviceable. A swing developed as the Stirling
landed and on leaving the runway the main undercarriage unit collapsed, damaging the bomber
beyond repair.

29 Oct 1941	218 Sqn	Wellington IC	X9833 HA-A	**Training**

Sgt Tomkins

Crashed 1250 at Washpit Farm, Rougham,
7 miles N of Swaffham, Norfolk. The accident
was attributed to engine failure and loss of control in the emergency
landing that followed. A fire broke out on impact and one crew member
was slightly hurt.

29-30 Oct 1941	106 Sqn	Hampden I	X3021 ZN-	Op: **Schiphol**

Sgt T L Panting   +
Sgt F R Lamin   +
Sgt G E Bradley   +
Sgt D C Cranston   +

T/o 2150 Coningsby. Crashed into the sea
off the Lincolnshire coast. The body of
Sgt Panting was recovered; his crew are
commemorated on the Runnymede Memorial.

	138 Sqn	Whitley V	Z9223 NF-	Op: **Special Duties**

F/L O J Oettle DFC   +
Sgt H F Rochford DFM RNZAF +
LAC W J Lee   +

T/o Stradishall. Stalled and crashed while
trying to land at base. Sgt Rochford RNZAF
had, until recently, served with 214 Squadron
and details of his award had appeared in the
London Gazette on 24 October 1941. He is buried in Haverhill Cemetery.

Note. It is believed that this was the first loss from 138 Squadron since its
formation from 1419 Flight. Information concerning losses from this Squadron
are difficult to ascertain, due to the secretive nature of its duties and the
sparse details recorded in its Operational Record Books. Despite the unusual
crew composition, A M Form 78 indicates the Whitley was destroyed during the
course of an operational flight.

31 Oct- 1 Nov 1941	7 Sqn	Stirling I	W7444 MG-G	Op: **Bremen**

P/O N E Winch
Sgt L Norvell
Sgt S J McNamara
Sgt N F Durban
Sgt G R Wood
Sgt H Paul
Sgt N J Stronell

T/o 1752 Oakington. Returned early due to
oxygen failure and crashed while trying to
land. No serious injuries reported.

31 Oct-	51 Sqn	Whitley V	Z9141 MH-J	Op: Hamburg

31 Oct-1 Nov 1941

51 Sqn		Whitley V	Z9141 MH-J	Op: Hamburg
F/L E A Barsby	+			T/o 1739 Dishforth. Last heard on w/t at
P/O S D Steel RNZAF	+			2152. Shot down by a night-fighter (Ofw Paul
Sgt J H Knight	+			Gildner, 4./NJG1) and crashed 2350 N of the
F/S E Warburton RCAF	+			dam on the Dutch island of Texel, where the
Sgt V Sature RCAF	+			crew are buried in Den Burg General Cemetery.

51 Sqn		Whitley V	Z9220 MH-V	Op: Hamburg
Sgt C A Guan RAAF	+			T/o 1738 Dishforth. Last heard on w/t at
Sgt W Bourke RAAF	+			0032 calling for help. All are commemorated
Sgt G O Williams	+			on the Runnymede Memorial. Sgt Guan RAAF
F/S A T Bradley RCAF	+			had recently been involved in a serious
Sgt S Burgess	+			crash during operations against Stettin.

76 Sqn		Halifax I	L9602 MP-N	Op: Dunkerque
F/S C S O´Brien RCAF	+			T/o 1917 Middleton St. George. Lost without
P/O N F McLean RNZAF	+			trace. All are commemorated on the Runnymede
Sgt C W Wood	+			Memorial. Prior to his death, F/S Flannigan
Sgt J R Johnson RCAF	+			had twice parachuted to safety.
F/S J Flannigan	+			
P/O F C Brooks RCAF	+			
Sgt J Mycock	+			

77 Sqn		Whitley V	Z6950 KN-	Op: Hamburg
Sgt H E Roberts	+			T/o 1652 Leeming. All are buried in Kiel
Sgt H R Elliott	+			War Cemetery.
Sgt W Partington	+			
F/S J M Boyd RCAF	+			
Sgt J H Stoll RCAF	+			

77 Sqn		Whitley V	Z6953 KN-	Op: Hamburg
Sgt A F C Couch	+			T/o 1656 Leeming. Lost without trace. All
P/O F Simpson	+			are commemorated on the Runnymede Memorial.
Sgt W Lowe	+			
P/O R J A Cleverdon RCAF	+			
Sgt W T Hall RCAF	+			

Note. From the five 4 Group casualties reported, not one man had survived.

115 Sqn		Wellington IC	X9873 KO-P	Op: Bremen
W/O J W B Snowden	pow			T/o 1750 Marham. Attacked by a night-fighter
Sgt H E Woolley RCAF	pow			(Ofw Paul Gildner, 4./NJG1) and crash-landed
Sgt A E Robinson	pow			on the Dutch island of Schiermonnikoog, from
Sgt P V Brazier RCAF	pow			where the crew were taken into captivity.
Sgt A W Clarke RCAF	pow			W/O Snowden was a very senior NCO pilot whose
F/S P J C Darvill	pow			service number suggests a career starting in
				the early 1920s.

1-2 Nov 1941

49 Sqn		Hampden I	AE224 EA-Z	Op: Anti-shipping
S/L D B Drakes	+			T/o 1948 Scampton. Shot down by flak off the
P/O V D Beaney	+			Frisian Islands. All are commemorated on the
F/S W A Watson	+			Runnymede Memorial. This was the first Hampden
P/O W H Cheetham	+			to be lost from a night anti-shipping operation.

78 Sqn		Whitley V	Z9152 EY-	Op: Kiel
S/L J Mercer	+			T/o 1732 Croft. Last heard on w/t at 0116 by
Sgt R F Duggan	+			Linton-on-Ouse. At the time the crew were in
F/L J R Campbell	+			contact with Bircham Newton. Presumed lost
Sgt T P Woodhouse	+			over the North Sea. All are commemorated on
F/S V G Wright	+			the Runnymede Memorial.

83 Sqn		Hampden I	AE358 OL-U	Op: Kiel
P/O A E Lloyd	+			T/o 1955 Scampton. Lost without trace.
Sgt W Powell	+			All are commemorated on the Runnymede Memorial.
Sgt D F Spindler	+			
Sgt J W Butler	+			

1-2 Nov 1941	102 Sqn	Whitley V	Z6749 DY-	Op: Kiel
	P/O V M Albrecht	+	T/o 1740 Topcliffe. Shot down by a night-	
	Sgt J Glover	+	fighter and crashed into the sea off the Dutch	
	Sgt J C Brooks	+	coast. All are commemorated on the Runnymede	
	Sgt P A Champion	+	Memorial.	
	Sgt D C Duguid	+		

	138 Sqn	Halifax II	L9612 NF-	Op: Special Duties
	W/C R Rudkowski	evd	Force-landed 0520 near Tormelilla, Sweden, while	
	F/O T Jasinski	evd	returning from operations over Poland. This was	
	F/O S Krol	evd	the first Mk.II to be lost from an operational	
	Sgt F Sobkowiak	evd	sortie and it is reported that the crew set fire	
			to the aircraft.	

Note. 138 Squadron records make no mention of this loss and the crew details reported have been supplied from a reliable private source in Holland.

2 Nov 1941	61 Sqn	Manchester I	L7520 QR-	Training
	P/O A I. Searby		Force-landed near Roxton, 7 miles NE of Bedford, after the port engine cut and all attempts to feather the airscrew failed.	

4 Nov 1941	88 Sqn	Blenheim IV	T1887 RH-	Training
	Sgt C C A Fuchs		Crash-landed 1100, due to hydraulic failure, near Swanton Morley airfield, Norfolk.	

5 Nov 1941	455 Sqn	Hampden I	AE434 UB-G	Transit
	Sgt Jones	inj	Landed 0740 Coltishall after a successful	
	Sgt Kirk	inj	mining operation. Left Coltishall mid-morning	
	Sgt Baynes	inj	to return to base and while doing so crashed	
	Sgt Shimmons	inj	1126 at Bassingham, 8 miles SW of Lincoln.	

5-6 Nov 1941	83 Sqn	Hampden I	AD850 OL-L	Op: Gardening
	P/O S Hartley	+	T/o 0105 Scampton to lay mines in Kiel Bay.	
	F/S A E Ward	+	Crashed in the sea SE of Mano Island, between	
	Sgt N I Cotterell	+	Hviding and Rejsby on the SW coast of Jutland,	
	F/S R B Turner	+	Denmark. All are buried in Fourfelt Cemetery.	

	109 Sqn	Wellington IC	T2565 HS-	Op: Special Duties
	P/O Bull	pow	T/o 1830 Boscombe Down on a special signals	
	Sgt N W MacKenzie	evd	investigation flight over France. During the	
	P/O Grisman	pow	course of the operation, the starboard airscrew	
	P/O H G Cundall	pow	fell off and the Wellington was abandoned at	
	Sgt J Gannon	pow	2046. P/O Cundall was on attachment from the	
	F/S W G Statham	pow	Telecommunications Research Establishment.	
	Sgt O A Sheffield	pow		

Note. 109 Squadron officially joined the ranks of Bomber Command on 6 August 1942, and at the time of the report shown above, the unit was conducting very sensitive radio trials. Its demise has been recorded on the official bomber loss cards, hence its inclusion in the 1941 analysis.

	144 Sqn	Hampden I	AD846 PL-	Op: Anti-shipping
	P/O D A Baker	pow	T/o North Luffenham. Hit by flak and crashed	
	F/O E L Shea RCAF	+	in the sea off Terschelling. The two airmen who	
	Sgt J S Crossley	pow	died are commemorated on the Runnymede Memorial.	
	Sgt R L Frank	+		

	144 Sqn	Hampden I	AE253 PL-	Op: Anti-shipping
	P/O F L Kidd	+	T/o North Luffenham. Lost in circumstances	
	Sgt P M Reed	pow	similar to those described above. Those who died	
	Sgt E Crowe	+	are buried in Sage War Cemetery.	
	Sgt J B Blackwood	+		

	144 Sqn	Hampden I	AE424 PL-	Op: Anti-shipping
	P/O L N Evans	+	T/o North Luffenham. Lost without trace. All	
	P/O H Walter	+	are commemorated on the Runnymede Memorial.	
	Sgt T G Miskin	+		
	Sgt G H S Bennett	+		

6-7 Nov 1941	50 Sqn	Hampden I	AE427 VN-	Op: Gardening

Sgt J Howett +
P/O P F J Boreham +
Sgt M G Bloomfield +
Sgt H W Fewkes +

T/o 0115 Swinderby. Hit by flak and crashed into Oslo Fjord. All are buried locally in the city's Western Civil Cemetery.

7 Nov 1941	226 Sqn	Blenheim IV	Z7455 MQ-	Training

Sgt F Emmett

Crashed 1600 while landing at Long Kesh airfield in Northern Ireland.

Chapter 10

Berlin

7-8 November 1941

No commander wishes to be associated with failure. Those that are tend to be treated unkindly by historians, and the accolades, oft as not, are reserved for those leaders who are perceived to have been successful.

But, going hand-in-hand with the kudos that awaits the successful commander is the lurking spectre of failure and, as our proud history shows, many prominent figures have been summarily dismissed in the aftermath of operations that fell short of expectation.

Air Marshal Sir Richard Peirse does not come into the latter category, but there are no doubts whatsoever that the events on 7-8 November 1941, and the searching enquiry that followed, were instrumental in causing his departure as Commander-in-Chief from High Wycombe early in January 1942.

On the night in question, 392 bombers were detailed for raids on mainland Germany, the channel ports of Oostende and Boulogne and a minelaying operation in Norwegian waters.

The numbers involved represented another record for the Command, exceeding by nineteen the record set less than four weeks previously. On that occasion, the end result had been disappointing with sixteen bombers lost, or destroyed in accidents associated with the various raids.

Originally, it was intended that Berlin would be raided by over 200 aircraft, but weather predictions were less than favourable. Strong winds and icing were forecast for large areas of northern Europe through which the bombers would have to pass.

However, Sir Richard was adamant that the operation should continue, and his decision provoked a strong protest from 5 Group. For the Hampden squadrons, Berlin was always a high risk target, even when the weather was at its best, and now in light of the current forecast, it would be suicidal to commit these aircraft to the German capital.

After some discussion, High Wycombe agreed to the removal of the 5 Group contingent, which instead would now visit Köln.

With fifty-five crews assigned to Mannheim plus the hotchpotch of secondary targets requiring their share of the bombers still available, the Berlin force was eventually reduced to 169 aircraft.

During the course of the next twelve hours the bomber crews strove to the best of their ability to carry out their instructions. It was an unequal battle waged between man and nature, resulting in less than half of those sent to Berlin from getting anywhere near the German capital.

By late morning on the 8th, it was all too painfully obvious that the operation had been a failure. Emerging from the de-briefing statements was a depressing picture of aiming points being obscured by cloud thus preventing any clear bombing results.

But, even more alarming was the fact that thirty-seven aircraft were missing. Never before had Bomber Command been notified of casualties of this magnitude.

At first there were few indications to explain such a high casualty figure. Wireless transmissions from three 102 Squadron Whitleys, that failed to return to Topcliffe had been picked up by various direction finding stations, these continuing almost until first light.

Therefore, it was a fairly safe assumption that all three crews were down in the sea.

But these, and the few others like them, were the exception and for the time being the fate that had befallen the majority could only be a matter of conjecture.

Reaction to the night's losses was swift in coming. The War Cabinet met and after some deliberation decided that the bombing offensive should be strictly limited, at least for the immediate future, while present policies were given a thorough review. This decision, signalled via the Air Ministry to High Wycombe, virtually placed Bomber Command on hold for the rest of the winter.

Meanwhile, in his preliminary report to the Air Staff following the events of 7-8 November, the Commander-in-Chief placed much of the blame on the inclement weather. At first this was accepted, but murmurings of disquiet persisted and by early December several amendments had been added to his original findings. None of these riders, however, fully satisfied the Air Staff, or the astute Secretary of State for Air, Sir Archibald Sinclair, who insisted that the Prime Minister be appraised forthwith.

What followed is now history and Sir Richard cleared his desk on 8 January 1942. His departure from the office that he had held for fourteen difficult months can only be regarded as less than happy.

Most certainly his cause was not helped by the extremely critical Butt Report, but the principal factor that determined his fate was the long run of heavy losses. Casualties on the scale suffered since mid-July could only be justified if these were commensurate with worthwhile results being achieved and, quite patently, this was not the case.

These final remarks should not be taken as a general criticism of the airmen of Bomber

Command. On their young and mainly inexperienced shoulders rested the aspirations of
any commander-in-chief. To the best of their
ability they had given, and would continue
to give, their all in the unrelenting night
bombing campaign.

7-8 Nov 1941	7 Sqn	Stirling I	N3677 MG-J	Op: Berlin

7 Sqn		Stirling I
F/O D B van Buskirk RCAF	+
Sgt J E Chadwick	+
Sgt S J Fenson	+
P/O G E Sweeney	+
Sgt D H Stronach	+
Sgt C Murch	+
Sgt D G Pack	+

N3677 MG-J   **Op: Berlin**

T/o 1731 Oakington. Last heard on w/t at 2044. Reported shot down by a night-fighter operating near Duisburg. All are buried in the Reichswald Forest War Cemetery.

7 Sqn		Stirling I
Sgt J W C Morris RAAF	+
Sgt M S Jacobs	+
Sgt C Walton	+
Sgt B Wallwork	+
Sgt P Johnstone	+
Sgt E O Brooks	+
Sgt G H Chesman	+

N6091 MG-K   **Op: Berlin**

T/o 1742 Oakington. Last heard on w/t at 2200. Shot down by flak and crashed between Hekelingen and Spijkenisse (Zuid Holland), 14 km SW of Rotterdam, where the crew are buried in the city's Crooswijk General Cemetery.

35 Sqn		Halifax I
P/O G Whitaker	+
Sgt R R Drummond	pow
Sgt E R Thomas	pow
Sgt A R Kilminster	pow
Sgt R F Thompson	+
F/S C R Witcher	pow
F/O M O Stephens RNZAF	pow

L9603 TL-P   **Op: Rover Patrol**

T/o 2007 Linton-on-Ouse on a Rover Patrol of the Ruhr with Essen as an objective. Shot down by a night-fighter (Oblt Herbert Lütje, III./NJG1) and crashed 0002 in the Imbos Forest (Gelderland) near Rozendaal, Holland. Those that died are buried in a private cemetery in the grounds of Rozendaal Castle.

51 Sqn		Whitley V
Sgt A W MacMurray RCAF	pow
Sgt A J Robottom	pow
Sgt C Kelly RCAF	pow
Sgt J H Telfer	pow
Sgt S J T Wilkins	pow

Z6839 MH-O   **Op: Berlin**

T/o 2229 Dishforth. Crashed 0615 between Bierum and 't Zandt (Groningen), two small towns some 8 km NW of Delfzijl, Holland.

51 Sqn		Whitley V
S/L P G S Dickenson	+
Sgt B S Walley	pow
P/O D A Simpson RCAF	+
Sgt A V Carpenter	+
Sgt W M Chambers RCAF	+

Z9130 MH-   **Op: Berlin**

T/o 2221 Dishforth. Presumed lost over the sea. The pilot and his RCAF observer are buried in Sage War Cemetery, but Sgt Carpenter and Sgt Chambers RCAF have no known graves.

57 Sqn		Wellington IC
Sgt S D C Gray	+
Sgt W F P Sellers RCAF	+
P/O E E Brown	+
Sgt E I L Grego	+
Sgt R F Whitton	+
Sgt W M Cullerne	+

Z8903 DX-   **Op: Rover Patrol**

T/o 2005 Feltwell on a Rover Patrol with Münster as its objective. Lost without trace. All are commemorated on the Runnymede Memorial.

57 Sqn		Wellington IC
Sgt A H T Cook RAAF	+
Sgt A McKillop	+
Sgt A C Crease	pow
Sgt J H D Howes	pow
Sgt A A Thomson	+
Sgt J L Ledsham	pow

Z8985 DX-   **Op: Rover Patrol**

T/o 2010 Feltwell on a Rover Patrol with Münster as its objective. Crashed near Haastrecht (Zuid Holland), 4 km SSE of Gouda. Those who died are buried in the Canadian War Cemetery at Bergen op Zoom.

58 Sqn		Whitley V
P/O E G Mounsey	+
Sgt K C Carr RCAF	+
P/O K B McGoun RCAF	+
F/S F M Legere RCAF	+
Sgt A G Kinnear	+

Z6818 GE-N   **Op: Rover Patrol**

T/o 1946 Linton-on-Ouse on a Rover Patrol of the Ruhr area and with Essen as an objective. Lost without trace. All are commemorated on the Runnymede Memorial.

7-8 Nov	58 Sqn	Whitley V	Z6972 GE-P	Op: Berlin

7-8 Nov
1941

58 Sqn		Whitley V
P/O K M Tuckfield	+
Sgt D Rowley-Blake	+
P/O C T Lane RCAF	+
Sgt A Scott	+
Sgt H F Stentiford RCAF	+

Z6972 GE-P   Op: Berlin
T/o 2242 Linton-on-Ouse. Believed down in the sea at 0742 in position 5417N 0135E. All are commemorated on the Runnymede Memorial.

58 Sqn		Whitley V
P/O D E W Brown	+
Sgt E F Gresham	+
Sgt B J Monk	+
Sgt N Fenton	+
Sgt J H Atkin	+

Z9205 GE-   Op: Berlin
T/o 2250 Linton-on-Ouse. Last heard on w/t at 0422, when the Whitley was plotted at 5402N 0947E. All are buried in Kiel War Cemetery.

75 Sqn		Wellington IC
P/O W R Methven	pow
Sgt J C McK Gibson RNZAF	+
P/O D A Webster RCAF	pow
Sgt A B Frisby	pow
Sgt T P Duffy RNZAF	pow
Sgt R Pattison	pow

X9951 AA-   Op: Berlin
T/o Feltwell. Sgt Gibson RNZAF is buried in the Reichswald Forest War Cemetery. It is reported that P/O Methven was repatriated before the end of hostilities.

75 Sqn		Wellington IC
Sgt J W Black RNZAF	+
Sgt T H Gray RNZAF	+
P/O E Lloyd RNZAF	+
Sgt L C Green	+
Sgt J D Thompson	+
Sgt C T Black	+

X9976 AA-   Op: Berlin
T/o Feltwell. Shot down by a night-fighter (Oblt Helmut Lent, 4./NJG1) and crashed 0121 at Oldeboorn (Friesland), 5 km E of Akkrum, Holland. All are buried in the Canadian War Cemetery at Bergen op Zoom.

78 Sqn		Whitley V
Sgt J W Bell	+
P/O G M McCombe	+
Sgt G T Webb	+
Sgt D Cameron	+
Sgt R Boucher	+

Z6948 EY-F   Op: Berlin
T/o 2231 Croft. Shot down by a night-fighter (Oblt Ludwig Becker, 4./NJG1) and crashed 0630 between Oudemirdum and Nijemirdum (Friesland), 20 km SSW of Sneek, Holland. Sgt Bell lies in Lemmer General Cemetery; the rest of the crew are buried in Nijemirdum General Cemetery.

78 Sqn		Whitley V
Sgt E J Sargent	+
Sgt E W Penn	pow
P/O J V Saunders RCAF	pow
Sgt T Hall	pow
Sgt T Paterson	pow
Sgt E G S H Freeman	pow

Z9151 EY-   Op: Berlin
T/o 2227 Croft. Sgt Sargent is buried in Berlin at the 1939-1945 War Cemetery.

99 Sqn		Wellington IC
P/O C G Gilmore	+
Sgt G W T Wiggs	+
Sgt I G Harrowby RNZAF	+
Sgt F H Sanders	+
Sgt A C F Harrop	+
Sgt E R Schofield	+

T2516 LN-   Op: Berlin
T/o 1728 Waterbeach. Crashed at Beilen (Drenthe), 16 km SSW of Assen, Holland. All are buried in Beilen General Cemetery.

99 Sqn		Wellington IC
F/L J P Dickinson	pow
Sgt R J Bell RAAF	+
F/O P R Searcy RAAF	pow
Sgt R B Martin RCAF	pow
Sgt A Featherstone RCAF	pow
Sgt J H Bowman	pow

T2554 LN-F   Op: Berlin
T/o 1721 Waterbeach. P/O Bell RAAF is buried in Becklingen War Cemetery, Soltau.

99 Sqn		Wellington IC
P/O W D Moore	pow
F/L H H Henderson	pow
F/O H A Goodwin	pow
Sgt A Mackenzie	+
Sgt R Dean	+
Sgt M G Bowen RCAF	pow

X9739 LN-   Op: Berlin
T/o 1722 Waterbeach. The two airmen who died are buried at Soltau in Becklingen War Cemetery.

7-8 Nov 1941

| 101 Sqn | Wellington IC | R1701 SR-K | Op: Berlin |

101 Sqn		Wellington IC
P/O W D C Hardie		+
Sgt B J Wrampling		+
P/O A L Miller RCAF		+
Sgt W Buchan		+
Sgt W Watson		+
Sgt R A Berry		+

R1701 SR-K — Op: Berlin
T/o 1733 Oakington. Last heard on w/t at 2015 indicating a ditching was imminent. At the time the Wellington was approaching the Dutch coast and three RN MTBs were sent out to search for the crew. No trace could be found and all are commemorated on the Runnymede Memorial.

102 Sqn		Whitley V
Sgt R C Matthews		+
Sgt R O Bryant RAAF		+
Sgt E M Leftly RCAF		+
Sgt R Brown		+
Sgt W Miller		+

Z6796 DY- — Op: Berlin
T/o 2214 Topcliffe. In response to a call asking for a bearing, Horsham responded at 0726, but received no acknowledgement. All are commemorated on the Runnymede Memorial.

102 Sqn		Whitley V
P/O B B P Roy		+
Sgt D R Pritchard		+
Sgt K Harwood-Smith		+
Sgt S Thomson		+
Sgt P H Stanton		+

Z6820 DY- — Op: Berlin
T/o 2203 Topcliffe. Last heard on w/t at 0743 calling for help. Presumed lost over the sea. All are commemorated on the panels of the Runnymede Memorial.

102 Sqn		Whitley V
Sgt T H Thorley		+
P/O J C A Allchin		+
Sgt V L Brown RAAF		+
Sgt J A Steeves RCAF		+
Sgt W C Clarke		+

Z9128 DY- — Op: Berlin
T/o 2207 Topcliffe. In response to a request for a bearing, the necessary information was transmitted at 0642, at which time the Whitley was believed to be nearly 100 km N of Borkum and on course for the east coast. All are commemorated on the Runnymede Memorial.

103 Sqn		Wellington IC
F/L E V Lawson		pow
Sgt C W Onions		+
Sgt A W Mills		evd
Sgt H Mossley		pow
Sgt W S C Partridge		pow
Sgt C L Williams		pow

X9794 PM- — Op: Mannheim
T/o 1827 Elsham Wolds. Crashed in the vicinity of Choloy (Meurthe-et-Moselle), 28 km W of Nancy, France. Sgt Onions is buried in Choloy War Cemetery.

106 Sqn		Hampden I
P/O D C Firth		+
Sgt W King		+
Sgt A Archer		pow
Sgt C Walton		pow

P1290 ZN- — Op: Gardening
T/o 0140 Coningsby to lay mines in Oslo Fjord. Hit by flak and crashed in the target area. The two airmen who died are buried in Oslo Western Civil Cemetery.

106 Sqn		Hampden I
F/L J Henderson DFC		pow
Sgt P A Ingram		+
Sgt J W Steven		pow
F/O C B Randall		+

AD760 ZN- — Op: Gardening
T/o 0025 Coningsby. Lost in circumstances similar to those reported above. F/O Randall is buried in Oslo Western Civil Cemetery, Sgt Ingram has no known grave.

106 Sqn		Hampden I
F/L T B Herd DFC		+
F/O B G McIver DFC, RCAF		+
Sgt H Sell DFM		+
Sgt S J H Jones		+

AD932 ZN- — Op: Gardening
T/o 0105 Coningsby. Last heard on w/t at 0845 calling for help. Believed down in the sea 48 miles E of Wick. Sgt Jones is buried on Kirkwall in the Orkney Islands; his three companions are commemorated on the Runnymede Memorial.

142 Sqn		Wellington IV
Sgt S A Hart		+
F/S T V S Wiggins RCAF		pow
Sgt F W Day		pow
F/S P W Duckers		pow
Sgt H J Gibson		pow
Sgt C L Dennes RNZAF		pow

Z1211 QT- — Op: Mannheim
T/o 1936 Binbrook. Shot down by a night-fighter (Oblt Egmont Prinz zur Lippe Weissenfeld of 4./NJG1) and crashed in the sea off Bergen-aan-Zee, Holland. Sgt Hart has no known grave.

7-8 Nov 1941	144 Sqn	Hampden I	AE238 PL-	Op: **Köln**

144 Sqn   Hampden I   AE238 PL-   Op: Köln

Sgt Woodhall
Sgt Pomroy
Sgt Tod
Sgt Lynch

T/o North Luffenham. Hit by flak and on return the Hampden crash-landed in the vicinity of Litchfield, Staffordshire.

149 Sqn   Wellington IC   X9878 OJ-A   Op: Berlin

Sgt S W Dane   +
Sgt P I Leeman   +
Sgt A C A Davis   +
Sgt H R Crowe RCAF   +
Sgt F Jenkinson   pow
Sgt J C Pengelly   +

T/o 1726 Mildenhall. Those who died are buried in the Reichswald Forest War Cemetery.

150 Sqn   Wellington IC   R1606 JN-G   Op: Mannheim

Sgt L J Atkins   +
Sgt V G Knighton   +
Sgt R A Bramley   +
Sgt S G T Farman   +
Sgt H Evans   +
Sgt W F Parsons   +

T/o 1820 Snaith. Believed crashed in the sea off the Dutch coast. Sgt Evans and Sgt Parsons are buried in Amsterdam New Eastern Cemetery; the rest of the crew are commemorated on the Runnymede Memorial.

214 Sqn   Wellington IC   X3206 BU-   Op: Berlin

P/O L B Ercolani
Sgt Hamilton
Sgt McLennan
Sgt Holdsworth
Sgt Weller
Sgt Fry

T/o Stradishall. Hit by flak which set light to the incendiaries and the fire was soon out of control. Distress calls were transmitted, after which the Wellington was put down in the sea. Three days later, the crew came ashore near Ventnor on the Isle of Wight.

Note. P/O Ercolani was connected with the Ercol Furniture Company. He was subsequently decorated with the DSO, Gazetted on 6 January 1942.

218 Sqn   Wellington IC   Z1069 HA-J   Op: Berlin

Sgt J R C McGlashan   pow
Sgt W Fraser   pow
Sgt A H Bowater   pow
Sgt R S C Stewart   pow
Sgt J Dobson   pow
Sgt F C Adams   pow

T/o 1733 Marham.

300 Sqn   Wellington IV   R1705 BH-U   Op: Mannheim

Sgt K Sobczak   pow
Sgt B Bilinski   pow
P/O P Kowalski   pow
Sgt J Budzynski   evd
Sgt S Konarzewski   pow
P/O Z Groyecki   evd

T/o 1839 Hemswell.

300 Sqn   Wellington IV   Z1271 BH-A   Op: Mannheim

Sgt P Nowakowski   pow
P/O W Radwanski   evd
F/O M Taras   evd
Sgt H Kudelko   pow
Sgt G Chrzanowski   int
Sgt Iwanowicz   pow

T/o 1843 Hemswell. Sgt Chrzanowski died on 15 June 1942, while being held in Vichy France. It is believed he is buried at Nice.

301 Sqn   Wellington IV   Z1277 GR-Z   Op: Mannheim

Sgt H Bolcewicz   pow
Sgt Z Lenczewski   pow
F/O W Kolanowski   pow
Sgt A Szczcpanowski   pow
Sgt B Wroblewski   pow
Sgt T Moryn   pow

T/o 1847 Hemswell. F/O Kolanowski was shot while trying to escape from Sagan.

7-8 Nov 1941	304 Sqn	Wellington IC	R1215 NZ-	Op: **Mannheim**

304 Sqn   Wellington IC   R1215 NZ-   Op: **Mannheim**

P/O T Blicharz   pow
P/O W Rekszczyc   pow
P/O J T Mondschein   pow
P/O J Jaworosiuk   pow
Sgt Lewandowski   pow
Sgt S Krzawiecki   pow

T/o 1803 Lindholme. Last heard on w/t at 2055 indicating that the target had been bombed. It is reported that P/O Mondschein was shot on 25 March 1944, following the mass break out from Sagan. He is buried in Poland at the Old Garrison Cemetery at Poznan.

405 Sqn   Wellington II   W5553 LQ-D   Op: **Berlin**

F/S A L D Hassan RCAF   +
P/O M K Solheim RCAF   +
Sgt R D Killin RCAF   +
Sgt C C Hynam   +
F/S C H Bell RCAF   +
Sgt G A McLeod RCAF   +

T/o 2321 Pocklington. Last heard on w/t at 0244 indicating the mission had been accomplished. All are buried at Soltau in Becklingen War Cemetery.

455 Sqn   Hampden I   P1201 UB-P   Op: **Rover Patrol**

P/O J A C Gordon RAAF   pow
P/O J D Cordwell   pow
Sgt M N Stokes   pow
Sgt E Holt   pow

T/o 1840 Swinderby on a Rover Patrol towards Köln. It is believed that P/O Gordon RAAF was the first Australian, serving in the RAAF, to be taken prisoner while serving with an RAAF bomber squadron.

455 Sqn   Hampden I   AE243 UB-B   Op: **Rover Patrol**

Sgt M A Jenkins   +
Sgt D R Rawlings   +
Sgt G A McGarvey   +
F/S K Morris   +

T/o 1830 Swinderby on a Rover Patrol towards Köln. All are buried in Heverlee War Cemetery, Belgium.

Chapter 11

In Limbo

8 November to 31 December 1941

Within twenty-four hours of sustaining the worst losses of the war so far, the Command was back over Germany, this time visiting the industrial centre of Essen. Some fires were started, but as the entire force did not exceed sixty aircraft, and with less than forty claiming to have reached Essen, little in the way of concentrated bombing was achieved.

Casualties were again high, considering the small numbers of aircraft employed. Six bombers missing from the main attack and two others lost from minor operations. Research since the war indicates that at least five of the missing crews were shot down by night fighters, thus providing chilling evidence as to how effective the Luftwaffe had become since General Kammhuber's arrival earlier in the year.

The order limiting Bomber Command activity took effect from mid-November and would remain in place for the rest of Sir Richard Pierse's tenure. Raids on coastal targets became the norm, with only occasional visits to the Ruhr.

Such restrictions, however, could not guarantee that losses would decrease and, taking 15-16 November as a convenient starting point, statistics show that 141 aircraft were written off in the remaining weeks of the year, the majority as a direct result of enemy action. Both Kiel and Emden were raided on this night, in the wake of which fourteen bombers had been added to the growing list of casualties. It had been a night of very severe frost and at least four of the fourteen crashed as a direct result of the heavy icing. Two, both Stirlings, were destroyed in departure accidents at Warboys and Oakington, while two Wellingtons crashed later as they tried to land.

Bombing successes were few and far between though the citizens of Hamburg underwent a disturbing night at the end of November when a force totalling nearly 200 aircraft raided the city in clear moonlit conditions.

A tremendous flak barrage greeted the raiders, but the majority pressed on through the bursting shells to deliver a good attack which left a number of large fires burning. The toll in achieving this was heavy; twenty aircraft lost and another two written off in a minor excursion to Emden. Seven from the twenty had quite simply disappeared without trace, while at least three crews which strayed over Kiel paid dearly for their mistake.

December was no less easy, despite the predominance of attacks being on the channel ports. Brest was heavily bombed by day on the 18th, and again on the 30th, both raids being strongly supported by fighter escorts. Nonetheless, the Luftwaffe claimed four Stirlings and a Manchester destroyed during the attacks on the 18th, and though their efforts came to nothing on the 30th, two Halifaxes were downed by flak and a third was shot about so badly that its crew were obliged to ditch south of the Lizard Point.

A third daylight raid during December also caused the Command heavy losses. Coming on the 27th, it witnessed the first Combined Operations raid of the war. The target was the German garrison on Vaagasö off the coast of Norway. It was a sharp engagement, during which the Commandos achieved their objective and were taken off by the navy with only light casualties. The bomber crews paid a heavy price with only one Hampden pilot surviving from a total of six Blenheims and two Hampdens destroyed. This fortunate airman owes his life to the crew of a passing destroyer which noticed his desperate plight and snatched him from the water.

In view of the events here reported, and the general tone set throughout the year, it would be wrong to imply that 1941 had been a good year for Bomber Command. True, the constant attention paid to the channel ports had played a useful part in thwarting the ambitions of the German High Command. The effectiveness of the three capital ships had been reduced, while the resources deployed for their protection would have served the enemy better elsewhere.

It is also true that considerable damage had been inflicted on Hamburg, Kiel and the inland port of Bremen, but apart from one or two isolated incidences, the Ruhr, which was regarded as the engine house of Germany's industrial power, had escaped serious harm.

Visits to Berlin, although giving a psychological boost to our populance which had suffered greatly in the Luftwaffe raids on our major towns and cities, had been quite unproductive.

All was not however lost. Adolf Hitler had effectively signalled Germany's eventual defeat when he declared war on America, just three days after the greatest industrial nation in the world was stung to the quick by Japan's surprise attack on Pearl Harbor. It is interesting to note that Stalin did not reciprocate by supporting America, the Russian dictator deciding to stay his hand and await developments.

Hope was also forthcoming in the continuing expansion of Bomber Command. Within the two Wellington groups improved designs were reaching the squadrons, while sufficient numbers of Halifaxes and Stirlings allowed a gradual build up in heavy bomber strength.

Whitleys were discarded by 10 Squadron in favour of the Halifax and 149 Squadron gave up its faithful Wellingtons and took in their place the Stirling.

Within 5 Group the Manchester, despite its shortcomings, was about to replace the long serving Hampden in two squadrons, but it was

the arrival on Christmas Eve of the first production Lancasters at Waddington which was to provide Bomber Command with its first real winner for the testing years ahead.

44 Squadron was ordered to bring the new aircraft to operational readiness and its potential as a key weapon in the Command's armoury was very soon realised.

Thus, it can be said, December 1941 proved to be one of the crucial turning points of the Second World War.

8 Nov 1941	97 Sqn	Manchester I	L7466 OF-N	Op: Air Sea Rescue
	F/L C P D Price DFC	+	T/o 1320 Coningsby to search for crews reported	
	P/O G H J Pickering	+	missing from the previous night's operations.	
	Sgt N J Weston RAAF	+	Last seen at 1600 in the search area, over the	
	F/S C Stanley DFM	+	North Sea. All are commemorated on the Runnymede	
	SGT A R A Dexter	+	Memorial. F/S Stanley gained his award for	
	SGT C R Bronson RCAF	+	service with 44 Squadron.	
	Sgt F W Manners	+		

8-9 Nov 1941	44 Sqn	Hampden I	AE377 KM-	Op: Dunkerque
	P/O W J Frost	+	T/o 1730 Waddington. Lost without trace. All	
	P/O F L Smith	+	are commemorated on the Runnymede Memorial.	
	Sgt T Copsey	+		
	P/O J Lindsay	+		

	49 Sqn	Hampden I	P1206 EA-K	Op: Intruder
	W/O C A Saunders DFM	+	T/o 1714 Scampton on an intruder sortie in	
	Sgt J M D'Arcy	+	the Bocholt area. Shot down by a night-fighter	
	Sgt S G Mullenger	+	and crashed 2107 into the IJsselmeer. Both	
	Sgt J E Kehoe	+	pilots are buried in Bergen General Cemetery;	
			their crew have no known graves.	

	51 Sqn	Whitley V	Z6567 MH-Z	Op: Essen
	S/L H F McCullagh	+	T/o 1752 Dishforth. Shot down by a night-fighter	
	P/O J A Nutt	+	(Oblt Egmont Prinz zur Lippe Weissenfeld, 4./NJG1	
	Sgt V F D Kirk	+	and crashed 2303 near Barsingerhorn, 20 km SSE of	
	Sgt J L Holloway	+	Den Helder, Holland. All are buried in Bergen or	
	Sgt C D Thomas	+	Zoom War Cemetery.	

	75 Sqn	Wellington IC	X9628 AA-	Op: Essen
	Sgt K M Smith	pow	T/o Feltwell. Crashed near Krefeld, where	
	Sgt W F French	pow	Sgt Thain was first buried in the Haupt Friedhof	
	Sgt L C Howe	pow	Since 1945, his remains have been taken to the	
	Sgt R J Rugg	inj	Reichswald Forest War Cemetery where they now	
	Sgt L G Eggar	pow	rest close to the grave of Sgt Rugg, who died	
	Sgt G M Thain	+	from his wounds on 15 November.	

	75 Sqn	Wellington IC	X9977 AA-	Op: Essen
	Sgt G S Nunn	+	T/o Feltwell. Shot down by a night-fighter	
	Sgt T Y Wyllie RNZAF	+	(Lt Werner Rowlin, III./NJG1) and crashed 2136	
	Sgt R Dundas	+	at IJzevoorde (Gelderland), 3 km E of Doetinchem	
	Sgt T E Elliott RCAF	+	Holland. All are buried in Loolaan General	
	Sgt A H Harrison RNZAF	+	Cemetery.	
	Sgt W Massey	+		

	75 Sqn	Wellington IC	Z8942 AA-	Op: Essen
	Sgt J S Wilson RNZAF	+	T/o Feltwell. Hit by flak and crashed 2215 at	
	P/O R O Foster RNZAF	+	Zuidland (Zuid Holland), 20 km SW of Rotterdam.	
	P/O R L O Ryder RAAF	+	Those who died are buried in the city's Crooswijk	
	Sgt J H Reid	+	General Cemetery. The sole survivor, Sgt Hope	
	Sgt Sir C T H Mappin	+	RNZAF, was killed on 19 April 1945 by Allied	
	Sgt L B H Hope RNZAF	pow	fighter bombers which attacked the prisoner of	
			war column in which he was marching. He is	

buried in the 1939-1945 War Cemetery at Berlin. Sgt Sir C T H Mappin was the 4th Baronet and son of T W and V M Mappin.

8-9 Nov 1941	102 Sqn		Whitley V	Z9212 DY-	Op: **Essen**

8-9 Nov 1941 — **102 Sqn** — Whitley V — Z9212 DY- — Op: **Essen**

Sgt G W McDonald +
F/O T H Taylor pow
Sgt A L Lord RCAF pow
Sgt T Rogers +
Sgt I Stein RCAF +

T/o 1728 Topcliffe. Shot down by a night-fighter and crashed in the vicinity of Köln, where those who died were buried in the Süd Friedhof. Since the war, their bodies have been taken to Rheinberg War Cemetery.

408 Sqn — Hampden I — AE433 EQ-D — Op: **Essen**

P/O E L Houghton RNZAF pow
P/O J C Monkhouse RCAF pow
Sgt A J Gallan pow
Sgt J E Woodward pow

T/o 1719 Syerston. Shot down by a night-fighter (Oblt Willi Dimter, III./NJG1) and crashed 2230 at Maasbree (Noord Brabant), 26 km NE of Helmond, Holland.

9-10 Nov 1941 — **9 Sqn** — Wellington III — X3280 WS- — Op: **Hamburg**

P/O H V Wilgar-Robinson +
Sgt R B Fielding +
Sgt R B How +
Sgt G H Dartnall +
Sgt W Smithson +
Sgt K Quick +

T/o 1730 Honington. Last heard on w/t at 2100 cancelling a distress call. Subsequently, the Wellington crashed in the Waddenzee off Vlieland, where P/O Wilgar-Robinson is buried. Apart from Sgt Dartnall, who is buried in Lemvig Cemetery, Denmark, the rest of the crew are commemorated on the Runnymede Memorial.

9 Sqn — Wellington III — X3352 WS- — Op: **Hamburg**

Sgt W E Pendleton inj
Sgt J Cartwright inj
Sgt A N Jenkins RCAF inj
Sgt H G Cawdron inj
Sgt W C Sadler inj
Sgt D S Nicholas inj

T/o 1731 Honington. Hit by flak in the port engine while N of the city. Reduced to a single engine, Sgt Pendleton brought his crew home, only to crash 2210 into a wood as he tried to land at East Wretham.

144 Sqn — Hampden I — AE311 PL- — Op: **Hamburg**

Sgt Nightingale
Sgt Sparks
Sgt Gailey
Sgt Ward
AC1 G Roberts +
AC2 F G Malin +

T/o North Luffenham. Crashed 2343 on return to base. The Hampden swung on touch down and collided with the airfield control caravan. The bomber crew escaped with little more than a severe shaking, but two airmen in the caravan were killed and a third injured.

408 Sqn — Hampden I — AE438 EQ-N — Op: **Oostende**

P/O J C Wilson RCAF +
P/O E B Te M Robertson + RNZAF
Sgt D F W Norton +
Sgt D V Markall +

T/o 1755 Syerston. Crashed near Westkerke (West Vlaanderen), 9 km SE of Oostende. All are buried in Westkerke Churchyard.

11 Nov 1941 — **49 Sqn** — Hampden I — X3135 EA- — **Training**

Sgt K Bryant +
AC2 W H Fulcher +

Crashed 1616 at Hackthorne Hall, 2 miles NE of Scampton airfield. The accident happened when the pilot turned steeply to the left and lost control. The Hampden exploded on impact.

115 Sqn — Wellington III — X3394 KO- — **Training**

Sgt G D H Dutton +
Sgt L H Pitt RCAF +
Sgt B E Dew +
Sgt R O Newbury +
Sgt R C Knott +
Sgt J L L Arthur +
F/L H S Mellows +

Crashed 1203 at Carol House Farm near Swaffham, Norfolk, during fuel consumption tests and cross country flying practice. F/L Mellows was a Medical Officer, who had accompanied the crew.

15 Nov 1941 — **88 Sqn** — Blenheim IV — Z7484 RH- — **Training**

Sgt K M Elkins

Collided with Blenheim Z7361, captained by Sgt K Smart RNZAF, while taxying at Swanton Morley airfield. Z7361 was repaired, only to be destroyed in a flying accident at Bicester on 21 December 1942, following transfer to 13 OTU.

15-16 Nov 1941

| 7 Sqn | | Stirling I | W7445 MG-V | Op: Kiel |

Sgt I H Hunter RNZAF — inj
Sgt A C Bennett RAAF — +
Sgt Helliwell
Sgt W D Topping — inj
Sgt A J Hansel — inj
Sgt T Bentham — inj
Sgt Hudson

T/o Oakington and crashed almost immediately into a house. Sgt Hunter RNZAF died shortly after the accident from his injuries. Glazed ice on the windscreen was a contributory factor in this crash.

| 15 Sqn | | Stirling I | N6097 LS-C | Op: Kiel |

P/O S P Edgehill
Sgt McMillan
Sgt Gahan
Sgt R J Cook
Sgt Sullivan
Sgt C J Du Preez
Sgt Sawyer

T/o 2220 Warboys but due to the mainplanes being covered in frost, the Stirling failed to gain height and crashed just beyond the airfield, clipping a line of trees in the process. The crew scrambled clear and soon afterwards the bomb load exploded, completely wrecking the aircraft.

| 50 Sqn | | Hampden I | P1152 VN- | Op: Gardening |

Sgt Young — inj
Sgt D McG Symes — inj
Sgt Bernard — inj
Sgt R St C Neale — +

T/o 2032 Swinderby for a mining operation in the nectarines region. Returned early due to icing, but the crew strayed from track and crashed 0200 into a hillside at Guisborough, 4 miles SE of Middlesbrough on Guisborough Moor, Yorkshire.

| 99 Sqn | | Wellington IC | L7873 LN-J | Op: Emden |

F/S T C B Patterson RNZAF — +
Sgt D E Hall — +
Sgt L R Townsend — +
Sgt R L Cooke — +
Sgt B J Dermody RCAF — +
Sgt W A McAllen RAAF — +

T/o 1720 Waterbeach. Lost without trace. All are commemorated on the Runnymede Memorial. As will be seen from the crew composition, three Commonwealth air forces were represented in this crew, which although not unique was quite rare.

| 99 Sqn | | Wellington IC | X9740 LN-O | Op: Kiel |

Sgt Russell — inj
Sgt Innes — inj
Sgt May — inj
Sgt Dipple — inj
Sgt Swann — inj
Sgt Humphries — inj

T/o 2116 Waterbeach. Turned back due to severe icing and while preparing to land, the aircraft crash-landed at Wilburton, 5 miles SW of Ely, Cambridgeshire. It is believed that the icing effected the instruments and the altimeter was showing a false reading.

| 99 Sqn | | Wellington IC | Z8975 LN-X | Op: Emden |

Sgt G A Farmery — +
Sgt F Peever RCAF — +
Sgt J O M Lobo — +
Sgt J Morris — +
Sgt R North — +
Sgt A E Nosworthy — +

T/o 1727 Waterbeach. Signalled target attacked, after which it is presumed to have crashed in the sea. All are commemorated on the Runnymede Memorial. Sgt Lobo's parents lived in Ceylon.

| 115 Sqn | | Wellington IC | X9888 KO-F | Op: Emden |

Sgt A C Homes — +
Sgt J M Horsley — +
Sgt R H Huckett — +
Sgt R W Platten — +
Sgt G R Ruscoe — +
Sgt F S Thomas — +

T/o 1732 Marham. Lost without trace. All are commemorated on the Runnymede Memorial.

| 115 Sqn | | Wellington IC | Z8848 KO-H | Op: Kiel |

P/O Stock
Sgt Weller
P/O Maher
Sgt Baker
Sgt Suckling
Sgt Roche

T/o 2148 Marham. Ditched 10 miles E of Whitby, Yorkshire, while returning to base. The crew were rescued by a destroyer crewed by Norwegian sailors.

15-16 Nov 1941	149 Sqn	Wellington IC	R1627 OJ-		Op: **Emden**

```
15-16 Nov    149 Sqn         Wellington IC    R1627 OJ-                Op: Emden
1941         Sgt R Bramhall            +       T/o Mildenhall. Lost without trace. All are
             Sgt J K Moss              +       commemorated on the Runnymede Memorial. This
             Sgt R V Bawden            +       was the last Wellington lost by 149 Squadron,
             Sgt B Ferguson            +       prior to conversion to Stirlings.
             Sgt J E King              +
             Sgt C Northcott           +


             150 Sqn         Wellington IC    T2618 JN-               Op: Emden
             P/O Leddra                        T/o 1730 Snaith. Believed force-landed
             Sgt Davenport                     0015 at Whitley Bridge, 3 miles W of the
             Sgt Baldwin                       airfield. Details of the crash are not
             Sgt Gray                          recorded in the Squadron records.
             Sgt Bright
             Sgt Guy


             214 Sqn         Wellington IC    Z8900 BU-               Op: Emden
             Sgt Campbell                      T/o 1719 Stradishall. Severely shot about
             Sgt Williams                      by a Me 110 over the Frisian Islands. The
             Sgt Herbert                       attack badly effected the controls and tore
             Sgt Pickthorne                    a six foot hole in the fuselage structure.
             Sgt Edington                      Bombs were jettisoned and despite severe
             Sgt Longden                       handling problems, the crew succeeded in
                                               returning to Coltishall where a safe landing
             was accomplished at 2205. Following a technical inspection, the Wellington
             was declared beyond economical repair.


             218 Sqn         Wellington IC    R1135 HA-N              Op: Kiel
             Sgt A Cook RAAF           +       T/o 2243 Marham. Crashed in the North
             Sgt K D Deadman           +       Sea. Apart from Sgt Drury, who is buried
             Sgt J B Drury             +       in Trondheim (Stavne) Cemetery, Norway,
             Sgt F C Reeve             +       the crew are commemorated on the Runnymede
             Sgt R N Hannam            +       Memorial.
             F/S R E Glenny            +


             218 Sqn         Wellington IC    Z8853 HA-H              Op: Kiel
             Sgt Forsyth                       T/o 2141 Marham. Encountered very severe
             Sgt Niblo                         weather conditions and crashed near Marske,
             Sgt Birks                         5 miles WSW of Richmond, Yorkshire.
             Sgt Gordon
             Sgt C L A Collins         +
             Sgt Slatford


             311 Sqn         Wellington IC    Z8966 KX-E              Op: Kiel
             Sgt S Linka               +       T/o 2129 East Wretham. Passed over the
             Sgt Lenc                          north of England on return and crashed in
             F/O Engel                         the Irish Sea, 20 miles SW of St. Bees Head,
             P/O J F Parolek           +       Cumberland. Two members of the crew were
             Sgt P Skutek              +       rescued; the rest are commemorated on the
             Sgt A Vaclavek            +       Runnymede Memorial.


             458 Sqn         Wellington IV    R1775                   Op: Emden
             P/O R J Furey RAAF        +       T/o 1717 Holme-on-Spalding Moor. Last heard
             Sgt A L Cox RAAF          +       on w/t at 2035. All are commemorated on the
             P/O W Goldman RAAF        +       Runnymede Memorial.
             Sgt D B Pepper            +
             F/S H W Duffield          +
             Sgt E Rowland             +


18 Nov       7 Sqn           Stirling I       N6087 MG-A             Op: Brest
1941         F/L J T O'Brien           +       T/o 1458 Oakington. Returning to base,
             Sgt J E Rose              +       the port outer engine caught fire and the
             Sgt J Devlin            inj       pilot decided to make an emergency landing.
             P/O J A Lopez RAAF      inj       While doing so, the bomber flew into telephone
             Sgt T Ryder            inj       wires and crashed near West Bluntisham, some
             Sgt M A Sullivan RAAF             12 miles NW of Cambridge. P/O Lopez RAAF died
             F/S P Comroe RCAF         +       soon afterwards from his injuries.
             Sgt A Grant              +
```

18 Nov   **7 Sqn**   **Stirling I**   **W7446 MG-S**   **Training**
1941   P/O M W Hardstaff   Landed Oakington on wet ground and while
                                    turning sharply to avoid running into an
aircraft parked on a dispersal pan, the undercarriage collapsed.

        101 Sqn   **Wellington IC**   **X9601 SR-V**   **Training**
        Sgt Hunt   T/o Bourn and crashed almost immediately
                                    due to partial instrument failure. The
Wellington caught fire and was damaged beyond repair.

21 Nov   **109 Sqn**   **Wellington IC**   **T2552 HS-**   **Training**
1941   F/L B P Hennessey   +   Crashed while trying to land at Oakington.
        P/O R M Lewin GC   +   P/O Lewin was awarded the GC for displaying
        F/S J A Bates   +   great valour, following an operational crash
        F/S J W Cornforth   +   in November 1940; his award being Gazetted
        F/S T D Snape   +   on 11 March 1941.
        Sgt D J Mackey DFM   +

22 Nov   **139 Sqn**   **Blenheim IV**   **Z7275 XD-**   **Training**
1941   P/O R Scott-Worthington   +   T/o 2104 Horsham St. Faith and crashed
        P/O D C Taylor   inj   almost immediately. P/O Taylor died the
        Sgt J Koller   inj   next day from his injuries.

        149 Sqn   **Stirling I**   **W7456 OJ-**   **Training**
        P/O C Lofthouse   T/o Mildenhall but a fire developed in
                                    one of the starboard engines and the pilot
crash-landed 1215 at Boxworth, 7 miles NW of Cambridge. This was the first
Stirling written off by the Squadron during its conversion programme.

23 Nov   **207 Sqn**   **Manchester I**   **L7300 EM-F**   **Transit**
1941   P/O A W Hills   Crashed 1530 while turning finals to land
        P/O F Roper RCAF   at Waddington. The pilot reported that
        P/O S E Patterson   the Manchester yawed to starboard and though
                                    he opened both throttles to full power, the
bomber struck the ground hard, whereupon it skidded into a lake known as
Fiskerton Lake, some 8 miles E of Lincoln. P/O Roper RCAF was an American
serving with the RCAF and he eventually completed a full tour of operations,
thus becoming the first American national to do so in Bomber Command service.
Subsequently, he transferred to the USAAF and rose to the rank of Lieutenant
Colonel.

24 Nov   **97 Sqn**   **Manchester I**   **R5792 OF-**   **Training**
1941   F/O H T Hill   +   Crashed 1155 at Walpole St. Andrew, 7 miles
        Sgt A C Smith   +   WSW of King's Lynn, Norfolk, following a
        Sgt J Newton   +   midair collision with Hurricane I V6864 from
        Sgt F Holt   +   57 OTU flown by Sgt G A Johnstone, who also
        Sgt F E Martin   +   died in the tragedy.
        Sgt J Few   +
        Sgt E C Hutton RAAF   +

        115 Sqn   **Wellington IC**   **Z8863 KO-G**   **Training**
        Sgt G R Bruce   +   Crashed 2 miles NW of March, Cambridgeshire,
        Sgt P M Taylor   +   following a low-flying accident during which
        Sgt H N O'Shea   +   the Wellington collided with a line of railway
        Sgt P G Crosbie   +   trucks on the March to Spalding line. In
        Sgt W M Evans   +   addition to the normal crew, three members
        Sgt E A Lawrence   +   of the ground staff had joined the flight
        Sgt J Dix   +   for air experience flying.
        Cpl J C Fox   +
        AC2 G S Wakefield   +

        458 Sqn   **Wellington IV**   **Z1246**   **Ground**
                                    Destroyed 2030 by fire on Holme-on-Spalding
                                    Moor airfield, Yorkshire.

| 25 Nov 1941 | 15 Sqn | Stirling I | W7450 LS-A | Op: **The Ruhr** |

Sgt J F Barron RNZAF
Sgt Shepherd
Sgt Cunningham
P/O V A Mulhall
Sgt Styles
Sgt Taylor
Sgt Coen
Sgt Jackson

T/o Wyton in an attempt to bomb the Ruhr using cloud cover. Turned back with failing engines and crashed 1225 following a heavy landing on Warboys airfield, Huntingdonshire. Sgt Barron RNZAF was later commissioned and when he was killed on operations on 20 May 1944, he was a Wing Commander decorated with a DSO & Bar, DFC and DFM.

| | 49 Sqn | Hampden I | AD759 EA- | Training |

Sgt R F Hough +
Sgt G E Smith +

Spun and crashed 1455 at Scamblesby, 6 miles SSW of Louth, Lincolnshire.

| | 142 Sqn | Wellington IV | Z1243 QT- | Training |

Sgt C M A B Brett +
Sgt C Jakins +
Sgt N Borrows +
Sgt H M Exley +
Sgt K W Light RAAF +

T/o Grimsby but climbed too slowly, stalled and crashed just to the SW of the airfield.

| 26-27 Nov 1941 | 75 Sqn | Wellington IC | Z1144 AA- | Op: **Emden** |

Sgt Giddens
Sgt Truscott
Sgt Smith
Sgt O'Grady
Sgt Davy
Sgt Rains

T/o 1830 Feltwell. Abandoned 2315, low on fuel and with engines misfiring, 10 miles N of Wrangle, a village on the Lincolnshire coast 8 miles NE of Boston.

| | 103 Sqn | Wellington IC | T2999 PM-P | Op: **Emden** |

P/O Ward
Sgt Wright
Sgt Kellough
Sgt Hyman
Sgt Harris
Sgt Thompson

T/o 1740 Elsham Wolds. Crashed 2205 in the circuit on return to base when the port engine cut and the Wellington was unable to maintain height. No injuries reported.

| | 106 Sqn | Hampden I | AE317 ZN- | Op: **Emden** |

Sgt W J Moss +
Sgt R H Breckell +
Sgt W L Ball +
Sgt J F Tarran +

T/o 1705 Coningsby. Crashed into the sea off the Dutch Frisian Islands. Sgt Tarran is buried in Sage War Cemetery, Germany; his companions have no known graves.

| | 214 Sqn | Wellington II | Z8373 BU- | Op: **Emden** |

F/S N G Hettrick RCAF +
Sgt M A Weavers +
P/O A D Moore +
P/O C D Cooling RCAF +
Sgt H J Cooper +
Sgt G L Hall +

T/o Stradishall. Lost without trace. All are commemorated on the Runnymede Memorial.

| | 218 Sqn | Wellington IC | Z1103 HA-A | Op: **Emden** |

Sgt Helfer
Sgt Taylor
Sgt Ross
Sgt Adamson
Sgt Purcell
Sgt England

T/o 1715 Marham. Ditched 2306 off Wells, Norfolk. The pilot decided to put the bomber down in the sea, rather than land on the beach which, he suspected, might be mined. After being picked up by the combined efforts of the Wells life boat and an RAF ASR, Sgt Helfer was told that he had been correct in his assumptions. Earlier, it is believed the Wellington was hit by flak.

| 27-28 Nov 1941 | 9 Sqn | Wellington III | X3287 WS- | Op: **Düsseldorf** |

Sgt W T Ramey RCAF   inj
Sgt G Armstrong RCAF   +
Sgt J Amphlett   inj
Sgt K W Stevens   inj
Sgt J Rutherford
Sgt P W Bilsborough   +

T/o 1713 Honington. Starboard engine caught fire while crossing the Dutch coast, homebound, and the Wellington was later abandoned over Herne Bay, Kent. Two of the crew fell into the sea and drowned; the injured were taken to the local Victoria Hospital.

27-28 Nov 1941	44 Sqn	Hampden I	AD933 KM-		Op: Düsseldorf

Sgt B D Moss
Sgt Ross
Sgt Seagoe
Sgt Hackett

T/o 1710 Waddington. Ran low on fuel and crash landed 0010 in a field near Honeybourne railway station, 5 miles E of Evesham, Worcestershire.

	144 Sqn	Hampden I	AE440 PL-		Op: Düsseldorf

P/O S T Farrington
Sgt Robinson
Sgt Martin
Sgt G Cornish

T/o North Luffenham. Crashed into high ground near Birdlip, 6 miles SE of Gloucester. Moments before the crash, the Hampden had broken through low cloud.

	408 Sqn	Hampden I	AE437 EQ-U		Op: Düsseldorf

F/O J A Caldwell   +
Sgt H E Marshall RCAF   +
Sgt E A Harry   +
Sgt R Crawley   +

T/o 1640 Syerston. At 2229 Heston d/f station acknowledged a call from this aircraft, asking for a bearing. Tragically, it is believed the crew misinterpretated the information sent by Heston and when last heard on w/t the Hampden was plotted in a 40 mile radius of 4730N 13W, some 270 miles off Brest and approximately 300 miles SW of Lands End. All are commemorated on the panels of the Runnymede Memorial.

28 Nov 1941	138 Sqn	Lysander III	T1771 NF-		Training

F/L A J de V Laurent   +
LAC J A M Harkness   +
AC1 J Roberts   +

Collided with trees while flying in poor visibility and crashed at Hungry Hill, Farnham, Surrey. F/L Laurent was a Frenchman serving in the RAF and he is reported to have died in the crash, though no burials details to date have been discovered. Believed to have been the first Lysander written off by a bomber squadron.

29 Nov 1941	214 Sqn	Wellington IC	X9752 BU-		Transit

Sgt S J Miller   +
Sgt A H Barford   +
Sgt Stewart   inj
Sgt A D Southall   +
Sgt R G C Walton   +
Sgt T A Quinn   +

Crashed 1 mile S of Oakington airfield, Cambridgeshire. It is believed the bomber, which had landed at Driffield three days previous following operations to Emden, suffered engine failure while flying at 500 feet in poor visibility.

30 Nov- 1 Dec 1941	10 Sqn	Whitley V	Z9166 ZA-O		Op: Emden

P/O M K Nelson RNZAF   +
Sgt G S Illingworth   +
P/O J S Knowles   +
Sgt W Webster   +
Sgt A F Wales   +

T/o 1648 Leeming. Last heard on w/t at 1900 while outbound. Presumed lost over the sea. The crew are commemorated on the Runnymede Memorial.

	35 Sqn	Halifax I	L9582 TL-T		Op: Hamburg

F/S J C Hamilton   pow
P/O C G Lythgoe   pow
Sgt W R Stapleford   pow
Sgt J A Longford   pow
Sgt A E Connor   pow
Sgt J P Henderson   pow
F/S J Collins   +

T/o 1726 Linton-on-Ouse. F/S Collins is buried in Hamburg Cemetery, Ohlsdorf.

	50 Sqn	Hampden I	P1202 VN-		Op: Hamburg

Sgt Williams
Sgt W J Johnston   inj
Sgt Smith
Sgt Caunce

T/o 1657 Skellingthorpe. Ran low on fuel and force-landed 0120 some 2 miles E of the airfield on return to base.

	58 Sqn	Whitley V	Z6506 GE-V		Op: Hamburg

Sgt A Whewell   +
Sgt G C Davies   +
P/O N M D Romilly RCAF   +
P/O E D Comber-Higgs   +
Sgt T H Marlowe   +

T/o 1651 Linton-on-Ouse. Lost without trace. All are commemorated on the Runnymede Memorial. Sgt Whewell was a member of P/O Law's crew that ditched in the North Sea in April 1941, and by coincidence, P/O Comber-Higgs was the sole survivor from the crash involving P/O Law after being recalled from Brest on 3 September 1941.

30 Nov– 1 Dec 1941	58 Sqn P/O H Knight P/O F D Hammersley Sgt G S H Mott Sgt D S Kay Sgt R L J Lizotte RCAF	Whitley V + + + + +	Z6507 GE-X	Op: Hamburg

T/o 1655 Linton-on-Ouse. Lost without trace. All are commemorated on the Runnymede Memorial.

58 Sqn	Whitley V	Z6575 GE-B	Op: Hamburg
F/S D G McKay RCAF	+		
Sgt J S Gearing	+		
Sgt J H K Deane	pow		
Sgt N S Bidwell RNZAF	pow		
F/O F Ivins	pow		

T/o 1706 Linton-on-Ouse. Those who died are buried in Hamburg Cemetery, Ohlsdorf.

58 Sqn	Whitley V	Z9211 GE-Q	Op: Hamburg
P/O Earp			
P/O McKenzie			
Sgt Carmichael			
Sgt Stewart			
Sgt Cairns			

T/o 1641 Linton-on-Ouse. Ditched off Grimsby, Lincolnshire, while returning to base. The crew were rescued by a passing trawler.

75 Sqn	Wellington IC	Z1099 AA-	Op: Emden
Sgt F C Harrison-Smith RNZAF	+		
Sgt D V Sizmur	+		
Sgt D McCready	+		
Sgt B D Meagher	+		
Sgt E H J Painter	+		
Sgt P Buckby	+		

T/o Feltwell. Shot down by a night-fighter (Ofw Paul Gildner, 4./NJG1) and crashed 2305 into the Waddenzee. Sgt Meagher is buried in Vredenhof Cemetery on the Dutch island of Schiermonnikoog; the rest are commemorated on the Runnymede Memorial.

76 Sqn	Halifax I	L9604 MP-W	Op: Hamburg
Sgt G R Herbert			
Sgt J H G Bingham			
Sgt Street			
Sgt M H Roberts RCAF			
Sgt J B Fanning			
Sgt Fulton			
Sgt M C Glover			

T/o 1718 Middleton St. George. Crashed 2335 on return to base. Subsequently, the Halifax was used for instructional purposes as 3161M.

77 Sqn	Whitley V	Z9299 KN-	Op: Emden
Sgt R B Vose RCAF	+		
Sgt P W Hewitt	+		
Sgt D B Grundy	pow		
Sgt R W Weymouth	+		
Sgt J W Woodroffe	+		

T/o 1650 Leeming. Those who died are buried at Oldenburg in Sage War Cemetery.

101 Sqn	Wellington IC	R1778 SR-G	Op: Hamburg
Sgt D A Willisson	+		
Sgt R St C Finch	+		
Sgt D E Williams	+		
Sgt J W Lamont	pow		
Sgt K Naylor	+		
Sgt L G C Dimond	pow		

T/o Oakington. Crashed 2000 in the North Sea approximately 70 kms WNW of Esbjerg, Denmark. The two survivors were rescued at 1000 on 2 December by the Danish fishing vessel 'Harmonie'. Both airmen were suffering from the effects of exposure and were taken to a hospital in Esbjerg for treatment.

101 Sqn	Wellington IC	R3295 SR-P	Op: Hamburg
Sgt P Winfield	pow		
Sgt W L Johnson RCAF	pow		
Sgt I G Davies	pow		
Sgt T A Cooke	pow		
Sgt A W J Cleeve	pow		
Sgt A L R Heath	pow		

T/o 1640 Oakington. Ditched off Schiermonnikoog in the Dutch Frisian Islands.

Note. Sgt Heath, who was born in Burma in 1920, was studying at the Slade when war broke out. On his release from captivity, he returned to his art studies and at the time of his death in 1992, he was recognised as one of the best abstract artists to have worked in the United Kingdom since the war. Daily Telegraph, 28 September 1992.

30 Nov–	**102 Sqn**	**Whitley V**	**Z6800 DY-**	**Op: Hamburg**
1 Dec 1941	S/L J G Walker	+	T/o 1647 Dalton. Hit by flak and crashed	
	Sgt C T R Anderson	+	near Kiel, where those who died are buried	
	Sgt J A Groom	+	in the local War Cemetery.	
	Sgt P A Taylor	+		
	Sgt J Williamson	pow		

102 Sqn	**Whitley V**	**Z9281 DY-**	**Op: Hamburg**
Sgt E P Pike		T/o 1640 Dalton. Abandoned after running	
Sgt J B Robinson		out of fuel and straying N of track. The	
Sgt G H Marks		Whitley came down at Springholm, 11 miles	
Sgt D C Grieve		WSW of Dumfries, Scotland.	
Sgt G Williams			

106 Sqn	**Hampden I**	**P1228 ZN-L**	**Op: Hamburg**
Sgt A J Moore	+	T/o 1620 Coningsby. Lost without trace.	
Sgt A J W Parker RNZAF	+	All are commemorated on the Runnymede Memorial.	
Sgt T F Gowan	+		
Sgt D D Jones	+		

106 Sqn	**Hampden I**	**AT115 ZN-**	**Op: Hamburg**
Sgt F E Rolfe	+	T/o 1640 Coningsby. Lost without trace.	
Sgt A E Hill	+	All are commemorated on the Runnymede Memorial.	
Sgt J Goodbrand	+		
Sgt H Griffiths	+		

142 Sqn	**Wellington IV**	**Z1202 QT-**	**Op: Hamburg**
F/S K W Barnfield	+	T/o 1817 Grimsby. Lost without trace. All	
Sgt S L Innes RCAF	+	are commemorated on the Runnymede Memorial.	
Sgt F Fishwick	+		
Sgt J O Edmonds	+		
Sgt G P Hughes	+		
Sgt R O Dowling	+		

142 Sqn	**Wellington IV**	**Z1292 QT-**	**Op: Hamburg**
Sgt A Gilmour	+	T/o 1757 Grimsby. All are buried in Kiel	
Sgt J H Lucking	+	War Cemetery.	
Sgt W J Lewis	+		
Sgt J S Saunders	+		
Sgt J Butterworth	+		
F/S F Sumner	+		

214 Sqn	**Wellington IC**	**Z8953 BU-**	**Op: Hamburg**
Sgt M J Fitzgerald	+	T/o Stradishall. Crashed in the North Sea.	
Sgt J R Boland	+	Sgt Boland is buried in Den Burg General	
Sgt I A Flower	+	Cemetery on the Dutch island of Texel; his	
Sgt G J W Fleming	+	five companions have no known graves.	
Sgt R W Ebsworth	+		
Sgt H L Loveday	+		

304 Sqn	**Wellington IC**	**X3164 NZ-**	**Op: Hamburg**
P/O J Zajac		T/o 1638 Lindholme. Ditched 2225 some 20	
Sgt Garstka		miles E of Great Yarmouth, Norfolk, after	
P/O Maczynski		returning on one engine. The Wellington	
Sgt Strzyzewski		floated for seven minutes, thus enabling	
F/O Klewicz		the crew to get into their dinghy without	
Sgt Pokrzywa		difficulty.	

405 Sqn	**Wellington II**	**W5476 LQ-H**	**Op: Hamburg**
S/L R C Bisset DFC & Bar	+	T/o 1721 Pocklington. Last heard on w/t	
F/S A J Knight RCAF	+	at 1835 indicating the crew were returning	
P/O R A Mather RCAF	+	to base. Presumed lost over the sea. All	
Sgt W L Evans	+	are commemorated on the Runnymede Memorial.	
F/S C E Hillmer RCAF	+	S/L Bisset, a Canadian serving in the RAF,	
Sgt R P Mann RCAF	+	was an experienced bomber pilot and had	
		been engaged on operations since the early	
		days of the war, at which time he was serving	
		with 102 Squadron.	

30 Nov- 1 Dec 1941	455 Sqn Sgt J Shannon RAAF P/O A G Sands RAAF Sgt A C Shorey Sgt V E Towers	Hampden I + + + +	P1272 UB-R T/o 1654 Swinderby. All are buried in Hamburg Cemetery, Ohlsdorf.	Op: **Hamburg**

	455 Sqn Sgt C J H Blunt Sgt L G Manning Sgt A H Gee Sgt E Waller	Hampden I + + + +	AE430 UB-M T/o 1652 Swinderby. All are buried in Kiel War Cemetery.	Op: **Hamburg**

**2 Dec
1941** **7 Sqn** Stirling I N3701 MG- Op: **Air Sea Rescue**

S/L D J H Lay DFC T/o Oakington. Returned to base in marginal weather and the pilot landed, by mistake, downwind. After touch down, the Stirling collided with an obstruction which smashed the bomber's undercarriage, causing damage that was deemed to be beyond economical repair.

**5 Dec
1941** **82 Sqn** Blenheim IV L9268 UX- **Training**

P/O F W Wilson inj Crashed 1815 while landing at Bodney airfield,
P/O E Forbes inj Norfolk.
Sgt Christmas

**6 Dec
1941** **9 Sqn** Wellington III X3289 WS- **Training**

S/L W I C Inness Caught fire in flight and the starboard
Sgt D S S Welch inj engine eventually fell from its mountings. Still burning, the bomber was force-landed between May Day Farm and High Lodge, Brandon, Suffolk. Sgt Welch, who was occupying the rear turret, was taken to Ely Hospital for treatment.

	110 Sqn Sgt V H Langrish F/O D H Ivens Sgt A E Bailey P/O E L V Stanley	Blenheim IV + + + +	Z7962 VE- T/o 1130 Bicester and crashed just beyond the airfield. The accident was attributed to incorrect trim tab settings.	**Training**

**7-8 Dec
1941** **10 Sqn** Whitley V Z9162 ZA-Y Op: **Dunkerque**

Sgt J W Barber T/o 1659 Leeming. Returned to base with its
Sgt R W B Blanchard bomb load intact and crashed 2240 while trying
Sgt Archer to avoid a collision with a 77 Squadron Whitley.
Sgt Waterworth The 10 Squadron aircraft smashed through the
Sgt Brewer roof of a house at Londonderry on the western edge of the airfield. The wreckage caught fire but the crew escaped with only minor cuts and abrasions.

	61 Sqn S/L J L Riley Sgt C L Wells P/O R Adcock Sgt J V Randall F/S J Wilson Sgt J Crawford Sgt J B Leigh RNZAF	Manchester I + + + + + + +	L7494 QR- T/o 1742 Woolfox Lodge. Exploded and crashed into the sea off Boulogne. Sgt Wells is buried in Boulogne Eastern Cemetery; the rest have no known graves.	Op: **Boulogne**

	82 Sqn P/O T McS Wilson Sgt R Johnston RAAF Sgt F C Hubbard	Blenheim IV + + +	V5876 UX-J T/o 2343 Bodney. All are buried in the Canadian War Cemetery at Adegem, Belgium.	Op: **Oostende**

Note. This was the first Blenheim to be lost on a night bombing sortie since 101 Squadron lost two crews raiding Brest on 3-4 April 1941.

	83 Sqn P/O A L Parsons Sgt B A Basevi P/O D Jacobs Sgt G Wiscombe	Hampden I pow + + pow	AE191 OL-Z T/o 0213 Scampton. Ditched in the North Sea. Two died before rescue was effected and their bodies were committed to the sea by their comrades. Both are commemorated on the Runnymede Memorial.	Op: **Aachen**

7-8 Dec 1941	99 Sqn	Wellington IC	Z8958 LN-	Op: Aachen

99 Sqn — Wellington IC — Z8958 LN- — Op: Aachen

Sgt Firth — inj
Sgt Collings — inj
Sgt Jarvis — inj
Sgt Macdonald — inj
Sgt Maconochie — inj
Sgt V L Lloyd — +

T/o 0225 Waterbeach. Shortly after take off the starboard engine caught fire and the Wellington crashed 0241 into a field on the edge of the airfield, as the crew tried to make an emergency landing.

104 Sqn — Wellington II — Z8426 EP-E — Op: Dunkerque

Sgt R K Anson — +
P/O B N Murdoch RNZAF — +
P/O W K Hayne RAAF — +
Sgt W W Covey — +
Sgt R Turner — +
F/S H B McGarrow — +

T/o 2005 Driffield. Lost without trace. All are commemorated on the Runnymede Memorial.

144 Sqn — Hampden I — AD791 PL- — Op: Aachen

Sgt F K Calcutt — +
Sgt A H Lawrence RCAF — +
Sgt R E Hirons — +
Sgt G Barnes — +

T/o North Luffenham. All are buried in Heverlee War Cemetery, Belgium.

11 Dec 1941 — 144 Sqn — Hampden I — AE353 PL- — Op: Brest

P/O C B Payne — +
F/O A J B Monk RCAF — +
P/O A L Smiley RNZAF — +
P/O J H Dunn RCAF — +
Sgt C E Gailey — +

T/o North Luffenham. Believed damaged while over the target and later crashed in the sea off the Sussex coast. F/O Monk RCAF is commemorated on the Runnymede Memorial.

11-12 Dec 1941 — 10 Sqn — Whitley V — Z9188 ZA-V — Op: Köln

P/O J H Kenny — inj
Sgt E C Hoskin — +
P/O Burgess — inj
Sgt Taylor — inj
Sgt Clarke — inj

T/o 1630 Leeming. Crashed 0143 on Eavestone Moor between Pateley Bridge and Ripon, Yorkshire, after being caught in a severe down draft. This was the last Whitley lost by 10 Squadron prior to converting to Halifaxes.

35 Sqn — Halifax I — L9600 TL-U — Op: Köln

P/O H D Buckley — +
Sgt G L Grigg — +
Sgt R W G Kent — +
F/S I R Bell — +
Sgt F W Crocker — +
Sgt M V Wakeling — +
Sgt L W Ketteringham — +

T/o 1712 Linton-on-Ouse. Presumed to have crashed in the sea off the Belgian coast. Sgt Ketteringham is buried in the Churchyard at Bredene, 2 km E of Oostende. The rest of the crew are commemorated on the Runnymede Memorial.

57 Sqn — Wellington IC — T2959 DX- — Op: le Havre

Sgt D A Watson — +
Sgt P L Gurd RCAF — +
Sgt E R Carter — +
Sgt J M McKenzie RCAF — +
Sgt S H Jackson — +
Sgt R P Manwaring — +

T/o 1625 Feltwell. Crashed 2050 some 200 yards W of Roudham station, 3 miles from East Wretham airfield, Norfolk.

218 Sqn — Wellington IC — W5727 HA-V — Op: Brest

Sgt Brewerton
Sgt Longmore
Sgt Cox
P/O Taylor
Sgt Williamson
Sgt McDonald

T/o 1520 Marham. The port engine caught fire, while outbound, and the crew were ordered to bale out. Satisfied all had left the Wellington, Sgt Brewerton crash-landed 1620 at Upavon airfield, Wiltshire. Repairs were started, but the airframe was eventually converted for instructional purposes as 3333M and issued to the Airborne Forces Training Unit.

408 Sqn — Hampden I — AE148 EQ-B Bar — Op: Gardening

P/O W F Hull RCAF — +
Sgt D L Todd RNZAF — +
Sgt S Jamieson — +
Sgt L Harding — +

T/o 1715 Balderton for a mining operation in Kiel Bay. Crashed at Sanderum, 5 km SW of Odense, Denmark, where the crew are buried.

Date	Squadron / Crew	Aircraft	Serial / Details
12 Dec 1941	106 Sqn F/L H D Webber + Sgt S V Crowhurst RNZAF + Sgt F Norman + Sgt T Robson-Scott +	Hampden I	AE391 ZN- **Op: Gelsenkirchen** T/o 1040 Coningsby. Crashed between Oberhausen and Osterfeld, Germany. All are buried in the Reichswald Forest War Cemetery.
13 Dec 1941	44 Sqn W/C S T Misselbrook DSO + Sgt A H G Gumbley RNZAF + Sgt L D Leggett DFM + F/O H J Jeffcoat +	Hampden I	AE196 KM- **Op: Gardening** T/o 1300 Waddington to lay mines off Brest. Lost without trace. All are commemorated on the Runnymede Memorial.
	144 Sqn P/O D McLaren + Sgt R J Pulham + Sgt T J Pearce + Sgt A H Taylor + Sgt R A P V Atkinson +	Hampden I	AD921 PL- **Op: Gardening** T/o North Luffenham to lay mines off Brest. Lost without trace. All are commemorated on the Runnymede Memorial.
14 Dec 1941	150 Sqn Sgt M D Lewis	Wellington IC	Z8849 JN- **Air Test** Overshot and crash-landed 1145 at Snaith, slightly injuring one member of the crew.
14-15 Dec 1941	83 Sqn P/O The Hon W R C B Parker + Sgt H Standen inj Sgt C Love + Sgt L King inj	Hampden I	P5393 OL-T **Op: Gardening** Collided on the ground at Scampton with another Hampden as both aircraft taxied towards the runway. The impact caused the mine aboard P5393 to explode, wrecking both aircraft.
	83 Sqn Sgt J M Thompson Sgt J Ryan Sgt J Rooney Sgt P N Foster	Hampden I	AE374 OL-R **Op: Brest** Wrecked in the circumstances previously described. It is believed the crew escaped serious injury.
	408 Sqn Sgt R W Sterling + Sgt J C Tomlin RCAF + Sgt W R Williams + Sgt C G Gibson +	Hampden I	P5392 EQ-W **Op: Cherbourg** T/o 0032 Balderton. Crashed 0327 at New Farm, Longdown Enclosure, 2 miles SE of Lyndhurst Road Station and 4 miles SW of Totton, Hampshire.
	408 Sqn Sgt J L Vaughan RCAF + Sgt R L Thompson RCAF + Sgt B Howells + Sgt W Oates +	Hampden I	AT133 EQ-X **Op: Cherbourg** T/o 0030 Balderton. Lost without trace. All are commemorated on the Runnymede Memorial.
15-16 Dec 1941	50 Sqn Sgt W J Young + Sgt D A Ferguson + Sgt F A White + Sgt E W Armer +	Hampden I	AE380 VN- **Op: Oostende** T/o 1757 Skellingthorpe. Presumed crashed in the sea off the Belgian coast. Sgt Young is buried in Oostende New Communal Cemetery; his crew have no known graves.
16-17 Dec 1941	102 Sqn F/S W G Caldwell RCAF + Sgt D G Jack RAAF + Sgt F E Baldock + Sgt G E Thompson + Sgt W A Evans RCAF +	Whitley V	Z6973 DY- **Op: Dunkerque** T/o 1643 Dalton. Hit by flak and crashed in the sea. All are commemorated on the panels of the Runnymede Memorial.
	218 Sqn Sgt Vezina Sgt Harding P/O Brown Sgt Willett Sgt Toynbee-Clark Sgt Crump inj	Wellington IC	X9785 HA-O **Op: Brest** T/o 1840 Marham. Starboard engine failed and after his crew had baled out, Sgt Vezina crash-landed at Holm Farm near Powerstock, 4 miles NE of Bridport, Dorset. It is believed that those who parachuted landed in the vicinity of Chilfrome Mill, a few miles ENE of the Wellington. Sgt Crump broke a leg when he landed awkwardly.

16-17 Dec 1941	304 Sqn	Wellington IC	R1064 NZ-	Op: Oostende

304 Sqn — Wellington IC — R1064 NZ- — Op: Oostende

S/L J Blazejewski +
F/O H Szczodrowski +
F/O J Komlacz +
Sgt B Golabek +
Sgt K Suwalski +
Sgt H Rutkowski +

T/o 1657 Lindholme. Last heard on w/t at 1905 by Manston, calling for assistance. Presumed lost over the sea. Some bodies were recovered from the water and burials have taken place in cemeteries in Belgium and France.

305 Sqn — Wellington II — Z8427 SM-W — Op: Oostende

Sgt Cusowski
Sgt Lemkrych
F/O Gebik
Sgt Gorny
Sgt Gora
Sgt Zwienka

T/o 1759 Lindholme. Crashed 2115 at Crowtree Farm in the Lindholme circuit, due to a faulty altimeter setting, which led the pilot to think he had 500 feet to go before landing. Four of the crew were treated in Doncaster Military Hospital.

17-18 Dec 1941 — 44 Sqn — Hampden I — AD868 KM- — Op: Brest

P/O T L Kaschula +
Sgt J G Henderson +
Sgt E Wade +
Sgt K E Hall +

T/o 1830 Waddington. Presumed lost in the sea off the French coast. F/O Kaschula is buried in Camaret-sur-Mer Communal Cemetery. His crew have no known graves.

Note. This was the last Hampden lost by 44 Squadron, prior to receiving the first Lancasters issued to Bomber Command.

78 Sqn — Whitley V — Z9129 EY- — Op: le Havre

P/O H G Bedford
Sgt Howell
P/O Ponds
Sgt Oliver
Sgt Parks

T/o 1643 Croft. While flying at 6500 feet the starboard engine caught fire. Prompt action by the crew quelled the fire, but the Whitley lost height and was successfully ditched 1850 off Spithead.

18 Dec 1941 — 7 Sqn — Stirling I — N3680 MG-Y — Op: Brest

F/L B Parnell MiD +
Sgt K R Taylor RNZAF +
Sgt J H M Pulford +
P/O N F Durban RCAF +
F/S R Wheatley +
Sgt M A Sullivan GM, RAAF +
Sgt T P Wright +

T/o 0940 Oakington. Shot down by Me 109s off the French coast. All are commemorated on the Runnymede Memorial.

7 Sqn — Stirling I — N6095 MG-K — Op: Brest

P/O G T Heard
Sgt P E Normanville
Sgt T A Ward inj
Sgt D K Haynes
Sgt G W Robinson
Sgt E B Dobson
Sgt H Inman inj

T/o 0947 Oakington. Hit by flak and was badly shot about by Me 109s, wounding two members of the crew. A safe return to base was accomplished, where the Stirling was declared beyond repair.

7 Sqn — Stirling I — W7436 MG-D — Op: Brest

S/L L W V Jennens pow
Sgt F K Lister RAAF pow
Sgt J C Webb pow
Sgt E V Smith pow
F/S W M Baker RCAF +
Sgt F V Davis pow
Sgt J Towns +

T/o 0948 Oakington. Shot down by Me 109s and crashed at Plouguerneau (Finistère), 24 km N of Brest. The two airmen who died are buried in Plouguerneau Communal Cemetery.

15 Sqn — Stirling I — N3665 LS-S — Op: Brest

F/L G G Heathcote MiD +
F/S W H O'Neill RCAF +
Sgt J F Bente +
F/S R Exelby MiD +
Sgt D G Penman +
F/S C P Gouding RNZAF +
P/O E L Smith +
F/S J Peters +

T/o 0950 Wyton. Last seen over the target with smoke pouring from one engine and trying to repel a strong fighter attack. Believed to have crashed near Plouguerneau (Finistère), 24 km N of Brest. Apart from P/O Smith, the crew are commemorated on the Runnymede Memorial. F/L Heathcote came from a military background, his father being Brigadier General C E Heathcote CB, CMG, DSO.

18 Dec 1941	15 Sqn	Stirling I	W7428 LS-Z	Op: Brest

F/O G Bunce	+	T/o Wyton. Last seen with its port wing
F/S J L Ruthven RCAF	+	burning furiously and continuing to fight
Sgt D Ferguson	+	off attacks from Me 109s. All are named
P/O R N Chancellor	+	on the panels of the Runnymede Memorial.
Sgt K A Jeffreys	+	
F/S W Wooldridge	+	
Sgt R Shearer	+	
Sgt P G Osman	+	

35 Sqn	Halifax II	V9978 TL-A	Op: Brest

W/C B V Robinson DFC		T/o 0959 Linton-on-Ouse. Hit by flak over
Sgt Larson		the target and crippled so badly that the
F/O A Abels		crew were obliged to ditch 1315 approximately
Sgt Hood		60 miles off the English coast. After landing
Sgt Burtonshaw		in the water, the Halifax floated for twenty
Sgt H Mennell		minutes. At the time, it was thought this
F/O R C Rivas	inj	was the first time a Halifax had been ditched

but, unknown to the authorities, S/L Williams of 76 Squadron had successfully put his Halifax into the sea off la Rochelle on 24 July 1941.

49 Sqn	Hampden I	AE354 EA-S	Training

Sgt J Bow	Overshot the Scampton runway and crashed 1200. Weather conditions are described as poor at the time of the accident. No injuries reported.

97 Sqn	Manchester I	L7490 OF-U	Op: Brest

W/C D F Balsdon	+	T/o 0930 Coningsby. Hit by flak in the
F/S G E A Pendrill DFM	+	target area, which wounded F/L Wright.
Sgt H Bischlager RCAF	+	On return to base the Manchester stalled
Sgt J L Gibson RCAF	+	and crashed. The flak damage is believed
Sgt F Y D Kerr	+	to have been a contributory factor. F/S
Sgt R T Bray	+	Pendrill was an experienced pilot and had
Sgt L W Jones	+	gained an immediate DFM for devotion to
F/L R A Wright	+	duty on recent operations.

97 Sqn	Manchester I	R5795 OF-W	Op: Brest

P/O N G Stokes	+	T/o 0934 Waddington. Shot down by Me 109s
Sgt G P Thomas RAAF	pow	and came down in the sea roughly 6 kms off
Sgt T M Wade RAAF	pow	Brest. Those who died are commemorated on
F/S I Hewitt RCAF	pow	the Runnymede Memorial. P/O Stokes was an
Sgt M R Heinish RCAF	+	Australian serving with the RAF.
Sgt G G Fell	+	

18-19 Dec 1941	78 Sqn	Whitley V	Z9277 EY-	Op: Brest

P/O J F Beadle	T/o 1553 Croft. On return to base, the crew
Sgt Cox	were unable to obtain any response to their
P/O Franklin	w/t calls asking for a bearing. Subsequently,
Sgt White	the pilot broke through the cloud in order to
Sgt Gale	establish his position and in doing so he
Sgt Kendall	crashed 2130 into high ground at Simon's Seat, 17 miles WNW of Harrogate, Yorkshire.

78 Sqn	Whitley V	Z9308 EY-	Op: Brest

Sgt J A Attwell RCAF	T/o 1607 Croft. Crash-landed 1630 at Keanley
Sgt Martin	Sides Farm near Harwood, Durham, after the
Sgt Howitson	starboard engine lost power. No injuries
Sgt Turpin	reported.
Sgt Johnston	

21 Dec 1941	106 Sqn	Hampden I	AE151 ZN-	Op: Intruder

F/S R S Hartgroves	pow	T/o 1210 Coningsby. Crashed at Schoonebeek
P/O A Carter	+	(Drenthe), 14 km S of Emmen, Holland. P/O
Sgt R Yearsley	pow	Carter is buried in Oud Schoonebeek General
Sgt D Martin	pow	Cemetery.

22-23 Dec 1941	405 Sqn	Wellington II		W5560 LQ-M	Op: **Wilhelmshaven**

405 Sqn Wellington II W5560 LQ-M Op: **Wilhelmshaven**

Sgt Mather
Sgt R N Lonergan RAAF
Sgt Skuthorp
Sgt Dodds
Sgt Campbell
Sgt G A Tilley

T/o 1710 Pocklington. Returned early with failing engines, but was ordered to divert to Lindholme. While approaching the runway the Wellington crash-landed at 1955, no injuries being reported.

23-24 Dec 1941

75 Sqn Wellington IC Z8834 AA- Op: **Brest**

F/S L L Bentley RNZAF +
Sgt T W Burke inj
Sgt H Ives inj
Sgt K C Wilkes inj
Sgt W H Olrod inj
Sgt S V Hardman inj

T/o Feltwell. Crashed 2345 near Elveden, Suffolk, 4 miles SW of Thetford, Norfolk. The accident happened as the crew awaited their landing instructions.

---

305 Sqn Wellington II W5374 SM-J Op: **Köln**

Sgt H Rozpara +
F/O S C Golacki +
F/O A Nowak +
Sgt E Baracz +
Sgt Z Kurowski +
P/O J Siwiec +

T/o 1732 Lindholme. Crashed at Sibbertoft, 14 miles NNW of Northampton. All are buried in Newark Cemetery.

Note. Names and initials have been checked against a copy of the original Register of Service Burials.

---

27 Dec 1941

50 Sqn Hampden I AE369 VN- Op: **Combined Ops.**

Sgt L F Redfern +
Sgt D H Roberts +
Sgt L R Brockett +
Sgt A V W Sherwin +

T/o 0543 Wick to support Allied Commandos at Vaagsö. Shot down by flak off Maaloy Island. Sgt Redfern is buried in Trondheim (Stavne) Cemetery, Norway; his crew are commemorated on the Runnymede Memorial.

---

50 Sqn Hampden I AE428 VN- Op: **Combined Ops.**

Sgt R N Smith
Sgt J D Williams +
P/O R Watson +
Sgt D Bell +

T/o 0529 Wick and lost in circumstances similar to those previously described. Sgt Smith was picked up by a British ship, possibly HMS Kenya, which is reported to have recovered the body of Sgt Williams. After formal identification, his body was committed back to the sea and his name appears on the Runnymede Memorial, as do those of P/O Watson and Sgt Bell. Sgt Bell had previously served with 23 Squadron, flying in Blenheims during the Battle of Britain.

---

82 Sqn Blenheim IV V6455 UX- **Training**

P/O T A M Jack inj
Sgt E Kerr inj
Sgt H Slater inj
P/O J F Graham inj
Sgt Broadhurst

T/o 1120 Bodney and crashed almost immediately.

---

110 Sqn Blenheim IV V6429 VE- Op: **Combined Ops.**

P/O J B MacLeod +
P/O H G Harris +
Sgt T E Anstey +

T/o Lossiemouth to support Allied Commando landings at Vaagsö. Shot down while attacking shipping off the Norwegian coast. All are commemorated on the Runnymede Memorial. P/O Harris was the Curate of Leigh-on-Sea, Essex, between 1938 and 1940.

---

110 Sqn Blenheim IV V6448 VE- Op: **Combined Ops.**

P/O D M Jenkinson RCAF +
P/O R J McLachlan RCAF +
Sgt R C Hawkes +

T/o Lossiemouth. Lost in circumstances similar to those reported above. All are commemorated on the Runnymede Memorial.

---

110 Sqn Blenheim IV Z7317 VE- Op: **Combined Ops.**

F/L R T Blewett RNZAF +
P/O M Murphy +
Sgt J L Bell +

T/o Lossiemouth. Lost in circumstances similar to those reported above. F/L Blewett RNZAF is buried in Sola Churchyard, Norway; his crew are commemorated on the Runnymede Memorial.

27 Dec 1941	110 Sqn	Blenheim IV	Z7442 VE-	Op: Combined Ops.

| 27 Dec 1941 | 110 Sqn | Blenheim IV | Z7442 VE- | Op: Combined Ops. |

Sgt N Kaby +
P/O R C Davis RNZAF +
Sgt N Coatesworth +

T/o Lossiemouth. Lost in circumstances similar to those previously reported. Sgt Kaby is buried in Trondheim (Stavne) Cemetery; his crew are commemorated on the Runnymede Memorial.

114 Sqn Blenheim IV V6227 RT-Z Op: Combined Ops.

F/S R W Fisher RAAF +
Sgt J Williamson +
Sgt W F G Fletcher +

T/o 0925 Lossiemouth to support Allied Commando landings at Vaagso. Collided with another Blenheim while attacking Herdla airfield and crashed in the target area. All are buried in Bergen (Mollendal) Church Cemetery, Norway.

114 Sqn Blenheim IV Z7500 RT-H Op: Combined Ops.

Sgt K A Davis +
Sgt J J B Ward +
Sgt J E Kitley +

T/o 0930 Lossiemouth. Lost in the circumstances described above. All rest alongside their fellow airmen at Bergen.

Note. These were the heaviest casualties suffered by 2 Group since mid-October when seven aircraft were lost while attacking shipping targets. Furthermore, in respect of 110 Squadron and 114 Squadron, twenty-seven Blenheims had failed to return from operations during 1941; from this total one airman had survived.

27-28 Dec 1941 57 Sqn Wellington IC Z1097 DX- Op: Düsseldorf

W/O T Purdy DFM +
Sgt M J Cronin RNZAF +
F/O R C Scarlett RAAF +
Sgt S Barraclough pow
Sgt R F Aldous +
Sgt W J Poulton +

T/o 1700 Feltwell. Shot down by a night-fighter (Hptm Werner Streib, I./NJG1) and crashed 2030 near Someren (Noord Brabant), 11 km SSE of Helmond, Holland. Those who died are buried in Woensel General Cemetery.

58 Sqn Whitley V Z6841 GE-F Op: Düsseldorf

P/O M J H Hunt RNZAF +
F/S J J Lynch RCAF +
Sgt E F E Hodges +
Sgt R A Johnson +
Sgt I Allan +

T/o 1656 Linton-on-Ouse. Lost without trace. All are commemorated on the Runnymede Memorial.

58 Sqn Whitley V Z9210 GE-J Op: Düsseldorf

Sgt R A Scott +
Sgt K E Stewart +
Sgt F J Goat RCAF +
Sgt E S Briggs +
Sgt R I Rhodes +

T/o 1657 Linton-on-Ouse. All are buried in the Reichswald Forest War Cemetery.

75 Sqn Wellington IC Z8971 AA- Op: Brest

Sgt Machin
Sgt Thompson
Sgt Buckby
Sgt Bolshaw
Sgt Clements
Sgt Bourne

T/o Feltwell. Crashed on Dartmoor while returning to base. No injuries reported.

77 Sqn Whitley V Z6956 KN- Op: Düsseldorf

W/O C H Grace pow
Sgt A B Wiggins pow
P/O C W Murphy RCAF pow
F/O R J Kimbell pow
Sgt W A Blackburn +

T/o 1644 Leeming. Sgt Blackburn is buried in the Reichswald Forest War Cemetery.

77 Sqn Whitley V Z9226 KN- Op: Düsseldorf

P/O A D Scott-Martin +
P/O J N Chisholm +
Sgt P G Clark +
Sgt S G Thompson +
Sgt W Jowett RCAF +

T/o 1652 Leeming. All are buried in Rheinberg War Cemetery.

27-28 Dec	77 Sqn		Whitley V	Z9306 KN-S	Op: Düsseldorf
1941	P/O C A C Havelock	+		

27-28 Dec 1941

77 Sqn — Whitley V — Z9306 KN-S — Op: Düsseldorf

P/O C A C Havelock +
F/S E D Ozment RCAF +
Sgt R Shuttleworth +
Sgt D M Godard RCAF pow
Sgt E Fieldsend +

T/o 1653 Leeming. Shot down by a night-fighter (Ofw Paul Gildner, 4./NJG4) and crashed 1957 at Zwarte Haan (Friesland), 16 km NW of Leeuwarden, Holland. Those who died are buried in Het Bildt (Sint Jacobiparochie) General Cemetery.

78 Sqn — Whitley V — Z9276 EY- — Op: Düsseldorf

P/O Shattock
Sgt Wado
Sgt Lee
Sgt Newman
Sgt Lyndon

T/o 1740 Croft. Crashed 1845 after colliding with h/t cables at Foxholes, 10 miles N of Driffield, Yorkshire. The accident was caused by icing of such severity that an emergency landing was inevitable. A fire broke out on impact, injuring three members of the crew.

101 Sqn — Wellington IC — Z1115 SR- — Op: Düsseldorf

P/O G K K K Pelmore +
Sgt J D Anderson +
Sgt O E Rance +
Sgt P C Williams +
Sgt S Johnson +
Sgt D S Edmond +

T/o 1700 Oakington. All are buried in Rheinberg War Cemetery.

138 Sqn — Whitley V — Z9385 NF- — Op: Special Duties

Sgt J R Petts RCAF +
F/S A W Reimer RCAF inj
Sgt G R S Gordon +
Cpl H A Pickering +

T/o Stradishall. Crashed on return to base. F/S Reimer RCAF died from his injuries on 12 January 1942. Along with Sgt Gordon, he is buried in Haverhill Cemetery.

28-29 Dec 1941

49 Sqn — Hampden I — AE419 EA-T — Op: Hüls

Sgt A C Watt +
Sgt E G Sawdy +
F/S E C Atkinson +
Sgt H W Wisdom +

T/o 1741 Scampton. Lost without trace. All are commemorated on the Runnymede Memorial.

51 Sqn — Whitley V — Z9202 MH-P — Op: Emden

Sgt F G W Roberts +
Sgt J H Durning RCAF +
Sgt O H Burchell RCAF +
Sgt R A Priestley +
Sgt H J Groom +
Sgt E A Spicer +

T/o 1724 Dishforth. Believed shot down by a night-fighter operating off the Dutch coast. All are commemorated on the Runnymede Memorial.

144 Sqn — Hampden I — P1295 PL-L — Op: Hüls

Sgt J W Woodall +
Sgt E B Whitaker RNZAF +
Sgt A Collier +
Sgt J F Skingsley +

T/o North Luffenham. Presumed lost over the sea. Two bodies were later recovered and Sgt Whitaker RNZAF and Sgt Skingsley now rest in the Old Communal Cemetery overlooking the harbour at Cherbourg. Their two companions are commemorated on the Runnymede Memorial.

144 Sqn — Hampden I — AD804 PL- — Op: Hüls

Sgt T E Barnett pow
Sgt T S Jones pow
Sgt W R Cheesman +
Sgt W Gilbey pow

T/o North Luffenham. Crash-landed at Doetinchem (Gelderland), Holland, where Sgt Cheesman is buried in Loolaan General Cemetery.

311 Sqn — Wellington IC — T2553 KX-B — Op: Wilhelmshaven

Sgt A Siska pow
Sgt J Tomanek +
F/O J Mohr +
F/O J Scerba pow
Sgt R Skalicky +
Sgt P Svoboda pow

T/o 1716 East Wretham. Crashed in the North Sea W of Petten (Noord Holland), 20 km SSW of Den Helder, Holland. F/O Mohr is buried in Bergen General Cemetery; the rest of those who died are commemorated on the Runnymede Memorial. F/O Scerba was repatriated on 16 September 1944.

28-29 Dec 1941	405 Sqn	Wellington II	W5561 LQ-J	Op: **Emden**

405 Sqn   Wellington II   W5561 LQ-J   Op: **Emden**

Sgt E J Williams RNZAF   +
Sgt D J Gordon   +
F/S J C Donkin RCAF   +
Sgt R James   +
Sgt W Langhorne   +
F/S J R F Bourgeau RCAF   +

T/o 1705 Pocklington. All are buried at Oldenburg in Sage War Cemetery.

408 Sqn   Hampden I   P1165 EQ-B   Op: **Hüls**

P/O S B K Brackenbury   pow
    RCAF
Sgt D W Thane RNZAF   +
Sgt D T Williams   +
Sgt P F Isaac   +

T/o 1855 Balderton. Shot down by a night-fighter (Oblt Emil Woltersdorf, III./NJG1) and crashed 2 km E of Winterswijk (Gelderland), Holland. Those who died are buried in the local cemetery.

29 Dec 1941

10 Sqn   Halifax II   L9614 ZA-   **Training**

Sgt W W Tripp RCAF   +
Sgt W C Green   +

T/o 1510 Leeming for a night training exercise and collided with another Halifax, captained by the Squadron's Commanding Officer.

10 Sqn   Halifax II   V9981 ZA-   **Training**

W/C Tuck

Damaged beyond repair after being struck by the Halifax identified above.

30 Dec 1941

10 Sqn   Halifax II   R9374 ZA-K   Op: **Brest**

F/S L Whyte
Sgt E Allen
Sgt J K Corke
Sgt G R Kent
Sgt C Charlton
Sgt Wood
F/L R J Roach   +

T/o 1102 Leeming. Hit by flak at 1411 over Brest and moments later was savagely attacked by a Me 109, which killed F/L Roach. At 1431 the badly damaged Halifax was ditched some 80 miles S of the Lizard Point, Cornwall, and the survivors were rescued at 1930 by an RN MTB and taken into Penzance. F/L Roach is commemorated on the Runnymede Memorial.

Sgt Kent was destined to have a long career in 4 Group, during which time he served on 76 Squadron and 640 Squadron, ending the war with a DFC and DFM.

35 Sqn   Halifax II   V9979 TL-E   Op: **Brest**

S/L S A Middleton DFC   +
P/O R A F Frew   +
Sgt A S Greenwood   +
P/O L J P Foster   +
Sgt P C G Maflin   +
Sgt J A Orton   +
Sgt M G Kipling   +

T/o 1125 Linton-on-Ouse. Hit by flak and crashed in the target area. All are buried locally in Kerfautras Cemetery.

76 Sqn   Halifax II   L9615 MP-X   Op: **Brest**

P/O D S King RCAF   +
Sgt W R Gates RCAF   +
Sgt P D Randall   +
Sgt S M Wilson RAAF   +
Sgt L Blair   +
Sgt H J Toski   +
Sgt F Eaton   +

T/o 1122 Middleton St. George. Hit by flak and crashed in the sea off the French coast. All are commemorated on the Runnymede Memorial. Buenos Aires born, P/O King RCAF had recently survived a Whitley crash while serving with 78 Squadron.

Appendix 1

Bomber Squadron Losses 1941

Sqn	Type	Op.	Non-op.	Grnd	Sqn	Type	Op.	Non-op.	Grnd
7	Stirling I	37	2	1	138	Lysander III		1	
9	Wellington IC	23		1		Whitley V	1	1	
	Wellington III	5	1			Halifax II	1		
10	Whitley V	36	1		139	Blenheim IV	34	7	1
	Halifax II	1	2		142	Wellington II	5	1	
12	Wellington II	15	1	1		Wellington IV	4	1	
15	Wellington IC	4			144	Hampden I	48	1	
	Stirling I	24	3		149	Wellington IC	29	2	
18	Blenheim IV	27	5	1		Wellington II	1		
21	Blenheim IV	37	6			Stirling I		1	
35	Halifax I	23	2	1	150	Wellington IC	17	2	
	Halifax II	2			207	Manchester I	15	5	
40	Wellington IC	31	1		214	Wellington IC	25	3	
	Wellington II	1				Wellington II	3		
44	Hampden I	35	5	1	218	Wellington IA		1	
49	Hampden I	29	4			Wellington IC	32	1	
50	Hampden I	44	6			Wellington II	2	1	
51	Whitley V	43	1		226	Blenheim IV	18	5	
57	Wellington IC	30	1	1	300	Wellington IC	11		
	Wellington II	2				Wellington IV	2	1	
58	Whitley V	37			301	Wellington IC	10	3	1
61	Anson I		1			Wellington IV	2		
	Hampden I	21	1		304	Wellington IC	10	3	
	Manchester I	3	2		305	Wellington IC	6	1	
75	Wellington IC	33	1			Wellington II	8	2	
76	Halifax I	13	2		311	Anson I		1	
	Halifax II	1				Wellington IA		2	
77	Whitley V	38	2			Wellington IC	12	1	
78	Whitley V	42	2		405	Wellington II	18	2	1
82	Blenheim IV	32	4	2	408	Hampden I	9		
83	Hampden I	39	3		455	Hampden I	5	1	
88	Blenheim I		1		458	Wellington IV	3		1
	Blenheim IV	6	3	1	1459	Whitley V	2	1	
	Boston III		1						
90	Fortress I	3	2	1		Total	1341	156	15
97	Hampden I	1							
	Manchester I	10	4						
99	Wellington IA		1						
	Wellington IC	29	2						
	Wellington II	3							
101	Blenheim IV	7	1						
	Wellington IC	15	1						
102	Whitley V	45	2						
103	Wellington IC	21							
104	Wellington II	15	3						
105	Blenheim IV	18	4						
106	Hampden I	43	5						
107	Blenheim IV	15	2						
109	Wellington IC	1	1						
110	Blenheim IV	16	4						
114	Blenheim IV	13	6						
115	Wellington IC	38	2						
	Wellington II	1							
	Wellington III		1						

Note. The statistics appearing below the column headed Grnd indicates aircraft destroyed in ground incidents.

941 Totals

ype	Op.	Non-op.	Grnd	Total
nson I		2		2
lenheim I		1		1
lenheim IV	223	45	5	275
oston III		1		1
ortress I	3	2	1	6
alifax I	36	4	1	41
alifax II	5	2		7
ampden I	274	26	1	301
ysander III		1		1
anchester I	28	11		39
tirling I	61	6	1	68
ellington IA		4		4
ellington IC	377	25	3	408*
ellington II	74	10	2	86
ellington III	5	2		7
ellington IV	11	2	1	14
hitley V	244	10		254
otal	1341	156	15	1515*

Indicates losses not covered by the hree headings.

1939-1941 Combined Totals - Revised

Type	Op.	Non-op.	Grnd	Total
Anson I	1	11		12
Battle I	148	40	28	217*
Blenheim I	11	11		23*
Blenheim IV	541	107	19	670*
Boston III		1		1
Fortress I	3	2	1	6
Halifax I	36	4	1	41
Halifax II	5	2		7
Hampden I	481	85	1	567
Hereford I		2		2
Lysander III		1		1
Manchester I	28	11		39
Master I		1		1
Stirling I	61	7	1	69
Wellington I	3	11	1	15
Wellington IA	45	13	1	59
Wellington IC	483	34	4	524*
Wellington II	74	10	2	86
Wellington III	5	2		7
Wellington IV	11	2	1	14
Whitley I		2		2
Whitley II		2		2
Whitley III	9	6		15
Whitley IV	5	2		7
Whitley V	381	16	9	408*
Total	2331	385	69	2795*

Appendix 2

Group Losses 1941

	Sqn	Code	Type	Op.	Non-op.	Grnd	Remarks
1 Group	12	PH	Wellington II	15	1	1	
	103	PM	Wellington IC	21			
	142	QT	Wellington II	5	1		
		QT	Wellington IV	4	1		
	150	JN	Wellington IC	17	2		
	300	BH	Wellington IC	11			
		BH	Wellington IV	2	1		
	301	GR	Wellington IC	10	3	1	
		GR	Wellington IV	2			
	304	NZ	Wellington IC	10	3		Operational 25–26 Apr 41
	305	SM	Wellington IC	6	1		Operational 25–26 Apr 41
		SM	Wellington II	8	2		
	458		Wellington IV	3		1	Operational 20–21 Oct 41
			Total	114	15	3	
2 Group	18	WV	Blenheim IV	27	5	1	
	21	YH	Blenheim IV	37	6		
	82	UX	Blenheim IV	32	4	2	
	88	RH	Blenheim I		1		Joined Group 8 Jul 41
		RH	Blenheim IV	6	3	1	
		RH	Boston III		1		
	90	WP	Fortress I	3	2	1	Operational 8 Jul 41
	101	SR	Blenheim IV	7	1		To 3 Group May 41
	105	GB	Blenheim IV	18	4		
	107	OM	Blenheim IV	15	2		
	110	VE	Blenheim IV	16	4		
	114	RT	Blenheim IV	13	6		
	139	XD	Blenheim IV	34	7	1	
	226	MQ	Blenheim IV	18	5		Joined Group 26 May 41
			Total	226	51	6	
3 Group	7	MG	Stirling I	37	2	1	Operational 10–11 Feb 41
	9	WS	Wellington IC	23		1	
		WS	Wellington III	5	1		
	15	LS	Wellington IC	4			
		LS	Stirling I	24	3		
	40	BL	Wellington IC	31	1		
		BL	Wellington II	1			
	57	DX	Wellington IC	30	1	1	
		DX	Wellington II	2			
	75	AA	Wellington IC	33	1		
	99	LN	Wellington IA		1		
		LN	Wellington IC	29	2		
		LN	Wellington II	3			
	101	SR	Wellington IC	15	1		Joined Group May 41
	115	KO	Wellington IC	38	2		
		KO	Wellington II	1			
		KO	Wellington III		1		
	138	NF	Lysander III		1		Administered by Group
		NF	Whitley V	1	1		
		NF	Halifax II	1			

	Sqn	Code	Type	Op.	Non-op.	Grnd	Remarks
3 Group	149	OJ	Wellington IC	29	2		
		OJ	Wellington II	1			
		OJ	Stirling I		1		
	214	BU	Wellington IC	25	3		
		BU	Wellington II	3			
	218	HA	Wellington IA		1		
		HA	Wellington IC	32	1		
		HA	Wellington II	2	1		
	311	KX	Anson I		1		
		KX	Wellington IA		2		
		KX	Wellington IC	12	1		
			Total	382	31	3	
4 Group	10	ZA	Whitley V	36	1		
		ZA	Halifax II	1	2		
	35	TL	Halifax I	23	2	1	Operational 10-11 Mar 41
		TL	Halifax II	2			
	51	MH	Whitley V	43	1		
	58	GE	Whitley V	37			
	76	MP	Halifax I	13	2		Operational 12-13 Jun 41
		MP	Halifax II	1			
	77	KN	Whitley V	38	2		
	78	EY	Whitley V	42	2		
	102	DY	Whitley V	45	2		
	104	EP	Wellington II	15	3		Operational 8-9 May 41
	405	LQ	Wellington II	18	2	1	Operational 12-13 Jun 41
			Total	314	19	2	
5 Group	44	KM	Hampden I	35	5	1	
	49	EA	Hampden I	29	4		
	50	VN	Hampden I	44	6		
	61	QR	Anson I		1		
		QR	Hampden I	21	1		
		QR	Manchester I	3	2		
	83	OL	Hampden I	39	3		
	97	OF	Hampden I	1			
		OF	Manchester I	10	4		Operational 8-9 Apr 41
	106	ZN	Hampden I	43	5		
	144	PL	Hampden I	48	1		
	207	EM	Manchester I	15	5		Operational 24-25 Feb 41
	408	EQ	Hampden I	9			Operational 11-12 Aug 41
	455	UB	Hampden I	5	1		Operational 29-30 Aug 41
			Total	302	38	1	

Appendix 3

Squadron Bases 1941

	Sqn	Base	Arrived	Remarks
1 Group	12	Binbrook, Lincolnshire	in situ	
	103	Newton, Nottinghamshire	in situ	
		Elsham Wolds, Lincolnshire	11 Jul 41	
	142	Binbrook, Lincolnshire	in situ	Wellington IV, Oct 41
		Grimsby, Lincolnshire	26 Nov 41	
	150	Newton, Nottinghamshire	in situ	
		Snaith, Yorkshire	10 Jul 41	
	300	Swinderby, Lincolnshire	in situ	
		Hemswell, Lincolnshire	18 Jul 41	Wellington IV, Oct 41
	301	Swinderby, Lincolnshire	in situ	
		Hemswell, Lincolnshire	18 Jul 41	Wellington IV, Oct 41
	304	Syerston, Nottinghamshire	in situ	
		Lindholme, Yorkshire	19 Jul 41	
	305	Syerston, Nottinghamshire	in situ	
		Lindholme, Yorkshire	20 Jul 41	Wellington II, Jul 41
	458	Williamstown, New South Wales	8 Jul 41	Formed
		Holme-on-Spalding Moor, Yorkshire	25 Aug 41	Wellington IV
	460	Molesworth, Huntingdonshire	15 Nov 41	Formed, Wellington IV
2 Group	18	Great Massingham, Norfolk	in situ	
		Oulton, Norfolk	3 Apr 41	
		Horsham St. Faith, Norfolk	13 Jul 41	
		Manston, Kent	16 Aug 41	
		Horsham St. Faith, Norfolk	27 Aug 41	
	21	Bodney, Norfolk	in situ	
		Lossiemouth, Morayshire	27 May 41	Detached Coastal Command
		Watton, Norfolk	14 Jun 41	
		Manston, Kent	17 Jul 41	
		Watton, Norfolk	25 Jul 41	
		Lossiemouth, Morayshire	7 Sep 41	Detached Coastal Command
		Watton, Norfolk	21 Sep 41	
		Luqa, Malta	26 Sep 41	Detached Mediterranean
	82	Bodney, Norfolk	in situ	
		Lossiemouth, Morayshire	18 Apr 41	Detached Coastal Command
		Bodney, Norfolk	3 May 41	
		Luqa, Malta	11 Jun 41	Detached Mediterranean
		Bodney, Norfolk	Jun 41	
	88	Swanton Morley, Norfolk	8 Jul 41	Joined Group
		Attlebridge, Norfolk	1 Aug 41	Boston III, Oct 41
	90	Watton, Norfolk	7 May 41	Reformed, Fortress I
		West Raynham, Norfolk	15 May 41	
		Polebrook, Northamptonshire	28 Jun 41	
	101	West Raynham, Norfolk	in situ	To 3 Group, May 41
	105	Swanton Morley, Norfolk	in situ	
		Lossiemouth, Morayshire	5 May 41	
		Swanton Morley, Norfolk	21 May 41	
		Luqa, Malta	28 Jul 41	Detached Mediterranean
		Horsham St. Faith, Norfolk	8 Dec 41	Mosquito IV, Nov 41
	107	Wattisham, Suffolk	in situ	
		Leuchars, Fifeshire	3 Mar 41	Detached Coastal Command
		Great Massingham, Norfolk	11 May 41	
		Luqa, Malta	20 Aug 41	Detached Mediterranean

	Sqn	Base	Arrived	Remarks
2 Group	110	Wattisham, Suffolk	in situ	
		Horsham St. Faith, Norfolk	16 Feb 41	
		Wattisham, Suffolk	15 Mar 41	
		Manston, Kent	26 May 41	
		Wattisham, Suffolk	9 Jun 41	
		Luqa, Malta	1 Jul 41	Detached Mediterranean
		Wattisham, Suffolk	28 Jul 41	
		Lindholme, Yorkshire	15 Sep 41	
		Wattisham, Suffolk	20 Sep 41	
		Lossiemouth, Morayshire	23 Dec 41	
		Wattisham, Suffolk	28 Dec 41	
	114	Oulton, Norfolk	in situ	
		Thornaby, Yorkshire	2 Mar 41	Detached Coastal Command
		Leuchars, Fifeshire	13 May 41	Detached Coastal Command
		West Raynham, Norfolk	19 Jul 41	
	139	Horsham St. Faith, Norfolk	in situ	
		Luqa, Malta	May 41	Detached Mediterranean
		Horsham St. Faith, Norfolk	Jun 41	
		Oulton, Norfolk	13 Jul 41	
		Manston, Kent	27 Aug 41	
		Oulton, Norfolk	7 Sep 41	
		Horsham St. Faith, Norfolk	23 Oct 41	
		Oulton, Norfolk	5 Dec 41	Embarked Far East, Dec 41
	226	Wattisham, Norfolk	26 May 41	Joined Group
		Swanton Morley, Norfolk	9 Dec 41	Boston III, Nov 41
3 Group	7	Oakington, Cambridgeshire	in situ	
	9	Honington, Suffolk	in situ	Wellington III, Oct 41
	15	Wyton, Huntingdonshire	in situ	Stirling I, Apr 41
	40	Wyton, Huntingdonshire	in situ	
		Alconbury, Huntingdonshire	2 Feb 41	Part to Malta, Oct 41
	57	Feltwell, Norfolk	in situ	
	75	Feltwell, Norfolk	in situ	
	99	Newmarket, Cambridgeshire	in situ	
		Waterbeach, Cambridgeshire	18 Mar 41	
	101	West Raynham, Norfolk	May 41	Joined Group
		Oakington, Cambridgeshire	1 Jul 41	
	115	Marham, Norfolk	in situ	Wellington III, Nov 41
	138	Newmarket, Cambridgeshire	25 Aug 41	Reformed
	149	Mildenhall, Suffolk	in situ	Stirling I, Nov 41
	214	Stradishall, Suffolk	in situ	
	218	Marham, Norfolk	in situ	
	311	East Wretham, Norfolk	in situ	
	419	Mildenhall, Suffolk	15 Dec 41	Formed, Wellington IC
Group	10	Leeming, Yorkshire	in situ	Halifax II, Dec 41
	35	Linton-on-Ouse, Yorkshire	in situ	Halifax II, Dec 41
	51	Dishforth, Yorkshire	in situ	
	58	Linton-on-Ouse, Yorkshire	in situ	
	76	Linton-on-Ouse, Yorkshire	12 Apr 41	Reformed, Halifax I
		Middleton St. George, Durham	4 Jun 41	Halifax II, Dec 41
	77	Topcliffe, Yorkshire	in situ	
		Leeming, Yorkshire	5 Sep 41	
	78	Dishforth, Yorkshire	in situ	
		Middleton St. George, Durham	7 Apr 41	
		Croft, Durham	20 Oct 41	
	102	Topcliffe, Yorkshire	in situ	
		Dalton, Yorkshire	15 Nov 41	Halifax II, Dec 41
	104	Driffield, Yorkshire	1 Apr 41	Reformed, Wellington II
	405	Driffield, Yorkshire	23 Apr 41	Formed, Wellington II
		Pocklington, Yorkshire	20 Jun 41	

	Sqn	Base	Arrived	Remarks
5 Group	44	Waddington, Lincolnshire	in situ	Lancaster I, Dec 41
	49	Scampton, Lincolnshire	in situ	
	50	Lindholme, Yorkshire	in situ	
		Swinderby, Lincolnshire	19 Jul 41	
		Skellingthorpe, Lincolnshire	26 Nov 41	
	61	Hemswell, Lincolnshire	in situ	Manchester I, Jun 41
		North Luffenham, Rutland	17 Jul 41	
		Woolfox Lodge, Rutland	Nov 41	
	83	Scampton, Lincolnshire	in situ	
	97	Waddington, Lincolnshire	25 Feb 41	Reformed, Manchester I
		Coningsby, Lincolnshire	10 Mar 41	
	106	Finningley, Yorkshire	in situ	
		Coningsby, Lincolnshire	23 Feb 41	
	144	Hemswell, Lincolnshire	in situ	
		North Luffenham, Rutland	17 Jul 41	
	207	Waddington, Lincolnshire	in situ	
		Bottesford, Leicestershire	17 Nov 41	
	408	Lindholme, Yorkshire	24 Jun 41	Formed, Hampden I
		Syerston, Nottinghamshire	20 Jul 41	
		Balderton, Nottinghamshire	9 Dec 41	
	420	Waddington, Lincolnshire	19 Dec 41	Formed, Hampden I
	455	Williamstown, New South Wales	23 May 41	Formed
		Swinderby, Lincolnshire	6 Jun 41	Hampden I

Appendix 4

Bomber OTU and Conversion Flight Losses 1941

OTU	Type	Op.	Non-op.	Grnd
10	Anson I		3	
	Whitley III		1	
	Whitley V		19	
11	Anson I		1	
	Wellington I		6	
	Wellington IA		3	
	Wellington IC	1	21	1
12	Wellington I		1	
	Wellington IA		1	1
	Wellington IC		11	1
13	Blenheim I		7	
	Blenheim IV		22	
14	Anson I		2	1
	Hampden I		30	
	Hereford I		1	
15	Anson I		1	
	Wellington I		2	
	Wellington IC	2	20	
16	Anson I		6	
	Hampden I		42	1
	Hereford I		1	
17	Anson I		2	
	Blenheim I		5	
	Blenheim IV		33	
18	Anson I		2	
	Wellington I		2	
	Wellington IA		2	
	Wellington IC		8	1
19	Anson I		3	
	Whitley IV		7	
	Whitley V		15	
20	Anson I		4	
	Wellington I		3	
	Wellington IA		3	
	Wellington IC		18	
21	Anson I		3	
	Wellington IC		12	
22	Anson I			1
	Wellington IC		6	
23	Wellington IC		5	
25	Anson I		3	
	Hampden I		18	
	Manchester I		1	
	Wellington IC		7	
27	Anson I		1	
	Wellington IA		1	
	Wellington IC		11	
	Total	3	376	7

Flt	Type	Op.	Non-op.	Grnd
26	Stirling I		3	
28	Halifax I		1	
	Total		4	

Note. A M Form 78 shows the Halifax as belonging to 1652 Conversion Unit which did not form until January 1942.

1941 Totals

Type	Op.	Non-op.	Grnd
Anson I		31	2
Blenheim I		12	
Blenheim IV		55	
Halifax I		1	
Hampden I		90	1
Hereford I		2	
Manchester I		1	
Stirling I		3	
Wellington I		14	
Wellington IA		10	1
Wellington IC	3	119	3
Whitley III		1	
Whitley IV		7	
Whitley V		34	
Total	3	380	7

1940/1941 Combined Totals - Revised

Type	Op.	Non-op.	Grnd
Anson I		48	2
Battle I		30	
Blenheim I		21	
Blenheim IV		85	
Halifax I		1	
Hampden I		127	1
Hereford I		10	
Manchester I		1	
Stirling I		3	
Wellington I		36	3
Wellington IA	1	28	2
Wellington IC	3	120	3
Whitley II		1	
Whitley III		6	
Whitley IV		9	
Whitley V		41	
Total	4	567	11

Appendix 5

Bomber OTU and Conversion Flight Bases 1941

OTU	Base	Arrived	Remarks
10	Abingdon, Berkshire	in situ	Used codes EL RK UY ZG
	Stanton Harcourt, Oxfordshire	in situ	Satellite
	Mount Farm, Oxfordshire	23 Jul 41	Satellite
11	Bassingbourn, Cambridgeshire	in situ	Used codes KJ TX
	Steeple Morden, Cambridgeshire	Oct 41	Satellite
	Tempsford, Bedfordshire	20 Dec 41	Satellite
12	Benson, Oxfordshire	in situ	Used codes FQ JP
	Mount Farm, Oxfordshire	in situ	Satellite until 23 Jul 41
	Chipping Warden, Northamptonshire	10 Jul 41	Main base
13	Bicester, Oxfordshire	in situ	Used codes FV KQ XJ
	Hinton-in-the-Hedges, Northamptonshire	in situ	Satellite
14	Cottesmore, Rutland	in situ	Used codes AM GL
	Woolfox Lodge, Rutland	in situ	Satellite until Sep 41
	Saltby, Leicestershire	Aug 41	Satellite
15	Harwell, Berkshire	in situ	Used codes EO FH KK
	Hampstead Norris, Berkshire	in situ	Satellite
	Mount Farm, Oxfordshire	24 Jul 41	Satellite
16	Upper Heyford, Oxfordshire	in situ	Used codes GA JS XG
	Croughton, Northamptonshire	in situ	Satellite
17	Upwood, Huntingdonshire	in situ	Used codes AY JG WJ
	Warboys, Huntingdonshire	17 Apr 41	Satellite
18	Bramcote, Warwickshire	in situ	Used codes EN VQ XW
	Bitteswell, Leicestershire	30 Jun 41	Satellite
19	Kinloss, Morayshire	in situ	Used codes UO XF ZV
	Forres, Morayshire	25 Jan 41	Satellite
20	Lossiemouth, Morayshire	in situ	Used codes JM XL ZT
	Elgin, Morayshire	in situ	Satellite
21	Moreton-in-Marsh, Gloucestershire	20 Jan 41	Formed Used codes ED SJ UH
	Edge Hill, Warwickshire	21 Oct 41	Satellite
22	Wellesbourne Mountford, Warwickshire	14 Apr 41	Formed Used codes DD LT OX XN
	Atherstone, Warwickshire	5 Jul 41	Satellite
23	Pershore, Worcestershire	1 Apr 41	Formed Used codes BY FZ WE
	Defford, Worcestershire	25 Sep 41	Satellite
25	Finningley, Yorkshire	1 Mar 41	Formed Used codes PP
	Balderton, Nottinghamshire	14 Jun 41	Satellite until 14 Nov 41
	Bircotes, Nottinghamshire	14 Nov 41	Satellite
27	Lichfield, Staffordshire	23 Apr 41	Formed Used codes BB UJ YL

Note. Throughout 1941, the OTUs were mainly controlled by 6 Group at Abingdon and 7 Group at Brampton Grange, Huntingdonshire, the latter establishment shifting to Winslow Hall in Buckinghamshire on 1 September 1941.

18 OTU Principally concerned with the training of Polish Air Force personnel.
22 OTU Atherstone was later known as Stratford.

Flt	Base	Arrived	Remarks
26	Waterbeach, Cambridgeshire	Oct 41	Formed Stirling I
28	Leconfield, Yorkshire	Oct 41	Formed Halifax I
	Marston Moor, Yorkshire	Dec 41	
106	Waterbeach, Cambridgeshire	Dec 41	Formed Stirling I

Appendix 6

Escapers and Evaders 1940-41

The Escape Reports, as they are officially known, are held at the Public Record Office, Kew, and can be located in the War Office series of files (WO208). The files, or piece numbers, run from 3298 to 3327 inclusive, though one file, 3305, is closed to public scrutiny for the foreseeable future.

Each file contains approximately seventy to eighty reports, each report noting the circumstances of the escape, or evasion, from the time of take off to the date of the airman's return to the United Kingdom. Some reports are extremely well documented, while others are less revealing in their content.

It is believed that the airmen identified in this appendix, who were posted missing in 1940-1941, were involved in escapes from enemy occupied territory and the reference number of their reports, where known, have been appended.

Those reports containing the letter G in their identity· suggest the airman concerned escaped from within Germany, in most cases from a prisoner of war camp.

What is most important to remember is that each escape required considerable courage and a will to succeed on the part of the individual involved, while more often than not he was aided by many helpers, who quite literally risked their lives each time they gave shelter and assistance to those on the run.

Taking, for example, the famous Comète organisation, well over 150 of their number were executed, often after enduring months of cruel torture at the hands of the Gestapo and their henchmen. Despite the risk, the escape lines were kept open throughout the war, and thus each of the reports hereby shown are a reminder of the debt owed to those extraordinary men and women of the occupied countries of Europe who played their part in securing victory.

Sqn	Name	File	Report
9	Sgt R W Blaydon	3308	(-)714
	Sgt H W Bratley		
	S/L H E Bufton	3307	(-)610
	Sgt W F Crampton	3307	(-)627
	Sgt L D Goldingay		
	Sgt S M P Parkes		
	Sgt K B Read	3307	(-)626
	F/L J T L Shore	3307	(G)593
	Sgt R Vivian	3308	(-)713
	Sgt L R Willis	3308	(-)712
10	Sgt D D W Nabarro	3310	(G)891
12	Sgt Batty		
	Sgt G D Mansell		
	Sgt J L Newton	3307	(-)649
40	Sgt G H Easton		
	S/L B Paddon	3310	(G)805
	Sgt C Rofe		
	Sgt E Watson		
50	F/O J A Whitecross	3304	(-)379
51	Sgt J L Ives RCAF		
	Sgt H R Wilson RCAF	3308	(-)673
61	Sgt M J Joyce	3311	(G)947
76	Sgt C B Flockhart	3319	(G)1833
77	Sgt A Day RCAF		
78	Sgt H J Mott	3307	(-)607
82	Sgt S J Fulbrook		
	Sgt N J Ingram	3304	(-)375
	Sgt T J Watkins		
83	Sgt C B James	3308	(F)682
	Sgt D MacCallum	3304	(-)374
99	Sgt L Birk		
	Sgt J Dicks		

Sqn	Name	File	Report
99	Sgt R Dyer		
101	Sgt G Campbell	3307	(-)634
	Sgt H I Hickton	3310	(-)894
	Sgt J W Hutton	3308	(-)688
	Sgt L Pearman	3311	(-)928
	Sgt R W A Saxton	3310	(-)893
	Sgt L A Warburton	3308	(-)687
	Sgt J R Worby	3307	(-)633
103	F/O R Hawkins	3299	(F)77
	Sgt A W Mills	3311	(-)929
104	Sgt G T Woodroofe	3323	(G)2452
107	W/C B E Embry DSO	3299	(F)41a
	Sgt R W Lonsdale	3303	(F)278
109	Sgt N W MacKenzie	3308	(-)699
115	P/O A F McSweyn RAAF	3317	(G)1629
138	F/O T Jasinski	3307	(-)617
	F/O S Krol	3307	(-)616
	W/C R Rudkowski	3307	(-)668
	Sgt F Sobkowiak	3307	(-)670
139	Sgt Hale		
	Sgt T E Hyde		
	F/O N E W Pepper		
	S/L T G Tideman		
142	Cpl D J Barbrooke		
	S/L J F Hobler		
	Sgt R V T Kitto		
	Sgt A N Spear		
144	P/O B J A Rennie		
149	F/O H Burton		
	Sgt R A Hodgson DFM	3318	(-)1817
150	Sgt H Berry	3303	(F)296
	Sgt D L Phillips	3300	(F)133

Sqn	Name	File	Report	Sqn	Name	File	Report
150	LAC A K Summerson	3302	(-)237	300	Sgt J Budzynski	3308	(-)686
	F/O J G Vernon				P/O Z Groyecki	3307	(-)667
207	P/O H B Carroll	3307	(-)666		P/O W Radwanski	3308	(-)722
	Sgt G T Cox	3308	(-)694		F/O M Taras	3308	(-)721
	F/S K H L Houghton	3309	(-)788	305	Sgt M Kowalski	3307	(-)631
	DFM				Sgt S Tomicki	3307	(-)630
218	Sgt V G Haley	3308	(-)691	405	Sgt M H J Dalphond	3311	(-)907
	Sgt W H Harris				RCAF		
	LAC H B Jones				Sgt J S Paton RCAF		
	F/L H D Wardle	3311	(G)996		W/C P A Gilchrist DFC	3308	(-)672

Appendix 7

Prisoners of War 1939-41

Information concerning airmen who were taken prisoner of war can be found in a number of files at the Public Record Office, Kew. The principal source is AIR20 2336, which was compiled in late 1944 and lists the names of airmen known to have been incarcerated in German prisoner of war camps. The document is considered accurate to circa December 1944, though a few entries for 1945 are included.

The names are arranged in alphabetical order of officers and airmen of the RAF, including non-commonwealth airmen, followed by the officers and airmen of the RAAF, RCAF, RNZAF and SAAF air forces. The majority of entries show the camp (by code) in which the airman was being held in 1944, his prisoner of war number and his rank.

Identification of the camp codes appearing in this appendix have been added at the end.

Sqn	Name	Camp	Number
7	F/L G M Fuller	L3	3659
	S/L L W V Jennens	L3	1427
	P/O C I Rolfe	L3	3586
	F/L M C G Sherwood	L3	3646
	W/O W S Bellow	357	18300
	W/O J H Boulton	357	9554
	W/O L N Chappell	357	39234
	W/O C J Cobbold	357	9675
	Sgt J J Copley DFM	L6	9676
	W/O L E J Davenport	L6	9553
	W/O F V Davis	383	151
	W/O A Donaldson	L3	18333
	W/O B A A Fowler	357	35
	W/O D A Lloyd	357	23610
	W/O C MacDonald	L3	560
	W/O D S Merrells	357	42
	W/O D Y Neil	357	24393
	W/O D Owens	357	183
	W/O E V Smith	383	123
	W/O A Speakman	357	9555
	W/O R I Stone	357	32
	W/O J M Sutton	357	9556
	W/O C A Tout	383	34
	W/O J C Webb	383	126
	W/O T F M Williams	357	45
	W/O W P Wood	357	37
	F/S A Yardley	357	9557
	F/L C M Hall RAAF	L3	389
	W/O F K Lister RAAF	L7	901148
	F/L G S Edwards RCAF	357	39237
9	F/O D Bruce AFM	04C	1356
	F/L R V Derbyshire	L3	327
	F/L B A James	L3	2263
	S/L S G Pritchard	L3	384
	F/O P A W Thomas	L3	352
	F/L S W Webster	L3	2253
	W/O R F Akerman	L6	316
	Sgt G C Balch	357	585
	W/O R H Barratt	357	18299
	W/O R D Bews	357	536
	W/O J R Brown	357	484
	W/O B W Channings	357	589
	W/O E Collins	357	492
	W/O R R Mc Graham	L6	598

Sqn	Name	Camp	Number
9	W/O D R Greig	357	52
	W/O A K Griffiths	357	500
	W/O N D R Griffiths	L3	548
	W/O B Hanlon	357	599
	W/O A Hunt	357	355
	W/O B S Jacobs	357	602
	W/O T Lancaster	357	604
	Sgt S Murray	357	23606
	W/O C Murton	357	52562
	W/O H Newall	L4	377
	W/O R Parkin	L3	566
	W/O J M Pinkham	357	18298
	W/O J Pryde	357	39328
	W/O D B Reid	L3	610
	W/O H J Tomkins	L6	852
	W/O R M Trundle	L3	2253
	W/O S F Whitlock	357	617
	W/O H A Wink	357	18297
	W/O R P Wright	357	23608
	W/O R G Damman RAAF	357	592
	F/L J T Stickles RCAF	L3	23602
10	F/L W A K Carr	L3	122
	F/L D A ffrench-Mullen	L3	118
	F/L W M W Fowler	L3	1384
	F/L G M Frame	L3	1380
	S/L M M Kane	L3	3708
	F/L J D Margrie	L3	1381
	F/L P R M Runnacles	L3	10
	F/L P G Whitby	L3	1256
	W/O J P Atkinson	357	148
	W/O H W Bradley	L6	204
	W/O W D Chamberlain	357	325
	W/O B S Craske	L6	120
	W/O J W Davidson	L1	31977
	W/O P R Donaldson	L6	138
	W/O W Gardner	357	15
	W/O N J Gregory	357	39172
	W/O J Grounds	L6	9552
	W/O R R Hanson	357	18291
	W/O R M Holder	L6	9549
	W/O E R Holmes	357	218
	W/O H H Josliu	357	39176
	W/O A G W Miller	357	153
	W/O A Millington	L7	341

Sqn	Name	Camp	Number	Sqn	Name	Camp	Number
10	W/O H le Q Mourant	357	166	15	W/O R Harper	357	9649
	W/O R E Nicholson	357	303		W/O E C Haynes	357	23621
	W/O A S Shand	357	307		W/O R D Hooley	357	9587
	W/O A M Somerville	L6	229		W/O J D Jeffrey	357	97
	F/S J E Fulkerson RCAF	357	123		W/O W Jessop DFM	L6	556
	F/S N S Jones RCAF	357	9551		W/O J M Johnson	L3	23624
	F/S J W Meyers RCAF	4B	122		W/O W H Jordan	357	506
	WO2 J H Morgan RCAF	357	9550		W/O W C Moir	357	9662
	F/S S S Shapiro RCAF	357	103		W/O F R Pepper	357	13039
12	F/L T F S Brereton	L3	2264		W/O D Rees	L1	39183
	F/L G D Clancey	L3	596		W/O J Scott	357	13076
	F/L P W Cook	L3	1243		W/O F Smith	357	9
	S/L S S Fieldon	L3	3788		W/O R R Stewart	357	23617
	F/L R B Langlois	L3	653		W/O V N Taylor	L6	98
	F/L I A McIntosh	L3	104		W/O E L H Thomas	L3	5209
	F/L J F McPhie	L3	16247		W/O T S Thorkilsen	L6	39184
	F/L A W Matthews	L3	1261		W/O L C Titterton	L6	8
	F/L R C L Parkhouse	L3	469		F/L F Thompson RAAF	L3	3675
	F/L N M Thomas	L3	1401		F/S G Armstrong RCAF	357	39290
	W/O C S G Beavers	357	13399		W/O D B Annesley RNZAF	357	39182
	W/O H J E Burrell	11A	139375		W/O H N Guymer RNZAF	357	2
	W/O T S Campion	357	13085		W/O H G Hedge RNZAF	357	503
	W/O B T P Carey	357	13097		W/O L B McCarthy RNZAF	357	39180
	W/O N Cass	L6	24378	18	F/L B A Davidson	L3	123
	W/O L R Clarke	L6	21959		F/L D S Dickins	L3	2271
	W/O R A Copley	357	24364		F/L G H Hill	L3	3734
	W/O C B Elsdon DFM	L6	24379		F/O W A Staniland	L3	3736
	W/O N T W Harper	357	88		W/O P C Brewer	L3	110594
	W/O S I Harrison	357	217		W/O H D Cue	L3	110592
	W/O L R Lanfear	357	9577		W/O R J Fisk	357	139
	W/O R Ledgerwood	357	9580		W/O J Gilmour	L3	74
	W/O R P MacNaughton	L1	13048		W/O C N Harris	357	18280
	W/O J W McLarnon	7A	139328		W/O E E B Le Voi	L3	13071
	W/O A R Morris	L6	372		W/O L C Mitchell	357	745
	W/O W G Morton	357	24465		W/O L A F Parrish	357	112
	W/O G N Patterson	357	36841		W/O J C Sands	L6	640
	W/O F G Pett	357	24400		W/O D G Adams RAAF	357	9621
	W/O M D Smalley	357	21957		S/L A F H Mills RCAF	L3	3706
	W/O F T Spencer	L6	13086		WO2 J M Jarrell RCAF	357	68
	W/O J Stewart	357	231	21	S/L F L Campbell-Rogers	L3	3655
	W/O J G Thomson	L6	13337		S/L H D H Cooper DFC	L3	3795
	W/O H R W Winkler	357	21960		F/O D Graham-Hogg	L3	3656
	W/O J D Wright	L3	151		F/L G F Lowes	L3	3815
	W/O A H Smith RAAF	357	9638		F/L D MacDonald	L3	115
	F/L J W McCarthy RCAF	L3	3763		F/L W L MacDonald	L3	3745
	F/L W J Peat RCAF	L3	3779		S/L M L C McColm	04C	458
	F/S D C Jackson RCAF	357	24381		F/O R J McConnell	L3	410
	F/S T V Johnston RCAF	357	9576		S/L H J C Tudge	L3	1621
	WO2 C W Lewis RCAF	357	24375		W/O W D Barker	357	39292
	W/O K A Cometti RNZAF	L7	18670		W/O D E Bingham	357	11
	W/O R D Porteous RNZAF	8A	32409		W/O D E Bristow	357	483
15	F/L P F Eames	L3	160		W/O W H Eden	L6	87
	S/L T W Piper	L3	3647		W/O E A Goold	L6	9602
	F/L J E Russell	L3	527		W/O E W Green	357	499
	F/L T H B Tayler	L3	3666		W/O J R M Kemp	L3	24485
	W/O J D Aitken	L6	23623		W/O G J Langston	357	89
	W/O C S Aynsley	357	9585		W/O J Marsden	357	39299
	W/O B Beecroft	L3	10		W/O C G Penn	357	39258
	W/O R Booth	357	13061		W/O D J Roberts	L6	92
	Sgt J Brown	344	23622		W/O H Rowson	357	112
	W/O J B L Bunce	357	23622		W/O F J Soal	357	38313
	W/O G H Burland	L6	23618		W/O C Webb	357	76
	W/O W E M Davies	L3	594	35	S/L J H Barrett	L3	3794
	W/O J T Day	L6	3		F/L G A Eperon	L3	2870
	W/O J E Dodd	L3	9584		F/L P Langmead	L3	1631
	W/O H J Dunnett	L6	9583		F/L C G Lythgoe	L3	703

Sqn	Name	Camp	Number
35	F/L G S Williams	L3	3787
	Sgt T E Allasson	L3	9524
	W/O S R Arthur	L6	9536
	W/O E O T Balcomb	357	25
	W/O G D Barry	357	39259
	W/O R L B Beare	L6	9569
	W/O L W Bovington DFM	357	39258
	W/O F H Brown	357	39208
	W/O A E Connor	383	97
	W/O E W Constable	357	2783
	W/O R R Drummond	L1	24504
	W/O J N Gibson	357	118
	W/O A Gillbanks	357	9548
	W/O S D Greaves	357	22
	W/O H E Greene	357	9628
	W/O J C Hamilton	383	84
	W/O K Hartland	357	39202
	W/O J W Hays	357	9600
	W/O J P Henderson	L1	90065
	W/O A Henery	357	26
	W/O W T Hogan	L1	39236
	W/O E H Jackson	357	9594
	F/S R F Jackson	L1	9975
	W/O A R Kiddey	357	39225
	W/O A R Kilminster	L3	24494
	W/O J A Longford	L6	90090
	W/O A R P Mills	L4	9537
	W/O R G Mullally	L6	9538
	W/O J E Murrell	357	9595
	W/O J H F Ogden	383	524
	W/O H S Oldman	357	9539
	W/O A Osborne	357	9593
	W/O R Shaw	357	9603
	W/O W R Stapleford	383	96
	W/O A Urquhart	344	9596
	W/O W C Walters	357	24
	W/O E Wilkinson	357	9597
	WO2 J A Arnsby RCAF	357	9629
	F/S S T Fisher RCAF	357	9619
	F/L M O Stephens RNZAF	L3	685
37	F/L P A Wimberley	L3	633
	W/O T E S Alderwick	357	416
	W/O J A Burke	357	13111
	W/O J R Clark	L3	13070
	W/O G J W Grimson	L6	134
	W/O T Johnson	357	438
	W/O H A Jones	357	13066
	W/O E Lawson	L3	13072
	W/O H Ruse	357	13077
	W/O K R Say	357	194
	W/O J A Theed	L3	149
38	W/O J Hamilton	357	295
	W/O N Packer	357	1
	W/O W Stevens	L4	55
	W/O S A Williams	357	311
40	F/L F A Bowler	L3	573
	F/L R M Burns	L3	595
	F/L G C Conran	L3	694
	F/L H Heaton	L3	3764
	F/L R H Jacoby	L3	581
	S/L E H Lynch-Blosse	L3	472
	F/O S H Palmer	L3	475
	F/L G Parker	L3	1250
	S/L M E Redgrave	L3	1362
	F/L A B Trench	L3	587
	W/O J A S Abernethy	L6	18277

Sqn	Name	Camp	Number
40	W/O P Addison	L1	10
	W/O T Arnold	357	834
	W/O A C T Barter	357	23597
	W/O C D W Bartlam	357	109
	W/O J R Brooker	357	288
	W/O H Caldicott	357	487
	W/O M R Chouler	357	739
	W/O D R Clay	357	491
	W/O D F Darlow	L6	9633
	W/O T A Foreman	357	64
	W/O A Hammond	L6	501
	W/O F M Hotchkiss	357	185
	F/S A E Hough	L6	9611
	W/O G Hurford	L3	37338
	W/O E A Jewson	357	603
	W/O B Kay	L3	39279
	W/O A Macaskill	L6	6430
	W/O R C Moffatt	357	20260
	W/O J Moore	357	188
	W/O R Peacock	357	192
	W/O D E Peters	357	20261
	W/O D J Rice	L6	349
	W/O P Rockingham	357	18282
	W/O E Rodgers	357	110
	W/O V C Salvage	357	13076
	W/O J Shaw	L1	9
	W/O E Spencer	357	614
	W/O P H Steele	357	195
	W/O S D Swindells	357	39280
	W/O R C Thompson	L6	18669
	W/O S I Tonks	357	31113
	W/O J A Tracey	357	39276
	W/O J A Webster	L3	152
	F/S R Alldrick RCAF	357	43
	F/S J C Bredin RCAF	357	23595
	F/L L S Dunley RNZAF	L3	1348
	W/O A F Potter RNZAF	357	18276
44	F/L E G M Bond	L3	464
	F/L H P Clarke	L3	157
	F/L J F Clayton DFC	L3	3683
	F/L F G Dutton	L3	364
	F/L B Green MC	L3	121
	F/L T G Hynes	L3	248
	F/L P J S Shaughnessy	L3	3643
	F/L H R Stockings DFC	L3	477
	F/L S R Taunton	L3	255
	S/L N H J Tindall	L3	637
	F/L H J Vollmer	L3	259
	W/O J A Anderson	357	24362
	W/O J P A Bonett	357	24367
	W/O L R Brooks	L3	172
	W/O A J Clarke	357	44
	W/O V A Coveyduck	357	176
	W/O A Cross	357	179
	W/O W R Davidson	L3	13110
	W/O E W Dunkling	L6	494
	W/O J H R Edgar	L6	181
	W/O E L Farrands	L6	136
	W/O A Golston	L3	9529
	W/O R J N Hanslip	357	600
	W/O G E Harris	357	184
	W/O J E Hughff	L6	39143
	W/O J McEwan	357	443
	W/O E Martin	357	375
	W/O G W Niblett	357	24471
	W/O W F O'Brien	357	187

Sqn	Name	Camp	Number	Sqn	Name	Camp	Number
44	W/O J Rawson	344	9535	51	F/L B W Hayward	L3	204
	W/O P R Tebbutt	L6	449		F/L K N Holland	L3	1358
	F/S C W Townsend	L3	39144		F/L T F S Johnson	L3	1247
	W/O L H Wainwright	357	236		F/L P A Leuw	L3	3652
	W/O W P J Watson	357	13064		F/L A W MacKay	L3	3662
	W/O R M Wicker	357	238		F/L T K Milne	09C	206
	W/O F M Wilkes	357	199		F/L A C Peach	L3	334
	W/O D Windle DFM	357	393		F/L C D Roberts	L3	3737
	W/O F E Wotton	357	24457		F/L H B Robertshaw	L3	3741
49	F/L J H Green	L3	465		F/L J M Taylor	L3	256
	F/L J D Haskins	L3	246		F/L E R Templer	L3	3754
	F/L B A Mitchell	L3	105		S/L W H N Turner DFC	L3	332
	F/L J D Mundy DFC	L3	656		W/O R J Allen	L6	54
	F/L L Reavell-Carter	L3	107		W/O L J R Barber	357	37
	F/L J V Silverston	L3	252		W/O A E Bowes	357	170
	W/O W J Baird	L3	479		W/O D L Boyer	L3	357
	W/O A L Bryceson	357	486		Sgt F J C Brown	L3	173
	W/O C H Butcher	L6	207		W/O V W Bruce	357	485
	W/O R Cartwright	357	268		W/O F W Coles	357	23619
	W/O P C P Darwin	L3	9690		W/O J H Davis	L6	9652
	W/O D C Dunphy	L3	363		W/O J J W Eames	L1	543
	W/O R I Eastwood	L6	428		W/O D S Edmondson	L3	182
	W/O W L Evans	L6	273		W/O R Entwistle	L6	212
	W/O K N Farrow	357	215		Sgt J C Gowland	357	9636
	W/O H E Fisher	357	495		W/O F Hargreaves	L3	13032
	W/O T R H Hawkes	357	435		W/O V B Housego	357	277
	F/S F R Hibbert DFM	357	9688		W/O W F Hurst	L6	553
	W/O S N Hind	L6	9695		W/O J N A James	357	554
	W/O S J Hitchings	357	276		Sgt M F Johnson	357	279
	W/O L W Homard	357	435		W/O J A Kearey	357	187
	W/O S R Hoskins	357	32906		W/O W A Kelham	L3	221
	W/O F H Lindesay	L3	374		W/O J C W King	L3	6432
	W/O W K O'Leary	357	444		W/O A G Lowe DFM	357	163
	W/O F Phillips	L4	381		W/O A W G Lyne		3104
	W/O M G P Stretton	357	232		W/O A Mather	L6	510
	W/O E B Torpey	357	389		W/O H Maylin	357	280
	W/O L C Turnbull	357	285		W/O W H Mercer	L4	342
	W/O A S Winton	383	9673		W/O D G Pinney	357	24464
	W/O J H Wyatt	344	27055		W/O E H Platts	357	304
	W/O D Young	L6	454		W/O G M Porrett	L7	90106
50	F/L E R Abbott DSO, DFM	L3	1407		W/O G Raper	357	13062
	F/L D B Ainsworth	L3	462		W/O J B Ritchie	L3	13051
	F/L G J Cornish	L3	574		W/O A J Robottom	L6	24501
	F/L E C Maskell	L3	3738		W/O G B Smith	357	13057
	F/L R D Wawn	L3	1255		W/O C Snook	L6	569
	S/L F A Willan	L3	260		W/O A S Tarry	357	39147
	W/O F C Bailey	357	478		W/O J H Telfer	357	24499
	W/O F G Brook	357	264		W/O P J M Thomas	357	39148
	W/O H J Bushell	L6	206		W/O V Thompson	357	23605
	W/O A B Cox	357	270		W/O P E Tripp	357	77
	W/O B Dixon	L1	723		W/O J A Walker	357	39302
	W/O R E Drake	L6	596		W/O B S Walley	383	80
	W/O D F Endsor	L6	9559		W/O A R B Ward	357	67
	W/O D G Good	357	9560		W/O G P White	L3	235
	W/O D G Hamilton	357	332		W/O J B Whitworth	357	39150
	W/O H L Hurrell	L1	334		W/O S J T Wilkins	357	24517
	W/O I A MacDonald	L6	9561		W/O B J R Wilson	L3	13042
	W/O J E Martin	357	605		F/L J I Davies RCAF	L3	3790
	W/O R H L Smith	357	228		F/L F W Shorrock RCAF	L3	3740
	W/O F C Snook	357	612		F/O A G Trites RCAF	L3	158
	W/O T G Wake	357	24399		F/S L W J Hart RCAF	357	225506
	W/O R Williamson	357	9563		F/S Kelly RCAF	L7	90061
	W/O K W Wright	357	286		F/S A R Lacharite RCAF	357	23603
51	F/L A J Brewster	L3	1354		WO2 A W MacMurray RCAF	L4	24518
	F/L P G Brodie	L3	1242		F/S J P Magwood RCAF	L4	90064
	F/L F T Clayton	L3	3679		F/S C J Powell RCAF	357	23609

Sqn	Name	Camp	Number	Sqn	Name	Camp	Number
51	F/S D A Switzer RCAF	357	164	58	W/O J Gutteridge	357	39293
57	F/L H R Bewlay	L3			W/O K D Hall	357	274
	W/C H M A Day	L3	37		W/O B A Hammond	L6	109
	F/L G K R Drimmie	L3	5171		W/O H R Holmes	L6	66
	F/L G W S Ritchie	L3	526		W/O W Hughes	L6	278
	P/O J S Walters	L3	714		W/O J B Jones	357	23631
	W/O T P Adderley	357	43		W/O B J Kemp	L1	9571
	W/O S Barraclough	383	134		W/O F M Kerr	L3	440
	W/O T C Bartle	L6	24451		W/O R P London	L6	1338
	W/O R S Cairns	357	542		W/O H P Marguire	L6	61
	W/O B Cleaver	357	83		W/O J R Mirfin	357	13102
	W/O L W Collins	357	17		W/O C H Neary	L3	59
	Sgt A C Crease	357	24503		W/O T A Nichols	357	9606
	W/O N C Davies	L3	81		W/O J Overson	L4	9648
	W/O J C F Everett	L6	554		W/O L E Proctor	357	9572
	W/O A G Fripp	357	5752		W/O R D Roberts	357	18292
	W/O J R Harvey	357	18281		W/O R R Schofield	L6	3
	W/O M D Hennessy	357	16		W/O P J Sharpe	357	351
	W/O J H D Howes	357	24490		W/O F S Staley	357	54
	W/O G H Johnson	L6	9692		W/O C H Steven	357	398
	W/O L Jones	L6	24385		W/O R M Wade	357	451
	W/O J L Ledsham	357	24502		W/O R D Wagstaff	357	117
	W/O E Lloyd	357	82		W/O H Wilkinson	357	13106
	W/O D McCaig	L6	86		W/O N S Bidwell RNZAF	357	221
	W/O S McIntyre	3D	42	61	F/L L S Adams	L3	94
	W/O J Nelson	357	5755		F/L D M Barrett	L3	93
	W/O A A Norman	357	9682		F/L J G N Braithwaite	L3	9973
	W/O R Parish	L6	93		F/L D H Davis	L3	150
	W/O G G Patterson	357	512		F/L E C S Fewtrell	L3	96
	W/O L Pattinson	357	513		F/L A H Gould	L3	1269
	W/O C A Sapcote	357	18330		F/L J W W Graham	L3	39324
	W/O R Shuttleworth	357	72		F/L K Jones	L3	124
	W/O S T Starkins	357	516		F/L S B Morley	L3	106
	W/O A R Ward	357	36		F/L P D Tunstall	04C	258
	W/O M P Whitworth	357	88		F/L D A Young	L3	336
	F/L I H Collett RNZAF	L3	646		W/O W Asson	357	18290
	W/O C S Greager RNZAF	357	547		W/O L R Biddlecombe	357	74
	W/O W C Hayman RNZAF	L7	90078		W/O R Bonson	357	169
	W/O D L Jones RNZAF	357	557		W/O J I Boyce	L6	322
	W/O A G Sutherland RNZAF	357	570		W/O W J Brook	357	799
58	F/L A F Barralet	L3	318		W/O N M Campbell	357	39282
	F/L J H Frampton	L3	1337		W/O J F Cowan	L3	177
	F/L T H Hadley	L3	245		W/O K Downing	L6	17488
	F/L F Ivins	L3	700		W/O E V Gawith	L6	317
	F/L J K Lyon	L3	629		W/O C E Hawkes	357	18293
	F/L J Plant	L3	1126		W/O H G Hill	L6	133
	F/L R S Stamp	L3	353		W/O R L Hollidge	357	370
	F/L G E Walker	L3	1120		W/O F Johnson	357	337
	F/L R T C O White	L3	3778		F/S H G Johnson	L1	18318
	F/L F R Wilbraham	L3	3777		F/S B D McPherson	357	70
	W/O C Bamford	L6	18286		W/O A E Murdock	357	225
	W/O A E Barlow	357	397		W/O J N Prendergrast	357	305
	W/O H Booth	L6	354		W/O T A Ross	357	13037
	W/O F E Bowen	357	9604		W/O L Walker	L3	13099
	W/O C R D Browne	L6	9624		W/O J F Williams	357	390
	W/O J Buckfield	L3	13091		W/O J W Wootton	357	13055
	W/O W Bull	357	265		W/O G A Wright	L6	314
	W/O J P Caldwell	357	267	75	F/L L P R Hockey	L3	410
	W/O J S Cameron	357	39295		F/L H D Newman	L3	459
	W/O L E Carden	357	39291		F/L W J S Smith	L3	3796
	Sgt J Daniels	L6	326		W/O H Bell	357	24461
	W/O J H K Deane	383	83		W/O J S Brooks	357	50392
	W/O W S Donnelly	L6	18289		W/O G F Cole	357	6338
	W/O J L S Flanagan	L6	42160		W/O A Donaldson	L3	18333
	W/O A E Furze	357	56		W/O L G Eggar	L6	24505
	W/O A A J Goss	L6	9615		W/O M C Fenn	357	429

Sqn	Name	Camp	Number	Sqn	Name	Camp	Number
75	W/O W F French	383	95	77	W/O E H Alderton	357	23596
	W/O A B Frisby	357	24481		W/O V G Allen	357	13023
	Sgt A H Heard	L1	9653		W/O W G Best	357	13104
	W/O L C Howe	357	24507		W/O N C Bizley	357	39201
	W/O S J G Isherwood	357	24462		W/O A Bocking	357	482
	W/O L I A Millett	357	106		W/O D Bradley	357	39221
	W/O R Pattison	383	121		W/O D V Browne	357	13087
	W/O D Polley	357	104		W/O E W Budd	L6	539
	W/O C Simpson	357	150		W/O G C Carter	357	39212
	W/O K M Smith	357	24508		W/O G B Clarke	L6	269
	W/O G Thorpe	L3	5399		W/O W Cowie	L6	13080
	W/O H Watson	357	9644		W/O J A G Deans	L6	271
	F/O L E Peterson RCAF	357	9630		W/O S A Evans	L3	39220
	F/L E M Sangster RCAF	L3	659		W/O R E Fletcher	357	39
	F/L D A Webster RCAF	L3	688		W/O H Fraser	357	39230
	F/S H A D Stanley RCAF	357	24459		W/O D H Gilbert	357	498
	F/S J B Stephenson RCAF	357	24396		W/O C H Grace	383	133
	W/O R B Blakeway RNZAF	L6	39332		W/O D B Grundy	L6	90139
	W/O T P Duffy RNZAF	357	24539		W/O W H E Harwood	357	39203
	W/O J M Garrett RNZAF	357	597		Sgt F A Hill	357	275
	W/O L B H Hope RNZAF	357	24510		W/O T S Hull	L6	552
	W/O R G Morgan RNZAF	357	23614		W/O M F Hurlston	L6	504
	W/O D G B Protheroe RNZAF	357	446		W/O T F Keeley	357	507
					W/O J W Lambert	357	5751
	W/O D J Pyman RNZAF	357	24469		W/O D N Lee	357	559
76	F/L C C Cheshire	L3	3712		W/O J Masters	L1	13078
	F/L J G Ireton	L3	3649		W/O A Morris	L6	32
	F/L N W McLeod	L3	3650		W/O M A Oliver	357	13033
	F/L N F Trayler	L3	661		W/O W Petch	357	39198
	S/L W R Williams	L3	3644		W/O W R Taylor	357	3035
	W/O R W P Alexander	357	24359		W/O D Thomas	357	9578
	W/O W A I Bone	357	143		W/O W F Thuell	357	23611
	W/O L J Butler	357	28		W/O A B Wiggins	383	132
	W/O T A Byrne	357	137		W/O D G Young	357	619
	W/O D Cotsell	357	24336		F/L C W Murphy RCAF	L3	1433
	W/O J W Duffield	383	89		F/S M B C Delaney RCAF	357	75
	W/O W A Finlayson	L6	48		WO2 D M Godard RCAF	L4	90104
	W/O E C Gurmin	357	111		F/S W J Haslam RCAF	357	39238
	W/O P H T Horrox	357	153	78	F/L G C Brown	L3	355
	W/O W H Hunt	357	24374		F/L J A Cant	L3	3711
	W/O S Jones	L3	15		F/L J R Denny	4B	361
	W/O K R F Kenworthy	357	109		F/L R E H George	L3	331
	W/O N Kershaw	L6	27		F/L B V Kerwin	L3	372
	W/O J S Lipton	357	39157		F/L J B T Loudon	L3	471
	W/O G H Patterson	L4	1276		F/L R C Mordaunt	L3	754
	W/O B Phillips	357	23		W/O L A Beckett	357	419
	W/O J H Pitt	357	9679		W/O S Cawkwell	357	323
	W/O L A Roberts	357	24371		W/O J E Everson	L1	365
	W/O G J Smalley	357	110		W/O E G S H Freeman	L4	24480
	W/O G W S Taylor	357	135		W/O J Geary	L6	160
	W/O L A Thompson	357	64		W/O T Hall	357	24491
	W/O A H J Turner	357	188		W/O W E Kerr	L6	161
	W/O R C Wash	357	134		W/O J W Knight	357	373
	W/O J R Wedderburn	357	21		W/O A M McMillan	357	841
77	F/O D G Baber	L3	3765		W/O J W Massie	L3	376
	F/L D Blew	L3	594		W/O T Paterson	357	24489
	F/L J B J Boardman	L3	620		W/O E W Penn	357	24500
	F/L C R Hubbard	L3	466		W/O E W Wilmore	357	453
	F/L I A Kayes	L3	3684		F/L J V Saunders RCAF	L3	682
	F/L R J Kimbell	L3	1428	82	F/L R M Biden	L3	239
	F/L A C Meigh	L3	2267		F/L J C Breese	L3	91
	F/L J E Simmonds	L3	1634		F/L R A G Ellen	L3	162
	F/L J Tilsley	L3	38		F/L F W S Keighley	L3	1275
	F/L J S B Tyrie	L3	530		F/O R J McConnell	L3	410
	F/L G M Wiltshear	L3	392		F/L R C D McKenzie	L3	1248
	W/O H J Agnew	L6	262		F/L B T J Newland	L3	1617

Sqn	Name	Camp	Number
82	F/L G P Robertson	L3	2268
	F/L T E Syms	L3	1288
	F/L K S Toft	L3	126
	S/L N Wardell	L3	1688
	W/O D A Adams	L6	202
	W/O A Avery	357	147
	W/O D Blair	L6	203
	W/O J F H Bristow	357	171
	W/O W H M Butcher	357	357
	W/O V J Dance	L6	180
	W/O K W J Farley	L6	213
	W/O J Ferguson	357	366
	W/O T Graham	357	183
	W/O W Greenwood	357	294
	W/O J Houston	357	13107
	W/O K Howard	357	220
	W/O H Humphreys	357	57
	W/O J W H Parsons	357	191
	W/O W J P Sheppard	357	732
	W/O A A Stanley	357	84
	W/O H H Williams	357	30663
	W/O K H Wright	357	201
83	S/L A O Bridgman DFC	L3	1264
	F/L S Carter	L3	1386
	F/L J B Leetham	L3	3784
	F/L I M Muir	L3	165
	F/L A R Mulligan DFC	L3	166
	F/L D B Organ	L3	3766
	F/L A L Parsons	L3	39646
	F/L N H Svendsen DFC	L3	1387
	W/O W Barber	L6	168
	W/O L C Coldwell	357	39251
	W/O P H Draper	L6	9620
	W/O H C Gabbitas	357	177
	W/O E W E Gough	L6	24380
	W/O D C Hedley	357	24369
	W/O V W Kent	357	39206
	W/O J Lawrence	357	9528
	W/O J Leakey	357	301
	W/O H Logan	L3	9542
	W/O G Mitchell	L4	24387
	W/O R B Olliver	L6	9541
	W/O J F Payne	357	9543
	W/O L W Sadezky	357	9581
	AC2 F A Stone	L3	196
	W/O P J Tointon	L6	197
	W/O G Wiscombe	L3	24785
	W/O W G W Younger	357	455
88	F/L A J Madge	L3	631
	F/L A W Mungovan	06B	324
	Sgt A C Collyer	L1	13056
97	F/L R S Ayton	L3	1346
	F/L M G Geoghegan	L3	3720
	F/O J A Little	L3	3717
	F/L J N Nunn	L3	39318
	W/O R Anderson	357	5
	W/O J N Ashmore DFC	L3	23627
	W/O J Bryce DFM	357	11
	W/O W J Chantler	L3	24
	W/O D J Harvey	357	0001
	W/O R G W Hodgkinson	357	142
	W/O R W Jones	357	113
	W/O P W Ratcliff	357	23626
	W/O L Robinson	357	133
	W/O E W R Sykes DFM	357	26
	W/O W Wood	L6	23625

Sqn	Name	Camp	Number
97	W/O W Wotherspoon	357	24457
	W/O G P Thomas RAAF	383	122
	W/O T M Wade RAAF	L7	90153
	WO2 I Hewitt RCAF	383	90129
	W/O G L Scott RNZAF	383	90063
	W/O A G Smith RNZAF	L3	23593
99	F/L J D Agrell	L3	1636
	F/L H G De Forest	L3	367
	F/L J P Dickinson	04C	670
	F/L H A Goodwin	L3	671
	F/L P A Goodwyn	L3	521
	F/L J R Hoppe	L3	371
	F/L E A Masters	L3	1630
	F/L J F Palmer	344	525
	F/L J L Scott	L3	272
	S/L D C Torrens	L3	529
	F/L F H Vivian	L3	638
	F/L R A G Willis	L3	108
	W/O E H Berry	357	534
	W/O J H Bowman	357	24498
	W/O R E Bush	L6	356
	W/O H J Casselden	357	174
	W/O E Coleman	357	9681
	W/O R H Davis	L6	39151
	W/O W W Hall	357	39213
	W/O F A Hard	L6	39241
	W/O D H Harley	357	5
	W/O H F Heritage	L3	296
	W/O A A Jenner	357	555
	W/O W Kershaw	357	39240
	W/O G Kilburn	357	6423
	W/O H G Lewis	357	18327
	W/O K A R MacArthur	357	77
	W/O H Mahoney	357	39149
	W/O C J Scanlon	357	78
	W/O A J Smith	357	568
	W/O W Stogdale	357	39243
	W/O J L Trask	357	9674
	W/O A L Walker	357	198
	W/O R M Williams	L3	6436
	W/O C H C Wright	L6	394
	F/L P R Searcy RAAF	L3	683
	F/S M G Bowen RCAF	L4	24383
	F/L A Featherstone RCAF	L3	24993
	F/L R B Martin RCAF	L3	24516
	Sgt R I Gemmill RCAF	357	39226
	F/L J McB Kerr RNZAF	L3	1359
101	F/L W Barrett	L3	641
	F/L R C Carroll	L3	643
	F/L G A D Imeson	L3	650
	W/O J M Atkinson	L3	24377
	W/O R L Betts	357	24382
	W/O L D A Bolton	357	24401
	W/O V I Bowden	344	24372
	W/O R H Cage	357	24360
	W/O A G Chelmick	357	209
	W/O A W J Cleeve	383	92
	W/O T A Cooke	383	87
	W/O I G Davies	383	91
	W/O R St C Finch	L3	94
	W/O A L R Heath	357	93
	W/O E J Hesmondhalgh	357	50
	W/O J W Lamont	L7	1039
	F/S H Martyn	L6	224
	W/O J Parkington	357	24389
	W/O F M Smith	L3	49

Sqn	Name	Camp	Number	Sqn	Name	Camp	Number
101	WO2 W L Johnson RCAF	383	90092	102	W/O J Williamson	L3	82
	F/S R T Wood RCAF	357	176		W/O C Wood	357	200
	W/O J R Ritchie RNZAF	357	24390		W/O F W Penn RAAF	357	39317
102	F/L R F Beauclair	L3	154		F/S A L Lord RCAF	357	24484
	F/L J C W Bushell	L3	156	103	F/L F Hugill	L3	1127
	F/L G W Cole	L3	3739		S/L J A Ingram DFC	L3	10
	F/O I P B Denton	L3	3654		F/L E V Lawson	L3	3223
	F/L G T Glover	L3	510		F/L J N Leyden	L3	1125
	F/L E G Libbey	L3	579		F/L W R Oldfield	L3	3760
	F/L D F M MacKarness	L3	102		F/L H J Sellers	L3	1622
	F/L L Miller DFC	L3	24		F/L A W Sulston	L3	3723
	F/L K H P Murphy	L3	207		F/L M C Wells	L3	331
	S/L S S Murray	L3	60		W/O G Avery	357	111
	F/L A Z Pengelly	L3	380		W/O G Beardsley	357	112
	F/L R G Poulter	L3	1382		W/O T H Bowen	357	62
	F/L D N Sampson	L3	3733		W/O H F Bullock	344	13050
	F/L T H Taylor	L3	687		W/O N W Clyde	L6	9686
	F/L A B Thompson	L3	59		W/O H Dunn	L6	39395
	W/O E Alderton	357	101		W/O E C Easton	L6	23
	W/O L Askham	357	73		W/O S E T Hamblin	357	2
	W/O J N D Bailey	357	39166		W/O W D King	L6	9666
	W/O V H Barr	357	13100		W/O G F Lewis	357	289
	W/O L Barrows	357	39142		W/O C H Lowne	357	222
	W/O H G Benfield	357	39		W/O H Mossley	L3	248022
	W/O B N Booth	357	39199		W/O W S C Partridge	L3	249078
	W/O W K H Bowden	L6	39199		W/O C L Williams	11A	
	W/O E H Bros	L6	13043		W/O J G Wright	L6	9671
	W/O S A Burry	357	1	104	S/L H Budden DFC	L3	3709
	W/O K S Carter	L6	41		S/L D M Strong	L3	3793
	W/O J I Charlton	357	590		W/O J A Chubb	357	9634
	W/O B A Cotton	357	6422		W/O N S Fisher	357	9661
	W/O J M Culley	L1	39168		Sgt J D Morgan	357	9567
	W/O N W Davies	L6	39200		W/O C K Mousley	L4	138
	W/O D L Dick	L3	52559		W/O R Ritson	357	9617
	W/O E W G Dickey	L6	9599		W/O L G Smalley	357	124
	W/O W M Featherstone	357	14		W/O D Storer	357	139
	W/O J Fisk	357	75		F/L H T Beare RCAF	L3	3781
	W/O C P Followes	357	330		F/S D F Sugden RCAF	357	114
	W/O W R Gibson	357	40	105	F/L E J Clelland	L3	358
	W/O J F Graham	L3	13112		F/L D G O´Brien	L3	597
	W/O E L G Hall MBE	357	13116		W/O M J Cowley	L6	359
	W/O J D Hamilton	357	100		W/O D F Eastwick	L6	13079
	W/O R V Harnett	L6	31		W/O A W H Hadley	357	65
	W/O G A Hartley	L6	601		W/O J S H Heape	357	502
	W/O A W Hawkes	357	131		F/S S R Wright	L6	13074
	W/O C A Hill	L6	2	106	F/L J Henderson DFC	L3	676
	W/O A Lakin	357	39215		P/O R A Walker	L3	1388
	W/O K G Lewis	357	102		F/L J M Wood	L3	664
	W/O J J McCurdy	357	606		W/O H Birtwhistle	357	6434
	W/O D Magee	L1	13065		W/O J H Cook	357	127
	W/O K P Marlow	357	107		W/O M C Curties	357	9558
	W/O T Michie	357	343		W/O F W Davies	L6	9660
	W/O J F M Moyle	357	607		W/O S A T Davies	L3	593
	W/O A Nicholas	357	136		W/O J Harker	L3	6435
	W/O J R Nicholson	L6	13040		W/O R S Hartgroves	383	130
	W/O C F Pacey	357	3		W/O J Henderson	357	39224
	W/O F Potts	357	23592		W/O G Luke	L1	9533
	W/O H Radley	357	347		W/O G V Lynn	357	144
	W/O N J Ranson	L3	39174		W/O E R H Lyon	357	9530
	W/O K J Read	357	193		W/O W F Osborne	357	608
	W/O N W J Scott	357	105		W/O J A S Philson	357	9637
	W/O J Urquhart	L6	47		W/O N T Powell	357	23594
	W/O T A Vermiglio	357	128		W/O G B Stanton	L1	9531
	W/O B R Wallace	357	39169		W/O J W Steven	357	24492
	W/O C Warner	L6	13098		W/O C Walton	L7	75
	W/O R C Watchorn	357	23598		W/O R J West	L6	616

Sqn	Name	Camp	Number
106	W/O R J K Woodroofe	357	9632
	W/O R G Woodwards	357	162
	W/O R Yearsley	383	136
	F/L B D Campbell RCAF	L3	1637
107	F/L C Y Buckley	L3	114
	F/L W H Culling	L3	104
	F/L E T Fairbank	L3	1373
	F/L J P North-Lewis	L3	128
	F/L J P Quirke	L3	167
	F/L J W Stephens	L3	519
	F/L W Welburn	L3	716
	F/L T A Whiting	L3	2266
	W/O G A Allison	357	146
	W/O S L Bain	L6	145
	W/O G F Booth	357	154
	W/O L F Brand	357	421
	W/O A Brown	357	422
	W/O R Buckingham	357	39158
	W/O C M Chown	L6	39186
	Sgt C E Coote	357	287
	W/O E H B Cotton	357	1345
	W/O L G Dicks	L6	39267
	W/O B R George	357	367
	W/O G R Griggs	L6	431
	W/O D C Hawkins	357	80
	W/O G C G Hawkins	357	131
	W/O H E Hunt	357	125
	W/O M Kelly	357	39187
	W/O V G L Luter	357	13054
	W/O K E Murray	357	85
	W/O E T Perry	357	445
	W/O M Roberts	357	9601
	W/O F A S Roche	357	82
	W/O T Scott	357	6427
	W/O L J Slattery	357	84
	W/O A E W Smith	357	39178
109	P/O H G Cundall	L3	5809
	W/O J Gannon	357	24475
	W/O O A Sheffield	357	24511
	W/O W G Statham	S8B	24474
110	S/L K C Doran DFC & Bar	L3	501
	S/L D B Gericke	L3	1341
	F/L E R Mullins	06B	504
	F/L G O M Wright	L3	599
	W/O J Fancy	357	13081
	W/O R Lowe	357	2669
	W/O E C Parker	L3	190
	W/O W W Street	357	21990
114	F/L J B P Hanlon	L3	163
	W/O A Stevenson	357	230
115	F/L J Barker	L3	1370
	F/L G T Dodgshun	L3	508
	F/L W Hetherington	L3	1383
	F/L W H C Hunkin	L3	125
	F/L D F Laslett	L3	511
	F/L F L Litchfield	L3	3716
	F/L N R Shuttleworth	L3	3816
	F/L A J J Steel	L3	1281
	F/L S W Wild	L3	108263
	W/O D A Boutle	357	39536
	W/O G T Buckingham	357	6425
	W/O C Clark	L6	143
	W/O A G S Colley	L3	142
	W/O P J C Darvill	L3	24466
	W/O T L Davidson	L6	39175
	W/O H Dickson	L6	141
115	W/O M G Dunne	L6	39288
	W/O W L Flower	L6	13082
	W/O D W Fraser	357	36
	W/O E A Gibbs	357	39179
	W/O H D Glendinning	L6	13038
	W/O R H Hilton-Jones	357	65
	W/O G W Hogg	357	34
	W/O E F Lambert	L3	70
	W/O A S Lawson	L6	85
	W/O L W Ludlam	357	13117
	W/O J J MacGregor	357	135
	W/O E E Mason	357	9564
	W/O R P Mogg	357	302
	W/O A B Morgan	357	33
	W/O T E F Mutton	357	9565
	W/O T W Oliver	357	39254
	W/O W J Reid	L6	6426
	W/O A E Robinson	L1	24454
	W/O J W B Snowden	L1	24467
	W/O K E Squire	357	9566
	Sgt M B Wallis	344	6428
	Sgt J A Williams	357	9645
	W/O A McB Kerr RAAF	357	182
	F/S P V Brazier RCAF	357	24455
	F/S A W Clarke RCAF	357	24453
	WO2 H E Woolley RCAF	L6	24456
139	F/L K J Macintosh	L3	704
	F/L A C MacLachlan	L3	40
	S/L E Sydney-Smith DFC	L3	3651
	F/L R A White	L3	3798
	W/O E G Caban DFM	357	9621
	W/O G Coast	357	9971
	W/O K R Coles	357	6
	W/O K Fenton	357	39204
	W/O A A Fuller	357	39209
	W/O H R Hale	357	31
	W/O R W McDonald	L3	39207
	W/O J W Middleton	344	26857
142	F/L R McD Durham	L3	3722
	F/L J R Gibbon	L3	3732
	F/L A D Gosman	L3	3713
	F/L A G Middleton	L3	411
	F/L B W Peryman	L3	413
	F/L M H Roth	L3	333
	F/L H H Taylor	L3	584
	W/O W F Algie	357	13059
	W/O R W Cornwall	L3	396
	W/O F W Day	L6	24512
	W/O P W Duckers	L6	24486
	Sgt L Firth	L6	146
	W/O H J Gibson	357	24497
	W/O A J Godsell	357	13109
	W/O T Greenall	357	16123
	W/O D J Holliday	357	520
	W/O K S Holman	357	145
	W/O R E Hotchkiss	357	186
	W/O S Lang	357	2692
	W/O H Long	357	2665
	W/O H Morris	357	13073
	W/O G Thompson	357	234
	Sgt R J Utteridge DFM	L6	741
	W/O D A Whiting	357	20096
	WO2 T V S Wiggins RCAF	357	24514
	W/O C L Dennes RNZAF	357	24487
	W/O J Jackson RNZAF	L6	148
144	F/L M T H Adams	L3	3751

Sqn	Name	Camp	Number	Sqn	Name	Camp	Number
144	F/O D A Baker	L3	665	149	W/O K C H Rawlings	357	609
	F/L R B Barr	L3	18391		W/O R W Saywood	357	226
	F/L R D Baughan	L3	634		W/O K K Sterrett	357	23613
	F/L R S A Churchill	L3	243		W/O W J Thew	357	13075
	F/L R M Coste	L3	20		W/O D Westmacott	357	35
	F/L W C Hartop	L3	1349		W/O F J Woods	357	12
	F/L A E Hayward	L3	3752		F/L P L Dixon RAAF	L3	3657
	F/L H O Jones	L3	507		W/O W J R Culpan RNZAF	L6	23615
	F/L I H Kingwell	L3	651		W/O J N Grace RNZAF	357	18332
	F/L I C Kirk	L3	1276		W/O C McK Laird RNZAF	L3	300
	F/L I G St C Pringle	L3	3755		W/O T E Schofield RNZAF	357	18296
	S/L C G C Rawlins DFC	L3	6424		W/O A B Witton RNZAF	L3	313
	F/L H A T Skehill	L3	1253	150	F/L K C Edwards	L3	3645
	F/L P Stevens	L3	3786		F/L D E T Osment	L3	506
	W/O T E Barnett	383	138		F/L A C Roberts	L3	327
	W/O J R Blake	357	23607		W/O G Busby	357	38248
	W/O G F Bottomley	357	39281		W/O G W Clifford	357	13058
	W/O S C Brown	357	23601		W/O C Davies	L6	157
	W/O C W Carter	357	17		W/O H Dodsworth	L6	155
	W/O J S Crossley	357	24477		W/O J D Elder	L6	156
	W/O D H Dunt	L6	725		W/O D Meyrick	357	13053
	W/O J Erskine	L6	23604		W/O A W Rultand	357	18162
	W/O R L Galloway	L6	5760		W/O R K Rye	357	13046
	W/O W Gilbey	L7	137		W/O W G Slade	357	13093
	W/O A E Jones	L1	13047		W/O G J Springett	357	5754
	W/O T S Jones	L7	90137		W/O J W Whittingham	357	159
	W/O L A Parker	L1	90138		W/O E W McConchie RNZAF	357	154
	W/O A W Payne	357	9579	207	W/C N C Hyde	L3	628
	W/O D Perritt	357	284		F/L W J Lewis	L3	3785
	Sgt P M Reed	L6	24478		F/L H T Morgan	L3	524
	W/O J K Scouller	357	18		F/L D E Pinchbeck	L3	636
	W/O W G Smith	L3	13103		W/O E G Ball	L6	129
	W/O H Thompson	357	9573		W/O C N Barron	357	4
	W/O J E Wiggall	357	18392		W/O W Buck	L3	538
	F/L R F C Featherstone RCAF	L3	1345		W/O D A Budden	L3	540
					W/O J A Cheeseman	L6	24356
149	F/L M G Butt	L3	241		W/O J R Currie DFM	357	126
	F/L M J Fisher	L3	1245		W/O A S Duncan	L3	20
	F/L D A McFarlane	L3	250		W/O G T J Fomison	357	545
	F/O G M R Smith	L3	253		W/O P Gurnell	357	549
	F/L P F R Vaillant	L3	1283		W/O C F Hall	L6	9586
	F/L L K S Wilson	L3	2547		W/O W Hart	357	6433
	W/O M E Adams	357	4		W/O L W Hedges	L6	550
	W/O V G Anderson	357	18283		F/S D Kingston	357	9589
	W/O J Bailey	357	290		W/O E A C Lee	L4	37
	W/O H G Barnes	357	263		Sgt W J J McDougall	L3	561
	W/O P Blackburn	357	223		W/O W M McGregor DFM	357	22
	W/O A Botten	357	321		W/O S E Panton	357	28
	W/O D H G Connolly	357	210		W/O P C Robson	357	567
	W/O N J V Cownie	357	211		W/O A Ross	L4	115
	W/O J J Eldridge	L6	13069		W/O A D Smith	344	39539
	W/O J Fender	L6	216		W/O J A Taylor	357	571
	W/O G E Forsyth	357	13108		W/O A Wappett DFM	357	141
	W/O W Harrison	357	18284		W/O J Wells DFM	L1	572
	W/O L W Hatherly	4B	260523		WO2 R B MacLeod RCAF	357	9588
	W/O K Holden	357	297		WO2 E S Miller RCAF	357	9591
	Sgt G A Johnston	4B	222428	214	F/L J G Crampton	L3	1632
	W/O C G Jones	357	23612		F/L M M Marsh	L3	1344
	W/O G D K Jones	357	39232		P/O I K Woodroffe	L3	1343
	W/O M T Kenny	357	18294		W/O J I Burbridge	357	18331
	W/O A Lawson	357	33		W/O D F Cooper	357	9699
	W/O C Morgan	357	18279		W/O J W B Follitt	357	9691
	W/O A R Peacock	L4	283		W/O H Gillies	357	25
	W/O F J Pennicott	L1	2435		W/O L Hancock	357	18328
	W/O F W Price	357	13		W/O C W Heathman	357	24384
	W/O C F Pummery	11A	138981		W/O R Instone	L6	9697

Sqn	Name	Camp	Number	Sqn	Name	Camp	Number
214	W/O A N Jones	L6	18329	300	W/O H Kudelko	4B	24521
	W/O H E Jones	357	39271		F/S L Maciej	L3	39140
	W/O J A Key	357	24386		W/O P Nowakowski	4B	24488
	W/O C W G King	357	24366		W/O M Przybylski	L6	9546
	W/O R Mutch	357	24388		W/O K Sobczak	357	39534
	W/O A Saxton	357	24391		W/O A Suczynski	L3	39266
	W/O B L Tillotson	357	13		W/O M Sztul	4B	39264
	WO2 H R Boyd RCAF	357	24402		W/O W Weinberg	4B	18275
	F/S M A Johnson RCAF	L6	39260		W/O S Winek	L1	39139
	W/O J R Fry RNZAF	357	12	301	F/L E Hubicki	L3	1390
218	F/L D A J Foster	L3	576		F/L L Kozlowski	L3	1391
	F/L A J Hudson	L3	329		F/L J Palka	L3	1627
	F/L A M Imrie	L3	505		F/L J Riedl	L3	657
	F/L H M Murray	L3	1130		W/O Z Baderski	L1	90
	W/O F C Adams	357	24476		Sgt H Bolcewicz	4B	24522
	W/O R J Alexander	357	785		Sgt M Borodej	L1	24428
	W/O R Barnard	L1	152		Sgt J Bujak	L1	39219
	W/O A E Binnie	357	39159		W/O L Cieslak	L1	24429
	W/O K R Birchenough	357	9416		W/O A Dydo	L1	39216
	W/O L Booth	357	9641		W/O D Dziegiel	L1	39245
	W/O A H Bowater	357	24468		W/O I Gacon	4B	91
	W/O W J Bowhill	357	24363		W/O M Hasinski	L3	39195
	W/O L Dobson	L6	24473		W/O Z Idzikowski	4B	39217
	W/O A Ellis	L6	742		Sgt A Klee-Berg	4B	39372
	W/O T S Evans	344	27365		F/S Z Lenczewski	357	24496
	W/O J D Howard	357	219		W/O A Mlodzik	L1	24431
	W/O H G Huckle	357	23632		F/S T Moryn	357	24523
	W/O P L Jones	357	24357		W/O A Stalewski	L3	24430
	W/O A R Langley	357	24370		W/O A Szczcpanowski	357	24506
	W/O A Learmonth	357	23629		W/O A O Weiss	357	39211
	W/O I H Leitch	357	9647		W/O B Wroblewski	4B	24519
	W/O D MacDiarmid	L1	24392	304	F/L T Blicharz	L3	666
	W/O J R C McGlashan	357	24452		F/L W Rekszczyc	L3	681
	W/O R Moodie	L3	9654		W/O J Jaworosiuk	L1	24433
	W/O A Parfitt	357	511		W/O S Krzawiecki	L1	24432
	W/O R K Pridham	357	23628		W/O T E Wady	357	0014
	W/O R Purdy	357	39621	305	F/L K Jaklewicz	L3	1367
	W/O E S Spong	357	72		F/L A Jastrzebski	L3	352
	W/O L Stephens	357	23630		F/L M Marcola	06B	3704
	W/O R S C Stewart	357	24470		F/L J Nogal	L3	342
	W/O P Stubbs	357	18818		S/L S Scibior	L3	3811
	W/O N H Thompson	357	13068		W/O J Debiec	4B	39218
	W/O A J Condon RAAF	357	23634		W/O T Kasprzyk	4B	103983
	W/O W Fraser RAAF	357	24450		F/S S Lewek	4B	39141
	W/O J Clark RNZAF	357	733		Sgt J Mikszo	4B	39214
	W/O C F Dare RNZAF	357	3610		W/O M Minta	4B	39247
226	F/O R G Drake	L6	174		F/S E Olenyn	L4	39137
	F/L F M V Johnstone	L3	3758		W/O W Sieminski	357	39261
	S/L C E S Lockett	04C	409		W/O T Zuk	357	103982
	W/O R S Annan	357	13101	311	F/L E Busina	04C	401
	W/O A R Carvell	357	23635		F/L O Cerny	L17B	3663
	W/O R Evans	L6	9547		F/L F Cigos	04C	402
	W/O C S Hart	L1	13092		F/L V Kilian	L3	3771
	W/O R J Jones	L1	13105		F/L K Krizek	L3	407
300	F/L W Cebrzynski	L3	1366		F/L Z Prochazka	L3	3770
	F/L J Janicki	L3	3814		F/L K Trojacek	L3	3769
	F/L P Kowalski	L3	679		S/L E J M Vesely	04C	662
	F/L M Kozinski	L3	1628		F/L J Zafouk	04C	3661
	F/L W Krupowicz	L3	1393		W/O F Knap	L3	39285
	F/L J Kuflik	L4	39268		W/O F Knotek	4B	315
	F/L S T Sedzik	L3	1368		W/O G Kopal	4B	441
	F/L W A Sojka	L3	1369		W/O G Nyc	357	39284
	W/O J Artymuik	L1	39265		W/O F Petr	4B	24448
	Sgt B Bilinski	L3	24513		W/O V F E Prochazka	4C	24472
	Sgt J Danielewicz	L1	51		W/O A Siska	4C	39654
	W/O S Konarzewski	383	90062		W/O K Stastny	4B	39287

Sqn	Name	Camp	Number
311	W/O J Suza	L3	24446
	W/O P Svoboda	344	24976
	W/O P Uraba	4C	450
	W/O F B Valnerova	4B	24441
	W/O A Zabrs	L3	18350
	Sgt J Zvolebsky	L1	24449
405	F/L R G M Morgan	L3	3653
	F/L W B Towler	L3	3812
	W/O D J Clayden	357	9669
	W/O J S Courtnall	357	9575
	W/O W C Dossetter	L3	184
	W/O T F Dougall	L6	9657
	W/O J Emsley	L6	9665
	W/O E Jones	357	39257
	W/O J Lord	357	9659
	W/O D S MacLeod	L6	140
	W/O J W Murfin	357	57
	W/O R Perkin	357	9608
	W/O G A Pruette	357	71
	F/S R S Skan	357	55
	W/O V R J Slaughter	357	39253
	W/O D B Thrower	L6	39303
	F/S R H Westburg	357	18394
	F/L R F Terry RAAF	L3	2685
	F/L T R Kipp RCAF	L3	3667
	F/L W K Mackay RCAF	L3	3780
	F/L J S Saunders RCAF	L3	9582
	WO2 C W Forman RCAF	357	9670
	F/S J N Kirk RCAF	357	185
	WO2 P S McNutt RCAF	357	9620
	F/S W Menzies RCAF	357	76
	F/S I B Quinn RCAF	357	175
408	W/O A J Gallan	357	24515
	W/O J E Woodward	357	24509
	F/L S B Brackenbury RCAF	L3	1413
	F/L J C Monkhouse RCAF	L3	124
	F/L E L Houghton RNZAF	L3	677
455	F/L J D Cordwell	L3	668
	W/O E Holt	383	116
	W/O M N Stokes	L6	90085
	F/L J A C Gordon RAAF	L3	672
458	W/O P G E A Brown	357	24443

Camp locations:

O4C	Oflag Saalhaus Colditz
3D	Stalag Berlin-Steglitz
4B	Stalag Mühlberg-Elbe
4C	Stalag Wistritz bei Teplitz
6B	Stalag Nieuweschans Emsland
7A	Stalag Moosburg-Isar
8A	Stalag Gorlitz
9C	Stalag Muhlhausen
11A	Stalag Altengrabow
17B	Stalag Gneizendorf
344	Stalag Lamsdorf
357	Stalag Kopernikus
383	Stalag Hohen Fels
L1	Stalag Luft Barth Vogelsang
L3	Stalag Luft Sagan and Belaria
L4	Stalag Luft Sagan and Belaria
L6	Stalag Luft Heydekrug
L7	Stalag Luft Bankau-Kreulberg
O6B	Possibly corruption for 6B
O9C	Possibly corruption for 9C
L17B	Possibly corruption for 17B

Note. Of the locations shown above, O4C at Colditz and L3 at Sagan are, perhaps, the best known of the prisoner of war camps. Colditz gained notoriety as the camp in which the most persistent escapers were held and Sagan is remembered for the mass escape of officers in late March 1944, after which many of those who were recaptured were, on Hitler's orders, handed over to the Gestapo and executed.

Appendix 8

Internees 1939-41

Aircraft of the warring nations that landed in neutral countries were impounded and their crews interned. Such a fate befell at least six RAF bomber crews prior to May 1940 though their crews are thought to have been released prior too, or shortly after the the German invasion of the west.

During 1941, it is believed that at least six bombers landed, or crashed, in neutral territory while engaged on bombing duties and a seventh aircraft came down in Sweden during clandestine operations over Poland. The names of their crews, where known, and their subsequent fates are appended below.

Sqn	Name	Country	Remarks
9	Sgt R W Blaydon	Vichy France	See Appendix 6. Reported killed in action 8 August 1944, while serving with 582 Sqn.
	Sgt H W Bratley	Vichy France	See Appendix 6.
	Sgt L D Goldingay	Vichy France	See Appendix 6.
	Sgt S M P Parkes	Vichy France	See Appendix 6.
	Sgt R Vivian	Vichy France	See Appendix 6.
	Sgt L R Willis	Vichy France	See Appendix 6.
18	F/O C M P Kempster	Belgium	
	LAC R G St James-Smith	Belgium	Missing from operations 13 April 1941.
	Sgt F L Smith	Belgium	Missing from operations 15 August 1940.
	Sgt J J F Talbot	Belgium	
	Sgt A W S Thomas	Belgium	
51	P/O Gibson	Sweden	
	Sgt Morgan	Sweden	
	Sgt Troughton	Sweden	Injured and admitted Trälleberg Hospital.
	Sgt Willson	Sweden	
	Sgt Wilson	Sweden	
57	Sgt Gilmore	Belgium	
	AC1 T J Jervis	Belgium	Killed in action 9 July 1940.
	Sgt Turnidge	Belgium	
77	F/O W P Copinger	Holland	
	F/O T J Geach	Holland	Killed in action 29 May 1940.
	AC2 R B Barrie	Holland	
	LAC S H E Caplin	Holland	
82	Sgt N J Ingram	Vichy France	See Appendix 6.
	Sgt F H Miller	Vichy France	
	Sgt W E W Whiteman	Vichy France	
99	P/O J S Trotter	Belgium	
	F/O O L Williams	Belgium	Killed in action 22 May 1940.
	P/O R A G Willis	Belgium	Taken prisoner 5-6 July 1940.
	AC2 C G Ashman	Belgium	
	AC2 W Cockburn	Belgium	
	Sgt A R Mattick	Belgium	
102	F/O W C G Cogman	Belgium	Believed drowned SS Abukir 28 May 1940.
	P/O A W Mack	Belgium	
	Sgt G J Henry	Belgium	
	AC1 A Steel	Belgium	
	Cpl S R Wood	Belgium	
103	Sgt M B Brown	Eire	
	Sgt A C Dalton	Eire	
	Sgt L C Draper	Eire	
	Sgt A Virtue	Eire	
	P/O J P S Calder RCAF	Eire	
	P/O R G Keefer RCAF	Eire	

Sqn	Name	Country	Remarks
106	Sgt N J Newby	Eire	
	Sgt D Reid	Eire	
	Sgt F W Tisdall	Eire	
	Sgt J Wakelin	Eire	
300	P/O W Radwanski	Vichy France	See Appendix 6.
	F/O M Taras	Vichy France	See Appendix 6.
	Sgt G Chrzanowski	Vichy France	Reported died 15 June 1942 and buried Nice.
	Sgt Iwanowicz	Vichy France	Reported as a prisoner of war, but no trace in AIR20 2336.
	Sgt H Kudelko	Vichy France	See Appendix 7.
	Sgt P Nowakowski	Vichy France	See Appendix 7.

Additions and Corrections to Volume 1 (1939-40)

Since publication of Volume One, a number of corrections, and additions, have been received. These are appended below in a simple format of page identification, serial and the revised, or additional information.

I am extremely grateful to all who have taken the trouble to write to me on the subject of bomber losses and, I trust, this extra material will enhance the details gathered thus far in the series.

Page	Serial	Addition/Correction
14	L4268	4 Sep 39
16	K9271	Believed shot down by Josef Scherm of JG52, who was killed by the return fire.
	N6206	Believed shot down into the German Bight by Lt Helmut Henz of II./JG77.
	N6212	Believed shot down by Fw Klaus Faber of I./JG1, operating in the Osnabrück area.
17	L4127	F/O Beck and Sgt Sproston are buried in Sage War Cemetery, P/O Turner has no known grave.
20	L1415	Crashed between Niederemmel and Wehlen, shot down by Hptm Werner Mölders of III./JG53.
	L6694	Crashed near Malborn.
24	R2699	LAC J T Warriner +
26	K7260	Berkshire.
27	N2943	Sgt D J Kirkness +
28	L1410	WV-B; may have been shot down by Fw Goltzsche of I./JG77.
	P4859	Shot down 1257 into the North Sea 200 km N of Terschelling by Hptm Falck of 2./ZG76.
29	N6211	Shot down 1610 off the Frisian Islands by Hptm Falck.
30	N3004	LN-I
31	N9824	P/O A C Manaton +
	K8960	P/O P R Johnson +
		P/O H B Hunter +
32	L4873	Crashed Foel Wen some 9 miles SW of Llangollen, Denbigh.
		Sgt R J Harbour +
		AC2 K C Winterton +
39	N1387	AC1 I Pacey
42	L8875	WV-S
47	L8860	Believed shot down by Oblt Schäffer of II./JG26 and crashed 1700 near Kessel (Limburg), Holland.
49	P2202	Sgt F Robson pow
	L9175	Believed shot down by Oblt Homuth of I./JG27.
51	P2204	Believed to have crashed at Eigenbilzen.
52	P2193	Crashed at Noirefontaine.
54	L9180	Crashed 0800 near the road to Baasrode from Dendermonde.

Page	Serial	Addition/Correction
54	L5516	Delete + against both crew.
66	P4980	Sgt Bowles.
	R3157	Shot down by flak, Abt.I./29.
68	N1361	Insert 78 Sqn EY-F, borrowed by 58 Sqn.
	P2356	Crashed at Springen, 21 km NW of Wiesbaden, Germany.
69	L7793	On Oostende-Steene airfield. Crew evacuated on SS Abukir; LAC Dear and AC1 Stanhope rescued by HMS Greyhound.
	L5514	Between Ucimont and Botassart.
72	N2993	Sgt P F Kay +
		Sgt E A Revell +
		Sgt B Raper +
		LAC M Pelling +
		Sgt A D F O´Driscoll +
74	N2253	LAC G F Lewis pow
77	P4339	Sgt S J Golding +
79	N1460	Believed crashed 0200 at Leveringhausen.
	N1499	Believed crashed Neukirchen-Vluyn.
		226 Sqn MQ-N
81	R3688	P/O S G Esson +
	L8754	P/O T C Prescott +
83	L4112	P/O N E Hore pow
	P4341	Crashed Schipluiden (Zuid Holland), 5 km SW of Delft.
	R3731	Shot down 1620 by Oblt Georg Schneider of 9./JG54 who was killed by the return fire.
	R3776	Shot down off the Dutch coast by Lt Bob of 9./JG54.
85	R3170	Sgt G F Sexton +
90	N1424	Crashed Antwerpen-Deurne.
91	R3597	Sgt D V Malpass +
		Sgt J N Routledge +
93	L9469	P/O C H Robinson +
94	P9275	LN-O Sgt K R Sellwood +
	R3895	S/L M N McF Kennedy pow
		Shot down by Oblt Armin Schmidt of II./JG77.
	L5502	Crashed 1 km SW of Audembert.
	L5528	LAC G A Hall +
95	L5568	Sgt B C Long MiD +
	L5433	Sgt G C Brams +
		Sgt J W Mallard +
	L9239	Crashed near Macqueville.

Page	Serial	Addition/Correction
95	L9239	Sgt D J Spencer +
		Sgt O P Evans +
96	P4357	Sgt G H McCrory +
	L5113	Sgt F J Tremeer +
	L5597	GR-; crashed 7 miles NE of Coventry.
97	P9244	Sgt J H Swift +
98	T1933	Sgt L R Youngs +
99	P4982	P/O S P Swensen +
	N1501	KN-N
	P5056	KN-Y
100		Amend 77 Squadron to read 77/102 Squadrons and add: LAC K E New + LAC B Ash +
	P1333	EA-F; crashed at Alphen (Noord Brabant), Holland.
101	R3892	Crashed at Zuiderweg 31, Beemster (Noord Holland), 12 km SE of Alkmaar.
	L5503	Mid A Taylor RN pow
	T1929	Sgt W L Smith +
102	R3276	T/o 2308 Marham.
104	L9326	Sgt F Little +
	L1489	Crashed at Hayhills Farm, Silsden, 4 miles NW of Keighley, Yorkshire. Sgt Smalley was rescued by a Home Guard soldier.
105	P2123	F/O D A A Romans
	L8796	Sgt A R Coburn + Sgt Robbins
106	L9188	Sgt J W K Allen +
107	P4290	P/O D A A Romans
	R3163	F/O Burton escaped from his prison camp in May 1941.
108	P9245	Apart from Sgt Brown.
109	L5010	S/L(A) R A De Sandoval Sievier RN +
	L8848	HA-J
	T1894	Shot down off Den Helder, Holland, by Lt Wuebke of 9./JG54.
	P5042	KN-K
110	P2121	Crashed just to the W of Burcht (Antwerpen) on the W bank of the Schelde.
111	L9339	Shot down 2143 by 4./Flak Rgt 37 and crashed, on fire, into the sea off Oostende.
	R3160	Delete four and insert five.
112	L4049	OL-A
	L7788	KX-E
	P5046	T/o 2000 Linton-on-Ouse.
	L5351	Sgt J Waronski + Sgt K Paliwoda +
	L7788	Emergency landing 0435 near Leidschendam (Zuid Holland) 10 km SW of Leiden. Sgt Kunka shot himself with a Verey pistol and died the next day. Wellington later test flown at Rechlin.
113	T2472	Delete no injuries. P/O M I Nichols +
	P6905	Crashed 0535 SW of Swaffham.

Page	Serial	Addition/Correction
114	N3640	Sgt R Jackson inj
		Sgt A A Griffin inj
		P/O J W Murray inj
		Sgt A C Nicholson inj
		Sgt E L Roberts inj
		AC2 J F Wood inj
	R3164	P/O H R Bjelke-Peterson pow
	R3168	P/O E A Jelley +
115	N6191	Sgt S Walters died from his injuries.
117	T1881	LAC H Key +
118	L5499	BH-Y F/O D Gebicki + Sgt E Morawa + Sgt T Egierski + All buried Newark Cemetery.
120	L7844	KX-T; shot down by Lt Ludwig Becker of II./NJG2 and thus became the first Allied bomber to be shot down by a radar guided night-fighter. Sgt E Novotny pow Sgt A Sestak pow
	N2771	S/L J Vesely + Sgt J Albrecht + P/O J Matousek + P/O J Slaby + Sgt F Zapletal + P/O Truhlar inj
	N2773	P/O M Vejrazka +
	L7786	Sgt K Lang +
122	P5073	Amend III./NJG2 to read 3./NJG2. Fw Hans Hahn was killed on 12 October 1941, when his Ju 88C collided with an Oxford near Grantham. He is buried in the German Military Cemetery at Cannock Chase, Staffordshire.
123	L5356	F/O S Firlej-Bielanski + Sgt G Goebel + Sgt T J Szmajdowicz + All buried Newark Cemetery.
	X3027	Shot down by Lt He⋯ Völmer of I./NJG2.
127	T4151	Whitley V
	R3289	Delete Point, insert Pond.
	T2470	Sgt S A Wormald + Sgt T H Sansum ⅃
129	L7852	Delete IJsselmeer, insert near the Zuidscharwoude (Noord Holland), 200 metres W of the Vegetable Auction Hall.
	T4208	Crashed Lettele (Overijssel) 10 NE of Deventer, Holland.
131	T1890	Crashed at Peutie in the NE suburbs of Brussels.
133	T4160	Sgt V G Sullivan +
134	X3064	Crashed Spital-in-the-Street, 10 miles N of Lincoln.
138	T1897	Shot down by 1.Batterie, Abt.74.
139	T4226	Sgt Ross is buried Hannover. Rest have no known graves.
141	P1304	ZN-Y